D1246823

THE ROLE OF THE CHINESE ARMY

The Royal Institute of International Affairs is an unofficial body which promotes the scientific study of international questions and does not express opinions of its own. The opinions expressed in this publication are the responsibility of the author.

The Institute gratefully acknowledges the comments and suggestions of the following who read the manuscript on behalf of the Research Committee: John Erickson, Ellis Joffe, and Hugh Tinker.

The Role of the Chinese Army

JOHN GITTINGS

Issued under the auspices of the
Royal Institute of International Affairs

OXFORD UNIVERSITY PRESS

LONDON NEW YORK TORONTO

1967

Oxford University Press, Ely House, London W.1

GLASGOW NEW YORK TORONTO MELBOURNE WELLINGTON
CAPE TOWN SALISBURY IBADAN NAIROBI LUSAKA ADDIS ABABA
BOMBAY CALCUTTA MADRAS KARACHI LAHORE DACCA
KUALA LUMPUR HONG KONG TOKYO

PRINTED IN GREAT BRITAIN AT THE BROADWATER PRESS, WELWYN GARDEN CITY, HERTFORDSHIRE

Contents

Abbreviations

CB:	US Consulate-General, Hong Kong, *Current Background*
CC:	Central Committee
CFCP:	*Chieh-fang-chün Pao* (Liberation Army Newspaper)
CFJP:	*Chieh-fang Jih-pao* (Liberation Daily), Yenan, 1941–7
Communist China (dates):	Union Research Institute, Hong Kong, *Communist China*, 1955, 1956, 1957, 1958, 1949–59, 1960
CPV:	Chinese People's Volunteers
CQ:	*China Quarterly*
CSM:	*Christian Science Monitor*
ECMM:	US Consulate-General, Hong Kong, *Extracts from China Mainland Magazines*
FE & *FE*(2):	*Summary of World Broadcasts*, Part V: *The Far East*, Nos. 1–862, 26 Apr. 1949–14 Apr. 1959. 2nd series (renamed Part III: *The Far East*), No. 1, 15 Apr. 1959– .
JMJP:	*Jen-min Jih-pao* (People's Daily)
KMT:	Kuomintang
KTTH:	*Kung-tso T'ung-hsün* (Bulletin of Activities)
KTTH (Cheng):	J. Chester Cheng, ed., *The Politics of the Chinese Army: a Translation of the Bulletin of Activities of the People's Liberation Army*, Hoover Inst. on War, Revolution, and Peace, Stanford Univ., Calif., 1966
MAC:	Military and Administrative Committee
MCC:	Military Control Committee
MAO, I–IV:	Mao Tse-tung, *Selected Works*, Peking trans., vols. i–iv
NCDN:	*North China Daily News*
NCNA:	New China News Agency
NDC:	National Defence Council
NDYL:	New Democratic Youth League
NPC:	National People's Council
NYHT:	*New York Herald Tribune*
NYT:	*New York Times*
PA:	*Pacific Affairs*
PR:	*Peking Review*
Peabody Report:	Brig. Gen. P. E. Peabody [Chief of US War Dept., Military Intelligence Service], 'The Chinese Communist Movement, 5 July 1945', in US Senate, Committee on the Judiciary, *Hearings on the Institute of Pacific Relations*, pt 7a, app. 2 (82nd Congress, 2nd session)
PLA:	People's Liberation Army
PRMC:	People's Revolutionary Military Council
SAC:	State Administrative Council
SCMP:	US Consulate-General, Hong Kong, *Survey of the China Mainland Press*
US Relations with China:	US Dept of State, *United States Relations with China*, 1949
YCL:	Young Communist League

Preface

There can be no salvation for China until the military is brought under proper control. . . . Proper control of the military may not mean instant realization of orderly government, but orderly government is dependent on proper control of the military. China has suffered at the hands of the militarists in the recent past and still suffers today. She will continue to suffer unless a future régime is able to dominate instead of be dominated by the militarists.[1]

'POLITICAL power grows from the barrel of a gun'. This well-known dictum of Mao Tse-tung finds confirmation in the historical experience of China's political development since the decline of the Manchu dynasty in the nineteenth century. This decline was accompanied by a steady growth of militarism and by a corresponding inability on the part of the central authorities to control it effectively. The future of the Republic of 1912 was determined in the last analysis by those who commanded the armies. This central fact of political life led to the fragmentation of the Republic and to the rise of the warlords. The Nationalist cause of Sun Yat-sen led a precarious life, in constant danger of obliteration, until it too took a leaf out of the warlords' book and set about organizing its own independent source of military power. The communists in turn were at first a purely political body without independent military backing, relying upon the armies of the Nationalists with whom they formed a united front. When the front collapsed in 1927, they too drew the inevitable conclusion, and began to construct the Red Army which eventually brought them to power.

During the nineteenth century the Manchu dynasty faced two separate threats to its existence, each of which would have been sufficient on its own to bring about the dynasty's overthrow. First was the growth of popular unrest and insurgency culminating in the Taiping rebellion (*c.* 1850–65). This would not have been so difficult to contain, nor would it have been so widespread, if the dynasty had itself maintained the vigour and dynamism of its earlier years. But the Manchus already had em-

[1] Ch'ien Tuan-sheng, 'The role of the military in Chinese government', *Pacific Affairs*, Sept. 1948, p. 251.

barked upon the familiar path of decline which marks the penultimate stage of the dynastic cycle—rising population, corruption at the imperial court, inability to cope with natural disasters, and general inflation. Another familiar feature of this decline was the growing ineffectiveness of the armed forces upon which the dynasty relied—the Manchu Banners and the predominantly native Green Standards.

In order to stem the Taiping flood (and also that of the Nien and Mohammedan rebellions), the imperial court had reluctantly to allow military power to devolve into the hands of the provincial authorities who were immediately concerned. Thus the complex system of checks and counterbalances, by which the dynasty controlled the army, and its jealous refusal to delegate military control outside its own hands, began to break down. Popular armies, such as Tseng Kuo-fan's Hunan Army, Tso Tsung-t'ang's Ch'u Army, and Li Hung-chang's Anhwei Army, were manned, officered, and led from within the regions in which they operated. Furthermore, because of the imperial court's chronic reluctance to provide adequate finance, the provincial leaders of these armies were allowed to draw upon provincial taxes and other sources of revenue. A new kind of military force was being created with strong regional associations, in which personal loyalty was generated as much between the soldier and his general as between the soldier and his emperor.

Although the picture is complicated by a constant process of disbandment and re-formation, the regional armies of Tseng, Li, and others provided the nucleus from which the new-style armies emerged at the end of the nineteenth century, which themselves were the forerunners of the warlord armies of the Republic. Attempts by the throne to resuscitate the Green Standards as an effective counterbalance and to secure control of the new armies were largely unsuccessful. Perhaps of greater importance, a significant proportion of the officer élite which staffed the new armies had originated in the regional armies, and graduated in time to serve under the warlords or to be warlords themselves. A complex net of relationships, formed in the new armies before 1911, linked many of the leaders of the military cliques which emerged under the Republic and helped bring about its demoralization and virtual disintegration between 1915 and 1927.

The other threat which the Manchu dynasty faced in the nineteenth century came from beyond China's frontiers. This threat from the Western powers possessed an ambiguous quality which was totally outside anything that China had previously experienced. Here was an alien invasion—in the widest sense of the word—which could not be assimilated in the way that the Mongols and Manchus themselves had been. It came from the sea rather than from the familiar source of danger of China's inner frontiers. It brought with it political and economic concepts which contributed materially to the break-up of imperial China. In the military sphere, the Western impact upon China added a new factor to those which had previously governed Chinese military thinking. Traditionally China had always looked upon her armed forces more as a means of maintaining internal law and order than as a means of defence against external aggression. This in part explains the relatively low level at which they were maintained, a level at which they were also inhibited from presenting an overt threat to dynastic rule. The presence of the Western powers knocking upon the doors of China, and the example of advanced Western military technology, meant that the new Chinese armies were both stronger and technologically more sophisticated than any that China had previously known. Their capacity to intervene decisively in the course of internal political developments was that much greater. Military 'self-strengthening' in the last decades of the nineteenth century brought Western equipment and techniques to China. To the extent that the process of self-strengthening was carried through more vigorously by regional leaders such as Li Hung-chang than by the imperial authorities, the tendency towards regional military autonomy was further accentuated.

The military problems which any aspirant to the control of China faced in the twentieth century were therefore threefold. First, it had to muster sufficient armed force with which to launch itself upon the road to power. In the climate of endemic warlordism, which persisted even after 1927 when China was apparently united under Kuomintang rule, it was not difficult to raise troops of one sort or another, from secret societies, from defectors and bandits, or from the dispossessed and unemployed. It was another thing altogether, at a time when the reputation of the Chinese soldier was deservedly lower than ever before, to ensure that one's forces secured popular support in the area in which they operated. While the government in power could afford the luxury of garrison armies who were loathed by the civilian population, an insurgent army had little chance of surviving, and none of expanding its power, if it did not enjoy a large measure of popular support. Unless such an army could move among the people, in the Maoist phrase, as fish in water, it would be left high and dry. The question of political control was part of the same problem. Insurgent operations demanded a high degree of initiative and autonomy among the guerrilla units involved, yet at the same time their actions had to be closely co-ordinated if they were to be effective. The question could not simply be solved by mechanistic systems of control, unless it embodied some sort of common ideals or ideology which would provide moral cohesion as well as organizational cohesion.

The second problem arose once victory had been achieved. The transformation of an insurgent force from a revolutionary army into an established regular army of national defence was extremely complex. It raised important social, political, and economic questions, as well as those of a purely technical nature. How much could be afforded for national defence, at a time when the country's peacetime reconstruction should be the top priority? Would the old system of political control prove adequate when the original revolutionary incentives no longer existed? Would a civilian population which had by and large accepted the burden of armed forces, when those forces could reasonably claim to be fighting on its behalf, show itself to be as tolerant of them when they moved into garrisons and had to be fed without showing anything tangible in return?

The third problem was peculiar to China's international situation in the twentieth century. It was no longer enough to run down one's armed capability to the minimum point at which internal law and order could be preserved. Regardless of the political complexion of the new Chinese government, it had to reckon with the international facts of life. In the world of the cold war, this meant in particular the United States and the Soviet Union. This was as much a problem of foreign as of defence policy, but regardless of what alliances were or were not formed, it was almost inevitable that some measure of military modernization and technological improvement would have to be carried out. An army which had successfully fought through a civil war was hardly capable as it stood of defending China's frontiers. In the meantime, China could not afford to stand apart from both of the major power blocs simultaneously. A reliable ally had to be found who would provide the essential military and political guarantees to safeguard China's security.

How has the Chinese communist party tackled these three successive problems? Two decades of revolution proved its ability to deal with the first—that of organizing a military apparatus, of maintaining political control over it, and of winning popular support for it. This essential basis for political and social integration of the communist army was not established overnight. The theory behind it had been worked out and to some extent put into practice during the Kiangsi Soviet period and even earlier. But it was weakened by the Red Army's decimation during the Long March, and by policy disputes within the party leadership. It was during the subsequent Yenan period of the anti-Japanese war that the political and social roles of the army finally crystallized along now familiar lines. The years 1941–4 in particular, when the communist areas were pressed hardest by Japanese blockade and encirclement, were the army's most formative period, perhaps out of sheer necessity. The revolutionary model which in recent years the army has been exhorted to revive strict political control, the practice of economy and participation in production work, scrupulous attention to public relations, expansion of the militia, democratic behaviour within the army itself, etc.—is pre-eminently that of these years. By 1944 the army had reached a point both of numerical and qualitative strength which provided the foundation for its rapid expansion in the last year of the war against Japan and in the civil war which followed.

The second and third problems are still with the Chinese communists today. The civil war marked the People's Liberation Army's revolutionary watershed, after which an entirely new situation had to be faced. Little hesitation was shown in choosing the Soviet Union as China's 'reliable ally'. The PLA's modernization, on the other hand, might have been accorded a slightly lower priority if war had not broken out in Korea. The Korean war speeded up the process of modernization, and encouraged a drift away from the revolutionary model. This was followed by two years of 'regularization', in which conscription, systems of ranks and awards, and all the other trappings of a professional army were introduced. The reaction against excessive professionalization, and against the uncritical acceptance of the Soviet model, gathered momentum during the years 1956–9, culminating in a major upheaval with the dismissal of the then Minister of Defence, P'eng Teh-huai. This reaction had its counterpart in the self-reliant philosophy of the Great Leap Forward, and the rejection of the Soviet Union both as a political ally and as an economic model. Since 1959 a new and generally more successful attempt has been made to restore the essentials of the PLA's revolutionary model—especially the political control structure—while de-emphasizing those aspects which are less relevant under modern conditions. A high point was reached in 1964, when the entire Chinese nation was exhorted to 'Learn from the PLA'. But since then relations between the party and the army have shown fresh signs of strain, and may be leading once again to serious friction.

Looking back at the whole period since 1949, and taking into account the difficulties which the communist leadership has faced, its handling of the army must be judged at least a qualified success. It has survived some negative tests of great importance. China has not been 'dominated by the militarists' at any time since 1949, and there is apparently little fear of military regionalism. The hand-over of military to civil government in the areas dominated by the PLA at the time of victory was accomplished without perceptible difficulty in the space of four years. While sections of the PLA leadership at times clearly resent important aspects of party policy, they have not resorted to extreme measures to challenge the régime. The PLA does not share the odium usually attached to the military in recent Chinese history; its reputation among the civilian population is remarkably high. Military morale has not been destroyed by party interference, although it reached a low point during the Great Leap Forward.

Nevertheless, if one examines the record of the past seventeen years since 1949, and the attempts made by the party to solve the problems of military management, it is clear that a major contradiction exists in China's military policy which is probably incapable of being definitively resolved. This is the contradiction between the need to construct a modernized army capable of sophisticated defence in the modern world, and the need to ensure that such an army preserves its revolutionary character and remains receptive to political control. In theory it should be possible to establish the right balance between these two priorities. In practice the history of the PLA since 1949 reveals a perpetual state of imbalance. This contradiction can be described in other words as one between command and control, between the unity of command which is essential for military morale and efficiency, and the primacy of political control which is essential for political stability. This conflict is not peculiar to a communist society; it would be inherent in any country with the divisive geo-political features which have always been characteristic of the old China, combined with the unhappy experience of political instability which was characteristic of modern China in the nineteenth and twentieth centuries until the communist victory. But the conflict is probably accentuated by the emphasis placed in a communist society upon the army as the ultimate sanction for political power, by its prominent role in the hierarchy and apparatus of the power structure, and by the absence in modern China of a military tradition of obedience to central authority.

This contradiction between 'revolutionization' and 'professionalization', between control and command, is not confined in China to the PLA alone. It is only one aspect of the wider problem which faces the veteran communist leadership today, in its attempt to apply revolutionary standards in undiluted form to a modernizing and developing society. The success or otherwise of this attempt as applied to the PLA will have implications for the whole of Chinese society. In a certain sense, the PLA is the testing-ground for the leadership's fervent belief that 'revolutionary successors' can be found to hold high the banner of the thought of Mao Tse-tung for China's future generations.

Whether or not this belief is justified remains to be seen. It is because the PLA's position in China must be looked at in the light of this unresolved question that it is impossible to draw any hard and fast conclusions about the future role of the PLA. The story of the PLA since 1949 would suggest that the problems presented by the role of the military in Chinese society should not prove unmanageable, although by the same token they are unlikely ever to be solved for good. So far these problems, although caused by major conflicts of interest and priority, have been successfully contained within a framework of general unity and party loyalty. There is a degree of flexibility in the apparently inflexible Chinese political system which allows for the modulation of policy just short of the point where conflict might otherwise break out. Alarmist prognostications of conflict between the party and army by outside observers have so far proved unjustified—Pekinologists are prone to read too much into legitimate policy differences in China. Disagreement is too often seen as a 'struggle for power'; dismissal is too often regarded as a 'purge'. There is always a temptation to exaggerate the seriousness of conflict in a closed political system like that of China, where so little is knowable and so much has to be inferred.

One might therefore reasonably forecast that we shall continue to see in China as a whole the kinds of oscillation between revolutionary and modernizing (or 'Maoist' and 'revisionist') postures of which the PLA's experience up to now is an example. This process of oscillation will incline more and more towards the latter posture, although it may take several decades. This at least is the expectation of those in the West who believe that China must eventually submit to the process of peaceful transition which at present she so vehemently resists. (If they are wrong and Mao is right, then the revolutionary/modernizing dialectic will eventually lead to the opposite conclusion.) In either case, the Chinese political structure should prove sufficiently flexible to withstand the strain.

Yet the Cultural Revolution, which is in full swing at the time of writing, must raise some doubts as to whether the conclusions drawn above are not over-optimistic. For the first time since 1949 differences over policy have arisen which have not been satisfactorily resolved within the existing party framework, and which have spilled over into the streets and the public press. Furthermore, the intensity of the campaign seems to have come very close to crossing the border beyond which party loyalty can no longer ensure automatic obedience.

The inherent conflict between the professional and political roles of the PLA has never been more clearly displayed than during the course of the Cultural Revolution. Despite the attempts of many Western analysts, it is impossible to define what part exactly the PLA has played in the Cultural Revolution. It all depends on what section of the PLA one is referring to, since it has shown during the course of the Cultural Revolution clear signs of a split personality. On the one hand, the Minister of Defence himself, together with a number of his leading colleagues, have emerged with added power and prestige as the prime movers in the campaign for political orthodoxy. Yet at the same time certain sections of the PLA—especially those of a technical nature—have displayed more discontent with party policies than at any time since 1959. Meanwhile at least one senior executive officer—the chief of staff, Lo Jui-ch'ing—and possibly others, appears to have been dismissed for his inability to reconcile conflicting military and political priorities, thus once again demonstrating the inherent difficulties of command at a senior level.

If therefore the passing away of the present veteran Chinese communist leadership continues to be accompanied by such extreme political trends as the Cultural Revolution has displayed, we may expect these divisive pressures on the PLA to increase accordingly. We may also expect to see a substantial growth in the PLA's political influence—a possibility which is not as paradoxical as it may sound. For in any political upheaval, as in the Cultural Revolution, where one party faction has invoked the authority of the PLA in support of its own claims, the army's prestige and political leverage will thereby be enhanced. This same increase in prestige may also be a unifying factor in the PLA, cancelling out the divisive pressures which have given rise to it. This may well be true of the army's role in the Cultural Revolution itself. The exalted role assigned to the PLA by the party leadership may serve to mollify those elements in the PLA which would otherwise be most critical of the actual policies at stake. And even though the PLA acts in the name of the leadership and purports to be a paragon of obedience to the party, it is likely in the process to become more independent of party control.

The problems described above constitute the central theme of this study of the PLA. I am well aware that I have treated many aspects of this theme in a rather superficial way, but in view of the comparative absence of published research on this subject, I hope that it may at least encourage others to look at some of the problems in greater detail. This is not strictly a military history; it does not provide a blow-by-blow account of the PLA's record in battle. Nor does it deal in any great detail with Chinese military strategy as such. This would require a full-length study in itself, taking into consideration the entire spectrum of Chinese foreign policy since 1949. The emphasis is rather upon the changing character of the PLA since 1949, the fluctuating position which it occupies in the scale of national priorities, its relationship with the communist party, and its economic and social roles.

The time-span of this study is roughly that of 1946–65, i.e. from the outbreak of civil war to the present day. A detailed analysis of the communist army before the civil war is beyond the scope of this study, both for reasons of space and because it would require much more intensive research, using primary materials of a rather intractable nature, than has yet been done (apart from Chalmers Johnson's work on *Peasant Nationalism and Communist Power*). I have however discussed at some length two aspects of the army's tradition without which its subsequent development can hardly be understood. These are the evolution of the political control structure, which is still essentially unchanged, from the army's earliest days (Chapter 5), and the mechanics of popular mobilization in the anti-Japanese war, which provided the model for mobilization, with some modifications, in the civil war and to a lesser extent during the Korean war (Chapter 3). The basic point of departure is however the civil war. This was the culmination of the PLA's revolutionary struggle, embodying all the features which it had acquired over the previous two decades. Its victory marked both the peak of its success, and also the start of a totally new phase in its development—the transformation from a revolutionary army to an established regular army of national defence.

The chapters are arranged in rough chronological order, with a few important exceptions, since they are also grouped as far as possible according to theme. Chapters 1–2 provide a straight narration of the PLA's development in the civil war and the problems which this created in the first year of the People's Republic. Chapters 3–5 deal with the historical background to the PLA's political and social roles, the origins of political control and of the techniques of popular mobilization. The theory and practice of modernization during and after the Korean war, and its connexion with Sino-Soviet relations, is described in Chapters 6–7. The party's subsequent reaction against professionalism, and its attempts to resurrect revolutionary practices in the PLA, culminating in the expansion of the militia and the 'officers to the ranks' movement during the Great Leap Forward, are dealt with in Chapters 8–10. Chapters 11–12 bring the story up to date with the strategic reappraisal and the restoration of political control which has taken place since 1959. The final two chapters examine the evolution of the military leadership, its character and status, from 1949 to the present day. The bibliography is 'select' by design, and those who wish for fuller information should consult the specialized bibliographies listed therein. The tables of statistical and other information make no claim to be authoritative; hard facts about the PLA's strength, organization, and personnel have to be deduced from isolated references in the Chinese press and should be treated with caution.

Acknowledgements

THIS book was written at Chatham House, and could not have been completed without assistance from many members of the staff. I would like in particular to thank Mr A. S. B. Olver for giving me the opportunity to write it. Miss Judith Trotter and Mrs Janet Pickering have both in turn cheerfully satisfied my immoderate demands on the Press Library, and their help was invaluable. Miss Hermia Oliver edited the manuscript with her customary skill and patience.

An earlier version of Chapter 10 and parts of Chapter 12 were originally published in the *China Quarterly*, April–June 1964. Chapter 14 was published in the April–June 1966 number of the same journal.

I am grateful to Dr Jerome Ch'en for helpful suggestions on the contents, and to my father for pertinent advice on the style. My colleagues in the Chatham House Working Group on China and the World have assisted me towards a better understanding of the problems of contemporary China. I am indebted to Professor Hugh Tinker and Professor John Erickson for their perceptive comments on the typescript. I am particularly grateful to Mr Ellis Joffe, who also read the typescript, for his detailed and expert criticism. Needless to say, I alone must take responsibility for the final product.

My wife has made useful comments on the manuscript, and has helped with the index. She has also provided the pleasure in life without which no work is worth doing.

London   J. G.
June 1966

I
Strategy of the Civil War, 1946–9

To whom should the fruits of victory in the War of Resistance belong? It is very obvious. Take a peach tree for example. When the tree yields peaches they are the fruits of victory. Who is entitled to pick the peaches? Ask who planted and watered the tree. Chiang Kai-shek squatting on the mountain did not carry a single bucket of water, and yet he is now stretching out his arm from afar to pick the peaches. . . . We say, 'You never carried any water, so you have no right to pick the peaches. We the people of the Liberated Areas watered the tree day in day out and have the most right to gather the fruit'.[1]

THE contest for the 'fruits of victory' in China after the defeat of Japan in August 1945 led directly to the outbreak of civil war a year later between the communist and Nationalist forces. Both sides sought to secure positions of strength from which to negotiate, or if necessary to fight. At the time of Japan's surrender, the Nationalist armies possessed a superiority, at least on paper, over those of the communists estimated at five to one. They also had a virtual monopoly of heavy equipment and transport, and air power.[2] Yet their forces were mainly confined to Central and South China, while the communists were better placed to extend control in East and North China from their existing border areas. Manchuria was in the hands of the Soviet occupying forces, and open to communist penetration. From its

[1] Mao Tse-tung, 'The Situation and Our Policy after the Victory in the War of Resistance against Japan, 13 Aug. 1945', *MAO IV*, p. 16.
[2] *US Relations with China*, p. 311. Communist forces in 1945 totalled 900,000 of whom 600,000 were regulars. Nationalist official estimates claimed a total of 5 million or more. But as one observer wrote. "Five million have been claimed, but it seems safe to accept a figure of about 1,500,000 for reasonably modern, effective troops' (Randall Gould, in *CSM*, 4 Jan. 1945). The true ratio of Nationalist/communist regular forces is therefore nearer 3 : 1. Nationalist estimates were inflated throughout the civil war. In autumn 1947 the official figure was 4,557,362. 'Actually there is probably not a single high military figure in Nanking who knows exactly how many men there are in the armed forces, for the Chinese army has not yet developed a scientific method of personnel accounting' (*NYT*, 31 Oct. 1947). The true figure was again estimated by observers as 1,500,000 (*NYHT*, 11 Dec. 1947).

capital of Yenan in Shensi province, the communist leadership lost no time in consolidating its position.

On 11 August 1945, one day after Japan's surrender, the Army General Headquarters in Yenan ordered its forces to advance on all fronts and to immobilize and disarm all Japanese troops whom they met. This was the culmination of an offensive, timed to coincide with the final phase of the war, which had begun the previous month.[3] This offensive had two clear objectives; first to dominate the means of communication and transport throughout North China, and to increase the territory of the communist border areas, and secondly to establish a communist presence in Manchuria itself. In North China four separate armies advanced to secure a stranglehold over the main arterial railways. This was so successful that Nationalist troops could only be moved over most of North China by air.[4] In Manchuria—or the North-east, as it is generally known—more than 100,000 communist troops arrived in a well-prepared operation. They joined forces with the existing guerrilla fighters in the North-east, and also recruited from former Chinese prisoners of war.[5] By February 1946 the

---

[3] The communist forces under Yenan's control comprised:
  (a) The Eighth Route Army, about 600,000 strong, located in North and North-west China.
  (b) The New Fourth Army, about 280,000 strong, located in East and Central China.
  (c) 20,000 guerrilla troops along the East river and on Hainan island in South China.
  The CCP, CC first called for an offensive on 7 July (*Ti-san-tz'u kuo-nei ko-ming chan-cheng ta-shih yüeh-pao* (1961), p. 1). On 9 August, the day after the Soviet invasion of Manchuria, Mao Tse-tung issued a statement calling on all forces to 'forcibly expand our liberated areas and reduce the areas under military occupation' (Liao Kai-lung, *From Yenan to Peking* (1954), p. 8). On the 10th, Japan surrendered and Chu Teh ordered the communist forces to receive and expedite the surrender of Japanese troops.

[4] *CFJP* (Yenan), 12 Aug. 1945: Orders of the Eighth Route Army General Headquarters. These orders revealed quite clearly Yenan's intention both to move into the North-east and to extend its control in the North. Other troops were to move into Inner Mongolia. These orders were also broadcast by Yenan radio. Later allegations that these were conspiratorial moves, undertaken secretly, are therefore unfounded.

[5] Eighth Route Army forces had begun to extend operations into the North-eastern province of Liaoning in 1944, setting up the Hopei–Jehol–Liaoning Border Area astride the main Peking–Liaoning railway. In March 1945 an American observer in Yenan reported that 'the most important fighting' was taking place in Eastern Hopeh, Chahar, and Liaoning, and that this was 'apparently intended to establish a *cordon sanitaire* between China and Manchuria and is being conducted with unusual determination and ferocity' (*Peabody Report*, p. 2372).

combined total of pro-communist forces in the North-east, now under the name of the 'Manchurian Democratic Joint Army', was given as 300,000, including 100,000 regulars.

Negotiations between the communists and the Nationalists, concerning a political settlement and the formation of a coalition government, had broken down in February 1945. They were resumed at the end of August, when Mao Tse-tung himself came to the Nationalist capital of Chungking. In one form or another, they pursued a tortuous path for the next year and a half, but by July 1946 they had already effectively broken down again, and major clashes in the same month heralded the beginning of the civil war. Much has since been written on both sides claiming lack of good faith by the other in these negotiations. The Nationalists are accused of using the peace talks 'as a smoke screen to start a civil war'. The communists are charged with having intended from the very start 'to overthrow the National Government of China and to seize sovereign power through armed rebellion'.[6] But the question of good faith is almost meaningless, since the aims of both parties were basically incompatible.

As students of classical Chinese history have often commented, from time immemorial the kingdoms based on what is now Shensi province in the west of China have pursued a 'horizontal' strategy, which sought to link Shensi to the sea along the Yellow river plain. This was the basis of the state of Ch'in's strategy in the Warring States period, and equally so of the communist strategy in 1945.[7] If they had allowed the Nationalist armies unimpeded

n.5 *cont.*

Guerrilla forces already in Manchuria totalled over 150,000, according to NCNA (London), 9 July 1947. For details of their organization, see Evans Fordyce Carlson, *The Chinese Army* (1940), pp. 44-45; Li Tu and others, *Tung-pei ti hei-an yü kuang-ming* (1946), pp. 34-53.

100,000 is the figure generally given for the number of communist troops moved in after August 1945; q.v. *MAO IV*, p. 84; *NYT*, 15 Mar. 1946; according to Hung-ch'i p'iao-p'iao she, ed., *Chieh-fang chan-cheng hui-i-lu* (1961), p. 162, 50,000 political cadres were also sent to Manchuria.

The total of 300,000 by the end of 1945 is reported in *NYT*, 16 Feb. 1946; NCNA (London), 9 July 1947.

[6] Ho Kan-chih, *A History of the Modern Chinese Revolution* (1959), p. 449; Chiang Kai-shek's message to the Chinese people, 9 Oct. 1949, in *China Handbook, 1950* (New York, 1950), p. 283.

[7] 'A study of the map of North China will show that these rival plans embody abiding strategic verities conditioned by unchanging geographical facts, which will remain true in all ages. Similar plans were framed in the civil wars of 1923-30, and during every contest between the western hill provinces and the great eastern

access through North China to Manchuria, they would have been more vulnerable to Nationalist encirclement than at any time since the end of the Long March. Similarly, the southern states of China have traditionally pursued a 'vertical' strategy, designed to establish north–south control and to contain the enemy in the west. However foolish Chiang Kai-shek's decision to occupy Manchuria afterwards appeared in tactical terms, the alternative would have been to abandon it to communist control and accept a *de facto* partition between north and south. The strategic importance of Manchuria and the North had been clearly underlined in the war against Japan.[8]

These strategic realities were reflected in the negotiations. Mao Tse-tung was prepared to withdraw units of the New Fourth Army from Central China to north of the Yangtze. The Nationalists agreed in principle, but blocked the transit of some of these units, fearing that they would be used to reinforce communist strength in the North and Manchuria. It was this action which sparked off major hostilities in July 1946, and virtually signalled the end of serious negotiations. In North China agreement was reached upon the military balance of Nationalist and communist forces to be achieved, but not on a political settlement. Mao Tse-tung would not surrender his existing political control in the North; Chiang Kai-shek refused to recognize Yenan's pre-eminent position, and insisted on the right to appoint his own officials throughout the North. In Manchuria the communists did not contest the Nationalist right to re-enter the region, but insisted that any political settlement or government should be a coalition on which they and their sympathizers were represented. Indeed, they established a provisional government of their own.[9]

---

plain, the "horizontal" and "vertical" plans of the ancient Chou strategists reappear in all essentials unchanged' (C. P. FitzGerald: *Son of Heaven; a Biography of Li Shih-min, Founder of the T'ang Dynasty* (Cambridge UP, 1933), p. 51, quoted in L. M. Chassin, *La Conquête de la Chine par Mao Tse-tung* (1952), p. 61.

[8] One Nationalist source comments that the Chinese people regard the North-east as 'China's lifeline'. 'They remember only too well that it was from these bases in the North-east that the Japanese steadily infiltrated south of the Great Wall and undermined the foundations of the National Government. Their feelings are succinctly expressed in the current phrase . . . "No North-east, No China" ' (*China Newsweek* 7 Mar. 1946, quoted in RIIA, *Survey of International Affairs: The Far East, 1942–46*, p. 199).

[9] On 26 December 1945 a provincial government was organized for Kirin province, under the governorship of General Chow Pao-chung. Similar bodies were later organized for the other North-east provinces. In August 1946 communist head-

The procedural manœuvres of the negotiations were over-shadowed by one dominant fact—the deep suspicion and hostility which both parties felt towards each other. As General Marshall reported on his return in January 1947 after over a year of attempts at mediation, 'the greatest obstacle to peace has been the complete, almost overwhelming suspicion with which the Chinese Communist Party and the Kuomintang regard each other'. Of the two, the communists were probably the more anxious to reach a political settlement, since this would leave them free—as Mao Tse-tung put it—to resume their work of 'legal struggle' in the cities, the villages, and the Nationalist army.[10] This was of course precisely what the Nationalists feared. The Kuomintang, for its part, confident in its military superiority, was more prepared to fight. Yet rather than accept a settlement which weakened their own position and left them vulnerable to attack in the future, the communists too preferred to fight.[11]

SUMMARY OF THE CIVIL WAR

Communist historians divide the strategy of the 'third revolutionary war' (the civil war, 1946–9) into three successive and logically consecutive stages. The formal outbreak of war occurred in July 1946, with the virtual breakdown of peace negotiations and the rapid spread of fighting through Central, North, and North-east China.[12] From July 1946 until June 1947 is known as

quarters in Harbin encouraged the creation of a 'Provincial Supreme Administration for Democratic Manchuria', which adopted a programme of coalition government and agrarian reform. See further *NYT*, 16 Feb., 9 & 11 May 1946; *NYHT*, 10 May 1946; *CSM*, 26 Aug. 1946.

[10] Personal statement by General Marshall, 7 Jan. 1947, in *US Relations with China*, pp. 686–9; Mao Tse-tung, 'Policy for Work in the Liberated Areas for 1946', in *MAO IV*, pp. 75–79.

[11] For detailed accounts and analyses of the course of Kuomintang/communist negotiations, see further *US Relations with China*, ch. 5; Tang Tsou, *America's Failure in China, 1941–50* (Chicago, 1963), chs. 8 & 10.

[12] In early July Nationalist offensives were launched against (*a*) Li Hsien-nien's army in north Kiangsu, (*b*) five major rail arteries in north China. In General Marshall's opinion, 'the Government was washing its hands of any democratic procedure and was pursuing a dictatorial policy of military force' (*US Relations with China*, p. 169). Military and government leaders spoke openly of civil war: Ch'en Li-fu, Minister of Information, compared the communists to 'a bad appendix that has to be removed to preserve life' (*NYT*, 22 July 1946). On the 28th the Nationalist government rejected a final offer of unconditional cease-fire by Chou En-lai. On the same day, in an inner-party directive of the CCP, CC, Mao Tse-tung issued a call to 'Smash Chiang Kai-shek's offensive by a War of Self Defence' (*MAO IV*, pp. 89–92).

the 'defensive stage of the People's War of Liberation'. While the Nationalist troops cleared their lines of communication in North China and captured the major cities of Manchuria, communist forces followed a policy of strategic withdrawal and mobile warfare, abandoning the towns for the country. In Central China 60,000 troops led by Li Hsien-nien broke through the Nationalist encirclement and withdrew into Shensi province. All of Manchuria south of the Sungari river was deliberately left to the Nationalists. Lin Piao's forces were concentrated north of the river, where as much of their time was spent in clearing the local bandits, restoring light industry, and in promoting land reform as in fighting the Nationalist army.[13] The emphasis throughout the communist war zones was on consolidation; the war at this stage was one of attrition. The dominant strategy established by Mao Tse-tung was to scale down the enemy's numerical superiority by attacking his weakest points, not to win territory for its own sake. 'So long as we are able to wipe out the enemy's effective strength on a large scale', wrote Mao, 'it will be possible to recover lost territory and seize new territory.'[14] In March 1947 the wartime communist capital of Yenan in Shensi province was abandoned to the Kuomintang without a shot fired. This well-publicized but empty victory marked the peak of the Nationalist all-out offensive and of the communist strategic withdrawal.

In the summer of 1947 the second stage began—that of a limited counter-offensive. This move was based upon the assumption—which proved to be correct—that the Kuomintang, by throwing its forces into Manchuria, had seriously over-extended its lines of communication and left its rear vulnerable to attack. The counter-offensive was therefore directed principally at the soft underbelly of Central China—Hupeh, Honan, and Anhwei—and at the major north–south railways in the North.

---

[13] A recent account quotes Lin Piao as having said: 'All the towns south of the Sungari can be given to Chiang Kai-shek. They will be burdens on his back—once occupied they must be defended. With so many towns to defend, his strength will be dissipated and we can destroy them one by one. . . . Our present task is to set up sound bases and settle north of the Sungari. We must clear the land of bandits, and send several tens of thousands of cadres into the country to arouse the masses' (Chou Ch'ih-p'ing, 'Comrade Lin Piao in the North-east War of Liberation', in Hung-ch'i p'iao-p'iao she, ed., *Chieh-fang chan cheng hui-i-lu* (1961), pp. 161–92, trans. in *SCMM* 217).

[14] Mao Tse-tung, 16 Sept. 1946, 'Concentrate a Superior Force to destroy the Enemy Forces One by One' (*MAO IV*, p. 106).

In July–August 1947 PLA troops crossed the Yellow river in three separate prongs and infiltrated southwards to set up new base areas in Central China.[15] By the end of the year PLA units threatened the railways from North China into Manchuria and were about to cut permanently the lines both to the north and south of Mukden. With the capture of Shihchiachuang in November, two communist base areas joined hands across the arterial Peking–Hankow railway in Hopei.[16] The central strategy was still to conduct mobile warfare, and to erode the KMT's effective strength, while extending the area of battle. The counter-offensive was intended to draw out and dissipate the enemy's strength and not to occupy territory.[17]

An essential part of this strategy was the winning of popular support in the liberated areas, both old and new. It was necessary to 'carry through the land reform, develop production, practise economy and strengthen the building of war industry—all for victory at the front'.[18] The winter of 1947 saw the launching of a new and more radical programme of land reform, large-scale recruitment for the coming year, and a major political and organizational overhaul of the armed forces and party.

By the summer of 1948 the Kuomintang army was clearly on the defensive, with 300,000 troops tied up in Manchuria, another 100,000 in Tsinan (Shantung), its reserves depleted and

---

[15] In July 1947 50,000 troops led by Liu Po-ch'eng crossed the Yellow river east of Kaifeng and infiltrated across Anhwei into the Tapieh mountains, lying above the Yangtze slightly to the east of Wuhan.

In August 20,000 troops of the Taiyueh army led by Ch'en Keng crossed the Yellow river from south Shensi and set up bases on the Honan–Shensi–Hupeh border south of Loyang.

In the same month eight columns of the East China Field Army led by Ch'en Yi moved into the area of south Honan vacated by Liu Po-ch'eng and liberated the Shantung–Anhwei–Kiangsu Border Area, harassing the Lunghai railway between Kaifeng and Hsuchow.

These three advances struck respectively at the west, central, and east zones of Central China above the Yangtze. According to communist claims, they immobilized some 90 out of the 160 or more KMT divisions in the field (Chang Chün-ying, *Ko-ming yü fan-ko-ming ti chüeh-chan* (1961), pp. 63–64).

[16] In November five columns of the Shansi–Chahar–Hopei Field Army led by Nieh Jung-chen captured Shihchiachuang, and thus joined up the Shansi–Chahar–Hopei and Shansi–Hopei–Shantung–Honan Border Areas.

[17] See the inner-party directive drafted by Mao Tse-tung of 1 Sept. 1947, 'Strategy for the Second Year of the War of Liberation', which stated: 'Make wiping out the enemy's effective strength our main objective; do not make holding or seizing a place our main objective. . .' (*MAO IV*, pp. 141–6).

[18] Ibid.

with political unrest in Nanking. By contrast the communists had used with profit the lull in fighting during the winter and spring. The excesses of the land reform programme, which brought new recruits in hundreds of thousands to the PLA, had been curbed. A start had been made with strengthening party and army discipline in preparation for a co-ordinated offensive. PLA troops were trained in positional warfare and their officers instructed on how to cope with urban administration with the same offensive in view.

Four major campaigns by the PLA against KMT defensive positions during the months September–December 1948 were to change the balance of forces in favour of the PLA and to render the KMT's stake in North China untenable. The third and final stage of the war, that of an all-out strategic offensive, had begun. The first demoralizing blow was struck on 24 September 1948, with the capture of Tsinan in Shantung, its garrison of 100,000 troops and an estimated 50,000 rifles. Meanwhile in the Liaohsi–Shenyang campaign, lasting from 12 September to 2 November, a successful communist attack on Chinchow, supply base for the Nationalists in Manchuria, led to a breakdown of command and co-ordination between the Nationalist units and the complete collapse of the KMT in the North-east. With the loss of Manchuria, the rest of North China was doomed. The capture of Tientsin (15 January 1949) was soon followed by the surrender of Peking, with 250,000 troops commanded by Fu Tso-yi, a week later. The way south to the Yangtze was cleared by the Huai-Hai campaign (6 November 1948–10 January 1949) in which more than 600,000 PLA troops gained control of Central and Eastern China to the north of the Yangtze, putting out of action almost their own strength in Nationalist forces.

This series of decisive and unexpected victories over a period of four and a half months effectively signed the Kuomintang's death warrant. They had created, in the words of Mao Tse-tung, 'a momentous change in China's military situation' by which for the first time the PLA's effective strength exceeded that of the KMT and the prospect of victory within the near future had become very probable.[19] The KMT's political morale and military cohesion was shattered; Fu Tso-yi's surrender in Peking paved

---

[19] See the NCNA commentary of this title, written by Mao and dated 14 Nov. 1948 (*MAO IV*, pp. 287–8).

the way for many similar actions by KMT commanders during 1949. As one independent American source commented at the time, 'The events of the last year, and more specifically those of the last four and one-half months, have resulted in such over-whelming losses to the Nationalist government that, acting alone, its military position has declined beyond possible recoupment'.[20]

A short respite from fighting was provided in the first quarter of 1949 by the peace negotiations between the communist government in Peking, and the delegation sent by Acting President General Li Tsung-jen. These negotiations finally broke down on 20 April, with the Nationalists' rejection of the CCP's proposals. (These were virtually in the form of an ulti-matum, demanding abolition of the Nanking government and reorganization of all its troops.) A day later the Second and Third Field Armies began to cross the Yangtze, for which they had trained since the Huai-hai victory. With only nominal opposi-tion from the demoralized Nationalist armies, the major towns of the Yangtze valley area fell in quick succession: Nanking (23 April), Hangchow (3 May); Wuhan (17 May); Shanghai (27 May). Meanwhile the First Field Army under P'eng Teh-huai resumed its advance into the North-west. Once Lanchow, the capital of Kansu province, had been captured (on 26 August) the remaining North-western provinces lost no time in surrender-ing.

In August a new offensive was launched in the south, and the entire Chinese sea-board including Kwangtung province had fallen into communist hands by the autumn. This only left the western provinces of Kweichow, Szechwan, Yunnan, and Sikang. Szechwan was the last to surrender (on 27 December), thus com-pleting the 'Liberation' of the Chinese mainland by the end of the year. Only the island of Hainan (captured the following April), Tibet, and Formosa remained on the list of 'unfinished business'.

COMMUNIST EXPECTATIONS OF VICTORY

Unlike so much of Chinese communist historiography, their periodization of the third civil war closely resembles the actual sequence of events. Furthermore, each new stage was forecast

---

[20] Report of US Dept of the Army, Intelligence Division, in *US Relations with China*, pp. 322–3.

and anticipated by them in their public pronouncements, and where these forecasts erred, it was invariably on the side of caution. As early as December 1945 General Yeh Chien-ying had told the foreign press that the communists could fight for ten years in the case of a showdown with the Kuomintang. If full-scale war developed, the communists would not depend upon outside supplies. They would do as they had always done before, acquiring most of their weapons and supplies by capturing them in battle.[21] As one observer reported from Yenan during the early months of the Kuomintang offensive,

... The Communists have an extraordinary capacity for laughing off immediate reverses and talking in terms of 'inevitable' victory in the long run. They count heavily on their high morale, their toughness, their discipline, their reform program and the meat-grinding tactics of their guerilla armies to wear down opposition.[22]

This confidence was based upon a strictly dialectic analysis of the class nature of the war. Reduced to its simplest terms, this meant—in the words of Chou En-lai—that 'as time goes on, the KMT will get weaker and weaker despite American support, while the Communists will grow stronger because they have the support of the people'. The fundamental political and economic contradictions which faced Chiang Kai-shek would in themselves make a communist victory inevitable, provided only that the communists were successful in 'winning the masses'. Time was on their side, and Chou forecast that they could fight for twenty more years.[23]

Unlike Nationalist spokesmen, who confidently predicted victory within six months or at the latest one year, there was no inclination on the communist side to underestimate the difficulties which lay ahead, and at the start of the war Mao emphasized that it should be planned for 'on a long-term basis'.[24] A year later, in the summer of 1947, when the PLA had begun their limited counter-offensive against the Nationalists, Mao spoke of the need to consolidate the liberated areas, to carry out land reform and build up production and industry. 'Only by doing this can we support a long war and win victory in the whole country.'[25] Victory continued to be seen as a long-term objective.

---

[21] *NYT*, 3 Dec. 1945.   [22] A. T. Steele, in *NYHT*, 9 Oct. 1946.
[23] *NYT*, 25 Sept. 1946.   [24] *MAO IV*, p. 90.   [25] Ibid., p. 145.

In their official pronouncements, the communists had no scruples about revealing their strategic plans, and the progression from defensive through counter-offensive to annihilation was clearly foreseen, although it was expected to take much longer than it did. Thus at the height of the Kuomintang onslaught in North China and Manchuria in the winter of 1946, a communist spokesman told the Western press that the government's offensive would continue for at least several months, after which the communists would shift to the offensive. He also joined Chiang's American advisers in pointing out that 'the Government's thinned-out communication lines were vulnerable to attack at virtually any point'.[26] Almost at the start of the war, the military correspondent of the communist New China News Agency (*Hsin-Hua She*) had published what was in retrospect a substantially accurate account of 'the weaknesses of Chiang's army', outlining the five weak points which would lead to the KMT's ignominious defeat. This article pointed to the inherent contradictions between the KMT's grandiose strategic plan and its manpower resources, between the same plan and the tactical requirements of the situation, and between the central and provincial armies. Chiang himself was criticized for issuing 'a stream of subjective orders' which conflicted with the actual situation in the field. The KMT army's morale was said to be seriously defective, and it was over-dependent on its supplies and lines of communication.[27]

Until the capture of Yenan and the withdrawal of the communist delegation from Shanghai in February–March 1947, foreign correspondents had no difficulty in informing themselves upon communist strategy. Chu Teh and Chou En-lai talked freely of plans for a mobile war of attrition, in which the PLA would not attempt to hold cities and defend fixed lines but would concentrate on destroying the Nationalists' manpower. Chu warned that if the Kuomintang continued to 'trade troops for towns', their offensive would come to a halt within half a year, and made it clear that Yenan would be evacuated rather than defended at any cost.[28]

[26] *NYT*, 6 Nov. 1946.

[27] *Tung-pei Jih-pao*, 22 Aug. 1946, *in* Tung-pei jih-pao she, *Chung-kuo chü-ta pien-hua ti i-nien* (Mukden, 1947), pp. 41–43.

[28] Interviews with Chu Teh in *Daily Worker*, 3 Jan. 1947; *NCDN*, 24 Feb. 1947; *NYT*, 8 Mar. 1947.

The fullest exposition of communist strategy was given by Mao Tse-tung in his speech of 25 December 1947 on 'The Present Situation and Our Tasks' to the party's Central Committee. Mao enumerated ten principles of operations for the coming counter-offensive against the Nationalists. The main objective was to wipe out the enemy's effective strength, and not to seize or hold land or towns. Until the balance of power had changed in its favour, the PLA would confine itself to operations against dispersed and isolated forces. Enemy concentrations would be left until later. Similarly, operations against large towns would be avoided for the time being. Mao emphasized that battles of attrition in which the PLA would only break even should be avoided; battle should only be joined when the PLA was able to bring a numerically superior force into action. The principal form of combat should be mobile warfare; enemy strongpoints and cities should be left alone unless they were weakly defended. The PLA should look to the enemy for its supply of arms and of personnel. 'Our army's main sources of manpower and material are at the front.' These principles, said Mao, were the result of the PLA's long revolutionary experience. Even Chiang Kai-shek, he claimed, had attempted to counter them by distributing communist military literature to his generals and field officers. But he lacked the support of the people, and 'no army opposed to the people can use our strategy and tactics'.[29] As the American ambassador, Leighton Stuart, aptly commented on this speech,

Mao's elaboration of Communist military tactics and strategy is a remarkably candid explanation of how precisely Communist armies operate as far as the Embassy has been able to determine. It is perhaps a mark of Communist contempt for Nationalist military thinking and intelligence that the Communists have so little hesitation in explaining their strategy, which, it must be admitted, has to date not been without success.[30]

'SELF-RELIANCE' AND RELATIONS WITH THE SOVIET UNION

Although in retrospect the course of communist victory may assume an air of inevitability, and although the communist leaders never appeared to waver from their belief in final suc-

[29] *MAO IV*, pp. 157–71. The original speech, which differs slightly from this version, is trans. in NCNA (London), Suppl. No. 3. Chinese text in Chieh-fang she, ed. *Mu-ch'ien hsing-shih ho wo-men-ti jen-wu* (1949), pp. 17–34.
[30] Stuart to Marshall, 9 Jan. 1948 (*US Relations with China*, pp. 840–1).

cess, one should not underestimate the magnitude of their decision to embark upon the civil war, without any significant measure of external aid, rather than seek any further compromise with the KMT.

Events had moved with unexpected speed in the two years before the civil war began; in 1944 the end of the war against Japan had seemed a long way off, whether viewed from Washington, Chungking, or Yenan. As late as January 1945 Mao Tse-tung continued to speak of a period of 'two to three years' before Japan would be defeated.[31] In an editorial for New Year's Day 1945, the communist newspaper *Chieh-fang Jih-pao* observed that in spite of great achievements by the United States in the Pacific, the Japanese land army was still very strong. It foresaw victory over Hitler in Europe in 1945, but in the Far East 'it will inevitably be a fiercer and harder battle than in 1944'.[32] Events also moved rapidly in the diplomatic field. In the hey-day of Soviet-American co-operation, Mao Tse-tung and his colleagues in Yenan also hoped for assistance from the United States. Throughout the summer and winter of 1944, informal and friendly contacts were maintained between American and communist officials, both in Chungking, and in Yenan where the Allied Observers' Group was stationed. The communists viewed with favour American attempts—especially those made by General Hurley—to provide political mediation between Yenan and the Nationalist government. They also hoped to obtain military aid from the United States—in this their hopes were unduly encouraged by some American officials on the spot.[33] At one point, Yenan even suggested that Mao Tse-tung and Chou En-lai should travel secretly to Washington to confer with President Roosevelt.[34] In the winter of 1944 Yenan also shared the widely held opinion in China that the allied offensive would involve American landings on the China coast, and expected that this would entail co-operation between the communist guerrillas in North China and the American forces.[35]

[31] *MAO III*, p. 250.   [32] *CFJP*, 1 Jan. 1945.

[33] Useful information on contacts between American officials and the Chinese communists in 1944–5 is included in C. F. Romanus & R. Sutherland, *United States Army in World War II, China–Burma–India Theater*, vol. ii: *Stilwell's Command Problems*; vol. iii: *Time Runs Out in CBI* (Washington, 1956 & 1959), passim.

[34] Gen. Hurley to Pres. Roosevelt, 14 Jan. 1945 (US Dept of State, *Foreign Relations of the United States: The Conferences at Malta and Yalta, 1945* (1955), pp. 346–51).

[35] Mao Tse-tung wrote that 'the whole anti-fascist war has had great successes; it is

Policy decisions were, however, taken in Washington in the first months of 1945 which meant both that there would be no landing on the China coast, and that support for Chiang Kai-shek's National government would be America's primary aim in China.[36] By August 1945, when the Soviet Union invaded Manchuria, it was clear that Yenan could expect no special treatment from the United States. Yet support from the Soviet Union also proved to be of equivocal value. In Manchuria it allowed the communists to take over a certain amount of Japanese arms, and to entrench their position before Nationalist forces arrived. But at the same time the Soviet Union did not hesitate to conclude an alliance with the National government, as well as denuding Manchuria of large quantities of equipment and machinery on the grounds that it was legitimate 'war-booty'.[37] The Soviet Union appeared willing at the most to save the communists from total isolation in the North, and to strengthen their bargaining position in Chungking. It may also have wished to see Manchuria under communist control as a buffer state in sympathetic hands. Nevertheless at the diplomatic level it worked together with the United States to bring about negotiations between the communists and the KMT, and was clearly opposed to a resumption of hostilities. Soviet policy was intended to strengthen its influence with the Nationalist government, and reaffirm its rights in Manchuria and Outer Mongolia, not to further the cause of the Yenan communists as such. Stalin privately advised the communists 'to join the Chiang Kai-shek government and dissolve their army'. There is nothing to suggest that Yenan's decision to fight to the bitter end met with the slightest approval from Moscow.[38]

It is not therefore surprising that the theme of 'self-reliance'

---

now possible to accomplish the overthrow of Hitler next year. We . . . must co-operate with the Allied offensive. America has already attacked Leyte island, and it is possible that she will land in China' ('The tasks for 1945', *CFJP*, 16 Dec. 1944).

[36] On American strategy in the Pacific, see J. R. M. Butler, ed., *Grand Strategy*, vi: *October 1944–August 1945*, by John Ehrman (London, 1956), chs. 6–8. On American policy towards aid to the communists, see the State Dept paper on 'US Short and Long Range Objectives in China', 27 Feb. 1945, in *Time Runs Out in CBI*, p. 337.

[37] On Soviet policy towards China in 1945–6, see the detailed account in Charles B. McLane, *Soviet Policy and the Chinese Communists, 1931–46* (Columbia UP, 1958), ch. 5.

[38] Stalin's advice is reported in the writings of two Yugoslav communist leaders: Milovan Djilas, *Conversations with Stalin* (London, 1963), p. 141; Vladimir Dedijer, *Tito* (New York, 1953), p. 322.

was constantly stressed by the communist leaders in Yenan. Although, said Mao, they had friends all over the world, 'we stress regeneration through our own efforts'.[39] In the same mood, Chou En-lai told a foreign reporter in February 1947 that 'the Communists from now on are working out their own problems without any foreign mediation—from Russia, Britain, the US or any other country'.[40]

Yenan's feeling of isolation was reflected in its analysis of the current international scene. There was, according to Mao Tse-tung, no question of a break between the Soviet Union and the West. On the contrary, it was likely that there would be a wide measure of compromise between them on some issues, including certain important ones. The dominant political contradiction in the world was not between the capitalist world and the Soviet Union, but between the following three groups: the American people and the American reactionaries, Britain and America, and China and America. Thus the course of events in China set the pattern for events of the international scene. Just as in China a united democratic front was struggling against US imperialism and domestic reactionaries, so, according to Yenan's argument, battle would be waged on a world-wide scale between the people and the reactionaries in the capitalist countries, and in their colonies. The Soviet Union did not play a very prominent part in this typically Sino-centric view of world affairs, and it was merely said that 'this united front will undoubtedly have the sympathy and moral support of the socialist Soviet Union'. This analysis had the effect of enhancing the significance and relevance of the Chinese civil war to the world at large, while accommodating and explaining a situation in which the Soviet Union gave no more than 'moral support' to the Chinese communists, although American aid to the Nationalists took more tangible form.[41]

[39] *MAO IV*, p. 20.

[40] *NYT*, 23 Feb. 1947. See also *NCDN*, 24 Feb. 1947, where Chu Teh is quoted as saying that China could solve her own problems without any assistance or advice from any other country. Chu also denied any connexion or special affiliation between the Chinese and Russian communist parties. Chou En-lai was also reported as saying 'They [the Soviet Union] made too many mistakes for us in the early days' (*NYT*, 9 Sept. 1946).

[41] See Mao Tse-tung, 'Some Points in Appraisal of the Present International Situation, April 1946', in *MAO IV*, pp. 87–88; Lu Ting-yi, 'Explanation of Several Basic Questions Concerning the Post-war International Situation', *CFJP*, 4–5 Jan. 1947, trans. in *US Relations with China*, pp. 711–19.

It was in this early phase of the civil war that Mao Tse-tung first used the phrase 'paper tiger' to belittle the significance of America's monopoly of the atomic bomb.[42] Mao's analysis of the international situation was designed to counteract the 'pessimism' of some party members who, we are told, 'overestimated the strength of imperialism, underestimated the strength of the people, feared US imperialism and feared the outbreak of a new world war', and therefore by implication feared the consequences of embarking upon the civil war.[43] We do not know who held such pessimistic views, although the frequency of references to them in Mao's writings suggests that they were both fairly numerous and were located in the higher ranks of the party. As the war progressed, the 'pessimists' appear to have doubted the advisability of launching the counter-offensive against Central China, and there is some indirect evidence to suggest that they favoured accepting a *de facto* partition of China and the establishment of a separate communist regime in the North.[44] Most of

[42] Mao Tse-tung first advanced his thesis that 'all reactionaries are paper tigers', and that the atomic bomb itself was a paper tiger in his 'Talk with the American Correspondent Anna Louise Strong' of August 1946 (*MAO IV*, pp. 97–101). He also expressed the view that all-out war between the Soviet Union and the US in the immediate future was improbable and that the struggle between socialism and imperialism would take place in the 'vast zone' outside the USSR and the US which embraced 'many capitalist, colonial, and semi-colonial countries in Europe, Asia and Africa'.

It has been pointed out that this amounted to 'Mao's first independent assessment of the global situation confronting the international communist movement', and that it 'constituted Mao's justification, from the viewpoint of the international Communist movement as a whole, of his acceptance (in July 1946) of all-out war with Chiang and placed the revolutionary war in China within the context of the world struggle between the socialist and imperialist camps' (Tang Tsou and Morton H. Halperin, 'Maoism at Home and Abroad', *Problems of Communism*, July–Aug. 1965, p. 3).

[43] *MAO IV*, p. 88 n. See also NCNA (N. Shensi), 7 Nov. 1947, 'A Spark Can Kindle a Mighty Flame', editorial on the 30th Anniversary of the October Revolution, summarized in NCNA (London), 2 Dec. 1947: 'The fact that the chief danger for the working class now lies in underestimation of its own forces shows that "paper tigers" can still confuse a section of the people and even some of the vanguards of the working class. The market for "paper tigers" has shrunk to an unprecedented extent but not as much as it should have done. . . . The Chinese people are now waging a great revolutionary war whose aim is to overthrow the rule of American imperialism and its "quisling" Chiang Kai-shek in China. Great victories have been won. New victories will continue to be won until a new China is established. We do not stand alone. We have the friendship of all anti-imperialist countries and peoples. But we emphasize self-reliance. Relying on our own organized strength we can overthrow our enemies.'

[44] In a directive of October 1946 Mao referred to 'those Comrades in the Party who

these doubts appear to have been allayed by the spring of 1948, when the PLA's counter-offensive began to pay off. As the prospects of victory loomed into sight, the advocates of 'pessimistic' policies within the communist party appeared to have fallen silent.[45] If, as has sometimes been suggested, Stalin continued to urge caution upon the Chinese communists as late as the summer of 1948, he was singularly ill advised.[46] Whatever doubts some party members may have had earlier in the civil war, by then it must have been abundantly clear that total victory was in their grasp.

THE CONSEQUENCES OF RAPID VICTORY

Ever since the outbreak of formal civil war, the Chinese communist leadership had insisted—at least in their public statements—that ultimate victory was inevitable. It was not, however, until the spring of 1948, following Liu Po-ch'eng's advance into Central China, communist gains in the Yellow river plains, and the partial isolation of KMT garrisons in Manchuria, that the Central Committee permitted itself to forecast victory within a given period of time. 'It should be possible', wrote Mao in a circular for the Central Committee, 'to wipe out the entire

---

are gloomy about the future of the struggle owing to their inadequate understanding of the favourable situation at home and abroad' (*MAO IV*, p. 117). In February 1947 he wrote that 'the myth that the offensives of the reactionaries cannot be smashed should have no place in our ranks' (ibid. p. 123). In December 1947 Mao told the Central Committee that 'we should rid our ranks of all impotent thinking. All views that overestimate the strength of the enemy and underestimate the strength of the people are wrong' (ibid. p. 173).

Two resolutions were passed at the same meeting of the Central Committee which suggest that some members had favoured reopening negotiations with the KMT and establishing a separate regime in the North. It was decided—

(1) 'That every effort should be made to carry the Chinese people's revolutionary war uninterruptedly to complete victory and that the enemy should not be allowed to use stalling tactics (peace negotiations) to gain time for rest and reorganization for a fresh attack on the people.'

(2) 'That the time was not yet ripe for the formation of a revolutionary central government, which was to be considered only when our army had won greater victories, and that the promulgation of a constitution was even more a question for the future' (ibid. p. 159 n.)

[45] In March 1948 Mao referred to the 'Right deviations' of 'overestimating the strength of the enemy, being afraid of large-scale US aid to Chiang Kai-shek, being somewhat weary of the long war, having certain doubts about the strength of the world democratic forces . . .' but said that these were no longer the main deviations; they were 'not difficult to correct' (ibid. p. 220).

[46] C. P. FitzGerald, *Revolution in China* (London, 1952), pp. 103–5; Max Beloff, *Soviet Policy in the Far East* (London, 1953), pp. 60–61.

Kuomintang army in about five years (counting from July 1946).'[47] It was estimated that numerical parity with the KMT would be reached by spring 1949, and that the PLA would destroy about 100 Nationalist brigades a year. This assessment was repeated at the Central Committee's meeting in September 1948, which also decided that during 1949 'the whole of the PLA will continue to operate north of the Yangtze river and in northern China and the Northeast'.[48] It was calculated that in spite of enemy losses exceeding 3 million since the war began, the KMT would still be able to raise the same number before defeat sometime in 1951, and that the PLA would have to double in size over the next three years in order to ensure victory.

The same note of caution can be found in an NCNA editorial of this period, which warned that:

... because China is almost equal to Europe in area and population, because her social development is complicated and uneven and because American imperialism and the KMT reactionary forces are so deeprooted in China's soil, the Chinese revolution cannot be completely victorious through one, or even several simple struggles. It can only be won step by step. The positions of the enemy cannot be taken all at the same time and the reactionary forces can only be exterminated one by one. The Chinese people must prepare for several years continued hard struggle; at least three or four years may be required to liberate and unify all China on a democratic basis. In the course of the struggle certain temporary, partial respites or zig-zag advances may occur.[49]

As it turned out, the Yangtze was crossed in April the following year, Nanking was liberated in the same month, Shanghai in May, and total victory achieved at least a year and a half before it had been predicted. The turning-point was marked by the three great offensives of autumn and winter 1948, and on 14 November Mao for the first time forecast that 'only another year or so may be needed to overthrow it [the KMT] completely'. The military situation, he wrote, had reached 'a new turning-point' and the balance of forces had undergone a fundamental change. The PLA, long superior in quality, was now superior in quantity as well, having grown to 3 million while the whole of the KMT forces now numbered only 2,900,000.[50]

There is no doubt that victory came to the communist leader-

[47] *MAO IV*, p. 225.   [48] Ibid., p. 273.   [49] NCNA (N. Shensi), 19 Aug. 1948.
[50] *MAO IV*, p. 287.

ship much earlier than they expected, although their cautious statements also reflected a refusal to compete with the extravagant forecasts of the Nationalist government. As Ch'en Yi told an audience in Shanghai shortly after he took control of the city:

> We have facts to support our statement that the war will be ended within a year. As everybody knows, we are very cautious in our military predictions and are inclined to err on the conservative side. It is more likely that total victory shall be gained in a shorter time.[51]

Although the speed of their success was gratifying, it created serious problems of administration and control for the new communist government in its first year of power. Chief among these was the rapid expansion of the PLA, the lack of trained cadres, and the extent of economic chaos throughout China.

In June 1948 the PLA numbered 2,800,000; two years later it had increased to 5 million. Nearly 80 per cent of these were 'young people', many of whom had defected from the Nationalist armies. Victory was hastened by the collapse of morale in these armies; this also meant that more KMT soldiers surrendered or let themselves be captured, while fewer got killed. According to PLA statistics, in the first two years of the war (1946–8) about 50 per cent of KMT losses were casualties (1,450,000 out of 3,090,000). In the third year (1948–9) losses were almost the same as for the previous two combined, but casualties amounted to less than 20 per cent of the total (571,610 out of 3,050,000). In the four years July 1946–June 1950, the PLA claimed that it had captured a total of 4,586,750 ex-KMT soldiers, and that a further 1,773,490 surrendered and crossed sides of their own free will. Whatever the precise accuracy of these statistics, their dimensions roughly indicate the size of the problem. The communist victories in 1949 created a reservoir of several million ex-KMT soldiers in need of either resettlement on the land or incorporation into the PLA. The steady rate of PLA expansion envisaged by Mao Tse-tung until 1951 had gone by the board.

The new administration was seriously short of trained cadres. This was an inevitable consequence of its rapid territorial expansion, and of the need for political cadres to consolidate party control over the new territory. The population of the liberated areas had grown from some 130 million in 1947 to 170 million a

[51] 'Mayor Ch'en Yi on the current situation', *Ta-kung Pao* (Shanghai), Aug. 1949 (US Consulate General, Shanghai, *Chinese Press Review*, No. 941, 3 Aug. 1949).

year later. It then leapt by over 100 million to almost 280 million in June 1949. Within the next year, the conquest of the remainder of the Chinese mainland had brought almost as many again under communist rule. The cadre problem was referred to by Liu Shao-ch'i in his May Day speech for 1950, in which he admitted serious shortcomings and errors in the work of cadres and promised a campaign of criticism and self-criticism among them.

The territory under our occupation is vast, and the various features of the work are heavy and complicated. We have insufficient experienced cadres and there are large numbers of new cadres. All these factors, together with no time for training, have caused many shortcomings and errors to arise in the course of attaining these great achievements.[52]

Two-thirds of the communist party's membership had joined since 1946, and for those stationed in the towns and cities there was the additional problem of working in an urban environment. Hitherto most cadres had been accustomed to working in rural areas.[53]

A large measure of economic disruption was obviously to be expected after a three-year-long civil war which itself followed eight years of resistance against the Japanese. However, the landslide victory of 1949 made things much worse. A more orderly progress would have allowed time for the rehabilitation of the North-east as an industrial base, and for the restoration of communications, production, and distribution systems in North and East China. As it was, these remedial measures had to take place concurrently with the much more onerous task of reviving the economy of Central and South China. It was aggravated by the natural disasters which hit China in 1949, as by the effects of spiralling inflation. PLA manpower demands—both for conscripts and for auxiliary service corps—also contributed to the dislocation of agricultural production.

ALLIANCE WITH THE SOVIET UNION

Finally, the rapid pace of victory in China required equally rapid decisions to be made in the field of foreign policy. It was in

[52] NCNA (Peking), 30 Apr. 1950 (NCNA (London), Suppl. No. 47). Henceforth all references to NCNA refer to stories datelined Peking, unless otherwise stated.
[53] Party membership increased from 1,348,320 at the end of 1946 to 4,488,080 at the end of 1949. A year later it had reached 5,821,604, according to official statistics published in *Shih-shih Shou-ts'e*, 25 Sept. 1956, trans. in *CB* 428.

the autumn of 1948, as the prospects of success drew dramatically nearer, that the communist leadership appears to have decided in principle to enter into alliance with the Soviet Union. In November 1948 major policy writings by Mao Tse-tung and Liu Shao-ch'i emphasized for the first time the need to lean to one side—the side of the Soviet Union.[54] On 15 February 1950 the Sino-Soviet Treaty of Friendship, Alliance and Mutual Assistance was signed in Moscow, after several months of hard negotiation.

There is little doubt that the alliance would have been concluded whether victory had come earlier or later. Neutrality was out of the question at a time of acute and world-wide cold war. So was alliance with the United States, the sponsors—albeit with some reluctance—of the losing side of the civil war. Whatever grievances the Chinese communist leaders might have over Soviet behaviour in the past, ideology and self-interest alike impelled them to alliance with their most powerful neighbour. It is difficult to imagine any circumstances under which a communist government in China would not have joined hands with the Soviet Union. Yet it is possible that if the communists had won with less haste, allowing them a more gradual extension of administration and economic control, they would have found it easier to negotiate a more satisfactory and 'equal' treaty. They might also have been able to do so without entirely turning their backs on the non-communist world (or without the latter doing the same to China).

In the event, the treaty was signed after two and a half months of hard negotiations between Mao Tse-tung himself and the Soviet leaders, in which he clearly did not obtain anything like complete satisfaction. Soviet rights in Manchuria were to be surrendered—but not for three years. The Soviet credit to China

---

[54] In an article for the Cominform journal *For a Lasting Peace, For a People's Democracy*, commemorating the 31st anniversary of the October Revolution, Mao wrote: 'Has not the history of these 31 years proved the utter hypocrisy and complete bankruptcy of all those who are satisfied neither with imperialism nor with the Soviet Union, of all those so-called "middle road" or "third force" attempts to stand between the imperialists counter-revolutionary front and the people's revolutionary fighting front against imperialism and its running dogs in various countries?' ('Revolutionary forces of the world unite against imperialist aggression', NCNA (London), Suppl. No. 11, 23 Nov. 1948). This sentence is omitted in the current *Selected Works* version (*MAO IV*, pp. 283–6). See also Liu Shao-ch'i, 'On Nationalism and Internationalism', NCNA (London), Suppl. No. 12, 28 Dec. 1948.

of US $300 million could hardly be described as over-generous. Outer Mongolia was formally recognized as independent of China; Soviet interests in Sinkiang were perpetuated in the form of joint-stock companies. China did not become the Soviet satellite which the American Secretary of State represented her as, but this was not the most 'equal' of treaties.

The major benefit which the treaty provided, and which Chinese leaders emphasized repeatedly, was the political and military backing of the Soviet Union at a time when China was at her weakest and most vulnerable. It was this aspect which was constantly underlined whenever the treaty was justified in the Chinese press, although before it had been signed, more attention was paid to the economic benefits which the 'lean-to-one-side' policy was expected to bring to China. After the Moscow negotiations the question of Soviet economic aid was given less prominence. In, for instance, an NCNA editorial of 15 February 1950 commenting on the treaty, the agreements on trade and economic credits were dismissed in a couple of sentences. The editorial implied that it was basically up to China to set her own house in order.

The Chinese people are brave and industrious. China is a country of vast territory, plentiful resources and huge population. Through hard struggle under the leadership of the Communist Party of China, in addition to the favourable condition of assistance from the Soviet Union, the great People's Republic of China is certain to be swiftly transformed into a strong, prosperous and industrialised country.

It emphasized the importance of Article 1 of the treaty, which provided for mutual military assistance in the event of an attack on either party by 'Japan or states allied with it'. It described this provision as providing 'explicit and weighty stipulations . . . against aggression'. China was no longer 'isolated' and the alliance would strike a great blow against American plans to 'undermine the peace of the Far East'.[55]

[55] NCNA editorial, 'The new era in Sino-Soviet friendship', 15 Feb. 1950.
    Art. 1 of the treaty reads in part: 'Both High Contracting Parties undertake jointly to take all the necessary measures at their disposal for the purpose of preventing a repetition of aggression and violation of peace on the part of Japan or any other State which should unite with Japan, directly or indirectly, in acts of aggression. In the event of one of the High Contracting Parties being attacked by Japan or States allied with it, and thus being involved in a state of war, the other High Contracting Party will immediately render military and other assistance with all the means at its disposal.'

Alliance with the Soviet Union gave China the military backing and diplomatic support necessary to enable her to relax her efforts in the military field and to embark upon the reconstruction of her economy. In the words of Mao Tse-tung, the Soviet Union was a 'valuable ally', whose acquisition made it possible to 'fulfil domestic construction, jointly oppose aggression of our enemies and build the foundation for establishing world peace'.[56] As Liu Shao-ch'i explained, 'the international conditions for carrying out our construction work are also very good'. The Soviet Union had provided China with a 'powerful ally', and this would free her from restraint in carrying out construction work. The alliance had created the 'peaceful environment' which China so urgently needed in order to stand on her feet again.[57]

[56] Address to the Chinese People's Government Council, 13 Apr. 1950.
[57] Liu Shao-ch'i, address to cadres at a meeting called by the National Committee of the Chinese People's Political Consultative Conference in celebration of May Day, 29 Apr. 1950 (NCNA (London), Suppl. No. 47, 8 May 1950).

2

From Liberation to the Korean War, 1949–50

Following the nationwide victory, to safeguard democratic reform and support economic recovery, our army liquidated the special agents of Kuomintang and armed bandits in the different parts of the country and took immediate steps to demobilize large numbers of troops and shift them to other work posts for participation in all kinds of national construction projects.

It should be specially pointed out here that just as the people of China concentrated their efforts in peaceful construction and our army effected extensive demobilization, the Korean War broke out.[1]

MANY of the special characteristics of the PLA which contributed most towards its success in 1949 began to become redundant almost as soon as it had been achieved. Its mobility, its loose organization and revolutionary enthusiasm, with which it had defeated a numerically superior but uninspired and largely immobile army, were no longer of such great importance in its new role as a permanent army of national defence. On the other hand it lacked almost all the specialized arms and expertise considered necessary for a modern army, it was grossly over-sized, and it had no effective structure of centralized control.

During the civil war the PLA's role had been arduous but relatively straightforward—to win popular support and to defeat an enemy which was clearly identifiable. Now its role was both less specific and more comprehensive—to protect China against 'foreign imperialists and Chinese reactionaries', as Mao Tse-tung warned the People's Political Consultative Conference on 21 September 1949. Internally the PLA had to garrison the length and breadth of the country in sufficient strength to maintain law and order and to prevent subversion and sabotage. Externally the PLA had to prepare itself to defend China against aggression which, however remote, was nevertheless a con-

[1] P'eng Teh-huai, Minister of Defence, speech to the 8th party National Congress of 18 Sept. 1956 (*CB* 422).

tingency to be taken seriously. By the very act of victory, the PLA had transformed itself from a free-wheeling revolutionary army to a predominantly garrison army of national defence. The *ad hoc* improvisations of the civil war had now to be replaced by careful and calculated planning for the future.

From the time of the communist victory until the Korean war, however, no immediate or positive steps were taken towards the modernization and reorganization of the PLA. Military policy during this year was essentially negative and short term. In the field of operations, it set out to achieve the limited objectives which still remained on hand—the occupation of Tibet, the invasion of Taiwan, and the pacification of 'bandits' and other dissident elements on the mainland. In terms of domestic policy, it sought to ensure that the requirements of the PLA did not conflict with—and were indeed subordinate to— China's immediate economic priorities. Thus the main emphasis was placed upon preparations for demobilization, and the diversion of part of the PLA into production work. This policy was pursued against the strategic background of the military guarantee which was implicit in China's alliance with the Soviet Union.

PLANS FOR DEMOBILIZATION

At the end of 1949 it was officially estimated that in the following year the PLA's strength would exceed 5 million, in addition to more than 3 million officials and teachers on the government payroll. The final liberation of the South-west, of Tibet and Taiwan was expected to increase this figure. During 1950, it was stated, only 'plans and preparations' could be made for demobilization and a heavy financial burden was therefore expected.[2] Military expenditure for 1950 was estimated at 38·8 per cent in the draft budget for that year, and even this figure was said to be artificially low. Many items under the separate budgetary category of administrative expenditure, such as locally raised war funds, transportation outlays, and the initial costs of setting up military control in the new liberated areas, should more properly have been included in the military appropriation.[3] Overall military and administrative expendi-

[2] 'Overcome financial difficulties and fight for stabilisation of commodity prices', NCNA, 4 Dec. 1949 (*FE* 34).
[3] Po Yi-po, report of 2 Dec. 1949 to 4th meeting of Chinese People's Government Council, in *New China's Economic Achievements, 1949–52* (Peking, 1952), pp. 39–45.

ture for 1950 was in fact estimated at 60 per cent of the total budget, covering a government payroll of 9 million military and civil employees. This payroll was deliberately kept at such a high level in order to implement the government's fixed policy 'to provide for large numbers of former KMT personnel, so that they would not be displaced and cause social disorder'.[4] There were frequent references to the heavy burden which this imposed, and in April 1950 Mao Tse-tung, commenting on a report by Ch'en Yun (the chairman of the Committee for Financial and Economic Affairs), listed three indispensable requirements for a 'fundamental turn for the better' in the overall economic and financial situation. These were the completion of land reform, a rational readjustment of industry and commerce, and 'big reductions in the Army and the governmental expenditure by the State'.[5]

In the same month some troops began to return from their terminal assignments south of the Yangtze to their original locations. It has been estimated that between the middle of May and early July, more than 60,000 troops from the Fourth Field Army in Central-South China returned home to Manchuria.[6] This transfer was explained at the time as forming part of the PLA's shift to production work. A cavalry division, for instance, reviewed in Peking on 2 April by Chu Teh, was said to be 'on its way back to Manchuria to take up garrison duty and to run a mechanized State farm and a stud farm'.[7] These moves were also a preliminary towards demobilization, since this would most naturally be effected in the troops' original recruitment area. Assignment to production appears to have been a half-way house towards demobilization, and the land armies which were later formed in this way were often soldiers only in name. According to the regulations of the Ministry of Public Security, 'people's armed personnel devoted to production careers' were not allowed to carry small arms or automatics, and could only carry weapons of any kind by licence from the local authorities.[8]

By June 1950 plans for demobilization had been speeded up, and in Mao Tse-tung's report of the 6th to the Central Committee, the prospect of partial demobilization in 1950 itself was raised for the first time.

[4] NCNA, 4 Dec. 1949 (see n. 2 above).
[5] Speech of 14 Apr. (NCNA, 21 Apr. 1950).
[6] Allen S. Whiting, *China Crosses the Yalu* (1960), p. 23.
[7] NCNA, 2 Apr. 1950. [8] Ibid. 27 June 1951.

On condition that it guarantees sufficient forces to liberate Taiwan and Tibet, consolidate the national defences and suppress the counter-revolutionaries, the PLA, while retaining its main forces, should demobilise part of its troops in 1950. This demobilisation must be carried out carefully, so that demobilised army men settle down in productive work when they return home. [9]

By this time, it was clear that the restoration of production had become the government's central preoccupation, and meetings of the party Central Committee and of the People's Political Consultative Conference in June were largely taken up with this theme. At the end of the same month the government's Committee for Financial and Economic Affairs adopted a plan of work which included the drafting of a first five-year plan for the years 1951–5. [10]

This growing concern with production may have prompted planning for measures of demobilization at an earlier date than hitherto thought feasible. On 24 June the State Administrative Council (SAC) and the People's Revolutionary Military Council (PRMC) were reported to have met to pass a 'decision on the work of demobilising part of the PLA in 1950'. [11]

The fact that these two bodies met and took such a decision

[9] Mao Tse-tung, 'The struggle for a basic turn for the better in the financial and economic situation of the state,' 6 June 1950, NCNA (London), Suppl. No. 50, 16 June 1950.

[10] 'China will have its first national economic plan next year', NCNA (London), 30 June 1950. The Committee for Financial and Economic Affairs decided to draw up 'an outline of the first five-year plan (1951–1955) to restore and build up the nation's economy and a plan for 1951'. However, a national planning conference for heavy industry, held in July, was reported to be 'strongly of the view . . . that it would be wrong to exaggerate the role of planning in the present stage of China's economy' (ibid. 26 July 1950). No further reference was made to a five-year plan. The idea may have been dropped because it was economically unsound at such an early stage of China's reconstruction, and also because the Korean war made it unfeasible. The concept of a five-year plan was revived in the spring of 1951, when the plan began to be drafted. It was put into effect in 1953, although it was not finally completed till February 1955. The ending of the Korean war was one of the reasons given for the timing of the plan. Its delay was said to be caused 'because we lacked research into our natural resources and had little statistical data at hand, and because we were faced with the co-existence of many forms of economy, our own lack of experience in drawing up long-term plans, and our very inadequate experience in construction work. (Also, looking from the overall situation of the nation, the armistice in the war of resisting American aggression and aiding Korea, which began in 1950, was realised only by the end of July 1953. . .)' (Li Fu-ch'un, chairman of State Planning Commission, 'Report on the First Five-Year Plan', *JMJP*, 8 July 1953, in *FE* Econ. Suppl. No. 172).

[11] NCNA, 24 June 1950, in *FE* 63.

indicates that it was of the greatest importance. Unfortunately no details are given of its contents. At dawn on 25 June, the day after this decision was taken, military action commenced on the 38th parallel in Korea. Even if at this early stage of the war, the Military Council still believed that it would be possible to start demobilization, it was obviously no longer politic to say so, with the outbreak of war on China's north-eastern doorstep. No further references to demobilization were made in July, or at the Army Day celebrations on 1 August, or subsequently, with one exception. On 11 August General Liu Po-ch'eng, chairman of the South-west Military and Administrative Committee, told the committee that

Part of the PLA in south-west China is to be demobilised. This will cut down Government expenditure and lighten the taxpayer's burden. Many demobilised Army men will soon return to their homes all over China. The People's Governments in the south-west will do everything possible to help them settle down.[12]

Thus in the South-west at least, the field of operations farthest removed from the scene of the Korean war, it was still intended as late as August 1950 to demobilize part of the Second Field Army (originally the Central Plains Liberation Army) and return it to its places of origin in Central China. There is no later reference to this proposal, and it seems unlikely that even the South-west PLA proved able to demobilize to any great extent.[13]

As a result of China's intervention in the Korean war, it seems certain that no significant amount of demobilization occurred in 1950. One official directive of December 1950 even suggests that previously demobilized soldiers were now liable to recall into the PLA. All provincial people's governments were instructed to issue 'new and rigid regulations about re-enlistment', and to ensure that these were 'energetically promoted to strengthen the fighting power of the army'.[14] There was no reduction in the

---

[12] NCNA (Chungking), 11 Aug. 1950.

[13] Of the 13 armies in the South-west Military Region, at least 3 were moved to Korea by the spring of 1951. (These were the 12th, 15th, and 60th armies, forming the Third Army Group of the CPV.) Two divisions of another army (the 52nd and 53rd divisions of the 19th army) took part in the invasion of Tibet in October 1950. Other troops were kept busy in Szechwan and Yunnan, two of the provinces worst affected by remnant KMT troops and 'bandits'.

[14] Joint Directive of the Ministry of the Interior and the General Political Department of the PRMC (NCNA, 23 Dec. 1950, in *FE* 90).

overall strength of the PLA until after 1951.[15] It was later stated that by 1954 almost 3 million troops had been demobilized; but the majority of these were apparently released in the latter part of the Korean war. Until 1953 very little reference was made either to demobilization itself or to the problem of resettling ex-soldiers which was later to become so important. The problem which was most discussed until then was the care of families and other dependants, while the soldiers themselves remained in service.[16] One must conclude that to a very large extent the PLA's plans for demobilization were thwarted and postponed by the advent of the Korean war.

PLA PRODUCTION WORK

Article 24 of the Common Programme of the People's Political Consultative Conference laid down that 'The armed forces of the Chinese People's Republic shall, during peacetime, systematically take part in agricultural and industrial production to assist in the work of national construction, on the condition that military tasks are not affected'. In a directive of 5 December 1949 issued by the Military Affairs Committee and signed by Mao Tse-tung himself, the PLA was ordered to take up a major share of the burden of production work as from spring of the following year. It was explained that this work was necessary in view of the severe damage inflicted upon the Chinese economy by the civil war, by the lack of capital, and the need for maximum use of manpower. The PLA, it was claimed, was especially suited to undertake production work, since the majority of soldiers came from the proletariat, possessed a high degree of political consciousness, and were expert in all kinds of productive skills. The tradition of productive work by the PLA dated back to the anti-Japanese war. Now that the civil war was over, it should again be revived.

It was emphasized that the PLA's participation in production should not be regarded as a short-term measure, but should take place within the framework of long-term planning for national reconstruction. Starting in spring 1950, each military region

[15] According to a resolution of the Standing Committee of the NPC, 14 Sept. 1956, '... since 1951 China has on separate occasions reduced its armed forces by a total of over 2,700,000...' (NCNA, 14 Sept. 1956, in *SCMP* 1373). This implies that no reduction took place in 1950.
[16] See further ch. 4, pp. 92–98.

D

should initiate a production movement on a planned basis and with a comprehensive rate of expansion in mind. In order to avoid any clash with civilian production requirements, the military regions' production plans should conform to those of the local people's governments, both in the choice of projects and in the raising of capital.[17] Any moneys borrowed for military production should be repaid with interest and all produce should be taxed according to civilian law. Private enterprise—opening shops and other commercial enterprises—was strictly prohibited, and all production plans should be carried out on a co-operative basis, with the participating soldier taking 40 per cent of any profits. Thus it was hoped to supplement the soldiers' pay and also to provide an incentive for production work.[18]

In line with this policy, a New Year's message for 1950 from the party Central Committee to the PLA and the Chinese people affirmed that 'The Chinese people must now shift its main effort "step by step" to peaceful construction; during 1950 efforts must be made to heal the scars of war and overcome financial and economic difficulties, to rehabilitate industrial and agricultural production and to restore communications.[19]

Ambitious plans were formulated for army participation in production on a nation-wide scale; it was said that only those units which had been assigned to 'combat duties' would not take part. Agriculture, handicrafts, construction and repair of factories, restoration of communications, irrigation works, and reclamation of barren land were among the fields in which the army could take part.[20] In North China over 50 per cent of the PLA was scheduled to take part in water-conservancy projects; while in Kiangsi province it was planned that each soldier would devote two months a year exclusively to production work.[21]

Army production was closely linked to the acute food crisis in

---

[17] This was not always observed. In a report to a meeting on financial and economic planning of the South-west MAC, its vice-chairman, Teng Tzu-hui, criticized government organs and army units for trying to 'do business or fight for profits with the people'. He repeated that their capital requirements should be approved through legal channels and that they should not enjoy preferential treatment of the kind extended to other State enterprises (Wuhan radio, 3 Dec. 1951, in *FE* 138).

[18] See 'Directive concerning military participation for 1950 in the work of production and reconstruction', NCNA 6 Dec. 1949 (*FE* 34).

[19] NCNA, 31 Dec. 1949 (*FE* 38).   [20] PLA radio service, 20 Jan. 1950 (*FE* 40).

[21] NCNA (London), 24 Jan. 1950.

China after the civil war. It was estimated that the country's overall food output for 1949 had dropped by 25 per cent as a result of that war, and that between 7 and 8 million people were waiting to be fed. Some 40 million had been affected in 1949 by natural disasters.[22]

Army production work was particularly necessary because much of China's skilled labour and technical expertise had been drafted into army service during the civil war. Furthermore, one of the first actions of the PLA on assuming military control in an area was to take possession of all essential services, thus assuming responsibility for their maintenance. On such public projects as irrigation and land reclamation, railways and roads, military labour units formed a 'shock-corps' nucleus to lead and direct the masses of civilian workers engaged on these projects. Army production work also had social implications, since it attempted to identify the PLA with the interests of the civilian population. Fifty per cent of army grain production in the Central-South Region, for instance, was to be set aside as public grain tax, and in Sinkiang army units made a token contribution of 1,500 tons of grain to the tax levied on the minority groups. Again in the Central-South, where conditions were particularly severe, a per capita deduction of one ounce in the daily rice ration was levied throughout the army 'for saving food to help the famine-stricken people'.[23] In the North-west region income from army production was earmarked to cover garrison food costs and administrative expenses.

Production work in 1950 varied from military region to region, according to the particular economic and military needs.[24] In North China army labour was mainly employed in water conservancy, and in the repair of some 400 engineering plants and workshops; 3,400,000 man-days were estimated to have been contributed by the PLA in repairing river dykes in the Hopei plain. Similarly, in Manchuria the PLA was mainly used to reopen mines, to repair buildings, bridges, roads, and rail-

[22] *NYT*, 15 Jan. 1950, quoting from the Shanghai *Ta-kung Pao*.
[23] Wuhan radio, 11 Mar. 1950 (*FE* 47). However, allowing for this deduction, army rations at 27 oz. per diem still compared favourably with the party and official entitlement of 23 oz., and a much lower non-official ration.
[24] In August 1950 the official figures for PLA cultivation of land were as follows: North-west—238,000 acres; Central-South—160,000; North—74,000; Manchuria—60,000; East—25,000; South-west—no figure given (*NYT*, 30 Aug. 1950).

ways. In the barren North-west and in the food-hungry Central-South, agricultural work predominated. On the East China sea-board, where preparations were in full swing for the invasion of Formosa, there was little evidence of PLA production work. There was also little activity in the South-west, whose army was responsible for the invasion of Tibet.[25]

Production work in Sinkiang province is a special case which will be considered later.[26] Here the PLA was used both to colonize the province and to open up and reclaim barren land, thus linking its security role as a garrison force to production work. Except in the case of Sinkiang, plans for PLA production virtually ground to a halt after the Chinese intervention in Korea. Reports of production work in 1951, other than in Sin-kiang, are confined to token gestures of solidarity with the civilian population. In the Central-South, troops were 'encouraged' to take part in spring cultivation 'in their spare time', and to join in irrigation work 'where possible'. The Third Field Army in East China helped peasants with summer harvesting and planting, using their afternoon nap and rest-time 'so as not to interrupt their military duties and training'.[27] In the South-west PLA labour was used in rail and road construction—projects on which army men worked included the Chungking–Chengtu railway, the road from Chungking to Lhasa, and the road connecting Sinkiang and Tibet—but these were essentially works of military rather than of civil significance. Throughout 1952–4 reports of PLA production work in China at large continued to be scarce.

'BANDIT' SUPPRESSION

The intention of the communist government to occupy For-mosa and Tibet was never at any time in doubt. On 2 September 1949 the NCNA had circulated an article under the title of 'Foreign Aggressors must not be allowed to annex Chinese terri-tory', which made it clear that the PLA 'must liberate all Chin-ese territory including Tibet, Sinkiang, Hainan and Formosa' and that not a single inch of territory would be permitted to re-main outside the realms of the People's Republic. Sinkiang was

[25] Between October 1949 and October 1951 320,000 troops led a total labour force of 10,370,000 to work on water-conservancy projects throughout China, accord-ing to Fu Tso-yi, Minister of Water Conservancy (*JMJP*, 30 Oct. 1951, in *CB* 147).
[26] See ch. 9, pp. 176 ff.
[27] Wuhan radio, 11 May 1951; Peking radio, 12 July 1951 (*FE* 109 & 117).

annexed by the end of the year, Hainan by the following April, which left Tibet and Taiwan on the list of unfinished business. The suppression of internal armed resistance was also a major operation; Mao in June 1950 referred to a total of 980,000 'bandit guerrilla forces' which had been 'annihilated' since the crossing of the Yangtze in April 1949, and admitted that there were still 'more than 400,000' to be disposed of.[28]

After twenty years in which they themselves had been often known as 'bandits' (except during the United Front period, the Red Army was usually described by Nationalist sources as '*kung-fei*' or 'communist bandits'), the communists now used the same indiscriminate term to describe all forms of armed opposition against them.

The 'bandit' problem was almost entirely confined to south of the Yangtze, where communist control was established at break-neck speed between May and December of 1949. It was admitted even in the inflated figures of 'bandit' statistics emanating from Taiwan that only a small percentage were located in Manchuria, North and East China.[29] According to communist figures, only 181 bandits were operating in Shantung during the months of May–August 1950, a total of not more than 14,000 in Honan for the entire year, and in Manchuria reference was made only to scattered pockets of resistance. In East China 90,000 bandits were said to have been eliminated in 1950, but the great majority of these were located in the seaboard provinces of Chekiang and Fukien south of the Yangtze and opposite Taiwan.[30]

The major afflicted area was the Central-South Military Region (Honan, Hupeh, Hunan, Kiangsi, Kwangtung, and Kwangsi), where a grand total of 1,060,000 'armed bandits' were 'inactivated' in the two years May 1949 to May 1951, and in the South-west (Sikang, Yunnan, Kweichow, Szechwan), where 558,863 were 'routed' in 1950, and a further half-million by

[28] Speech to CC of 6 June 1950 (NCNA (London), Suppl. No. 50, 16 June 1950).
[29] In January 1951 Taiwan sources claimed a total of 1,610,800 active bandits on the Chinese mainland. Of these, only 15,800 were alleged to be in Manchuria, and 110,000 in the North (*NYHT*, 28 Jan. 1951).
[30] Tsinan radio, 24 Nov. 1950; Wuhan radio, 8 Feb. 1951. Over 32,000 bandits were eliminated in Fukien in August–November 1950 (Shanghai radio, 15 Dec. 1950, *FE* 88), and 36,000 in Chekiang for the whole of 1950 (Hanchow radio, 29 Apr. 1951, *FE* 101).

1954.[31] Within these regions the trouble was localized to a few provinces. In the Central-South Kwangsi, Kwangtung, and Hunan accounted for the greater part of the total banditry; in the South-west it was confined in the main to Szechwan and Yunnan.[32] In the more sparsely populated North-west the total banditry reported over the four years 1950–4 was 90,000.[33]

The term 'bandit' covered a wide variety of types. According to the communist usage, it was applied to all forms of organized armed resistance in a given area once it had been officially 'liberated'. Most of those in the Central-South consisted of ex-KMT units which had taken to the mountains, as the large number of weapons captured with them indicates. Their morale was low, and almost half the total surrendered voluntarily.[34] Nationalist units were also reported in Yunnan and Kweichow, whence many crossed in Vietnam where they were disarmed by the French.[35]

Not all 'bandits' were necessarily pro-Kuomintang. They included independent bands of pirates on the Chekiang and Fukien coasts, and long-established guerrilla units in the mountainous border areas of South China. Attempts were made to control their operations from Taipei, under the supervision of Lieut.-General Cheng Chieh-min (successor to General Tai Li who headed the Nationalist secret police during the anti-Japanese war) and Mao Jen-feng, director of the security bureau in Taiwan. However, there was very little communication or co-

---

[31] Canton *Nan-fang Jih-pao*, 29 July 1951, in *SCMP* 147; Sun Ching-jui, 'Gigantic victory on the bandit-suppression front in the Central-South Region', Chungking radio, 31 Dec. 1950, in *FE* 90; Li Ta, 'Work undertaken and accomplishment achieved by the troops in South-west Military Region during the past three years', *Hsin-hua Jih-pao*, 1 Oct. 1952 (quoted in Shih Ch'eng-chih, *People's Resistance in Mainland China 1950–5* (1956), p. 48).

[32] 424,000 bandits were eliminated between January 1950 and June 1951 in Kwangsi, almost half the Central-South total (Wuhan radio, 22 July 1951); and 250,000 in Hunan (*SCMP* 1619). 52,650 were eliminated in Kwangtung between October 1950 and August 1951 (*CSM*, 3 Nov. 1951). In South Szechwan alone, 58,000 bandits were reported to be rounded up in the month of June 1950; 100,000 were eliminated altogether in Yunnan (*SCMP* 2180).

[33] Urumchi radio, 16 Mar. 1954 (*FE* 338).

[34] 1,066,899 'bandits' were inactivated in the Central-South, and 1,021,893 firearms captured with them. Just over 470,000 were stated to have surrendered or to have 'given themselves up for registration' (*Nan-fang Jih-pao*, 28 July 1951, in *SCMP* 147).

[35] *NYT*, 15 June 1951, reported that 55,000 had been disarmed and interned in Indo-China since December 1949.

ordination between the various resistance movements, which facilitated the task of the PLA in isolating and eliminating them. In Kwangsi it was reported that pro- and anti-Nationalist bandits fought among themselves for supremacy. The Nationalist claim that in the winter of 1950–1 there existed some 2 million guerrillas on the Chinese mainland who could be persuaded to join their ranks in an invasion of China must be regarded with great suspicion. Most independent observers were of the opinion that no effective control was exercised from Taiwan.[36]

Opposition in Szechwan centred on the Elder Brothers Society (*Ko-lao-hui*) and other secret societies which energetically resisted land reform and the restoration of centralized government. In August 1950 they and similar secret societies throughout China were outlawed. Members of such societies were required to register with local authorities and persuaded to resign their membership, and during the subsequent campaign against counter-revolutionaries, many secret society leaders were accused of subversive intrigues and executed.[37] In the North-west the PLA had to contend with a relatively small number of local-nationality guerrillas. The largest of these was led by Osman Bator, a former district governor, who organized a mixed force of ex-Nationalists and Kazakhs some 5,000 strong. Osman was captured in the summer of 1950, and it was claimed in July that the bandits had been reduced from over 20,000 to less than 100.[38]

The task of bandit suppression did not impose an excessive burden on the PLA, although it caused some alarm in the four provinces most badly affected. After the liberation of Hunan, bandits still controlled over a third of the towns and the majority of villages, including the whole of West Hunan except the major highways, and their hold was not broken until the end of 1950. Land and water communications were harassed throughout that year in Szechwan, Kwangtung, and Kwangsi. In the summer, following warnings by government leaders that the problem was still of serious dimensions, a tougher policy was put into opera-

[36] See reports *NYT*, 2 July 1950 & 1 Jan. 1951; *NYHT*, 16 Nov. 1950; *CSM*, 27 Jan. 1951.
[37] For an account of communist policy in Szechwan and *Ko-lao-hui* resistance, see G. William Skinner, 'Aftermath of Communist Liberation in the Chengtu Plain', *PA*, Mar. 1951.
[38] NCNA (Tihua), 16 July 1950, in NCNA (London), 17 July 1950.

tion throughout the country. We are told that in Kwangsi there had been 'deviationism which permitted unlimited leniency and made it impossible to suppress promptly and vigorously the ringleaders', and in Fukien 'excessive lenience' was criticized.[39]

The new policy was described as combining 'oppression and leniency'. Full-scale campaigns were launched in the affected areas, with participation by local militia units, and captured leaders were executed in exemplary fashion. At the same time greater emphasis was laid upon securing popular support. Land reform cadres were instructed to compromise in their work, reducing taxation and postponing collection, and new efforts were made in the autumn of 1950 to build up local self-defence, militia and vigilance units among the local population.

Armed resistance on the mainland did not appear to receive any encouragement from the Korean war and China's intervention in that war, whereas in urban areas opposition to the regime took heart from China's new predicament. The campaign against counter-revolutionaries which began in the winter of 1950 was primarily aimed at the urban population. Bandit suppression in the countryside was not intensified, and after final mopping-up operations most areas were reported to be basically clear by the summer of 1951. The major exception was the North-west, and especially Sinkiang where national minorities continued to resist government control. There is an obvious incompatibility between the two reports referrred to above that in July 1950 20,000 bandits had been reduced to less than a 100, and that by 1954 a total of 90,000 bandits had been 'eliminated'.[40] Outside the North-west, however, banditry as a form of organized armed resistance appears to have declined very rapidly after 1951. Those who subsequently opposed land reform or mutual-aid teams, or who were identified as belonging to secret societies or other prohibited organizations were usually described as 'counter-revolutionaries' or as 'Chiang Kai-shek spies', suggesting that their numbers were small and their degree of organization very limited. Except in the North-west, the actual numbers of those identified in 1952–3 as belonging to counter-

[39] NCNA, 9 May 1951 (*FE* 108); Shanghai radio, 15 Dec. 1950 (*FE* 88).
[40] Over-optimism had been frequently displayed during the course of the 1950 campaign, as when Teng Tzu-hui claimed in March that 'only a few' bandits remained in Kwangtung and Kwangsi (Peking radio, 9 Mar. 1950; *NYT*, 10 Mar. 1950).

revolutionary groups were in the hundreds or less in each instance.[41]

OCCUPATION OF TIBET

Preparations for the invasion of Tibet began in January 1950, as soon as the South-west had been liberated, under the personal supervision of Ho Lung, commander of the South-west Military Region. During the spring, troops were moved up to Kantzu, in the province of Chinghai close to the Tibetan border, where a 'patriotic' provisional government had been established. In October units from both the North-west and South-west Military Regions, amounting to some 40,000 men under the command of Chang Kuo-hua, crossed into Tibet and captured the garrison town of Chamdo in Eastern Tibet on 10 October with only token resistance.[42] The battle of Chamdo, such as it was, was the first and last engagement of any size fought by the PLA in its invasion of Tibet. Military resistance was out of the question for Tibet: their armed forces totalled a maximum of 8,000–8,500, possessing an adequate number of rifles but only about 50 artillery pieces, 250 mortars, and 200 machine guns. Its purpose, as the Dalai Lama later narrated, was 'to stop unauthorized travellers and act as a police force. It was quite inadequate to fight a war.'[43]

The capture of Chamdo served as a warning of the irresistible military strength which could be brought to bear upon the Tibetan government unless it conceded Peking's claims of sovereignty, rather than as the preliminary to full-scale military operations. Further advance by the PLA was suspended while negotiations took place. China issued several statements which promised magnanimous treatment, and pledged herself to

[41] See details in Shih Ch'eng-chih, *People's Resistance*, chs 3–4.

[42] See Chang Kuo-hua, 'Tibet Returns to the Bosom of the Motherland', *JMJP*, 25 Oct. 1962 (*SCMP* 2854). According to an eyewitness report in the *Manchester Guardian*, 20 Jan. 1951, Chamdo was captured without a single shot fired, after the troops and townsfolk had been terrified by a Chinese display of rockets and star-shells. General Ngaboo, who later collaborated with the Chinese, deserted the town during the night. According to the PLA's own statistics, only 180 enemy troops were killed and wounded in the entire campaign leading up to the fall of Chamdo; 894 were captured and 4,317 surrendered (NCNA, 8 Nov. 1950, military communiqué on entry of Chinese army into Tibet).

[43] Dalai Lama, *My Land and My People*, ed. David Howard (London, 1962), p. 73. For similar figures from a Chinese source, see *JMJP*, 23 Nov. 1950 (trans. in Ling Nai-min, *Tibetan Source Book* (Hong Kong, 1964), pp. 3–4).

acknowledge the political status of the Dalai Lama, to accord freedom of religion and to protect all lamaseries and temples. Negotiations took place in April–May 1951 in Peking, and on 23 May an agreement was reached for 'the peaceful liberation of Tibet'.[44] In July 1951 Chang Kuo-hua's troops resumed their advance without opposition, arriving in Lhasa on 26 October. A total Chinese garrison of over 20,000 men was soon installed in Lhasa,[45] and in February 1952 the Military Region of Tibet was established, with Chang Kuo-hua as commander.

The strategic purpose of the occupation of Tibet, as explained by the Chinese themselves, was twofold. It was 'to liberate our brothers in Tibet from imperialist oppression, and to consolidate the defences on the western frontiers of the motherland'.[46] At this early stage, no attempt was made to enforce social reform in Tibet. Article 11 of the Peking agreement laid down that there should be no 'compulsion' in 'matters relating to various reforms in Tibet', and this was at first observed. Initially, the main Chinese objective appears to have been to consolidate their control over Tibet without arousing open opposition, and they were to some extent successful in inducing the Tibetan leadership to collaborate.

The Peking agreement provided for the reorganization of the Tibetan army, 'step by step', in the PLA (Article 8). It also provided for the establishment of a Military and Administrative Committee (MAC) and a military region headquarters in Tibet, to be paid for by the Central People's Government. Integration of the army in the PLA was formally completed by February 1952, when the military region was set up. As in the case of provinces like Sinkiang and Kansu in China proper, some Tibetans were given nominal positions of authority in the military region, but real power rested in the hands of the commander and 1st and

---

[44] 'Agreement of the Central People's Government and the Local Government of Tibet on Measures for the Peaceful Liberation of Tibet', NCNA, 27 May 1951; Ling Nai-min, *Tibetan Source Book*, pp. 19–23.

[45] Chang Kuo-hua was joined in December by troops from the First Field Army led by Fan Ming, which had entered from Chinghai province in the north and crossed the Tangla mountains (Chang Kuo-hua, *SCMP* 2854; *The Times*, 12 Dec. 1951).

[46] 'Joint Political Mobilisation Directive on the Military Expedition into Tibet, South-west Bureau of the CCP Central Committee, South-west Military Region Command and Command HQ of the 2nd Field Army', NCNA, 1 Nov. 1950 (Ling Nai-min, *Tibetan Source Book*, pp. 6–7).

2nd political commissars (Chang Kuo-hua, T'an Kuan-san and Fan Ming), who were concurrently deputy secretaries of the CCP Work Committee for Tibet.[47] While the reorganization of the Tibetan army followed communist policy elsewhere in China the presence of a garrison and military headquarters in Lhasa, as well as many of the provisions of the Peking agreement itself, are reminiscent of the methods by which Chinese authority was asserted over Tibet in the Ch'ing dynasty. The precedent of a Chinese garrison and a Resident or *amban* in Lhasa may well have been prominent in the minds of the negotiators of that agreement.

The consolidation of 'the defences on the western frontiers of the motherland' proceeded almost unnoticed by the outside world. A detachment from the North-west province of Sinkiang was ordered into Tibet after the signing of the Peking agreement, and crossed into western Tibet during the winter of 1951, possibly pioneering the 'West Tibet' road which was later constructed from Sinkiang into western Tibet via Ladakh.[48] According to reports reaching the West from travellers into India from Tibet, these troops, who reached Ngari province on the Tibet Indian border, were reported to number between 2,500 and 10,000. Frontier controls along the border were tightened and construction began on the conversion of the main east–west Lhasa–Gartok road into a modern highway. A Chinese garrison was installed at Gartok reputedly numbering 750 men.[49] The construction of a highway network, which began immediately,

[47] See NCNA, 19 Feb. 1952 (Ling Nai-min, p. 461) for details of the military region personnel, and George Ginsbergs & Michael Mathos, 'Tibet's Administration in the Transition Period, 1951–4', *PA*, June 1959. The MAC was never established, owing to Tibetan opposition and to the November 1952 abolition of the MACs in China proper. The integration of the Tibetan army was not very effective, and Tibetan soldiers fought against the PLA in the 1959 revolt. On both these points see further G. Ginsbergs & M. Mathos, *Communist China and Tibet* (The Hague, 1964), pp. 53–56.

[48] Chang Kuo-hua *SCMP* 2854: 'Another fraternal force which left Sinkiang also crossed the snow-capped and wind-swept Kunlin Mountains, the uninhabited grassland, rapid rivers, and deep ravines, and arrived in the Ari [Ngari] area after a difficult march of several thousand li.'

[49] It was reported at the time that the Chinese advance from Sinkiang into western Tibet took place in the summer of 1951 before Lhasa itself had been occupied, and that the movement had started earlier in the spring, when remnant Sinkiang rebels led by the nationalist leader Ali Beg were pursued south into Tibet (see *The Times* & *Manchester Guardian*, 4 Sept. 1951; *Scotsman*, 19 Sept. 1951, reports from India).

closely followed the routes which the three invading army detachments had taken. These were: (1) from Yaan (Sikang) via Chamdo to Lhasa (2,300 km.); (2) from Sining (Chinghai) to Lhasa (2,100 km.); and (3) the West Tibet highway. The first two were officially completed in December 1954, and the last in 1957.

The occupation of Tibet was not affected by the developments in Korea. If anything, the threat of America's presence in Korea may have impelled the Chinese leadership to speed up the process of securing their western flank. It did not appear to impose a heavy burden in terms of manpower; the three prongs of the Chinese advance numbered at the most 10,000 each, or the equivalent of one army group. Yet the severe climatic conditions were said to have exacted a heavy toll on the soldiers involved, and the cost of supplying them was considerable. The construction of highways, bridges, and the airlifting of supplies was also disproportionately expensive. It was reported that it cost six catties of rice to transport one catty from Chengtu just as far as the Tibetan border. These difficulties may have contributed to the decision to reach Lhasa by negotiation rather than by fighting; but they also testify to the importance which the leadership in Peking attached to the restoration of Tibet to Chinese control.[50]

THE INVASION OF TAIWAN FRUSTRATED

The invasion of Taiwan, where Chiang Kai-shek and some half a million troops had taken refuge, was given greater priority by Peking than either Tibet or bandit-suppression. Yet of the three major military tasks for 1950, it was the only one not to be completed by the end of the year. In January major policy statements by both President Truman and Dean Acheson had indicated that the US would not become involved in the civil war or extend its protection to Formosa. On the 5th Truman announced that the US recognized China's legal claim to Formosa, and did not have 'any intention of utilizing its armed forces to interfere in the present situation'. Nor would the US government 'provide military aid or advice to the Chinese forces in Formosa'. On the 12th Acheson excluded by implication Formosa from the

[50] See *NYT*, 24 Mar. 1951 for report of difficulties encountered in the Chamdo campaign; also 'Tibet Today', *The World Today*, May 1951, pp. 202–9.

United States defence zone in the Pacific, remarking that it would be the greatest folly to undertake 'ill-conceived adventures' with the object of stopping communism and thus 'to deflect to ourselves the righteous wrath of the Chinese people'.[51]

Although these statements did not irrevocably commit the US to refrain from action in the case of armed invasion against Taiwan, they were generally taken in that sense, and most commentators agreed that Chiang Kai-shek now stood alone. This view was apparently shared in Peking. It is true that communist propaganda alleged that 'U.S. top brass-hats' were personally directing Nationalist bombing raids on Chinese cities, that an 'International Air Brigade' was being organized with American connivance; and pointed out that 'The Kuomintang gangsters are using war vessels supplied by America to blockade the China coast: they are using U.S. aeroplanes to bomb Chinese cities....'[52] Yet these allegations were not over-stressed, and the possibility that America might interdict the invasion was not even hinted at. After the fall of Hainan island at the end of April, America was described as 'disillusioned'. The liberation of Taiwan was presented not as a confrontation with US imperialism but as a final blow against Chiang Kai-shek's 'remnant brigands', which would restore 'peace and unity in the whole of China' and allow China at last to 'turn fully from war to peaceful construction'.[53]

The invasion was definitely planned for 1950, and it was described as the 'principal task' for that year. In March Chu Teh claimed that it was 'not far off''; army commanders of Ch'en Yi's Third Field Army had already begun to study amphibious techniques in January, and his troops were exempted from production work 'because they still have military tasks to perform'. The magnitude of the task was not underestimated, and General Su Yü (deputy commander of the Third Field Army and the officer designated to lead the invasion) admitted that it was 'an extremely big problem and will involve the biggest campaign in the history of modern Chinese warfare', emphasizing the need for careful preparation for amphibious warfare.[54]

[51] RIIA, *Survey of International Affairs, 1950*, pp. 344–5.
[52] Speech of 28 Feb. by Chu Teh to commemorate the Third Anniversary of the Taiwan Rising. See also NCNA, 24 Mar. & 3 May 1950.
[53] *JMJP* and *Kuang-ming Jih-pao*, 21 Apr. 1950, editorials, in NCNA (London), 24 Apr. 1950.
[54] 'Liberation of Taiwan in sight', *People's China*, 16 Feb. 1950.

Preparations for the invasion continued throughout May and June. There were signs that the experience of Hainan had induced a more realistic assessment of the difficulties of the task. The *People's Daily* forecast with some caution that 'it is not inconceivable that the Kuomintang remnants perched on Taiwan and other islands will also be extirpated before long'.[55] A large fleet of invasion barges was built, airfields were constructed in the provinces of Chekiang and Fukien to accommodate China's primitive air force, and cadres were trained for amphibious operations. According to outside observers in Taiwan and Hongkong, some 5,000 junks were assembled on the East China coast, and fishermen and sailors were mobilized to man them.[56] Some reports spoke of as many as thirty airfields under construction in the Yangtze valley and East China, and a radar network installed with Soviet assistance on the coast. One report alleged that an army of 15,000 paratroopers had been assembled, consisting in part of ex-Nationalist battalions. The total strength of General Ch'en Yi's invasion force was usually put at 300,000 or more. While two armies had been withdrawn from the Fourth Field Army in South China to be regrouped in their native North-east, the disposition of the Third Field Army remained unaltered, and it was reported that the two armies withdrawn from the Fourth had transferred their heavy equipment and skilled cadres to the Taiwan task force.[57] On the outbreak of the Korean war (25 June 1950) some observers believed that the invasion of Taiwan was imminent, others that it had been postponed till August, but all agreed that it was still on.[58]

President Truman's statement of 27 June put a new perspec-

[55] 21 Apr. 1950, editorial.

[56] It was believed by the command of the US Seventh Fleet that the invasion fleet would consist mainly of wooden-hulled junks, sampans, and fishing craft, 5,000–6,000 in number and carrying up to 250,000 troops. They were expected to cross under cover of darkness and in bad weather, landing in the early morning, and to operate in packs of up to 50 craft together, with primitive artillery sandbagged in the bows or on the high-poop sterns. These tactics had already been demonstrated in the crossing of the Yangtze river estuary and in the capture of Hainan island (Walter Karig and others, *Battle Report: The War in Korea* (New York, 1952), pp. 47–50.

[57] See for instance reports in *NYT*, 21 & 30 July 1950; *Observer*, 23 July & 6 Aug. 1950.

[58] Marguerite Higgins reported in the *NYHT*, 15 June 1950, that Gen. MacArthur's Tokyo headquarters had intelligence indicating that the invasion was postponed 'at least beyond midsummer, and probably longer'. There was still time, a very high American official 'believed', to take a 'strong stand' in Formosa.

tive on the situation in the Taiwan straits. In the circumstances of the attack upon Korea, it stated:

> The occupation of Formosa by communist forces would be a direct threat to the security of the Pacific area and to United States forces performing their lawful and necessary functions in that area.
> Accordingly I have ordered the Seventh Fleet to prevent any attack on Formosa. As a corollary of this action I am calling upon the Chinese Government on Formosa to cease all air and sea operations against the mainland.[59]

In a reply to Truman's statement, Chou En-lai, the Minister of Foreign Affairs, characterized it as 'a further act of intervention by American imperialism in the affairs of Asia' and called on the people of the East not to 'yield to threats' but to 'struggle against the warmakers'. However, he avoided any firm commitment to 'liberate Taiwan', merely saying that 'no matter what obstructive action the US imperialists may take, the fact that Taiwan is a part of China will remain unchanged forever'. This remark in itself implied a realization on the part of Peking that the obstruction would not be short-lived.[60]

Allen S. Whiting, in his study of China's decision to enter the Korean war, has shown that at this point Peking tacitly admitted 'the futility of attacking Taiwan as long as the threat of American intervention remained'.[61] Subsequent Chinese statements regarding Taiwan and the role of the Third Field Army reflected the beginning of a shift from an offensive to a defensive strategy. The struggle to liberate Taiwan began to be linked to the struggle against US imperialism as such, and the achievement of the former was now seen in the more long-term context of the latter. The liberation of Taiwan was also subordinated to the theme of the modernization of the PLA as the means of accomplishing the overthrow both of the 'American imperialists' and of Chiang Kai-shek. Thus an editorial in the Shanghai *Liberation Daily* stated that 'The people and army of East China … have not only the direct task of liberating Taiwan, but also the task of consolidating national defences and guarding the fatherland'. It went on to call on the army and people 'to build up a powerful navy and airforce, strengthen the training of ground forces, and

---

[59] Text in *NYT*, 28 June 1950.   [60] NCNA, 28 June 1950.
[61] *China Crosses the Yalu*, pp. 63–4. Shifts in Peking's policy towards the invasion of Taiwan are ably expounded in pp. 21–22, 49–50, 62–63, 80–84.

study the use of combined operations in modern warfare'.[62]
General Ch'en Yi himself took a similar long-term view in a
report of 16 July to the East China MAC's economic session, in
which he said: 'While we are preparing for the liberation we must
not relax our work of economic re-organization, because a strong
and prosperous China will contribute greatly to democracy and
peace in the world'.[63]

A REVERSAL OF POLICY AND PRIORITIES

By the winter of 1950, the entire framework of Chinese military
policy as formulated after Liberation had been turned upside
down. One may gain some idea of the radical nature of this reversal by comparing the situation as seen by Liu Shao-ch'i in his
May Day address for 1950 with the situation as it subsequently
appeared after the outbreak of war in Korea.

Liu's speech was generally optimistic in tone. Although he
admitted that there were still many difficulties to overcome, he
foresaw a 'future of unlimited splendour' for the new China. One
difficulty was the continued existence of Kuomintang reactionaries in Taiwan and other islands on the mainland. But the war
of liberation was 'coming to a victorious end', and the experience
of liberating Hainan would soon be successfully applied to the
operations against Taiwan. 'After the Liberation of Taiwan',
Liu forecast, 'the enemy bombing and blockade will naturally
come to an end. Military and administrative expenditure by the
State will be greatly reduced. And it will be possible to increase
greatly the volume of investment in economic reconstruction.'
References to American imperialism were few and in a minor
key. True, it was 'still helping the Chiang Kai-shek gang in
Taiwan and engaging in all sorts of conspiratorial and disruptive
activities against the new China', but this was not presented as a
major threat. On the contrary, the international conditions for
China's peaceful reconstruction were 'very good', due to the fact
that she had acquired a 'powerful ally' in the Soviet Union.

---

[62] NCNA (Shanghai), 5 Aug. 1950 (NCNA (London), 10 Aug. 1950). See also the
statement made in an appeal to the Nationalist army in Taiwan, that 'The PLA
is making full preparations for the battle to liberate Taiwan by building a powerful navy and airforce, and by further strengthening its ground forces'; 'People's
army is building up land, sea and air strength to liberate Taiwan', NCNA,
4 Aug. 1950.

[63] NCNA (Shanghai), 20 July 1950.

Imperialist provocations of wars of adventure would result in the doom of the imperialist system. With the Soviet Union as an ally, China was free from any restraint in carrying out construction work. The PLA's military objectives in the near future were the liberation of Taiwan and Tibet, the wiping out of bandits and enemy agents at home, the 'consolidation of national defence' and participation in production work. These were 'the foremost demands of the people at the present moment'.[64]

What was the situation six months later? Taiwan, far from being wide open to communist invasion, had its safety guaranteed by the Seventh Fleet of the United States. The basis for 'a joint defence of Formosa and for Sino-American military cooperation' had been established,[65] as Chiang Kai-shek proclaimed following General MacArthur's visit to Taiwan at the end of July. By the end of the year Nationalist officials had begun to talk optimistically of a roll-back policy of reinvasion.[66] Along the mainland coast opposite Taiwan, the PLA had begun to construct defensive positions and installations.[67]

The role of the US as a threatening force and as a potential aggressor against China was now dramatically upgraded in Peking. While Chiang Kai-shek receded into the background as a mere puppet of the United States, American imperialism moved up into the position of prime danger to China which it has occupied ever since. At first American encirclement of China was presented as largely passive, with the twin objects of blockading the mainland and of preventing the liberation of Taiwan. Thus Kuo Mo-jo wrote in the *People's Daily* on Army Day that

The American imperialists fondly hope that their armed aggression against Taiwan will prevent us from liberating it... Around China in particular their designs for blockade are taking shape in the pattern of a stretched out snake. Starting from South Korea, it stretches to Japan, the Ryukyu Islands, Taiwan and the Philippines and then turns up at Vietnam.[68]

---

[64] See n. 57, p. 23 above.

[65] Statement by Generalissimo Chiang Kai-shek, *NYT*, 2 Aug. 1950.

[66] Governor K. C. Wu of Taiwan predicted that the whole Fukien coast was open to attack 'any time President Truman rescinded his neutralization order' (ibid., 17 Dec. 1950).

[67] See reports of defensive preparations in Kwangtung province and Shanghai, ibid. 28 Nov. 1950; *South China Morning Post*, 7, 8, 18 & 29 Nov. 1950.

[68] *JMJP*, 1 Aug. 1950 (NCNA, 3 Aug. 1950).

E

During August and September, as the tide turned in Korea and United Nations forces counter-attacked until they had crossed the 38th parallel on 1 October, charges from Peking of active American 'aggression' against China rather than of passive containment increased in frequency, and the war in Korea began to be linked with the question of China's own security. Following China's intervention in Korea on or about 16 October, America was characterized without qualification as wishing to overthrow the People's Government: 'American aggression is aimed at Europe and Asia as two main targets. And, in Asia, their main objective is to seize China with her 475 million people. To seize China is to seize the whole of Asia.'[69]

American designs on China were compared with those of fascist Japan: 'Japanese fascism has been overthrown, America has become heir to its teachings'. American statements that they would not cross the Yalu into Manchuria were dismissed as double-talk, for, 'in the light of the experience afforded by history, such a statement is in fact a prediction that the US aggressors will push beyond the border of Korea'. Those who thought Chinese intervention in Korea would simply provoke the US into attacking China were reminded of the dangers of appeasement.

Some people may think in the following vein: 'Though the enemy has now marched his army on our Yalu and Tumen rivers, though his airforce has bombed and strafed our border areas, he has nevertheless not yet undertaken any large scale invasion of our territory. And it must be remembered that though the Japanese undertook their armed aggression in Korea in 1894, it was not until 1931 that they occupied the North-east, with a lapse of 37 years in between. Would it not be better, therefore, that we should strive our utmost not to afford any pretext under which the enemy might undertake an attack on us, and utilise the intervening period for the peaceful reconstruction of the nation?

Such reasoning is erroneous, because it presumes that the enemy which has started his attack will permit us an intervening period and environment for peaceful reconstruction, which is contrary to the facts. The US of today is different from the Japan of the past, and there is neither need nor possibility for the United States to stop at Korea for such a long time as Japan did... Let us recall the situations in 1931 and 1937. In those days the Chinese people did not give any aid to

[69] Ibid. 6 Nov. 1950, editorial: 'Why we must not tolerate our neighbour being savagely invaded' (*SCMP* 5).

Korea, and indeed did not even give aid to China's own compatriots who were oppressed. But the enemy still easily manufactured pretexts for his attacks.[70]

The occupation of Tibet and the task of bandit suppression had both already got under way without significant interference from the Korean war, but the invasion of Taiwan was tacitly postponed until the PLA should become sufficiently modernized to accomplish it, and until 'U.S. imperialism' as a whole should suffer defeat. In military matters, modernization took precedence over demobilization and production work; national defence over the needs of peaceful reconstruction. As far as the PLA was concerned, the Korean war brought it face to face with the task of its modernization and of its structural reorganization which might otherwise have been deferred until a later date.

[70] Ibid.

3
Popular Mobilization in the Revolution

It is the peasants who are the source of the Chinese army. The soldiers are peasants in military uniform, the mortal enemies of the Japanese aggressors.[1]

WHETHER or not the Maoist dictum that man, and not weapons, is the decisive factor in war still holds good in the nuclear age, there is no doubt that the communist success in the anti-Japanese and civil wars stemmed primarily from their successful mobilization of manpower. At a very rough estimate, slightly less than 1¼ million soldiers were recruited to the Eighth Route and New Fourth Armies in 1938–45. During the civil war of 1945–9 as many as 4¼ million had joined the PLA by June 1949, and a further million or so came over from the KMT in the following year. Before conscription was introduced in 1954–5, yet another 1½ million at a conservative estimate had been recruited in order to replace the losses caused by demobilization of war-weary veterans and by the Korean war. This gives a somewhat arbitrary but illustrative figure of 8 million recruited in the fifteen years 1938–53.[2]

Popular mobilization is the basis of Chinese communist control throughout the whole spectrum of society, and the system of mass organizations now familiar in modern China was already highly developed during the anti-Japanese war. There were mass organizations based upon occupation, age, or sex—for peasants, women, children, workers, teachers, merchants, and cultural workers—and there were those which were defined by function—stretcher-bearers' corps, self-defence, and militia. The civil and military organizations overlapped in membership; they had the dual purpose of mobilizing civilian support for the war and of arousing the same support for the policies of the communist party. These mass organizations did not have real political power, but they served as a channel of communication in both directions between the leadership and the people. 'The mass

[1] *MAO III*, p. 300.   [2] For detailed figures see Tables 1, 2, & 3 (pp. 303–5 below).

associations' real contribution to Chinese political life was not democracy but . . . the structuring of mass mobilization'.[3]

There was a well-defined dividing line between membership of a mass organization—even of the militia, which was essentially a civilian home guard—and membership of the guerrillas or field units of the regular army. The former were defined as 'not divorced from production' and stayed at home—while the latter were full-time soldiers, whether they served in their own locality, as did the guerrillas, or were fully mobile, as in the case of the field units. In either case, recruitment for the army was a more delicate operation than recruitment into the mass organizations, although it was made easier by the constant threat of Japanese oppression.

'The role played by the Japanese Army in bringing the Chinese Communists to power', observes Chalmers Johnson, 'has never been fully appreciated by foreign observers.'[4] Japanese hostilities against the communist areas, in particular the ruthless tactics of their 'three destruction' pacification campaigns (kill-all, burn-all, destroy-all), coupled with the effect of their propaganda which continually identified communism as the main enemy in China, only served to increase the existing support for the Chinese communists. It was a situation where the middle position of neutrality was virtually ruled out; one had to be either for or against. (The tacit truce on the front lines between the Japanese and Nationalist forces, on the other hand, which lasted from the end of 1938 until the launching of Operation Ichi-gō in spring 1944, had the dual effect of corrupting the integrity and efficiency of the Nationalist forces, and of encouraging collaboration.) The concept of nationalism and of struggle against the Japanese was no abstract idea; it was literally a matter of survival. To the peasant population of the communist-held border areas, there was a clear connexion between joining the army or one of the para-military organizations, and safeguarding the well-being and lives of one's family and village.

It was their sense of 'mortal enmity', as Mao described it in his speech 'On Coalition Government', which provided the basic incentive in the communist border areas for mobilization during the anti-Japanese war.

[3] Chalmers Johnson, *Peasant Nationalism and Communist Power* (1963), p. 90. The above account of popular mobilization is drawn from this source, pp. 89–91.
[4] Ibid., p. 31.

One should not, however, overlook the importance of the communists' economic and social policies in translating the peasants' latent anti-Japanese hostility into effective and co-ordinated action. As Professor George Taylor wrote at the time with reference to the communist Hopei–Shansi–Chahar Border Government:

> ... both Japanese and other foreign observers had agreed in thinking that there would be no mass opposition from the impoverished peasants of North China to the new Japanese-sponsored regime. . . . Provincial civil administration in the north was of the old-fashioned type—corrupt, inefficient, and conservative. Incompetent, untrained bureaucrats, in league with provincial military leaders, fattened on the peasantry and had no other contribution to make to the government than the collection or addition of more and more taxes. There was no conception of modern forms of government, no desire for change.

The provincial armies were poorly equipped, notoriously corrupt, and feared by the local peasantry.

The peasant of North China, therefore, hated the very name of government. . . . Such was the situation which the [Communist] Border Government took over and such were the foundations upon which it helped to build some kind of effective resistance to the Japanese invasion. Small wonder that it put so much emphasis upon two things—winning goodwill and active co-operation of the people and organizing an army which should revolutionize the relations between army and people.[5]

Moderate policies on the part of the communist government encouraged solidarity between the peasantry, the armed forces, and the government itself. All political elements except those of the right wing were associated in the process of government and administration, especially after 1941 when the 'tripartite' or 'three-thirds' system was introduced.[6] Ultimate authority rested

---

[5] George E. Taylor, *The Struggle for North China* (1940), pp. 98–100.

[6] The tripartite system established the practice that one-third of government officials in communist areas were CCP members, one-third were members of other parties, and the remaining third were 'independent'. The chief criterion was that all should be 'anti-Japanese and democratic'. According to Michael Lindsay, the Kuomintang were not entirely excluded, but 'those elected to the Government of the region are mostly of the liberal wing of the Kuomintang and they get on very well with the Communists' (Gunther Stein, *The Challenge of Red China* (1945), p. 299).

of course in the hands of the communist party, but wide areas of responsibility devolved on non-communist officials. Moderation was also the key-note of the communists' wartime land policy, which abandoned the drastic measures of redistribution and confiscation of land without compensation that had been enforced during the Kiangsi Soviet period. The new policy involved 'reduction of rent and interest rates on the one hand, and the guarantee of rent and interest collections on the other'. In other words, the existing system of land tenure was retained, but manifest inequalities within it were eliminated, and the position of landlords (except those who collaborated with the Japanese) was guaranteed.[7] A unified tax system, known as the 'progressive consolidated tax', was also put into effect, on the principle that 'those who have money give money', with the object of spreading the burden of taxation more fairly.[8]

COMMUNIST EXPANSION, 1937–40

Recruitment to the guerrilla and regular forces of the Eighth Route and New Fourth Armies proceeded rapidly during 1937–40, but at a rate which was never incompatible with the size of the population and of its resources. After the battle of P'inghsing-kuan in September 1937, no major fixed engagements took place with the Japanese during the next two years. As Mao himself admitted, until the fall of Wuhan in October 1938 the Japanese 'employed their main forces in attacking the Kuomintang front', and paid little attention to the base areas, 'believing that these amounted to only a handful of Communists engaged in guerrilla actions'.[9] This allowed the communists a breathing space in which to organize the base areas and to recruit soldiers. Between May 1937 and May 1940 over 300,000 were recruited to the Eighth Route Army in North China, and not quite 100,000 to the New Fourth Army in Central-South China.[10] These were not by any means raw recruits. Many former independent guerrillas and bandits, as well as ex-KMT troops, joined the communist forces whom they saw as the major resistance movement against the Japanese; this was especially true of the New Fourth Army,

---

[7] Conrad Brandt and others, *A Documentary History of Chinese Communism* (London, 1952), pp. 275–85. Decision of the CC on Land Policy in the Anti-Japanese Base Areas (28 Jan. 1942).

[8] Israel Epstein, *The Unfinished Revolution in China* (1947), p. 251.

[9] *MAO III*, p. 167.   [10] See Table 1 (p. 303).

which flourished in the chaotic situation in the Yangtze valley, where KMT troops, bandits, village militia, and communist forces fought over the same land. A number of these varied elements were in time assimilated into its ranks.[11]

Anti-communist writers have frequently claimed that the communists had no real intention of fighting the Japanese, and that they were solely interested in increasing their strength at the expense of the Kuomintang. Mao Tse-tung is often quoted as having said that communist policy should be one of '70 per cent expansion, 20 per cent dealing with the Kuomintang, and 10 per cent resisting Japan'. The authenticity of this statement is highly suspect,[12] and is made even less credible by subsequent events in which the communist forces became deeply involved in the war against Japan. It would, however, have made sense in a strictly military context in 1937–9, since it was during these years that the Eighth Route and New Fourth Armies concentrated their efforts on expanding their effective strength rather than on armed confrontation with the Japanese. A policy of large-scale

[11] 'Bandit' elements were allowed to join the Eighth Route Army guerrilla units on acceptance of the following conditions: (1) Fight the Japanese until they withdraw from China; (2) accept orders from the Eighth Route Army; (3) accept political indoctrination and political leaders; (4) avoid harming the people; (5) provide regular statements of income and expenditure; (6) accept the salary schedule of the Eighth Route Army (from $1 a month for fighters to $5 a month for commanders); (7) share the same type of food (Evans Fordyce Carlson, *Twin Stars Over China* (1940), pp. 251–2). For a detailed analysis of the build-up of guerrilla forces in 1938–9 see Wang Yu-chuan, 'The Organisation of a Typical Guerrilla Area in South Shantung', in Carlson, *The Chinese Army* (1940), pp. 85–130).

[12] Mao is alleged to have formulated this policy in a speech given to political workers from the Eighth Route Army in October 1937, on their departure from Yenan to fight in North Shansi (Freda Utley: *Last Chance in China* (New York, 1947), pp. 194–5). A portion of the alleged speech is reproduced in the same source. F. F. Liu has suggested that this document was brought over by the dissident communist leader Chang Kuo-t'ao on his defection to the Kuomintang in August 1938 (F. F. Liu, *A Military History of Modern China, 1924–49* (1956), pp. 205–6). Together with other purportedly secret communist documents, it was presented by the Nationalist government to the People's Political Council in Chungking in March 1941, at the time of the South Anhwei incident when the New Fourth Army had been dissolved and KMT/communist tension was at its height. The collection of documents was finally published in Chungking by the Supreme National Defence Council in 1944. Mao's alleged speech is therefore associated both with Chang Kuo-t'ao and with KMT attempts at the time of the South Anhwei incident to prove bad faith on the part of the communists. As reproduced by Freda Utley, it contains phrases which it is hard to imagine coming from the mouth of Mao Tse-tung. For instance: 'While waiting for an unusual turn of events, we should give the Japanese invader certain concessions'.

confrontation was hardly feasible until political stability was reached in the base areas and until the areas themselves had been enlarged, the population mobilized for armed resistance, and the guerrilla and regular forces expanded and organized for combat action.

In any case, by 1939 the expansion of communist activities in North China was giving serious concern to the Japanese. In the same year the Imperial General Headquarters in Tokyo issued orders to make the elimination of all communist and anti-Japanese forces in the base areas a first-line operation, and pressure on the border areas began to increase.[13] In 1940 Lieut.-General Tada, the commander-in-chief of the Japanese North China Expeditionary Forces, developed the so-called 'cage policy' to contain the communist base areas. Hundreds of miles of new roads were built, and a network of key points, fortified with blockhouses, trenches, and barbed wire, spread through Hopei and Shansi.

In an attempt to counteract the crippling effect of Japanese containment and blockade, the Eighth Route Army in North China launched what was known as the 'Hundred Regiments Offensive', lasting from 20 August to 5 December 1940. This offensive involved 115 regiments and 400,000 men supported by local militia in an all-out attack on the major Japanese communication lines in the North. Although it inflicted heavy damages on the Japanese, it was achieved at the cost of high losses in casualties and material, and it led to an intensification of countermeasures against the base areas.[14] The years 1941–2 were a lean period for the North China base areas, in which their population shrank by nearly half. There were major shortages of basic necessities, made worse by the economic blockade carried out both by the Kuomintang and by the Japanese. In the Yangtze valley the Kuomintang took the opportunity to strike at the New Fourth Army. This army was shattered in the South Anhwei incident of 4 January 1941, officially dissolved by the Chungking government, and was painfully reassembled and reconstituted by Liu Shao-ch'i in the following years.

[13] Johnson, *Peasant Nationalism*, pp. 53–60.
[14] Ibid., pp. 57–58; Stein, *Challenge of Red China*, pp. 135–6; Chung-kuo hsien-tai shih tzu-liao ts'ung-k'an, *K'ang-Jih chan-cheng shih-ch'i ti Chung-kuo jen-min chieh-fang-chün* (Peking, 1953), pp. 108–18.

THE PERIOD OF RETRENCHMENT, 1941–4

The Hundred Regiments' offensive had led to a reduction of some 25 per cent in the size of the Eighth Route Army, and between 1941 and 1944 recruitment in North China did little more than keep pace with the loss of effectives. This was a period of political rectification and economic reform, summed up by the policy of 'picked troops and simplified administration'. '... The base areas have shrunk and may continue to shrink for a period, and undoubtedly we cannot maintain the same enormous war apparatus as before', wrote Mao in a *Liberation Daily* editorial.[15] The reduction in regular strength was a deliberate measure to ease the burden on military taxation and to avoid excessive demands upon agricultural labour. It was intended to solve the contradiction known as that of the 'large fish in small water' (*yu ta shui hsiao*), which would otherwise lead to friction and resentment between the armed forces and the civilian population. This reduction in regular strength was compensated for by an increase in the number of local guerrillas and militia. In 1941 the number of local guerrillas and militia who were 'not divorced from production' at the level of *hsien* and below almost doubled. The advantage of the militia was that it could perform a military role without interfering with vitally needed production. It was also village based and self-supporting. Similar changes occurred in the communists' overall strategy; positional warfare involving regular units became more infrequent, while guerrilla activities with militia support, of small scale individually but persistently carried out over wide areas of enemy-held territory, sharply increased in number. Armed work teams were formed in the occupied areas to carry out political propaganda among the peasants and sabotage against the Japanese.[16]

In the border areas strenuous efforts were made to ensure that army-civilian solidarity was not weakened by the economic crisis, and that popular support was maintained for recruitment. In 1943 a 'Return-to-the-Front' movement was launched

to mobilise those who have deserted from the army or direct those whose vacations are over to return to the front. . . . Government offices of various grades and the mass organisations must not employ

---

[15] *MAO III*, p. 100.   [16] *K'ang-Jih chan-cheng . . .*, pp. 122–7.

those who should be at the front, and the cadres must not give shelter to such relatives of theirs.[17]

Preferential treatment was accorded to soldiers' families. These were to be helped with capital and labour, in order to ensure a satisfactory standard of living. They would be given priority in obtaining agricultural loans, and discounts in purchases from co-operatives and government stores. Discharged and disabled soldiers would also be encouraged and assisted to set up home and find employment.[18]

Throughout the anti-Japanese war the financial cost of maintaining a large regular army imposed a heavy burden of taxation upon the civilian population, as well as monopolizing the major part of the border areas' economic resources. For instance in early 1944, as much as two-thirds of the budget of the Shansi–Chahar–Hopei Border Region was devoted to military expenditure.[19] After the Hundred Regiments' Campaign, an attempt was made to reduce this burden by diverting as much of the army as could be spared to take part in production. Those forces which remained in the field were expected to practice economy to the maximum, and to assist the peasants in production whenever their duties permitted. In the Shen Kan Ning Border Region, the heartland of the communist territories, where military operations were confined to the defence of its frontiers, all five brigades garrisoning the area were put to production work. The production movement began here in 1940–1; by 1942 it had spread to all the communist bases in China. It was not confined to the army; every government official was expected to draw up his own production plan, and it was proudly boasted that Mao Tse-tung raised American onions while Chu Teh planted lettuce and cabbage in his vegetable patch.[20]

The star performer in the production movement was the 359th Brigade of the 120th Division, which had fought for several years behind enemy lines in North China, under the command of

---

[17] Lin Tsu-han, 'Annual Report of the Shensi–Kansu–Ninghsia Border Region Government for the Year 1943' in Stuart Gelder, *The Chinese Communists* (1946), p. 133.

[18] Ibid., pp. 132–3.

[19] *The tax system in a Chinese Communist Area* (London, mimeo. n.d.), p. 9 (summary of *hsien-hsing fa-ling huo-chi*, 'Finance' section, issued by the Executive Committee of the Shansi–Chahar–Hopei Border Region, 15 Dec. 1945).

[20] Harrison Forman, *Report from Red China* (1946), p. 66.

Wang Chen. In 1941 Wang and his brigade were recalled to garrison the Nanniwan district of Shen–Kan–Ning against Japanese positions on the opposite bank of the Yellow river. Wang's brigade was chosen to lead the campaign for economic self-sufficiency, under the twin slogans 'Organize for Production' and 'Move Your Own Hands'. The wasteland of Nanniwan, reclaimed and cultivated by the 359th Brigade, became the showplace of the movement. By 1944, when a party of foreign journalists visited Nanniwan and were much impressed by what they saw, the soldiers had been organized into co-operatives, and the Brigade possessed its own smithies, spinning and weaving factories, tailor shops, oil presses, and food-preserving plants.[21] In 1943 the 359th boasted that it had reclaimed 100,000 mow of waste land in that year—more than one-tenth of the total amount reclaimed in the border region—and that it had attained 'complete self-sufficiency'.[22]

Except for crack units like the 359th, it was not humanly possible for army and government personnel to become totally 'self-sufficient'. Taxation continued to be heavy—although it was generally agreed to be less than in pre-communist days.[23] As Mao Tse-tung admitted in a speech to senior cadres in December 1942: 'To meet the needs of the War of Resistance and national reconstruction, the people must shoulder such burdens, the necessity of which they very well realize.'[24] As far as one can generalize from the figures for Shen–Kan–Ning, participation by the armed forces in production did not succeed in decreasing the burden of taxation in cash or grain from the high level which it reached in 1941 at the peak of the economic crisis and the joint Japanese-Nationalist blockade. It did, however, manage to prevent that level from rising still higher, in spite of increased public expenditure and military commitments in the next three years. This was a considerable achievement in itself.[25] Of more funda-

---

[21] Ibid., pp. 37–45. Other accounts of Wang Chen's brigade are given in Stein, *Challenge of Red China*, pp. 52–59; Epstein, *Unfinished Revolution*, pp. 259–63.

[22] Lin Tsu-han, 'Annual Report of the Shensi–Kansu–Ninghsia Border Region Government for the Year 1943', in Gelder, *Chinese Communists*, pp. 111–39.

[23] *Peabody Report*, p. 2427.   [24] *MAO III*, p. 113.

[25] In 1943 the garrison troops of Shen–Kan–Ning were said to be 79·5 per cent self-sufficient, 'excluding grain' (Forman, *Report from Red China*, p. 74). This was an important proviso; the total grain requirement in 1944 of army and government agencies in the border region was 260,000 piculs, of which only 100,000 was self-produced. The remainder was supplied through the public grain tax (*MAO III*, p.

mental importance was the example which the army set by working on the land, and the contrast which this implied with the behaviour of the military under previous governments. It reinforced solidarity between the army and the people at a time when it came under exceptionally severe strain.

This feeling of solidarity was encouraged by the annual campaigns to 'support the government and love the people' and to 'support the army' which were first launched in 1943 at the time of the Spring Festival (Chinese New Year). These were formal occasions, celebrated by the exchange of gifts, by feasts and other ceremonial meetings, between army units and the local populace, when the army pledged itself to 'support the government and love the people', while the people promised to 'support the army'. These campaigns had been initiated in order to check a deterioration in relations between the army and the people which had developed during the lean years of 1941–2. Soldiers of the Eighth Route Army invited the local population to social meetings at which they 'danced the country dances together, invited each other to feasts, and all had a grand time'.[26] At these meetings, which were also attended by members of the local party organization and government, army leaders would publicly criticize their behaviour towards the civilian population, and

---

242). The volume of grain tax rose sharply in the first three years of the war; but the production movement helped to prevent it rising any further after 1941.

Public grain tax, Shen–Kan–Ning Border Region
(in piculs of millet)

1938	10,000
1939	50,000
1940	180,000
1941	200,000
1942	160,000
1943	170,000
1944	160,000

Sources: MAO III, pp. 113 & 242; Peabody Report, p. 2427.
The Peabody Report gives 180,000 piculs for 1940; Mao quotes a figure of 90,000.
Production by army and government agencies was nevertheless considerable, according to communist claims. In 1944 the troops produced 8 per cent of the total regional production of grain (Epstein, Unfinished Revolution, p. 265). In 1943 64 per cent of government expenditure came from government enterprises and army production; in 1944 70 per cent came from the same sources (Peabody Report, p. 2427).

[26] Lin Tsu-han, 'Report of Shen–Kan–Ning Border Region Government for 1943' (Gelder, Chinese Communists, pp. 120–3).

offer compensation for any damages or losses inflicted upon it.[27]

The concept of army-people unity in time of war inevitably placed a greater burden upon the people than upon the army. They were encouraged to contribute substantial aid in the form of 'gifts' to the armed forces; in 1943 these amounted in value to $4 million Border Region (equivalent to no less than two-thirds of total cash government expenditure in Shen–Kan–Ning).[28] These were, however, gifts in kind—firewood, food, vegetables, etc.—which a peasant economy could more easily afford than if the equivalent cash had been raised through direct taxation and then used to purchase the same goods. The people's second major obligation was to take care of the families of army servicemen, to help in the tilling of their fields, and to subsidize their living standards on a communal basis.

The significance of these two mass movements probably lay more in the psychological boost which they gave towards creating a much-needed sense of solidarity between the army, government officials, and civilians than in producing tangible benefits for any of the parties involved. Perhaps not every peasant said 'Your army is a good army, and your officers are good officers, and we hope that you will be stationed here forever'[29] but enough did so to ensure that the army did not lack that vital factor of popular support without which it could barely survive. The movements to 'support the army' and to 'love the people' became enshrined in the communist army's revolutionary tradition, and were revived under very different circumstances in post-Liberation China.

RENEWED MILITARY EXPANSION, 1944–5

The diversion of Japanese forces from North China in the spring of 1944 into Operation Ichi-gō against Nationalist territory in Central China, and their replacement by less experienced units from Japan, relieved pressure upon the communist base areas in the North for the first time since 1940.[30] The Eighth Route Army, and to a lesser extent the New Fourth Army, took

---

[27] *MAO III*, pp. 134–5.   [28] Lin Tsu-han, in Gelder; *Peabody Report*, p. 2427.

[29] Lin Tsu-han, in Gelder.

[30] Seven out of the 23 divisions in the China Expeditionary Army were shifted into Ichi-gō, including the 27th Division from Manchuria, the 110th from North China, and the 3rd Tank Division from Mongolia. In addition, the entire 12th Army of North China Area was employed south of the Yellow river to clear the Hankow line in the preceding Operation Kogo (Romanus & Sutherland, *Stilwell's Command Problems*, pp. 317–25).

advantage of this lull in hostilities to expand and reorganize, just as they had done in the previous lull of 1938–9. According to official statements from Yenan, the two armies combined almost doubled in size during the winter training period of 1944–5. There is little reason to doubt that this increase took place in roughly the dimensions given, although the exact figures are open to question.

In June 1944 the Eighth Route Army and the New Fourth Army together totalled about 475,000, of whom three-quarters were regular field units and the remainder guerrillas. By the end of the year their combined strength had reached just under 780,000, and at the Seventh Party Congress of April 1945 their total was said to be about 900,000. By the end of 1945 it had risen again to approximately 1,300,000.[31]

This expansion was achieved by regrouping guerrilla forces into regular army units, and replenishing the guerrillas' strength from the land-based militia. This three-tier system (militia-guerrilla-regular forces) of recruitment was the standard procedure, both during the anti-Japanese and civil wars, and again after Liberation during the Korean war. The figures suggest that the regular and guerrilla expansion during winter 1944–5 was achieved almost entirely by the transfer upwards of militia. The overall increase in regular and guerrilla forces was in the order of 405,000,[32] while in the second half of 1944 the militia's total

[31]

	Eighth Route and New Fourth expansion, 1944–5			
	South China Guerrillas	8RA	N4A	Total
end 1943	4,500	339,000	125,892	469,392[a]
June 1944	—	320,800	153,676	474,476[b]
end 1944	20,730	507,620	251,393	779,743[c]
March 1945	20,000	600,000	260,000	880,000[d]
end 1945	20,820	1,028,893	268,581	1,318,294[e]

[a] Wang Ping & Kao Fan, *Kuang-jung ti san-shih nien, 1927–1957* (1957), p. 36.
[b] Yeh Chien-ying, 'Report on the General Military Situation of the Chinese Communist Party in the War of Resistance', in Gelder, *Chinese Communists*, p. 94. Similar figures are given in *Peabody Report*, p. 2432–4.
[c] Wang & Kao.
[d] *K'ang-Jih chan-cheng shih-ch'i ti Chung-kuo jen-min chieh-fang-chün*, pp. 219–20.
[e] Wang & Kao.

[32]

	Regular	Guerrilla	Total
June 1944	346,000	129,000	475,000[a]
April 1945	600,000	280,000	880,000[b]

[a] *Peabody Report* p. 2448, figures based on communist statistics.
[b] The figure for regulars in spring 1945 is widely given in non-official sources as 600,000; *CSM*, 20 Feb. 1945 (Stein); *Daily Herald*, 4 Apr. 1945 (quoting US Foreign Service officer); *News Chronicle*, 17 Aug. 1945.

strength fell by approximately the same amount. Thus in the first stage of expansion, the regular and guerrilla units were strengthened at the expense of the militia, and the total burden of recruitment placed upon the civilian population was reasonably small. The second stage, which Mao Tse-tung called for in December 1944 in an article discussing 'the Tasks for 1945', involved the expansion of the militia itself. This proved more difficult. Mao had suggested a target for militia expansion of 5 per cent of the population or 4,500,000—well over twice its current size. By April 1945 the militia had restored the gaps left in its ranks by recruitment into the regular forces, but, by the end of the year, it had only added another 500,000 and was still far short of the target.[33] The greater part of this latter increase probably derived from militia units in Manchuria which were assimilated when communist forces moved in at the end of the war in the autumn of 1945. Absorption of guerrilla units in Manchuria would also account for the increase in the Eighth Route Army during the same period. From April 1945 until the end of the year there was virtually no expansion in the New Fourth Army in Central China, but the Eighth Route increased by 400,000 over the same time. This increase was almost entirely confined to guerrilla units.[34]

If this analysis is correct, the expansion of communist forces in 1944–5 becomes more credible than has sometimes been thought. The militia provided the key, first by supplying recruits for the regular and guerrilla units, and then by replenishing its own numbers. Overall expansion in the militia, regulars, and guerrillas combined amounts to some $1\frac{1}{2}$ million in the space of eighteen months. Here again, the major area of expansion takes

---

[33]

	Militia expansion
June 1944	2,130,000[a]
end 1944	1,685,384[b]
April 1945	2,200,000[c]
end 1945	2,687,698[d]

[a] Yeh Chien ying (Gelder, p. 94).   [b] Wang & Kao, p. 36.
[c] *MAO III*, p. 264.   [d] Wang & Kao, p. 36.
The 5 per cent target was specified in Mao Tse-tung, 'The Tasks for 1945', *CFJP*, 16 Dec. 1944.

[34] There were said to be over 150,000 guerrillas in Manchuria at the end of the war against Japan (NCNA (N. Shensi), 9 July 1947). Between June 1945 and June 1946 communist regular forces only rose from 600,000 to 612,000. In the same period guerrilla forces rose from 280,000 to 665,000 (figures for June 1945, cited above; figures for June 1946 in *MAO IV*, p. 223).

place in the militia, which accounts for 1 million of this total. The final increase is largely taken care of by the absorption of existing guerrilla units in Manchuria. At the end of 1945 a halt was called to recruitment. Mao Tse-tung wrote in an internal party circular that

The field armies of the Liberated Areas have already been formed in the main, and the regional troops are also quite numerous. Hence, for the time being, we should generally stop expanding the number of troops and should make use of the intervals between battles to stress the training of troops.[35]

Recruitment was not resumed until the summer of 1946, when the civil war broke out in earnest.

MOBILIZATION IN THE CIVIL WAR

A major factor behind the communist success in the civil war was their ability to raise adequate manpower to replace losses and expand capability without alienating popular support. The PLA expanded from just over 1,200,000 strong in July 1946 to 4 million exactly three years later. Since losses during this period totalled more than the army's original strength, this meant that the PLA had raised more than 4 million recruits within those three years, of whom about one-third were raised in the final year.[36] The rate of recruitment increased from year to year as the PLA turned from defence to offence, and in the second year a major recruiting drive was launched to prepare for the coming counter-offensive. In the first two years (1946–8) two-thirds of the PLA's manpower came from the peasantry, and only one-third from captured KMT troops. This achievement was all the more remarkable in view of the natural resistance of the Chinese peasant to military service, and it contrasted with the mounting difficulties which the Nationalist army experienced in replenishing its sources of manpower.

Recruitment of the dimensions carried out by the communists, and the mass mobilization of resources and labour which was needed to support the front could not have been achieved without major political, social, and economic reforms. The 'built-in incentive' of anti-Japanese solidarity, referred to earlier, which

[35] Mao Tse-tung, 15 Dec. 1945, 'Policy for Work in the Liberated Areas for 1946', ibid., p. 76.
[36] See Table 2 (p. 304).

F

eased the task of mobilization before 1945, was no longer relevant during the civil war when recruitment was again stepped up. A substitute for it was provided by the radical developments which took place in the economic and military policies of the communist areas.

The more radical programme of land reform, initiated in October 1947, was closely linked to recruitment for the PLA. During the anti-Japanese war and immediately afterwards, Yenan's policy for land reform had been confined to the reduction of rent and interest. In June 1946, with civil war now imminent, the Central Committee in its 'Directive on the Land Question' of 4 June had endorsed the principle of 'land to the tillers', in other words the confiscation and redistribution of land. At first this new policy was confined in the main to absentee and large landlords, or to those who had collaborated with the Japanese. The middle peasant was left undisturbed and concessions were made to the small and middle landlords. The Basic Programme of Agrarian Law, drawn up by a National Land Conference which met in September 1947 under Liu Shao-ch'i's Working Committee in Hopei, laid down a series of far more radical measures. These included abolition of landownership rights of all landlords, cancellation of all debts, total egalitarian distribution of all land, establishment of People's Courts and of 'real democratic rights for the people'.[37]

By enlarging the scope of land reform, the new programme at the same time vastly increased the number of beneficiaries from land redistribution and therefore the number of potential recruits. Land reform, as Mao had emphasized, was 'the most fundamental requirement for supporting a long war and winning country-wide victory',[38] and it provided an indispensable basis both for economic and military mobilization. Recruitment was encouraged by a provision in the Basic Programme which laid down that all PLA personnel whose home was in the countryside should be given land and properties equivalent to that of peasants for themselves and their families (art. 10, sect. c). It was claimed that thousands of farmers who had recently acquired land joined the People's Armies 'to protect their land and new democratic way of life' in the knowledge that 'only the victory of

[37] NCNA (London), Suppl. No. 1, 4 Nov. 1947.   [38] *MAO IV*, p. 145.

their armies can make their land and homes finally secure'.[39]
Recruitment drives under such slogans as 'everything for the
front' were launched among the newly emancipated peasants,
and registration centres were set up in the villages. During the
first two years of the civil war a total of 1,600,000 peasants were
recruited into the PLA. A large proportion of these came from
Manchuria, where in three years the same total (1,600,000) was
raised in that region alone, although North China was also a
major source.[40] One of the main tasks prescribed for Manchuria
in 1948 was 'the increasing of our manpower and material support of the liberation war of the whole country, to convert Manchuria, rich in manpower and resources, into the main base for
the liberation war of the whole country'.[41] This was to be
achieved by the completion of equal distribution of land within
six months in both the old and the newly liberated areas.

The question of the correct treatment of the rank and file became particularly important during 1947–8, when large numbers of peasants were being recruited. The point of such recruitment would be lost if it was carried out by compulsion, or if the
new soldiers were discontented and therefore likely to desert.
Recruits were in theory selected on a voluntary basis from
families which had benefited from land reform, on the so-called
'Three Not Wanted' system. ('The army does not want those
who don't come entirely of their own free will, those whose democratic spirit and high moral character cannot be fully vouched
for and those who are not in A.1 physical condition.') Volunteers
were doubtless encouraged by propaganda and by local social
pressure, and recruitment of a younger member of a family was
often seen as a *quid pro quo* in return for an allotment of land. One
observer reported that 'besides propaganda, family members
were mobilised to convince a prospective recruit that he should
enlist. If this did not work, then the whole people of the village

---

[39] NCNA (London), 9 July 1947; NCNA (Harbin), 23 Sept. 1947.
[40] NCNA (Mukden) 5 Sept. 1949. According to NCNA (N. Shensi), 16 Sept. 1948,
'several hundred thousand men, 99 per cent of whom are emancipated peasants,
joined the PLA from the North China liberated areas in the second year of the
war'. NCNA (Mukden), 25 Nov. 1947, reported that '23,000 peasants in East
Shantung who have obtained land from the land reform have recently joined the
Liberation Army. 12,000 have joined the local troops'.
[41] *Tung-pei Jih-pao* editorial, 14 Jan. 1948, in NCNA (N. Shensi) 27 Jan. 1948.

might be mobilised to break down the recruit's resistance and force him to join up'.[42] Once in the army, recruits began their course with a discussion on 'Why do we join the army? Why do we fight? and Why do we train?', and great efforts were made to make the new soldier feel at home.[43]

Army education attempted to instil a sense of class consciousness in the new recruit and to build up his morale. Soldiers were told that they were fighting in order to defend their newly acquired land, and to liberate themselves from oppression and exploitation by the old ruling class. Morale-raising meetings were held at which they were encouraged to 'Report their Grievances' (*Shuo k'u*), in other words to publicly recall and describe 'the oppression which they have suffered at the hands of the landlords and other oppressors of the old feudal society'. In another form of public self-criticism, known as the 'Triple Examination' (*San ch'a*), they discussed and analysed their class origin, their performance of duty, and their willingness and zeal to fight. It was claimed that

These under the leadership of the Chinese Communist Party, have greatly raised the level of political consciousness, improved discipline

---

[42] See the account of conscription methods in Jack Belden, *China Shakes the World* (London, 1949), pp. 341–6. Volunteers were given a feast by their village, decorated with a banner, and serenaded by gongs, cymbals and flutes. In this way 'the enlisted man got the idea that joining the army was not entirely a personal affair, but one in which he represented the whole village'. Period of service was for the duration of the war. If a man deserted, he was usually ostracized by his village. Only if he deserted three times was he turned over to the district magistrate for hard labour. See also the short story about popular conscription, 'Patriot', by Chao Shu-li, in *Chinese Literature*, No. 3, 1964. As during the anti-Japanese war, villagers were organized to take part in 'substitute ploughing', to help army dependants, and carry out work formerly undertaken by soldiers. During the civil war only members of the peasant union were acceptable as recruits, thus debarring landlords and rich peasants. (Isabel & David Crook, *Revolution in A Chinese Village* (1959), p. 75 n. 1.)

[43] 'Liberated areas train "brand new army" in Manchuria' (NCNA (N. Shensi), 6 Jan. 1948) explained that: 'Recruits are carefully selected under the "Three Not Wanted" system. The new army only wants the "flower of the peasantry".... Particular attention is paid to the social background of recruits to ensure that they are not loafers, potential fifth columnists or "landlord elements". Rigorous selection ensures that the new reserves are of the highest character and make rapid progress in modern combat training.' According to Belden (*China Shakes the World*, p. 343), once the new recruit had arrived: 'old soldiers rushed to pay their respects to the new soldier. Some helped him put on his uniform. Some gave him a haircut, or made him presents of hand towels and soap. A distinct effort was made to make the new soldier feel at home and among friends.'

and strengthened the spirit of solidarity among all ranks. . . . These discussions bring home sharply to the troops the nature of the present conflict in China and their role as a People's Army.[44]

During the winter of 1947, concurrently with the movements for land reform and party reform, a campaign was launched for 'military democracy' within the army. The concept of military democracy was described as:

an extremely important part of Chairman Mao Tse-tung's military thought. The winning or losing of a battle is often decided by the seizing of fleeting opportunities. It is therefore essential, through military democracy, to encourage initiative in all ranks.[45]

Initiative was encouraged by the restoration of the system of Soldiers' Committees at company level which had been abolished in the last year of the Kiangsi Soviet.[46] These committees were led by officers but elected by the rank and file. During training periods they met to discuss the purpose of the training programme, to criticize their performance, and to suggest improvements. Meetings were also held before battles and even while they were taking place, to discuss tactics and allocate combat assignments. After a military engagement, yet another meeting would hold a critical post-mortem, to evaluate its success or failure.[47] Soldiers were also given the right to nominate candidates for lower-level cadre posts—the equivalent of n.c.o.'s—subject to confirmation by superior officers. Under a scheme known as the 'junior instructors system', experienced men from the rank and file were promoted to act as training instructors.[48]

Military democracy was one of the so-called 'three democracies' whose practice was called for throughout the army. Economic democracy meant that soldiers took part through the soldiers' committee in deciding such matters as food distribution, mess arrangements, and budgeting. Political democracy gave

[44] 'Liberation Army prepared big spring offensive', NCNA (N. Shensi), 16 Mar. 1948. See also Mao Tse-tung, 7 Mar. 1948, 'On the Great Victory in the Northwest and On the New Type of Ideological Education Movement in the Liberation Army', *MAO IV*, pp. 211–17.

[45] 'Military democracy in the Chinese People's Liberation Army', NCNA (N. Shensi), 2 July 1948.

[46] See further ch. 5, p. 113.

[47] Mao Tse-tung, 30 January 1948 'The Democratic Movement in the Army', *MAO IV*, pp. 191–2.

[48] 'People's Army trains for capturing cities', NCNA (N. Shensi), 4 Oct. 1948.

them a say in approving the appointment of cadres and criticizing their behaviour. There were, however, definite limits within which these democratic rights were allowed to function. It was emphasized that the soldiers' representatives had 'the right to assist (but not to by-pass) the company leadership in managing the company's supplies and mess'.[49] It was also explained that

> While the commander must stress the development of democracy to enable his command to be closely combined with the broad rank and file and practical combat, the fighters and commanders of lower grades must on the one hand help to improve the command and administration and on the other hand observe discipline more consciously and obey orders to ensure a centralised command.[50]

Enthusiasm for military democracy might otherwise go beyond the bounds of legitimate criticism, and encourage dangerous tendencies towards egalitarianism, as occurred in the course of the land reform movement. One example of over-enthusiasm in the application of military democracy comes from the Shansi–Suiyuan Liberated Area, where the land reform programme led to a number of 'left' deviations which were subsequently criticized by Mao Tse-tung.[51] In a statement issued by the Peasants' Association of that area, welcoming the Basic Programme of Agrarian Law, the view was expressed that the People's Army was 'the peasants' own army' and that 'military force must be in the hands of the peasants'. It claimed that the supreme authority of the party over military and government organizations was subject to the right of supervision by the peasants themselves.[52]

[49] *MAO IV*, p. 191.
[50] 'Military democracy in the Chinese PLA', NCNA (N. Shensi), 2 July 1948.
[51] Mao Tse-tung, 1 Apr. 1948, 'Speech at a Conference of Cadres in the Shensi–Suiyuan Liberated Area', *MAO IV*, pp. 227–39.
[52] 'Open letter of the Provisional Committee of the Peasants' Association of the Shansi–Suiyuan Border Region', NCNA (Shansi-Suiyuan), 18 Nov. 1947. This document provides an extreme interpretation of the democratic movement and the land reform programme, of the kind which was later regarded as an example of 'left' deviation. It claimed that:
'The Communist Party has called upon us to develop our democracy and make a strict examination of all our cadres of all Government, Party, Military and public organisations. We peasants have the right to supervise and reform all departments and organisations, all Working Groups (groups of mass organisers), schools, factories or publicly owned shops whether they belong to the Party, the Government, army or the people. . . .

In addition to providing recruits for the regular army, the peasantry supplied numerous auxiliary workers for transport, communications, supplies, and first-aid purposes. These became needed in increasing quantities to maintain supply lines for the Field Armies as they moved into the counter-offensive, and recruitment was stepped up during the land reform campaign of winter 1947. Speaking to his officers on the importance of civilian auxiliaries, General Ch'en Yi, commander-in-chief of the East China Field Army, urged them to pay the greatest attention to their welfare and political education, and to master 'the science and art of organising such an army of hundreds and thousands of civilian workers'. He compared the creation of this civilian army with such historical achievements as land reform.[53] As in the case of regular recruitment, Manchuria again was a primary source of manpower, and it was claimed that under the slogan of 'everything for the front', almost 4 million had volunteered for service from the North-east in the first war year.[54] But under the stimulus of land reform, North China provided a larger share of the burden in the second year of the war. In the Shansi–Hopei–Shantung–Honan Border Region 700,000 were reported to have joined the voluntary services in 1948, and a further 500,000 joined in Shansi–Chahar–Hopei.

Migrations of civilian labour of such dimensions could hardly fail to interfere with agricultural production, and this was

---

'You have not only the right to examine all cadres and organisations, you have also the right and duty to reform and improve all organisations. You can improve the peasants' organisations, revise their constitutions and qualifications for membership. Democracy must be fully developed. No one can be permitted to monopolise the leading positions in the peasants' associations. It is your right to call peasant conferences at all levels . . . to elect your representatives and establish peasant associations. In this way all Party, Government Military and public organisations can be firmly built.

'Hence we suggest: bear your share of responsibility for the People's Army. This is the peasants' own army. From now on, no members of the landlord class, no rogues or traitorous elements, no feudalistic, rich peasants or evildoers are to be allowed to enter the People's Army or the People's Militia. Only peasants and other working people are qualified to join those organisations. Military force must be in the hands of the peasants. The People's Militia must be under the direct control of the peasants' associations so that it will really be the armed force that protects the peasants. The stronger the Army and the Militia, the quicker will be the defeat of Chiang Kai-shek, Yen Hsi-shan, Hu Tsung-nan and Fu Tso-yi.'

Abridged trans. in NCNA (London), Weekly Bull. No. 24. Full text in Mao Tse-tung and others, *Tsen-yang fen-hsi chieh-chi* (1948), pp. 15–20.

[53] NCNA (N. Shensi), 9 Dec. 1947.   [54] NCNA (Harbin), 23 Sept. 1947.

realized once the excesses of the land reform programme began to be curbed. In its inaugural issue of 15 June 1948 the *North China People's Daily* emphasized the importance of restoring production, and spoke of the need 'to improve ways of carrying out war services, so as to reduce the people's burden in manpower, materials and finance'.[55] Shortly afterwards the ratio of war-service workers to combatants in the Field Armies was reduced from 5:1 to 1:2 or 1:3.[56] Yet the need for such workers increased again during the large-scale offensives of the coming winter. The Liao-ning, Huai-hai, and Ping-chin campaigns were accompanied by a total of 5,390,000 civilian service workers, and over a million head of animal transport was contributed.[57]

The problem of returning civilian workers to their original localities continued to preoccupy the authorities throughout 1949. It was reported that over 100,000 civilian workers from North China were 'gradually returning home' in May 1949 after helping in the advance on Taiyuan, and it was hoped that they would be home in time for the spring planting. Another 200,000 were meanwhile returning to their farms in Shantung, North Kiangsu, and North Anhwei after working as 'auxiliary service volunteers' for the PLA's crossing of the Yangtze. Yet another 50,000 from Shantung continued with the PLA in the march southwards, while their women and children at home 'ground flour, sewed uniforms, and made shoes for the troops'.[58] The peasant population of North China was finally rewarded for its pains by a guarantee that, as from October 1949, they would be 'exempted from all war service work except farming'. From now on, according to the North China People's Government, they could 'best support the PLA by increasing their agricultural and industrial output'.[59]

ABSORPTION OF KMT FORCES

The recruitment of ex-KMT troops in the PLA had obvious advantages in diminishing the call on agricultural labour and the consequent depopulation of able-bodied peasant manpower.

[55] 'Present tasks of the North China Liberated Area', *Hua-pei Jen-min Jih-pao*, 15 June 1948 (NCNA (N. Shensi), 6 July 1948).
[56] NCNA (N. Shensi), 16 Sept. 1948.
[57] Chang Chün-ying, *Ko-ming yü fan-ko-ming ti chüeh-chan* (1961), p. 98.
[58] NCNA, reports of 3 & 29 May and 23 July 1949 (*FE*, 3, 7, 15).
[59] Ibid., 30 Aug. 1949 (*FE* 20).

At the same time it raised problems of discipline and of political control, especially in the third and fourth years of the civil war when the number of captured or surrendered KMT troops increased rapidly. According to communist statistics, out of a total of 4,150,000 Nationalist losses (captured, surrendered, or mutinied but excluding casualties) in the three years July 1946–9, nearly $2\frac{1}{2}$ million occurred in the last year. By June 1950 a further 2 million or more had been added.[60] This number of able-bodied but unemployed men called either for incorporation into the PLA or for resettlement, neither of which were entirely satisfactory solutions.

Communist policy on the eve of the 1947–8 counter-offensive was to seek replenishment of PLA strength chiefly from the enemy and the Kuomintang areas and only partly from the old liberated areas. It was envisaged that between 80 and 90 per cent of the men might be recruited, as well as a small number of junior officers.[61] By June 1948 the PLA had 'absorbed' a total of 800,000 KMT soldiers, as against twice that number of liberated area peasants, and had 'changed them into liberated fighters who have turned their guns against the KMT', a relatively manageable intake when spread over two years. A similar steady rate of expansion was planned for the next three years, involving a further 1,700,000 captured soldiers and 2 million peasants, reaching a total PLA strength of 5 million by June 1951.[62] In the event, this total was reached by the end of 1949. The unexpectedly rapid conclusion to the civil war speeded the process of recruitment from the KMT. As morale collapsed in the KMT armies, more Nationalist soldiers surrendered or let themselves be captured, while fewer were killed or wounded. According to the communists' own statistics, the number of troops who surrendered or came over to the PLA was negligible in the first two years of the war (less than 50,000) but increased dramatically in the second two years beginning July 1948 (644,000 and over 1 million in 1948–9 and 1949–50 respectively).[63]

[60] Ibid., 16 July 1949 (*FE* 14); Chang Chün-ying, p. 113.
[61] *MAO IV*, p. 145. This proportion was later reduced to 60 per cent (ibid. p. 272). The Double Tenth (10 Oct.) 1947 Manifesto of the Liberation Army specified that 'Those soldiers and officers of Chiang's army who lay down their arms will be accepted into our ranks if they wish or will be allowed to return home if they so desire" (NCNA (London), 28 Oct. 1947).
[62] *MAO IV*, p. 272.   [63] As n. 60.

The fall of Tsinan in September 1948—the first of the great series of victories in the North which marked the 'turning-point' of the war—was precipitated by the revolt of General Wu Hua-wen, commander of the 84th Division defending the south-west perimeter of the town, with 6,000 men. This defection 'upset the entire Nationalist plan' and allowed the communists to breach the perimeter.[64] The pattern of defection was to become almost standard. At Changchün in Manchuria, General Tseng Tse-sheng went over with 10,000 men in October. The fall of Changchün left the way for Lin Piao's army open to Mukden and thence into North China. Similar defections to the total of nine KMT divisions marked the Huai-Hai campaign in November–December 1948 which cleared the route to the Yangtze.[65]

In the closing stages of the war, it became a standard feature of communist tactics to negotiate for the surrender of KMT troops and their reorganization into the PLA. The best example of this procedure was seen in Peking, where on 22 January 1949 General Fu Tso-yi signed a surrender agreement whose terms provided for the reorganization of his 200,000 troops into the PLA. Twenty-five divisions were to be reorganized into independent divisions of the PLA. Officers who wished to go home would be allowed three months pay and free travel. They would be accorded equal treatment in land reform, and would not be punished for their past misdeeds. Those who wished to join the PLA would receive the same salary and treatment as regular PLA officers, but would be required first to undergo political education. This, according to Lin Piao, would necessitate 'a thorough transformation in their political nature and style of thinking'.

This agreement was more than a straightforward act of surrender. It was 'not merely a simple military reorganisation or merely a change in designation ... but was a political reorganisation'.[66] It prevented the disintegration of the KMT divisions into isolated and potentially dangerous units; they stayed in

[64] *NYT*, 24 Sept. 1948.
[65] Besieged KMT garrisons were bombarded with propaganda bombs and loud-speaker appeals. The message would run along these lines: 'Brothers! Lay down your arms which you never wanted to take up. .... Come over to us. If you want, we will send you home. Better still, you can join us and fight to free your homes as we have ours' (Belden, *China Shakes the World*, pp. 413–18).
[66] Gen. Lo Jung-huan, quoted in Robert R. Rigg, *Red China's Fighting Hordes* (Pennsylvania, 1951), p. 276.

formation and continued to maintain law and order in the Peking area until communist troops could take over, avoiding the usual chaos of an interregnum. Their officers were allowed to return home or to join the PLA without losing face (Fu Tso-yi himself was removed from the list of war criminals after making an appropriate apology to Chairman Mao and all the democratic parties).[67]

After the loss of Tientsin, Fu Tso-yi, isolated in Peking, had no alternative but to seek for peace. The communists hoped that his surrender would encourage the KMT armies south of the Yangtze to do likewise. 'The settlement at Peking', NCNA commented, 'has set a precedent—even by Kuomintang law—that the reactionary Kuomintang Nanking government will not be able to repudiate, even when it is applied to other places.'[68] The peace negotiations during January–April 1949 between representatives of Li Tsung-jen for the Nationalist government and the communists attempted to achieve on a nation-wide basis what had been agreed for Peking. At all stages of the negotiations, from the communist '8 Basic Terms' of 14 January to the draft Agreement on Internal Peace rejected by Nanking on 20 April, the communist position insisted upon virtual surrender by the Nationalists and reorganization of their troops.[69]

Hopes in Nanking of a *de facto* partition along the Yangtze river were dashed by repeated communist insistence that 'the peace which the people demand is a people's peace and not a peace with the Yangtze as the boundary line' and on the opening day of negotiations (2 April) a message from Mao Tse-tung cited Fu Tso-yi's surrender as the pattern for peace throughout China.[70] In his report to the second plenary session of the Central

[67] Reorganization terms in NCNA (N. Shensi), 1 Mar. 1949 (quoted in Rigg, pp. 275–6). See also NCNA, 15 Feb. 1949; *NCDN*, 3 Apr. 1949.
[68] 'Background to the Peace Settlement of Peiping', NCNA (N. Shensi), 15 Feb. 1949.
[69] The fourth of the 8 Basic Terms read: 'Reorganize all reactionary troops on democratic principles'. Section 4 of the draft Agreement on Internal Peace incorporated detailed plans for the reorganization of KMT troops 'on democratic principles'. KMT forces were to maintain law and order until the arrival of the PLA. They were then to move to designated areas and reorganize into regular units of the PLA. Officers and men were at liberty to return home, where they would not be discriminated against. Those who remained would be subject to PLA military and political discipline (*MAO IV*, pp. 318, 390–6).
[70] Lin Piao, 'We have the power to realise all Mao Tse-tung's 8 Peace Points', NCNA, 2 Mar. 1949 (*NCDN*, 3 Apr. 1949).

Committee (5 March 1949), Mao spoke optimistically of the possibility for solutions on the Peking pattern. He described this solution as unavoidable now that the main force of the enemy had been destroyed; it was also advantageous to the army and the civilian population since it avoided casualties and destruction. It was not, however, as effective as fighting in 'eliminating the vestiges of counter-revolution and liquidating its political influence', and the entire PLA should not relax its will to fight or belittle the enemy's strength.[71]

Following the breakdown of peace talks on 20 April, and the crossing of the Yangtze, the possibility of an overall 'Peking solution' receded. But the rate of defection throughout the last year continued to be high, and the communists later claimed that over 1 million had come over from the Nationalists in that year, apart from the capture of yet another million. Whenever possible, the communists continued to seek victory by negotiation rather than by fighting. Three of the most crucial victories were won in this way. The loss of Changsha in early August, which broke the Nationalists' defence line and left the way open to Kwangtung, was brought about by the defection of General Ch'en Ming-jen with 30,000 troops. On 19 September T'ung Chi-wu, governor of Suiyuan, surrendered the province with more than 40,000 men, directly exposing the whole of the North-west to communist take-over and isolating Moslem resistance led by General Ma Pu-fang and his son in Ninghsia province. (T'ung Chi-wu, a former subordinate of General Fu Tso-yi, had been 'neutralized' since Fu's surrender by secret agreement, and had been waiting for the opportune moment to make his defection public.)[72]

In Sinkiang, where the situation was complicated by the presence of the pro-Soviet and pro-Sinkiang autonomy Ili party, both the revolutionary army belonging to this faction and over 60,000 troops under Governor T'ao Chih-yueh also transferred their allegiance. In all these cases—no doubt as a concession to the fact that they had voluntarily assisted the communist cause by their defections—the armies involved were not dispersed or

---

[71] *MAO IV*, pp. 361-2.

[72] See ibid.: 'The Suiyuan pattern is deliberately to keep part of the Kuomintang troops wholly or nearly inert, that is, to make temporary concessions to these troops in order to help win them over to our side or neutralise them politically'. See also report in *NYT*, 21 Sept. 1949.

reorganized, but were incorporated into the PLA as separate units.[73]

[73] Ch'en Ming-jen's 1st KMT Army Group became the 21st Army Group of the PLA as part of the 4th Field Army. The Suiyuan Army became the 23rd Army Group, under direct administration from PLA headquarters. The Sinkiang Army joined the 1st Field Army as the 22nd Army Group, and the Ili rebels were incorporated as the 5th Army of the PLA in Sinkiang.

4
Popular Mobilization for the Korean War

To hold the victorious trophies of our revolution, to keep the dirty swines' lips from intruding through the fence of our beautiful garden, we expect all you revolutionary young workers to respond to the call of your fatherland![1]

IT is easy to deduce that the drain of manpower and resources to China caused by the Korean war was of the first magnitude. It is less easy to examine this in detail, given our very scanty knowledge of several crucial factors. In contrast with their behaviour during the civil war, the PLA headquarters (or rather the Chinese People's Volunteers Command in Korea) issued no statistics of any kind during the entire course of the Korean war regarding the CPV's strength, equipment, or casualties. Indeed this same attitude persisted after the signing of the armistice. The Chinese and North Korean refusal to furnish any information or assistance to the Neutral Nations Supervisory Commission and its inspection teams was to lead to the withdrawal of the Commission from North Korea in May 1956.[2]

In part this atmosphere of secrecy was created at the very start of the war by Chinese insistence that their forces were 'volunteers' and hence by the need to conceal their real designations as regular army units. Since the issues of rotation of troops and the build-up of forces were contentious questions both before and after the armistice, there was a further reason for maintaining silence on this score. We are therefore forced to rely almost entirely upon United Nations statistics, and these too are by no means free from error. There was a built-in bias towards exaggeration of communist strength, at first in order to explain

---

[1] Call for enrolment in military training schools, issued by the All-China Federation of Labour, quoted in *NYT*, 6 Dec. 1950.

[2] See *United Nations Command Report on the Neutral Nations Supervisory Commission in Korea*, 15 Aug. 1956, UN A/3167, for details of communist obstruction of the Neutral Nations Supervisory Commission.

UN losses during the first half of 1951 and later to provide ammunition for charges of bad faith against the communist side. Conversely, there was a tendency to exaggerate communist losses and casualties, especially by the American forces who both formed an overwhelming majority of the UN forces and dominated the UN Command. With this proviso in mind, the following figures for Chinese strength and losses during the Korean war may be suggested.

ESTIMATED RECRUITMENT FOR THE KOREAN WAR

By the end of October 1950 six Chinese armies had crossed the Yalu, totalling at least 180,000 men. Four more armies crossed in November, bringing the total to some 300,000. By January 1951 this had almost reached 500,000, and increased rapidly to 700,000 at the time of the summer offensives. Severe losses inflicted on the CPV during the two spring offensives and the advance to the 'Iron Triangle' of May–July 1951 were estimated to be of the order of 200,000, thus bringing the total down again to half a million.[3]

During the next year a steady build-up restored the strength of the CPV to roughly its previous level. At the highest estimate, the total number of communist forces in North Korea doubled from half a million in July 1951 to just short of one million a year later.[4] Since this figure included 200,000 North Korean troops, the total strength of Chinese regular units can be placed at between 700,000 and 800,000. This is confirmed by other calculations based upon the subsequent withdrawal of Chinese units from Korea.[5] It seems therefore that the overall strength of the CPV during 1951–4 may be placed at something in the order of 700,000 or more.

According to a UN Command release of 23 October 1953, CPV casualties—killed and wounded—to that date totalled 900,000, as against 520,000 among the North Korean forces.

---

[3] David Rees, *Korea; the Limited War* (London, 1964), pp. 136, 245–6, 258.
[4] *Daily Telegraph*, 11 June 1952, interview with Gen. Mark Clark; *The Times*, 20 Oct. 1952, quoting from a UN Command report to the General Assembly. Sir Winston Churchill told the House of Commons on 28 May 1952 that the 'enemy' was 'not far short of one million men' (HC Deb., vol. 501, col. 1360).
[5] The total cumulative withdrawal of CPV forces from Korea has been estimated at between 710,000 (*China Weekly*, No. 308, quoted in *Communist China 1958*, p. 181) and 770,000 (*Communist China 1949–59*, i. 231).

South Korean (ROK) losses were estimated at 1,313,836, but these included about 1 million civilian casualties. (North Korean civilian casualties were also estimated unofficially at about 1 million.)[6] The figure of 900,000 Chinese casualties is almost certainly exaggerated, and serious suspicions have been cast upon the methods of calculation employed by the UN Command.[7] The real figure is likely to be much lower, and one can only suggest an arbitrary reduction of the UN claim by one-third, arriving at a total CPV casualty list of 600,000.

This raises the question of the extent to which recruitment was necessary in China in order to maintain the strength of the CPV in Korea and to make good its casualty losses. Most unofficial estimates of recruitment into the PLA during the Korean war appear to be greatly exaggerated. (These range as high as 2,700,000 in 1951 alone,[8] or 4 million over the years 1951–3.)[9]

In 1950 the PLA's strength totalled 5 million. Over the next six years the same number of men were demobilized, and its strength fell in the same period to about 2¾ million. This figure had therefore to be supplied by recruitment, and almost half (1,330,000) was provided for by the two annual drafts of 1954 and 1955. The remaining half was consequently raised before 1954 during the Korean war. While the overall demobilization figure of 5 million presumably includes the wounded casualties of the Korean war who were retired from service, it obviously does not include the percentage of 'killed' casualties which had to be replaced. It follows that a proportion of the casualty figure for Korea must be added to the recruitment total during the war. This proportion cannot be precisely calculated, the more so since the total casualty figure itself is in doubt. At a very generous estimate, one could postulate that one-third of the casualty figure

---

[6] Rees, pp. 460–1; Leckie, *Conflict; the History of the Korean War* (New York, 1962), p. 406.

[7] In a review of Leckie, *Conflict*, in *International Review*, Spring 1963, H. F. Wood writes: 'In general, when dead Chinese soldiers were found after a battle, intelligence reasoned that there must have been many more that the enemy had evacuated. Having thus arrived at an arbitrary figure for fatal casualties, a statistical probability of wounded was worked out based on experience rather than evidence. Thus the UN estimates of enemy losses seem in retrospect to have been produced as much for the purpose of maintaining UN morale as for assessing enemy capabilities.'

[8] *Daily Telegraph*, 22 Aug. 1953.   [9] *Communist China, 1949–59*, i, 225.

estimated by the UN Command was 'killed'—i.e. 300,000. This suggests a very rough upper limit for total recruitment during the Korean war of approximately 1,750,000. Allowing for a wide margin of error, the real figure may therefore come anywhere between 1½ and 1¾ million.[10]

The 5-million strong PLA might legitimately be regarded as a more than adequate source from which to maintain an army of 700,000 in the Korean field, and with which to replace 600,000 or even 900,000 casualties. Why then was it necessary to recruit replacements on such a large scale? This was partly due to the effect of demobilization. Although, as has been shown, the Korean war temporarily checked plans for demobilization, it did not altogether halt them. By the end of 1953, almost 3 million men had been demobilized from the PLA, and while the majority of these were probably dismissed in 1953 itself after the cease-fire in Korea, a good proportion must have left while the war was still in progress.[11] The majority of these were probably war-weary veterans and ex-KMT troops—neither of which categories were suited for prolonged service with the PLA in China or with the CPV in Korea.

Secondly, the PLA lacked in quality what it made up for in quantity. The number of well-trained, experienced, and politically reliable troops was considerably less than its total strength. The PLA in China was divided into the original Field Armies and the local Garrison Armies (*Chün-ch'u tu-li- shih*). The former were first-line troops, veterans of the civil war. The latter, no doubt largely composed of ex-KMT manpower, were second-line troops at a lower state of readiness and capability. Estimates of the relative strength of these forces vary considerably, but in general they place the Field Army at between 2 and 3 million,

---

[10] For calculations and sources, see Table 3 (p. 305). In a recent interview with Stuart and Roma Gelder (*Evening Standard*, 31 May 1966), Marshal Ch'en Yi stated that 'we sent a million troops to Korea and suffered more than a hundred thousand casualties'. The figure of one million is consistent with my calculations if one allows for rotation of troops. Ch'en Yi's figure for casualties suggests a much lower estimate, even if it only applies to those who were actually killed.

[11] Report by P'eng Teh-huai to the NPC on the Draft Military Service Law (NCNA, 16 July 1955, in *SCMP* 1090). P'eng told the NPC that '. . . more than 1,570,000 military personnel have been demobilized since 1954', and that 'since the founding of the Chinese People's Republic, we have demobilized more than 4,510,000 persons from our armed forces'.Thus 2,940,000 were demobilized before 1954.

G

and the Garrison Army strength at between 1 and 2 million.[12] Heavy demands were already made upon the Field Armies for the performance of vital military duties in China itself—especially in Sinkiang and Tibet and in guarding the coastal frontiers. Field Army personnel were also used to provide the nucleus for the navy, air force, and other newly established service arms. If the Korean war had not broken out, it would probably have been possible to demobilize the greater part of the second-line troops and to maintain the Field Armies intact without any need for large-scale recruitment. But the Korean war imposed an additional burden upon the Field Armies' pool of skilled manpower, which could only be met by the mobilization of fresh reinforcements. These, unlike the existing second-line troops, had to be young, politically reliable, and capable of being trained to higher standards of military proficiency. The sheer volume of recruitment in China during the Korean war imposed a heavy strain upon the country's manpower resources, but its most important aspect was that it siphoned off a considerable proportion of skilled manpower which was urgently needed elsewhere in civilian life. This particularly affected high-school and college graduates, and qualified personnel in the fields of communications and medicine.

The mass element in recruitment was provided by the militia. The CPV was reinforced from the regular Field Armies; new

[12]
PLA Strength, 1950–4

	Total	Field Armies	Garrison Armies
1950	5,000,000[a]	—	—
1951	—	2,380,000[b]	—
	4,000,000[c]	2,500,000[c]	1,500,000
	—	2,100,000–2,500,000[d]	—
1952	4,700,000[e]	2,800,000[e]	1,900,000[e]
	5,000,000[f]	3,000,000[f]	under
	or less		2,000,000[f]
1953	4,600,000[g]	3,200,000[g]	1,400,000[g]
	—	2,800,000[h]	—

[a] *The Chinese PLA* (Peking, 1950).   [b] *CSM*, 8 Feb. 1951.
[c] *The Times*, 19 Mar. 1951, acc. British War Office.
[d] *NYT*, 14 Jan. 1951.   [e] Ibid., 30 Sept. 1952.
[f] *Daily Telegraph*, 11 Dec. 1952.
[g] Chin Ta-k'ai & Chang Ta-chüh, *Chung-kung chün-shih p'ou-shih* (1954), p. 17.
[h] Calculated from *Problems of Red China*, i(1954), p. 38.

soldiers were not recruited directly to the Korean front, but graduated from the militia through the garrison armies into the Field Armies, thus ensuring a steady flow of trained manpower into the regular units. The militia expanded rapidly during the first year of the Korean war, from 5 million in 1950 to 12,800,000 by September 1951.[13] A certain proportion of these recruits eventually passed into the regular PLA, and in the North-east, according to one report, this was as high as 70 per cent of the local militia.[14] It has been estimated that more than 1 million militiamen were eventually drafted to fill vacancies in the Field Armies.[15] Rank and file militia were required to take the following pledge: 'To help whole-heartedly the public security forces in suppressing counter-revolutionary elements and to be prepared, of their own volition, to proceed at any time to the Korean Front to fight'.[16] But the demands of the CPV in Korea involved more than the constant supply of cannon-fodder. Large numbers of officers and n.c.o.'s with technical expertise were required to staff the armies and to cope with the new and more sophisticated types of equipment supplied by the Soviet Union. The guerrilla-type qualities of the veteran cadre from revolutionary days were also less suited to the waging of positional warfare on a scale hitherto largely unfamiliar to the PLA.

ENLISTMENT OF STUDENTS AND SKILLED LABOUR

Some military academies had already been established at the time of Liberation; 6,000 students had enrolled at the North China Military Administrative University in Peking, while by September 1949 16,000 cadets had enrolled at the East China Military Region Military and Political Institute in Nanking, an institution which would provide 'youthful intellectuals' with military knowledge and would 'raise the cultural standards of veterans'.[17] In the same month a naval academy was opened in Nanking, while each of the other military regions established

---

[13] Chou En-lai, report of 23 Oct. 1951 to People's Political Consultative Conference (NCNA, 2 Nov. 1951).
[14] *Ta-kung-Pao*, 2 Aug. 1953, quoted in Chin & Chang, *Chung-kung chün-shih p'ou-shih*, p. 77.
[15] Ting Li, *Militia of Communist China* (1955), p. 133.   [16] Ibid., p. 107.
[17] Peking radio, 1 Sept. 1949 (*FE* 20). The East China Military and Political Institute subsequently became the PLA General Staff and War College, and the senior military academy in China.

staff colleges to train military and political cadres for the PLA.

A year later, under the stimulus of China's intervention in the Korean war, a campaign was launched to recruit military cadres which dwarfed all previous efforts. On 1 December 1950, a joint resolution of the PRMC and the SAC called for the enrolment of young students and workers in military cadres' schools. Recruits should be aged between 17 and 25, should have 'correct political thoughts, good character and a determination to aid in national defence'. They should be in good health, with at least junior college or higher secondary school education. The Ministry of Education was to help by setting up enrolment committees to screen students for training. Students from technical schools, with specialized qualifications in such fields as mechanical engineering, aerial navigation, civil engineering, electrical and marine engineering, and chemistry were particularly sought after. Students were enrolled in the first instance for the Aviation and Artillery Schools (1 year's training), the Naval School (2 years), and the Armoured School (8 months). Those who failed to satisfy the medical requirements for these schools or who were surplus to requirements were directed to the service schools—Medical, Supply, Signal Corps, as well as the Public Security School, the Foreign Languages and Russian Language Schools. By 10 January, exactly one month after recruitment began, it was claimed that more than 250,000 students and young workers had enrolled for military training, of whom over 50 per cent belonged to the communist party or to the New Democratic Youth League (NDYL).[18]

The purpose of this recruitment campaign had been to skim the technical and political cream of China's student and working population for the armed forces. Only in the south-west, where the economic situation was particularly bad, was it decided that workers should not volunteer, but should demonstrate their patriotism 'in the battlefront of production'.[19] A deliberate attempt was made to encourage the recruits to regard themselves as a new élite. The campaign was launched on the fifteenth anniversary of the student anti-Japanese demonstra-

[18] Joint Resolution of the PRMC and SAC, Tsingtao radio, 1 Dec. 1950 (*FE* 86); Regulations of the PRMC Political Dept (NCNA, 9 Dec. 1950); ditto, Peking radio, 26 Dec. 1950 (*FE* 89) & 22 Jan. 1951 (*FE* 93).
[19] Chungking radio, 24 Dec. 1950 (*FE* 89).

tions of 9 December 1935, and the *People's Daily* quoted from a speech by Liu Shao-ch'i made in 1944, the tenth anniversary of the demonstrations, to the effect that

In the present war to safeguard their Fatherland, they [students] occupy various important posts and struggle effectively for their 9th December aspirations. I believe that in the not distant future they will return to Peking, Tientsin, Shanghai and other places with the status of victors and masters. . . .[20]

The purpose of a second campaign, launched in June 1951 by the State Administrative Council and netting a further 270,000 students (no workers were recruited in this campaign), was more ambiguous. The lower age limit was lowered to 16, but it was 'not to be too rigid'. Physical requirements were also lower; 'as many as possible of those whose physique is not too far below the standards should be admitted'. This time it was lower secondary school graduates who were chiefly required, and the *People's Daily* stated frankly that one reason for this was that 'there is a surplus of junior middle [secondary] school graduates available'. This campaign appears to have been intended partly to absorb surplus student manpower as well as to provide cadre material for the army. Indeed, it has been suggested that many students went direct to the front without being given any cadre training.[21] At the same time a decision of the SAC directed that students graduating from institutes of higher learning should be 'allocated to posts in various forms of national construction work according to the needs of the departments and enterprises concerned', in order to eliminate unemployment or the misapplication of graduate talents. This measure, like that of recruitment into the PLA, was part of a conscious policy of labour direction for students. Some degree of direction would have been necessary in any case, to ensure that students were absorbed into jobs where they were most needed. Yet the siphoning off of a large proportion of China's student population into the PLA had serious implications, both for the educational system itself and doubtless for the

---

[20] NCNA, 9 Dec. 1950 (*FE* 87).
[21] Chin & Chang (*Chung-kung chün-shih p'ou-shih*, p. 87), claim that in many cases 'joining as a cadre' (*ts'an kan*) amounted to 'joining as a soldier' (*ts'an chün*). They quote from a speech by Yang Teh-chih, deputy commander of the CPV in Korea (*JMJP*, 16 Oct. 1953), in which Yang described how student recruits were sent direct to the front and learnt their military techniques there.

civilian enterprises which were deprived of their skilled services.[22]

While the second campaign for student enrolment was in progress, all entrance examinations to colleges had been postponed. Local education departments were ordered to co-operate with army political departments in selecting students. In spite of the emphasis upon 'voluntary' enrolment, some schools had started compulsory 'all-class enrolment'. In August 1951 both the Central-South and East China MACs were compelled to issue directives on 'the correction of confusion in educational activities'. 'Serious and chaotic conditions' had developed in the schools owing to 'the inadequate attention given to education by the various departments concerned'. This, they said, was not only an unnecessary loss of talent, but it had also caused dissatisfaction among the people, students, and teachers. No department or organization, it was emphasized, was allowed to assign teachers or students to activities outside school without prior approval from higher educational authorities.[23]

A similar directive from South-west China noted that the total number of students in the area was reduced by 23 per cent as compared with autumn 1950. 'There was a noticeable depletion in the sources for fresh students and teachers at high school level.' Henceforth the fundamental task for all education authorities was to be 'the completion of the schools' programmes'.[24]

[22] The 520,000 students who 'enrolled' appear all to have been accepted for service. The regulations issued by the General Political Dept of the PRMC on 9 Dec. 1950 specified that acceptance of volunteer students into the PLA depended upon the final approval of college recommendation committees and local enrolment committees (*FE* 87). But the published figures of 250,000 for the first campaign and 270,000 for the second campaign clearly refer to the number who were actually accepted for service in military cadre schools (Peking radio, 22 Jan. 1951 (*FE* 93), & 17 July 1951 (*FE* 118)). The number of those who originally 'volunteered' may have been much higher. The figure of 520,000 comprised almost 40 per cent of the total student enrolment for 1950–1 in schools of secondary and higher education. The fact that these enrolment figures did not rise appreciably from the low post-civil war rate of 1949 until the final year of the Korean war may be largely explained by the diversion of students into the PLA.

Leo A. Orleans, *Professional Manpower and Education in Communist China* (Washington, 1961), pp. 35, 61 gives the following figures for student enrolment:

	Secondary Education	Higher Education
1949–50	1,039,000	117,000
1950–1	1,305,000	137,000
1951–2	1,568,100	153,000
1952–3	2,490,000	191,000

[23] East China MAC Directive, Shanghai radio, 15 Aug. 1951 (*FE* 124).
[24] NCNA, 1 Sept. 1951 (*FE* 125).

Other sources of skilled labour were also depleted in the interests of the war in Korea. In July 1951, following a directive from the SAC on the need for the 'strengthening of public health personnel in national defence construction', a volunteer campaign was launched among medical staff throughout the country. (This decision was probably prompted by the increasing incidence of contagious diseases and epidemics among the troops in Korea.) The ratio of doctors in China at that time was only one to 10,000 of the population; 3,000 of these, or perhaps as many as 7–8 per cent of the total, were enrolled and accepted for service in Korea by the middle of 1951. By the end of the war, twice that number had served in Korea as volunteer civilian medical workers. Those who remained in China were urged to devote more of their time to work in the armed forces and among army dependants, giving their services free or at a nominal rate.[25]

Truck drivers and railway workers were also persuaded to volunteer, in order to keep the heavily hit supply lines open to the front, and to supplement North Korea's meagre resources of trained manpower. By the end of the war over 4,000 railwaymen from Shanghai alone had served in Korea.[26] Manchuria provided large numbers of peasants to act as stretcher-bearers and coolies—many of them veterans of similar volunteer units during the civil war.

THE VOLUNTEER MOVEMENT

The Korean war imposed a heavy burden on the Chinese government, already faced with the task of winning the support of a population of which more than three-quarters had only come under communist control in the past three to four years. The combination of continued internal unrest with a major external war meant that the need to secure mass support was all the more urgent, since the alternative would be doubly disastrous. It is no accident that all the major mass movements launched in the first years of the Chinese People's Republic except for land reform

[25] Report of Ho Chung, Deputy Minister of Health to SAC, 13 July 1951 (NCNA, 13 July 1951, in *FE* 118); Peking radio 19 July 1951 (ibid.); NCNA, 27 Oct. 1951 (*FE* 133). A Pakistani reporter who visited Peking wrote in February 1951 that Korean casualties were much greater than anticipated, and that hospitals in Manchuria were denuded of nursing staff (*NYHT*, 18 Feb. 1951).

[26] NCNA, 8 Nov. 1950 (*FE* 82); *Kung-jen Jih-pao*, 31 July 1953 (NCNA, 5 Aug. 1953).

were initiated after and not before China's intervention in Korea. The following are the major movements of this kind, with their dates of origin.

1. The Volunteer movement   November 1950
2. Resist-America and Aid-Korea leading to the Patriotic Pact movement and the Donation for Purchase of Planes and Heavy Artillery movement   November 1950
3. Suppression of Counter-Revolutionaries   February 1951
4. The 'Three-Anti's' (Anti-Corruption, Anti-Waste, and Anti-Bureaucratism)   September 1951
5. Increase Production and Practise Economy   October 1951
6. 'Five-Anti's' (Anti-Bribery, Anti-Tax Evasion, Anti-Fraud, Anti-Theft of State Assets, and Anti-Leakage of State Economic Secrets)   October 1951

All these movements were essentially aspects of the same attempt to secure total commitment by every segment of the population to the government's policies. They were coercive to the extent that in the last resort they were backed by political, military, or social sanctions. They were popular to the extent that they could not succeed without some measure of grass-roots support, whether induced by repeated pressure, or spontaneous, or a mixture of both. To examine all these campaigns in detail would involve one in considering the role of mass persuasion in Chinese communist government—a subject which deserves greater attention but which lies outside the scope of this study. Two of these campaigns, however, touched directly on the methods by which China supported the Korean war both materially and morally, and will therefore be considered below.

The call for volunteers for the CPV, whether from the militia or from the civilian population, was organized at the local level by the Volunteer Movement Committee, set up by the Military District and party authorities. Volunteers were called for at agitation meetings, and emulation contests were organized both on an individual and on a village basis. Families of those who refused to volunteer were visited by the committee in order to persuade them to 'send off' (*sung*) their sons to the army. If this failed, then a struggle meeting might be organized, while members of the youth group would sing songs satirizing the reluctant volunteers.[27] Public opinion was also mobilized to congratulate those who had volunteered. It is interesting to note that the object of such congratulation was usually the family of the volunteer rather than the volunteer himself—a recognition of the influential part which familial authority played in persuading young men to enlist. Social approval was formally accorded to such families by 'congratulation teams' organized among their neighbours, who would visit them with gifts and ceremonial banners. Students who volunteered for military training colleges were also congratulated by their colleagues. These held elaborate farewell parties, complete with red flowers, bands, and firecrackers, and visited the volunteers' families to make sure that they had no problems.[28]

Agitation meetings for recruitment were not of course designed to produce a random number of recruits on a voluntary basis. The exact number and qualifications required would have already been fixed, and the purpose of the meeting was to whip up sufficient popular enthusiasm so that subsequent drafting of recruits would not be resisted. This is illustrated by one particularly candid account of a recruitment meeting of a trade union branch in Peking.

The secretary of the branch spoke about the danger of American attacks towards the Manchuria border; the Americans were professing peaceful intentions while 'aiming a gun at our heart and preparing to pull the trigger'. Any Chinese volunteering was a true patriot; he would act as a 'sentry guarding our gates from the invaders'. The secretary finished his address amid complete silence. . . . One could feel how the audience began to realise that after one year's peaceful reconstruction China was again being threatened by her old enemy. . . . Suddenly someone shouted that he wanted to go to Korea . . . thereupon many other people rose to their feet. . . . After two hours had passed the trade union secretary said that it appeared to him that everybody wished to volunteer. This was 'magnificent but not practical'. He suggested that the branch should consider these applications and recommend who should be allowed to step forward. . . . Everybody would 'have a chance'.[29]

[27] Chin & Chang, *Chung-kung chün-shih p'ou-shih*, pp. 76 ff.

[28] See further Wen-hui C. Chen, *Wartime 'Mass' Campaigns in Communist China : Official Country-wide 'Mass Movements' in Professed Support of the Korean War* (1955), pp. 32–35. This monograph provides a detailed analysis of the various mass movements during the Korean war.

[29] NCNA, 9 Nov. 1950 (*FE* 82).

Recruitment in the countryside was closely linked to land reform—as it had been during the civil war and indeed as early as the Kiangsi Soviet.[30] The land reform movement of 1950–1, Chou En-lai later claimed, had caused 'an exceptional sharpening in the political consciousness of the peasants'. In order to 'safeguard the fruits of emancipation' they had sponsored the movement to resist American aggression, signed patriotic pacts, 'volunteered for the Army', increased production and made their 'patriotic public grain deliveries'.[31]

The land reform law of June 1950 included the by now customary special privileges for soldiers and their families. They would be exempted from the category of 'landlord' and their landholding would remain untouched unless it was markedly excessive (Art. 5). Active and demobilized soldiers, their families and camp-followers ('those who travel with the Army'), and the families of revolutionary martyrs, were entitled to equal shares in land and means of production (Art. 13 (c)). The term 'revolutionary army men' was redefined in a supplementary decision of the SAC to mean not only veteran PLA men, but also 'the commanders and fighters of the armed forces who have crossed over to the side of the revolution as from the date of their re-organisation into the PLA'.[32] As one analyst writes, 'the military advantage derived from land reform was certainly more than a mere incidental effect of the carefully engineered social upheaval'.[33]

THE RESIST AMERICA AND AID KOREA (RAAK) CAMPAIGN

Apart from the burden imposed upon the Chinese people by the need for recruitment and by their obligations towards army dependants, the greatest effect of the Korean war upon their daily life was undoubtedly the campaign 'To Resist America and

---

[30] Art. 2 of the Land Law of the Soviet Republic (Nov. 1931) stipulated that: 'The Red Army is the front rank fighter in the defence of the Soviet government and in the overthrow of the rule of imperialism and the government of landlords and capitalists. Therefore, each Red Army man must be given a plot of land, and the Soviet Government must see to it that his land is tilled, whether or not his home is in the Soviet district or in an area ruled by reactionaries' (text in Brandt, *Documentary History*, p. 225).

[31] See n. 13.

[32] *The Agrarian Reform Law of the People's Republic of China, 30 June 1950* (Peking, 1950).

[33] T. L. Wu, *Economic Survey of Communist China* (London, 1956), p. 135.

Aid Korea'. This campaign ultimately involved the entire body of China's population, operating simultaneously through all the mass organizations, the labour unions, and government services. It has been suggested that its primary purpose was 'to liquidate the last vestige of Western influence',[34] and it is true that under its aegis businesses were reorganized and sometimes sequestered and schools and hospitals divorced from Western control or influence. It was indeed closely linked to the concurrent movement for the Suppression of Counter-Revolutionaries. But its main purpose was to generate and diffuse a popular sentiment in support of the government's action in Korea, and in opposition to the United Nations intervention. It attempted to translate this into practical action by seeking to increase production, secure the payment of taxes, and stimulate productive efficiency by non-material incentives, namely by moral exhortations and by appeals to the nation's sense of patriotism.

In the first months of Chinese action in Korea, the movement was confined to two objectives: the increase of production in the North-east, and the coercion of business and commerce to pay its taxes and to raise the quality and quantity of its manufacture and transactions. In November 1950 it was reported that a vast patriotic emulation campaign was sweeping Manchuria under the slogan 'Our factory is our battlefield and our machines are our weapons'. Practically every factory in the North-east had drawn up 'anti-American aggression emulation targets'. Stakhanovite records were set up and then broken among the key industries of coal, iron, and steel. By January 1951 the emulation campaign had spread outside the North-east till it involved more than 1,200,000 workers in the rest of the country.[35]

Meanwhile meetings of businessmen and industrialists were convened in all the major towns, at which they demonstrated against American aggression and then signed 'patriotic pacts' in which they pledged themselves to increase production and to pay their taxes promptly. A typical letter from such a meeting in Chungking, circulated among businessmen in other cities, stated that:

In order to show our love for our Fatherland, we have decided to pay the taxes with great enthusiasm as a practical demonstration in

---

[34] Chou Ching-wen, *Ten Years of Storm* [1960], pp. 117–18.
[35] NCNA, 5 Nov. 1950 (*FE* 82); Peking radio 11 Jan. 1951 (*FE* 92).

the patriotic movement of Resist-America-Aid-Korea. . . . We are sure that you will consider the tax payment as one of your patriotic obligations. . . .

Other pledges included ones to 'refrain from speculation', to 'improve relations between labour and capital' and to send donations to Korea.[36]

Until the spring of 1951 the movement had been chiefly confined to promoting emulation campaigns in the factories and patriotic pacts in business and commerce. In April the national headquarters in Peking of the Resist-America-Aid-Korea Association instructed all towns and *hsien* to set up local branches, whose 'guiding units' should admit elements of all democratic parties, people's organizations, and patriotic democrats of all walks of life. On the same day it was announced that an agricultural emulation drive had been started.[37]

On 1 June 1951, following heavy Chinese losses in Korea, a nation-wide campaign was launched to provide funds for the purchase of heavy equipment (planes and guns) for the Chinese volunteers. It began by an NCNA interview with Liao Chengchih, recently returned from leading a 'comfort mission' to the troops in Korea, in which he frankly outlined the CPV's deficiencies in equipment. According to Liao, the CPV urgently needed more aircraft, tanks, guns, AA guns, anti-tank guns, lorries, and cars. It was also short of 'nutritive food in a form that could be carried easily', first-aid packages and medicines, and amenities such as radio sets, popular magazines, gramophones and records. The Chinese People's Committee for World Peace and Against American Aggression promptly called for the development of 'patriotic pacts' throughout the nation 'until all strata of the people integrated their day to day work with the various present political tasks of the country'.

The campaign for donations, which continued until the end of 1951, was measured in terms of the number of 'fighter planes' (or rather their cash equivalent) 'donated' by the Chinese people. By the beginning of 1952, a total of 5 billion yuan had been donated, equivalent to almost 3,152 fighter planes.[38] Tanks and guns were also donated, and the donors were allowed to affix their own names to the equipment. The question of who this

[36] Peking radio, 18 Jan. 1951 (*FE* 93).   [37] Peking radio, 3 Apr. 1951 (*FE* 103).
[38] NCNA, 31 Dec. 1951, 28 Feb. 1952.

equipment would be purchased from was never mentioned, and the very fact of this campaign carried with it an implicit criticism of the Soviet Union for failing to provide military equipment without payment.[39] However, it was never seriously pretended that these funds would be directly spent on arms purchases. Donations were paid directly in cash to the local branch of the People's Bank, and what happened to them thenceforward was never disclosed. The real purpose of the campaign appears to have been not so much to levy additional taxes as to stimulate production and to prevent inflation. As the final communiqué on the campaign was to comment, 'besides adding to the fighting strength of the Chinese volunteers . . . this campaign has accelerated the tempo and expanded the scale of the national programme of reconstruction'.[40]

Indeed, from the very outset of the campaign, it was constantly emphasized that the progress of the campaign should go hand in hand with increased production. As one Peking commentary observed, the drive for heavy equipment should be coordinated with 'raising production, improving business operation, promoting work efficiency and increasing incomes; in this way, the national reconstruction programme will be accelerated at the same time'. It continued, 'if every Government employee, student and worker worked one more day a month to contribute to the war chest, it would exert a great influence not only on the reinforcement on the front but also on national economic reconstruction'. Any form of coercive levies of funds, it was underlined, would merely destroy the attempt to raise productivity and lower the people's living standards.[41] The prospect of a cease-fire and armistice in Korea was not allowed to interfere with the progress of the campaign. Public opinion, it was claimed, was against any slowing down of the campaign and the *People's Daily* commented editorially that 'we cannot permit the possible development of the Korean situation to slacken our tasks in the least'. On the contrary, 'all people in the country must step up the present movement . . . since the job of consolidating our Fatherland is our long-term duty'.[42]

[39] One sign of Chinese dissatisfaction with the Soviet Union at this time was the total absence of any reference to that ally in the slogans for 1951's Army Day. See further ch. 6.
[40] NCNA, 31 Dec. 1951.   [41] Peking radio, 13 June 1951 (*FE* 113).
[42] 'The Korean situation and the patriotic movement in China', *JMJP*, 4 July 1951.

The campaign was prosecuted as before primarily through the trade unions and businessmen's associations, who pledged themselves to increase production and in many cases to contribute one day's additional unpaid labour each month. But patriotic pacts were also extended to the countryside, where emulation campaigns were launched to increase ploughing, planting of crops, and harvesting. It was in the country that the campaign ran into most difficulty. There were frequent reports that cadres in the field had prosecuted the campaign 'in name only', or had gone to the other extreme and levied forced donations. Cadres were accused of having shown themselves 'indifferent' to the campaign, of having simply copied examples of patriotic pacts from newspapers and failed to make sure that they were implemented. In North Anhwei 'leading cadres thought it enough to issue public statements, convene meetings and make general preparations'. In West Szechwan many production and donation plans were couched in 'vague terms'. In Central-South China responsible cadres were accused of having failed to 'lead the masses in patriotism' so that the donation movement was not properly co-ordinated with increasing production and improving management. Some people gave all their money to the arms fund, thus 'jeopardising their livelihood', while others made no contribution at all. The people of some villages in North Szechwan did not even know what the campaign meant. The vice-chairman of one village peasant association thought that *Kangmei Yuan-ch'ao* (Resist America Aid Korea) was a person. Some village cadres in the area had misappropriated funds, while others in South Szechwan had hoarded grain contributions against a rise in prices. In some places the campaign was used as an excuse to hold popular celebrations and festivities. Thus in one place in East Szechwan the propaganda corps spent over $3 million on 'drums and other musical instruments', while in Shanghai over $370 million had been spent on street decorations, musical bands, and loud-speaker installations, until the Shanghai party committee was compelled to forbid 'colourful display and extravagance'.

All these complaints reflect the difficulty of putting over a popular campaign among the peasant population of China, and the tendency of untrained cadres to distort the aims of the campaign and alienate popular support by arbitrary compulsion.

The bulk of donations to the campaign continued to come from industry and business, but in the country districts it seems to have created a certain amount of resentment and confusion, while showing very little financial return.[43]

How successful was the arms fund campaign itself in financial terms? From the outset of the Korean war until June 1951, when the arms fund campaign was launched, donations by private subscription to the war effort had totalled only 11 million yuan, while the subsequent arms fund campaign raised over 500 million yuan. This was equivalent to about one-tenth of the military budget for 1951 of just over 5 billion yuan. Since the major portion of defence expenditure in 1951 must be accounted for by the purchase of equipment from the Soviet Union, in this sense it can be said that the overt purpose of the campaign, to pay for aeroplanes and equipment, was justified.[44] As an extra-legal method of taxation, however, the campaign produced only one-sixteenth of the revenue raised by orthodox taxation,[45] and a slight increase in regular taxation would therefore have been equally productive.

The fundamental purpose of the Resist America Aid Korea movement must rather be seen in the context of its social and political effects upon popular support for government action. Among the Chinese people, pitchforked into a war with America so soon after the end of the civil war, at a time when China's resources of economic strength and of national morale were both gravely depleted, there was confusion and perhaps even opposition to China's intervention. The wisdom of taking on a redoubtable enemy like the United States was also doubted. The heavy burden which the Korean war threw upon China's economy and her reserves of manpower also created some doubts and dismay at the popular level. The techniques of mass mobilization, used so successfully during the revolutionary and civil wars against

---

[43] See reports from NCNA, 21 July & 8 Aug. 1951; Chungking radio, 15 Aug. & 27 Oct. 1951; Peking radio, 22 July 1951; *Chang-chiang Jih-pao*, 11 Aug. 1951; Wuhan radio, 27 July 1951 (*FE* Nos. 119, 120, 122, 124, 127, 133).

[44] Defence expenditure rose from 2·82 billion in 1950 to 5·06 billion in 1951. Meanwhile expenditure on compensation and pay for military and supporting personnel rose in the same period only from 0·96 billion to 1·33 billion (William W. Hollister, *China's Gross National Product and Social Accounts 1950–1957* (Massachusetts, 1958), pp. 102–3; Wu, *Economic Survey*, p. 97).

[45] Revenue from taxes in 1951 was 8·1 billion yuan (Wu, p. 97).

Japan and the Kuomintang respectively, were therefore re-applied through the medium of the RAAK movement. The political significance of the movement was stressed above all else at the time of its inception.

In the Resist-America-Aid-Korea, Protect Homes and Defend Country patriotic mass movement, now spreading like wild fire all over China, the people of all circles are not only spreading their patriotic ardour by speech, but also answering the call of the Father-land by concrete action. . . . With the successful raising of the level of political consciousness of the masses throughout the country, the people have been enabled to gain a better understanding of the true aggressive nature of American Imperialism; the counter-revolution-ary reactionaries have been completely dissipated; the confused state of mind which used to prevail in certain people as a result of temporary reverses in Korea, done away with; and the tendency towards racial inferiority complex, the inevitable product of imperialistic oppression during the past hundred years, got rid of, to make way for increased self-respect and self-reliance on the part of the Chinese people.[46]

At the conclusion of the campaign, Chinese statements again stressed its psychological importance in arousing mass enthusiasm in support of the war:

Besides adding to the fighting strength of the Chinese Volunteers by providing them with thousands of first-line planes and artillery, this campaign has accelerated the tempo and expanded the scale of the national programme of reconstruction. It has been a great encouragement to the Volunteers.

There is no over-estimating the political significance of this great patriotic campaign. The political consciousness of the masses in town and countryside has been raised to a level never reached before in the history of China. They not only understand fully that their security is inextricably linked with the fate of the Korean people, but also feel themselves as part of the struggle and are doing their duty for it.[47]

THE DEPENDANTS PROBLEM

The perennial problem of how to provide for army dependants and veterans assumed new proportions as a result of the Korean war. This was the third burden which the 'June 1st call' of the

[46] 'Keep up the effort to extend the scope and range of the Resist-US Aid-Korea, Protect Homes, and Defend Country Patriotic Movement', *JMJP* editorial, 28 Dec. 1950 (*SCMP* 38).
[47] NCNA, 31 Dec. 1951.

Resist America Aid Korea campaign asked the Chinese people to assume. (The other two were the patriotic pact and arms donation movements.)[48]

Some indication of the size of this problem may be gauged from the fact that over 10 per cent of China's farm land was owned or farmed by army dependants. In North China as a whole, 9 per cent of the population fell within the category of 'army dependants', while in some of the liberated areas which had supplied the PLA with manpower for many years the proportion was considerably higher. Both in its economic and social aspects, the problem was of major importance. It was economically essential that dependants should perform productive labour and that their lands should not be allowed to lie idle. It was politically and socially desirable that the army in Korea and elsewhere should be assured that their families were being looked after—in many cases they had volunteered for service on this assumption. Likewise, failure to take care of army dependants would only create unrest among the civilian population at home.

At first the problem was tackled simply by allowing village cadres to assign workers on occasion to help dependants in their cultivation, but this was soon rejected as leading to 'irresponsibility among subordinates, waste of labour and lack of safeguards for output'. In July 1951 a government directive specified the punishment of anyone 'guilty of affecting the livelihood of dependants of martyrs or soldiers by neglecting measures for assistance or harming the production of such persons'. It warned against the tendency to regard assistance for dependants as a 'personal favour'; on the contrary, it should be regarded as a 'routine', and officials at all levels should see that it was carried out. On the same day, the central government's North China Affairs Department complained of 'serious shortcomings in the task of supporting the army and rendering preferential services to army dependants' and reminded local authorities of the heroic

---

[48] *Hsin-Hua Yüeh-pao*, June 1951, p. 242 (quoted in Chen, *Wartime, 'Mass' Campaigns*, p. 30): 'We, the people, must be responsible for their [Chinese soldiers, militiamen, and workers in Korea] welfare through relief and aid to their families and to the invalid veterans. In the countryside we must cultivate the fields for them, while in the city we must help their families find employment. In both rural and urban areas we must help their children to go to school and help the families to overcome their difficulties.'

H

work done by the PLA which was 'made up of the best sons and daughters of the Chinese people . . . and was personally organised by the great leader of the Chinese people, Chairman Mao. . .'.

The adoption throughout China of the Yenan system known as 'substitute tilling' was urged. This was an attempt to systematize the community's expenditure of labour on behalf of dependants. Several methods were suggested—the 'assigned substitute' system by which a number of peasants were permanently assigned to till dependants' land and compensated by other neighbours in food and work, and the 'credit working system' by which the local authorities exacted food from designated peasants, which was then used for the relief of army dependants. The former system involved the making of contracts between substitute peasants and dependants either for output or for work, or sharing the crops in an agreed proportion. The latter system was more akin to corvée labour, under the direct control of the local authorities. In both cases, the burden of substitute farming fell directly upon the community, and government relief was reserved for cases of particular hardship. The guiding principle was that 'relief alone was not enough and that it must be accompanied by encouragement of productive work and self-help'.[49]

In spite of these measures, shortcomings in the work of preferential treatment continued, due both to the reluctance of cadres to enforce the work and of civilians to carry it out. In March 1952 the Ministry of the Interior called for the immediate inspection of 'substitute ploughing' in order to ensure the completion of spring ploughing, and in February the SAC had directed that further efforts should be made in the old revolutionary bases, where shortage of labour and general 'lassitude' had created a situation whereby the living standards of dependants were lower than the average. In North-west China 'poor leadership' was to blame. Summing up at the end of the year, the Minister of the Interior, Hsieh Chüeh-tsai, claimed that the living standards of the 'majority' of dependants were equal or above those of the locality. However, in 'some districts' they were still lower, their children were unable to go to school, schools for

[49] See: NCNA, 18 June 1951 (*FE* 114); ibid., 20 July 1951 (*FE* 119); ibid., 17 Nov. 1951, report by Minister of Interior, Hsieh Chüeh-tsai, to North China Magistrates Conference (*FE* 136). In 1954 about 20 per cent of all dependants in the country received government subsidies (NCNA, 17 Oct. 1954, in *FE* 398).

retraining disabled veterans were unsatisfactory, and some veterans were not well placed in their jobs.[50]

The connexion between preferential treatment for dependants and the raising of morale in the PLA and CPV was simple and direct. In the official version,

> many dependants have written to their children at the front about their happy life in their native places and have asked their children to deal determined blows against the American invaders in order to protect the happy life of their own families, to safeguard their farmland and to defend world peace.[51]

When the war ended, however, and the need for boosting morale at the front grew correspondingly less, so the emphasis upon preferential treatment modified significantly. The trend was away from substitute labour and government subsidies towards participation by the dependants themselves in production and the rehabilitation of veterans. In 1953 emphasis was placed upon mobilizing dependants to take part in mutual-aid teams and co-operatives. 'The major objective', according to a Ministry of the Interior circular of December 1953, 'should be to organise the dependants, demobbed men and personnel in production and to encourage them to join mutual-aid and co-op organisation.' The *People's Daily* complained that preferential treatment had 'given some individuals the impression that they can depend on others to do their tilling and that they can rely on the Government to give them subsistence'. Dependants should not rest upon their laurels, and cadres should realize that they could become useful members of the labour force and not take refuge in the excuse that they were 'hard to lead'. Government subsidies should not be given indiscriminately, since this 'did not help to solve the problems of their livelihood'.[52]

The drive to enrol dependants and demobilize soldiers in the co-operatives was both of economic and social value. It had 'not only improved the standard of living but had lessened the burden

[50] Directive of SAC (NCNA, 1 Feb. 1952, in *FE* 147); Directive of Ministry of Interior (NCNA, 16 Mar. 1952, in *FE* 153); Directive of NW MAC (Sian radio, 23 Apr. 1952, in *FE* 158); speech by Hsieh Chüeh-tsai (Peking radio, 31 Dec. 1952, in *FE* 213).

[51] NCNA, 28 July 1952 (*FE* 172).

[52] Ministry of Interior circular of 9 Dec. 1953 (Peking radio, 11 Dec. 1953 in *FE* 313); *JMJP* editorial, 1 Feb. 1954 (*FE* 326).

of the masses in tilling their lands for them; it had also been a factor in encouraging the masses to join mutual aid teams and co-ops'.[53] Meanwhile in the towns small-scale handicraft industries were set up to absorb dependants' labour. Thus in Nanking 40 factories covering 18 different trades were set up, employing some 1,300 dependants. Technical training courses for veterans were started in such industrial centres as Tsingtao and Tsinan, while political courses were instituted to rehabilitate veterans and 'to strengthen their understanding of the spirit and glory of labour'.

The emphasis thus shifted from government subsidy to self-help, as the burden of dependants and demobilized soldiers increased, while under peacetime conditions they no longer required such favoured treatment. Less was heard of society's duty to go out of its way to grant special privileges to dependants and demobilized soldiers; more was heard of the latter group's duty to integrate itself usefully into society. The size of this group had reached a total of 30 million by the end of 1956, of whom 5 million were demobbed servicemen. By 1959 another 2 million had been demobilized. The dependant problem was basically under control by 1954. The danger of any future increase in its size was minimized by the introduction of national service in that year. The various schemes for preferential treatment and assistance of army dependants by their own neighbours and communities took care of the great majority. By 1959 regular annual government subsidies were only necessary for three-quarters of a million dependants—about 4 per cent of the total. Temporary relief was granted when required to another 4,200,000—about 12 per cent of the total. The spreading of this burden over the country as a whole must be regarded as a considerable achievement.

From 1956 onwards concern was mainly displayed over the problem of the resettlement of demobilized soldiers. Out of the total of 7 million demobilized between 1950 and 1959, 5 million were resettled in the countryside, usually at their place of origin. Well over a million, specially chosen from those who had served as cadres in the PLA or who had technical qualifications, were directed to work in government offices, factories, mines, and industrial enterprises. Several hundred thousand were transferred in their original units to work in state and army farms in border

[53] Hsieh Chüeh-tsai, speech of 31 Dec. 1953 (*FE* 318).

areas such as Sinkiang, and another 200,000–300,000 were permanently disabled.[54]

The task of resettlement was not always easy. On the one hand there was a certain amount of prejudice against accepting demobilized servicemen back into service life. One newspaper commented that

> Though prejudice and discrimination against demobilized men have been severely criticized, people in certain quarters at the present still have not yet understood that resettlement of demobilized soldiers has a close bearing on enforcement of obligatory military service system, as well as on national defence and economic construction. These quarters still entertain the notion that 'good soldiers never get demobilized'. Some units required the ex-servicemen to go through a period of probation before accepting them. Even ex-soldiers who had been associated with the Party for as long as 10 years were not immediately admitted to trade unions but were told to try and win their membership. Demobilized men working in factories were not given the benefits of labour insurance when sick. Such prejudice and discrimination against demobilized servicemen absolutely cannot be tolerated, though the cases are few.[55]

This kind of prejudice was mainly met with in the towns, in offices and factories where the ex-soldier was felt to be an intruder. In the countryside resettlement met with fewer obstacles. Most ex-soldiers rejoined their families or kin, and the co-operativization programme made it easier to provide them with land. On the other hand the ex-soldiers themselves sometimes aroused resentment by their behaviour. They were warned not to hold the attitude that 'after being a soldier for so many years, it is unpromising to return home to become an ordinary person'. There were those who were used to a sheltered life in the army, with everything taken care of, and who were reluctant to return to the comparatively harder life of the country. Sex was another problem; some ex-soldiers were accused of spending all their resettlement grants on 'bad-quality idlers', and rushing into hasty

[54] Figures and calculations based upon the following: 'Some figures on care for servicemen and dependants', *CFCP*, 6 Nov. 1956 (*SCMP* 1441); 'Tung Pi-wu addresses Conference of Army Dependants and Veterans', NCNA, 17 Nov. 1956, (*SCMP* 1420); 'Great achievements accomplished in work of demobilization and relief in the past ten years', NCNA, 25 Sept. 1959 (*SCMP* 2108).

[55] 'Resettle speedily and properly the demobilized servicemen', *Kuang-ming Jih-pao* editorial, 19 Apr. 1956 (*SCMP* 1284).

marriage with the first eligible girl they met. They were also advised not to be conceited and look down upon the local cadres, and to accept the fact that their adjustment would take time.[56] In spite of these difficulties on both sides, however, there is no indication that friction between the ex-soldiers and the civilian community ever reached unmanageable proportions. Ex-soldiers were traditionally the staple source of banditry; this was now a thing of the past. Credit for this considerable achievement is due to the concerted efforts, made over a long period of time, by government agencies working together with local authorities and civilian communities, to solve the dependant and veteran soldier problem.

The way in which the mobilization of popular support and manpower was handled during the Korean war has much in common with the methods adopted during the revolution. The connexion between land reform and recruitment, the launching of a mass popular campaign, and the careful handling of the problem of dependants and demobilized servicemen, all owe much to past experience. Yet at the same time it was clear that mass mobilization was becoming a thing of the past. The Resist America Aid Korea campaign had a definite psychological value in raising national morale, but it no longer provided the same direct support to the PLA which similar mass movements in Manchuria and North China had provided during the civil war. The volunteer movement was less important in raising manpower for the PLA than the selective recruitment of skilled labour to service the growing technical requirements of the PLA. The Korean war can therefore be seen as a transitional phase in which the old revolutionary methods gradually lost their value, and which paved the way for the full-scale introduction of conscription and of the professionalization of the officer corps once the war was over.

[56] See further Hsieh Chüeh-tsai (Minister of the Interior): 'A few words to comrades who will soon be demobilized', *CFCP*, 29 Jan. 1957 (*SCMP* 1552); 'Return home, do production work and build new countryside of socialism', ibid., 24 Jan. 1957 (*SCMP* 1514).

5

The Political Control System

The Chinese People's Liberation Army is an armed organization built by the Chinese Communist Party to win victory in the revolution and realize socialism and Communism in China. Only under the leadership of the Party can our army grow into a powerful people's army, win victory in revolutionary wars, and fulfil the glorious task of defending the motherland. Whenever our army separates itself from the Party leadership, the revolutionary cause will suffer a loss. For this reason, we must resolutely fight against all tendencies towards separation from Party leadership. We must enforce a system of Party leadership.[1]

THE theme of party political control over the army has been a constant factor in its development from the Red Army on Chingkangshan in 1928 up to the PLA of today, and it is a theme with which Mao Tse-tung himself has throughout been closely associated. In general outline, the system of party control has remained essentially unchanged, although parts of it have at times received more emphasis while others have temporarily lapsed. The harmonious relationship between army and party during the revolutionary period cannot be fully appreciated without an understanding of the way in which party leadership was enforced, and it continues to be as relevant today as it was then. Over thirty years after its introduction, the political control system is still regarded as the infallible recipe for ensuring a harmonious relationship between the army, the party, and society in general.

The political control structure of the People's Liberation Army has as long a history as the army itself. It can be traced back to April 1928, when Chu Teh joined Mao Tse-tung on Chingkangshan and the Fourth Red Army came into existence, with Chu as commander-in-chief and Mao himself as political commissar. The system is based in its essentials on that of the Soviet

---

[1] 'Hold aloft the banner of the party committee system', *CFCP* editorial, 1 July 1958 (*SCMP* 1881).

Red Army, as first introduced by Trotsky when he took over control of the Commissariat for Military Affairs in March 1918. yet although the Soviet system was clearly regarded as the model, the immediate example before the Chinese communists was nearer home. Both the Whampoa Military Academy and the National Revolutionary Army had been established by the Kuomintang in 1924–5 under direct Soviet guidance at the time when Soviet influence was strong among the revolutionaries in Canton. The curriculum at the Academy (where Chou En-lai was deputy director of the political education department) was modelled along the lines laid down by Trotsky, and emphasized the importance of political instruction. When the Academy was reorganized as the Central Military and Political Academy in January 1926, its primary objective was to 'offer good political training to military officers'.[2]

The same system of political control was practised in the First Army Corps of the Nationalist army (which evolved from the Whampoa Academy) where for a short time most of the divisional political commissars were communist party members.[3] The system was extended as the Nationalist armies expanded, although by 1927 their rapid growth had diluted political control to the point where it was barely effective. The political commissar was supposed to operate down to company and platoon level, and was regarded as party representative of the Kuomintang with final jurisdiction over all party and political matters. Fifteen years later the Eighth Route Army admitted that its own system of political commissars followed KMT practice, stating in a troop indoctrination manual that 'the political commissar system is the successor to the Party representative system of the National Revolutionary Army at the time of the Great Revolution'.[4]

Although the actual structure of political control in the Soviet

---

[2] 'Plans on the Establishment of the Central Military and Political Academy', in C. Martin Wilbur & Julie Lien-ying How, *Documents on Communism, Nationalism, and Soviet Advisers in China, 1918–27* (Columbia UP, 1956), pp. 203–4. For further description of the Whampoa Military Academy see Liu, *Military History*, pp. 11–15; R. MacFarquhar, 'The Whampoa Military Academy', *Papers on China*, ix (Harvard Univ. E. Asia Program, Aug. 1955).

[3] All communist representatives withdraw voluntarily from the First Army in April 1926 following pressure by Chiang Kai-shek, the army's commander (Wilbur & How, p. 222).

[4] Quoted in Johnson, *Peasant Nationalism*, p. 80. See also Regulations of Political Departments in the National Revolutionary Army (Wilbur & How, pp. 200–2).

and Chinese (both Nationalist and communist) armies was very similar, there was some difference of emphasis in their original purpose. The Soviet commissar system had been established with the principal aim of supervising ex-Tsarist personnel—especially the officers of whom some 48,000 volunteered or were conscripted into the Red Army: all military orders were countersigned by the commissars, and they were empowered to countermand orders and even to arrest military commanders for counter-revolutionary activity.[5] Both in the National Revolutionary Army of the KMT and in the communist Red Army, emphasis from the start was placed as much upon the educational and propaganda roles of the political cadre as upon his supervisory role over the military leadership. Thus the purpose of the political department in the National Revolutionary Army was said to be to 'promote political education, instill a national revolutionary spirit, raise fighting capacity, solidify discipline, and realise Sunyatsenism in the Army',[6] and a communist document on the principles of political work described the ideal political cadre as a man with

high class consciousness, very determined and loyal, a regular party member with experience in political education and work. He must assume positive responsibility in his work, suffer hardship without complaining, and be an example to his unit in doing his own and others' work.[7]

It is with this creative use of political control as a means of conducting propaganda and raising army morale that Mao Tse-tung was associated from the earliest days of the communist army. Chu Teh later told Agnes Smedley that the Fourth Red Army's Political Department under Mao was 'the lifeline of the army', which prevented it from degenerating into militarism. Its purpose was 'to create an educated, conscious, iron revolutionary army dedicated to the liberation of the country and the emancipation of our people'. Compared with later developments, he said, the political work was primitive. Yet even under the most harassing conditions, the troops were taught their history of the revolution and of foreign aggression against China,

[5] Z. K. Brzezinski, ed., *Political Controls in the Soviet Army* (Harvard, 1954), pp. 3–6.
[6] Regulations of Political Departments in the National Revolutionary Army (Wilbur & How, pp. 200–2).
[7] Chin & Chang, *Chung-kung chün-shih p'ou-shih*, p. 72.

methods of mass leadership and organization, how to carry out propaganda with enemy troops, and the arts of singing and public speaking.[8]

Whilst on Chingkangshan in 1928, Mao is said to have pioneered the system of party representatives and party branches on a company basis, and to have insisted on the basic principles of democracy between officers and men, correct treatment of prisoners-of-war, and the building up of good relations with the local population.[9] It was also then that Mao first propounded the 'Three Rules and Eight Injunctions' which became the Red Army's disciplinary catechism. These survived with a few changes for the next twenty years until the civil war, and comprised the basic code for army/civilian relations at the time of Liberation.[10]

THE KUTIEN SPEECH

In December 1929 Mao Tse-tung delivered a speech to the Ninth Representative Conference of the Fourth Red Army at Kutien in Fukien province, which has since become the *locus classicus* in the Maoist scriptures on this question of party control over the army.[11] The Kutien conference was held at a time when

[8] Agnes Smedley, *The Great Road* (1956), p. 230.

[9] Ho Kan-chih, *Hist. Modern Chinese Revolution*, p. 191; see also Mao Tse-tung, 'The Struggle in the Chingkang Mountains', report of 25 Nov. 1928 to the CC where Mao criticizes the belief that 'the Party commissars can be abolished simply because our army is now called the Red Army', and claims that army democracy gives 'great satisfaction to the soldiers; the newly captured soldiers in particular feel that the camp of today and the camp of yesterday are worlds apart. They feel that, although they are materially worse off in the Red Army then in the White, spiritually they are liberated; therefore, they are reasonably content' (trans. from original version in Stuart R. Schram, *The Political Thought of Mao Tse-tung*, (London, 1963), p. 198).

[10] The final form of the Three Rules and Eight Injunctions was formulated on 10 October 1947 as follows:
The Three Main Rules: (1) Obey orders in all your actions, (2) Don't take a single needle or piece of thread from the masses, (3) Turn in everything captured.
The Eight Points for Attention: (1) Speak politely; (2) Pay fairly for what you buy; (3) Return everything you borrow; (4) Pay for anything you damage; (5) Don't hit or swear at people; (6) Don't damage crops; (7) Don't take liberties with women; (8) Don't ill-treat captives. (*MAO IV*, pp. 155–6, where the earlier version is also given.)

[11] A recent communist account claims that in this speech 'Comrade Mao Tse-tung summed up the vast store of experience gained in the building of the Army, drove away the influences of the old army, and put the Army on a true Marxist-Leninist

conditions in the Red Army were still disorganized. Its ranks included ex-warlord soldiers, peasant militiamen, raw recruits, bandits, and fugitives from justice. It was beset by lack of discipline, 'remnants of militarism', with some officers maltreating or even beating their men, and 'vagabondage', defined as 'a disinclination to settle down to the serious tasks of government'—probably a euphemism for banditry.[12] This desperate need to hold the army together and prevent its deterioration into yet another bandit force gave flesh and blood to the abstract principles of political control.

Mao's Kutien speech (which was passed as a resolution by the Army Conference) concentrated upon the creative use of political work in improving army solidarity and discipline, in establishing good relations with the civilian population, and in winning over the enemy.[13] His speech dealt in turn with the questions of 'erroneous conceptions' in the army, party organization, party education, army propaganda, soldiers' political training, special education of young soldiers, prevention of maltreatment of soldiers, favourable treatment of prisoners, and relations between military and political authorities within the army. The 'erroneous conceptions' give some idea of the disorganized state of the army at that time. They included the 'purely military viewpoint' which regards military and political affairs as opposed to each other, 'ultra-democracy' which breeds a reluctance to carry out party decisions, individualism, cliquism, and the 'desire to leave the army'. Some of these sins, and especially that of the 'purely military viewpoint', later became

---

basis, thereby making it the true army of the people. At that time, he pointed out that the army we had built up must be an army led by the Party and must be a tool for the realization of the political goal of the revolution. Thus, he set his face against any attempt to set up military work and political work in opposition, and he slashed the slogan prevalent then: "Command Headquarters Deals with the Public" ' [i.e. army units in the field need not concern themselves with good relations between themselves and the general public] (Chang Min, 'Notes on "Rectification of Incorrect Ideas in the Party"—an important historical work on the building of the party and the army"', *Hei-lung-chiang Jih-pao*, 30 Dec. 1959, in *SCMP* 2214).

[12] Edgar Snow. *Red Star Over China* (1963), pp. 168–9.

[13] The first section only of the Kutien resolution is reproduced in *MAO I*, pp. 105–16, under the title 'On Correcting Mistaken Ideas in the Party'. The full text is available in Mao Tse-tung, *Chung-kuo kung-ch'an-tang hung-chün ti-ssu-chün ti-chiu-tz'u tai-piao ta-hui-i chüeh-i-an* (1949).

a recurring motif in the party's attempt to maintain control over the army, and the Kutien resolution was quoted from whenever 'rectification' took place again in the army.[14]

Writing on party organization within the army, Mao emphasized the necessity for quality of membership and for political penetration down to the lowest level. Every company was to have a party branch, and every squad a party cell. He also formulated new conditions for entry into the party in order to raise the calibre of party members. Mao went on to examine in detail the mechanics of party education, listing ten different subjects which should be taught and eighteen different ways of putting them across. The same meticulous treatment was given to the question of army propaganda work. Here Mao stressed the need for versatility and for adaptability to circumstances; slogans and appeals should suit the place and the occasion. He pointed out shrewdly that 'women form half the population'; they were a potential revolutionary force which required special attention. Propaganda teams were controlled by the army political departments; they were urged by Mao to use a variety of techniques, including leaflets, wall newspapers, revolutionary songs, pictures, dramatized propaganda, the forming of Soldiers' Clubs, and many other devices which later became a standard part of the repertoire of political education. Special tactics were suggested for winning over enemy soldiers: They should be treated leniently, given good medical treatment, and allowed to return home or even back to the enemy camp once they had been effectively converted.

Political education of cadres and soldiers was the next subject to be given systematic treatment by Mao, who listed nineteen different types of material to be taught. These included what we

[14] In January 1944 the entire resolution was republished by decision of the CC as a *cheng-feng* ('rectification') document for army cadres, after a period of 'many years' in which it had not been used as propaganda material. It was said to be extremely relevant to the situation then current within the army of 'warlordism tending towards alienation' from the masses' (*Chung-kuo kung-ch'an-tang hung-chün . . .* introd. p. 2). Several articles were written between 1959–61 on the abbreviated version published in Mao's *Selected Works*, emphasizing its relevance to the struggle against 'the current incorrect ideas of the right opportunists' (Chang Min, *SCMP* 2214). In the PLA itself, Marshal Lo Jung-huan proposed that the full resolution should be republished, together with two other key documents, since they provided the right line with which to build the army, to combat revisionism and dogmatism (*KTTH*, 6 Feb. 1961 (Cheng, pp. 227–9)).

might regard as purely educational matters—health, literacy, and the like—as well as more overtly political subjects such as land reform and the aims of the revolution. Mao went into great detail on the methods to be adopted in carrying out political education, whether by special classes, lectures, informal conversation, or by exemplary behaviour. Special attention was to be given to the education of young soldiers; classes were not to exceed twenty-five, paper and ink was to be provided out of unit funds, and so on. Other important topics dealt with in the Kutien speech include the abolition of corporal punishment, the provision of better treatment for wounded soldiers, and the relationship between military and political army authorities.

The Kutien resolution is important not only because it is the first extended treatment of the question of political control and education by Mao or any other Chinese communist leader, but because it sets the pattern for the approach to this question throughout the army's subsequent history. Political work was, and still is, regarded as a totality which embraces all aspects of the army's everyday life, of its cultural, educational, and spare-time activities. It also dictates the way in which relations between the army and the civilian population, and within the army itself between officers and men, are handled. This all-inclusive interpretation of the nature of political work has recently been challenged in certain sections of the PLA, and has again been vigorously reaffirmed.

One can identify two distinct elements in the theory of party political control over the armed forces, as formulated by Mao in its earliest years and as practised since then. The first is that of political control itself, in the sense of maintaining control by the central party authorities over the military leadership, and of ensuring that party policies are carried out. The second, of equal importance, is that of political education and propaganda, by which support for the party's policies is secured within the army, and the triangular relationship between army, party, and people is kept on equable terms. The structure and apparatus of political control in the army can also be divided into two distinct and separate hierarchies, which roughly correspond to the functional division between control and education. Changes have occurred in the form of this apparatus over the past thirty years, which will be discussed later, but the following account seeks to describe its essential structure and role.[15] (See Table 4, p. 306, 'Political Control Structure of the PLA'.)

THE STRUCTURE OF POLITICAL CONTROL

The first hierarchy consists of the party committee. This is strictly a party body, which has no formal organizational links with the military authorities. It exists alongside of but independently from every level of the military structure down to regiment.[16] The party committee at any level is responsible solely to its superior party organization, and the chain of responsibility thus formed leads directly to the Military Affairs Committee of the Central Committee of the communist party. Apart from transmitting policy decisions received from superior authorities, the party committee also has sole jurisdiction over planning and policy-making at its own level. As defined by the Minister of Defence in 1956, its jurisdiction extends over 'all important matters in the army, such as important directives and orders issued by the higher organizations, the plan and arrangement of military, political and logistic tasks, the transfer and readjustment of working personnel etc. . . .'.[17] It effectively initiates or supervises all important decisions reached at its own or higher levels, except in time of emergency. It has been aptly described as 'the eyes, the ears, and the policy-implementing agents of the Party in the PLA'.[18]

The party committee of a given military unit will consist of the military commander of that unit, the political commissar, and one or more principal staff members (who must of course also belong to the party). It is elected by a meeting of all party members in that unit, although this is usually a formality. As in the case of party organizations in civilian life, those in the army have the usual powers of discipline or commendation over all party members within their jurisdiction. The committee take decisions

[15] This account relies heavily upon S. M. Chiu, 'Political Control in the Chinese Communist Army', *Military Review*, Aug. 1961; and Johnson, *Peasant Nationalism*, pp. 77–84.

[16] At battalion level, the party organization is known as the 'general branch' (*tsung chih pu*). The party structure continues down to the party branch (*chih pu*) in a company, and the party cell (*hsiao tsu*) in a platoon. Unlike the party committee at higher levels, the branch and cell comprise all party members in their unit.

[17] P'eng Teh-huai, 'The Chinese People's Liberation Army', speech of 18 Sept. 1956 (*CB* 422).

[18] Ralph L. Powell, *Politico-Military Relationships in Communist China* (1964), p. 9.

by consensus, which are then passed to the political commissar, or the military commander, or one of the staff departments for implementation, according to the nature of the decision. This system of leadership is described as one of 'individual responsibility by the commanders under the collective leadership of the party committee'. It means, according to P'eng Teh-huai, that all tasks, especially military operations, should be carried out on a sound basis and after careful deliberation. Collective leadership could also enable the leaders of various units to grasp the over-all situation and arrive at a unified view, and unified action of the troops could be better ensured.[19]

The committee's own regulations stipulate that it should not 'usurp the specific tasks that are within the functions and power of leading personnel, nor are party committees supposed to hinder leading personnel from handling an emergency situation'.[20] Yet is is clear that the need to report back to the party committee for subsequent approval is bound to discourage independent initiative. The main purpose of the system is not primarily to ensure military efficiency, although this is claimed for it as well—but to provide a 'genuine guarantee for the absolute Party leadership over the army and for the implementation of the Party principle and line', and to guard against such dangerous tendencies as 'purely military views, doctrinairism and warlordism'.[21]

The second political hierarchy consists of the Political Department (*cheng-chih pu*), which exists at all levels from the General Political Department (GPD) of the PLA Headquarters down to the Political Office (*cheng-chih ch'u*) in the regiment. Unlike the party committee, the Political Department is an integral part of the army's structure. It is regarded as the senior of the various departments (Rear Services, Cadres, etc.) which comprise a unit's general staff headquarters. It carries out the policy decisions of the party committee, and is responsible for the detailed implementation of measures intended to educate the rank and file of the army.

The Political Department (or Political Office at regimental level) is divided into a number of sub-departments, whose

[19] P'eng Teh-huai, in *CB* 422.
[20] 'Hold aloft the banner of the party committee system' (*SCMP* 1881).   [21] Ibid.

functions suggest the role which it is intended to perform. These were four in number before 1949—organization, propaganda, popular movement, and enemy work—in addition to a secretariat.[22] These are again divided into a number of branches. The propaganda sub-department, for instance, is split up into propaganda, education, and cultural branches. Since 1949 the Political Department has shared in the trend towards greater structural complexity. With the growing importance of education and literacy work in the PLA, culture and education has been established as a separate sub-department. The enemy work sub-department has been replaced by liaison and a security sub-department has been created with special responsibilities for intelligence and counter-espionage within the armed forces. Another important area, youth work, constitutes a section of the organization sub-department.[23]

The two hierarchies described above tend to merge at the lower levels of army organization—battalion, company, and platoon—and especially at the company level. Here the Political Department is represented in the person of an individual political officer, while the party structure is continued through the party group or cell.[24] The company political officer or 'in-

[22] The sub-departments' functions are given as the following:
  (a) Organization: army organization, statistics, appointment and dismissal of personnel.
  (b) Propaganda: propaganda and education in the army, cultural and recreational activities.
  (c) Popular movement: military-civilian co-operation, propaganda for civilians, army participation in production, investigation of civilian complaints against the army.
  (d) Enemy work: propaganda for Japanese and 'puppet' pro-Japanese Chinese troops, instruction in Japanese language.
  See further Johnson, *Peasant Nationalism*, p. 82; Lo Jui-ch'ing, 'Political Work in Anti-Japanese Military Forces', May 1939, excerpt trans. in Gene Z. Hanrahan, *Chinese Communist Guerilla Tactics* (Washington, 1952), pp. 125–31.
[23] See further Rigg, *Red China's Fighting Hordes*, pp. 71–72; Chin & Chang, *Chung-kung chün-shih p'ou-shih*, p. 69.
[24] The battalion political officer is known as the 'battalion political education officer' (*ying cheng-chih chiao-tao yuan*). The company political officer is known as 'company political instructor' (*lien cheng-chih chih-tao yuan*). They should not be confused with the political commissar (*cheng-chih wei-yuan*), who is the political officer in command of all units of regimental levels and above.
  Between 1927 and 1929 all political officers at any level went under the name of party representative (*tang tai-piao*). Between 1929 and 1931, they were all renamed political commissar. The present nomenclature has been in force since then (qv. *MAO I*, p. 103 n. 10).
  At the level of platoon, a 'political fighter' (*cheng-chih chan-shih*) assists the com-

structor' is appointed by the Political Department of his regiment. He is also in charge of the company party group. Thus he combines both the control and educational functions of the political system; he provides the essential link in the transmission belt between the decision-making process and chain of command, and the rank and file which carries out such decisions and commands. He is regarded as pivotal to the whole success of the system, and his duties range over the entire field of company activities.[25]

Political work at the company level is mainly carried out through the Soldiers' Club (*chü-le pu*), a mass organization to which all soldiers in the company belong.[26] This is run by a committee of 7–9 men elected by the entire company, under the supervision of the company political instructor. Its purpose has been recently described as

to develop political democracy, economic democracy and military democracy under centralized leadership, to organise extra-curricular

---

pany political instructor, by whom he is appointed. At the lowest level of squad, a 'political fighter' is also sometimes found. Both are selected from rank-and-file party members.

[25] One set of regulations, formulated during the anti-Japanese war, described the normal duties of the company political instructor as consisting of

(*a*) to be responsible for the entire company's political and cultural education and entertainment activity, and for the studies of company cadres;

(*b*) to lead the company in the work of strengthening itself; by eliminating tendencies towards defeatism and desertion; by scrutinizing the behaviour of new recruits and of prisoners, and raising their morale;

(*c*) to talk to the soldiers, to get to know their names, ancestry, origins, characteristics, political knowledge and interests; to prevent them developing tendencies towards cliquism and individualism and 'frontier mentality';

(*d*) to encourage cadres and fighters to render meritorious service (*li kung*) and to organize *li kung* emulation movements;

(*e*) (before battle) to collect information on the prevailing situation, to give rousing speeches and slogans, to raise the morale and belief in victory of the soldiers, to carry out education on battle discipline and prevent cowardice;

(*f*) (during battle) to note all changes in the situation, publicize news of victory among the soldiers, organize political squads to shout slogans and scatter propaganda in the front line;

(*g*) (after battle) whether victorious or defeated, to carry out propaganda explanation among the troops, and strengthen their resolve to carry on fighting; immediately select and publicize battle heroes; immediately rectify organizational defects, and encourage positive elements among the troops to join the party. (*Lien-tui cheng-chih chih-tao yuan kung-tso hsi-tse* n.d., in Chin & Chang, pp. 70–73.)

[26] The club was known as the Lenin Club during the Kiangsi Soviet period, and as the Soldiers' Club in the Yenan period.

I

studies and to expand mass cultural, physical culture, and health activities, so as to strengthen unity, re-inforce discipline and raise fighting capacity.[27]

The Soldiers' Club is a recreation centre for social and political activities, and it is through its agency that political and health education is given on almost every aspect of a soldier's life. These include hygiene, production, news bulletins, physical education, culture and recreation, political study, and 'evaluation', each of which is the responsibility of a separate subcommittee within the club.[28] These subcommittees are set up under the club's 7–9 men Management Committee, which is supposed to be in active liaison with their superior officers, and to represent their unit at army conferences.

The strength and effectiveness of the party's control in the army ultimately depends upon the number of party members within it. Although no figures are available, it seems likely that the great majority of officers or 'cadres' holding posts at regimental level or above are party members. All unit commanders of regiments and upwards have to belong to the party in order to serve on the appropriate party committee. The real strength or weakness of the party is felt to lie in the extent of its membership among the rank-and-file party branches or cells at company or platoon level.

Writing in 1928, Mao had suggested a 50–50 ratio of party members among the combat soldiers. This ambitious target was subsequently lowered to a ratio of 1 party member to 2 non-party men; this was regarded as the optimum ratio both for the Red Army and later for the PLA.[29] Even this ratio was not always

---

[27] 'Four sets of regulations on political work in company-level units of PLA promulgated for enforcement', NCNA, 21 Nov. 1961 (*SCMP* 2630).

[28] This is the present structure of the club subcommittees according to Chiu (*Military Review*, Aug. 1961). Lo Jui-ch'ing in 1939 lists the following subcommittees—hygiene, economic, wall paper, skilled swimming, learn characters, physical education, military-political education. Three other elected company groups also functioned at this time: the popular movement work group which carried out propaganda among the local inhabitants, the enemy work group, with the same task directed towards the enemy, and the serviceman's press association which assisted and censored the writing of letters home.

According to Chiu, the evaluation subcommittee 'directs specially appointed members of the squads to evaluate merits and demerits in the performance of duty. This latter is done regularly, even in the heat of battle, to serve as a means of encouragement or as a lesson for recalcitrants.'

[29] *MAO I*, pp. 84, 104, n. 15.

achieved. In 1950 it was down to less than 1 in 4 (1,200,000 out of 5 million) as a result of the influx of ex-KMT troops.[30] The task was complicated by the introduction of conscription, which meant that the great majority of servicemen were even younger than before and therefore less suited for party membership. Already in 1949 it was said that 'young people' formed nearly 80 per cent of the PLA; by 1960 the rank and file were described as being 'without exception youths'.[31] It was therefore through the youth organizations that strenuous efforts were made to increase party membership. One of the principal tasks of the NDYL was to establish itself as a youth political organization within the PLA, and later the CPV. By October 1950 it had a quarter of a million members within the PLA, rising to more than 1 million by June 1953.[32] NDYL work in the PLA was written into the League's constitution as being 'an important constituent part of the Party's political work (which) must be carried out under the direct leadership of the political organisations and the Party and with the instruction of the troop commanders'.[33]

POLITICAL CONTROL DURING THE REVOLUTION

These are the essentials of the political structure in the Chinese communist army during the revolutionary period (and afterwards). Yet the strength of such a complex system inevitably depends upon the strength or weakness of its component parts. How well it worked in practice during the Kiangsi Soviet and Yenan periods is a question which will require further research before a detailed answer can be given. In general outline, it appears that the system worked reasonably well. It is, of course, true that disputes took place over military policy between various factions within the party leadership, notably during the later part of the Kiangsi Soviet when the 'Third Leftist Line' predominated, and between the supporters of Mao and of Chang Kuo-t'ao in 1935 on the Long March, and perhaps on other occasions of which we are unaware. There was also rivalry between different party organs, especially between those in local

[30] Peking radio, 1 July 1950, reported in *South China Morning Post*, 3 July 1950.
[31] Report of Liao Cheng-chih to All-China Youth Congress (NCNA, 5 May 1949); 'Let the whole army do youth work' *CFCP*, 22 Sept. 1960 (*SCMP* 2360).
[32] NCNA, 26 Oct. 1950 (*FE* 80), and address by Hsiao Hua to the 2nd National Congress of the NDYL (NCNA, 24 June 1953, in *FE* 263).
[33] Constitution of the NDYL (NCNA, 7 July 1953, in *FE* 267).

government and those in the army. It was also difficult during the anti-Japanese war to maintain centralized and co-ordinated control over the army's guerrilla and regular units, scattered as they were among some nineteen liberated areas and linked at best by unreliable radio communications. The strategy of guerrilla warfare itself demanded a high degree of initiative and responsibility at the local level. Some degree of local autonomy persisted during the civil war, encouraged by the rapid expansion both of the army and of the battle areas. It was a phenomenon which, according to Mao, had both advantages and disadvantages. It allowed local party organizations and armed forces 'to bring their initiative and enthusiasm into play and to come through long periods of grave difficulties', but it also gave rise to 'certain phenomena of indiscipline and anarchy, localism and guerilla-ism, which were harmful to the cause of the revolution'.[34] Yet throughout the period of revolutionary struggle, as far as one can tell from the scanty evidence, there was no major challenge on the part of the army against the party leadership. It is even perhaps misleading to draw a hard and fast distinction between the two groups. All the major party leaders were at one time military commanders or political commissars, and conversely the upper echelons of military leadership were for the most part in the hands of veteran party members. The frequent practice whereby the posts of commissar and commander were concurrently held by the same person also tended to minimize conflict. As Ellis Joffe has observed, three reasons seem to account for the harmonious relationship between army and party leadership:

> First, both the military commanders and political commissars were veteran party members, with much the same experience and background in both political and military work. Second the close interrelation of political and military tasks in the mileau of insurrection gave little basis for conflict. Third, in many cases the commander and the commissar were one and the same person.[35]

Difficulties did, however, arise within the system of political control itself. There appears to have been an inherent conflict between the principle of 'democratic centralism', in other words of centralized party control exerted through the party committee,

---

[34] *MAO IV*, p. 273.   [35] *Party and Army* (1965), p. 68.

and the need under conditions of guerrilla war for considerable local initiative. In this conflict the powers of the political commissar were greatly enhanced. Party control continued to be exercised, but individually through the commissar rather than than collectively through the party committee. As one political officer described it in 1937, 'the political commissar is all-powerful in the policies of the army, and the political department is under his direction to carry out his plans'.[36] The army's party committee system apparently lapsed at the end of the Kiangsi Soviet period and during the Long March, with political control exclusively in the hands of the political commissar operating through the Political Department.

As communist power expanded in the North during the anti-Japanese war, local party 'political and military committees' were set up, dominated by the army forces controlling the area, and analogous to the 'military and administrative committees' set up after 1949 to enforce military control over the newly liberated areas. These were the highest source of military authority at the level within their jurisdiction. In order to curtail their power, the Central Committee decided in September 1942 to institute 'unified leadership of military, political and administrative affairs' whereby the 'political and military committees' were abolished, and the civilian party committee of a given area assumed control over all cadres and committees in local party organizations, military units, and government offices. Army political departments and administrative committees became subcommittees of the local party committee, whose secretary served concurrently as political commissar of the appropriate army unit.[37] This system again placed great emphasis upon the role of the political commissar (i.e. the party secretary). The party committee system as such within army units was not restored until 1947. The right of the elected committee of the Soldiers' Club to be consulted by its superior officers and to take part in army representative conferences was also restored at the same time.[38]

---

[36] Wang Shou-tao, chairman of the 15th Army Corps Political Dept. in 1937, reported in Nym Wales, *Red Dust* (Stanford, 1952), p. 79.

[37] CC Resolution on the Unification of Leadership in the Anti-Japanese War Bases, in Boyd Compton ed., *Mao's China, Party Reform Documents, 1942–4* (Seattle, 1952), pp. 161–76.

[38] Mao wrote in October 1948 that 'we . . . have restored the Party committee

Faced in recent years for the first time with major criticism of the party control system as such in the PLA, the Chinese leadership has attempted to present this criticism as the latest in a series of similar challenges which were made against the Maoist line in the revolutionary period. In fact, during that time, the main defects in the army's political structure were probably less in the sphere of political *control* by the party than in that of *education* and the maintenance of the triangular army-party-people relationship. The allegation, first made in 1958 in the *Liberation Army Newspaper*, that 'dominated by the third "leftist" line the Party abolished the system of Party leadership during the later stage of the Second Revolutionary War, thus causing loss to the army work' is unfounded in its literal sense.[39] An earlier account, written in 1945, although also giving Mao's side of the story against the Third Leftist Line which dominated the party centre towards the end of the Kiangsi Soviet, makes it clear that party *leadership* was maintained, and that it was the vital factor of political *education* within the army and among the people that was neglected.[40]

---

system at various levels of the army and the soldiers' committee system in the companies, both of which produced good results from 1927–1932 but were later abolished' (*MAO IV*, p. 271). On the abolition of soldiers' committees and soldiers' representative conferences, see also *MAO I*, p. 102 n. 3.

[39] 'Hold aloft the banner of the party committee system', 1 July 1958 (*SCMP* 1881). This editorial claims that 'during the early period of the anti-Japanese war, the political commissar system was abolished for a time'. I have been unable to find any confirmation of this. It is however quite possible that the political commissar system was abolished nominally during the early stages of the war against Japan as a United Front concession to the Kuomintang, which by that time was strongly averse to such systems. Lo Jui-ch'ing in his 'Political Work in Anti-Japanese Military Forces', written in 1939, stressed that political commissars should 'guarantee the thorough carrying out of each government policy and law for all military units'. But he also wrote that 'Political commissars within military forces should not be used "to keep watch over" armies. While some may believe this is a proper use of the political commissar system, it is not and should not be used in this manner. . . . The important duties of the political commissar ought to lie within the realm of political leadership within a military unit. All military affairs and military command must be handled by the military officer alone' (Hanrahan, *Chinese Communist Guerrilla Tactics*, p. 131). I am grateful to Mr Ellis Joffe for this interpretation.

[40] The 'Resolution on Certain Questions in the History of our Party', written by Mao Tse-tung and adopted by the Enlarged Seventh Plenary Session of the Sixth CC on 20 April 1945, claims that 'on the question of building the army, the exponents of the third "Left" line reduced the Red Army's threefold task to the single one of fighting and neglected to educate the Red Army on the correct relations between army and people, between army and government and between officers and men;

Deterioration in the army's political consciousness and in its relations with the people was hard to avoid at a time of desperate resistance against the Fifth Encirclement Campaign, of acute economic hardship, and of decline in morale resulting from the decision to abandon the Kiangsi Soviet and to embark upon the Long March. A similar deterioration again took place in 1942–4, when Japanese military pressure, coupled with the economic blockade on the border regions, was at its height. Just as the Rectification Campaign (*cheng-feng*), launched in 1942, was concerned not only with strengthening party leadership but also with eliminating 'bureaucracy' and 'dogmatism' and improving party-people relations, so the measures undertaken in the army at this time were above all directed at integrating the army with the population of the hard-pressed border areas and preventing the erosion of that popular support on which it depended for its continued survival. The main targets of these remedial measures were 'dogmatism' (*chiao-t'iao chu-yi*)—as in the case of the *cheng-feng* movement—and 'warlordism' (*chün-fa chu-yi*). In spite of its usual connotations, 'warlordism', as used then and more recently by the communist leadership, does not necessarily imply setting oneself up against the party. It is a style of behaviour associated particularly with the anti-popular Kuomintang-type of army which is 'isolated from the masses' and fails to observe the correct principles in its relations with the people. It is also characteristic of those officers who ignore military democracy, disregard the interest of their soldiers and inflict physical punishment upon them. It is obviously an attitude which leads to disrespect for party and government organs, but that is not its most significant feature.

At a meeting in the winter of 1942 of high-level and military cadres, convened by the Central Committee of the North-west party bureau, it was resolved that the army had developed certain bad tendencies, especially those of 'warlordism' and of 'dogmatism', and that rectification should be carried out. In April 1944 it was reported that substantial improvements had been made.[41] Methods of rectification included participation in the

---

they demanded undue regularization and opposed the then sound guerrilla character of the Red Army as "guerrilla-ism"; furthermore, they fostered formalism in the political work in the army' (*MAO III*, p. 207).

[41] See T'an Cheng, 'On the question of political work in army units', report to a meeting of high-level cadres of the North-west bureau, *CFJP*, 15 Apr. 1944.

production movement, the movement for 'military democracy', and the bilateral campaign to 'support the government and protect the people' (for the army) and to 'support the army' (for the people and government), all of which were first initiated in 1943.

The PLA's duty to live up to its name as a People's Army was a recurring theme as both the number of men under arms and the extent of territory under control expanded from 1945 onwards. In outlining the tasks for 1945, Mao admitted that 'the influence of militaristic habits of the troops of Chinese warlords still exists among our troops', and asked that such violations of military democracy as

> beating, cursing, neglecting the food supply, diseases and the other difficulties of the soldiers, not using patient education and persuasion in correcting mistakes of soldiers, punishing freely . . . insulting and shooting deserters etc. should be fundamentally rooted out

by the end of the year.[42]

In the winter of 1947 a new 'ideological education movement' was launched in the North-west Field Army under Mao's personal direction, and later extended to the other Field Armies and communist units. As victory drew near in the later part of 1948, the Central Committee initiated a series of measures, affecting local party and government organs as well as the army, to improve centralized control, to consolidate party organization, restore the party committee system, to set up procedures of regular reports to the party centre, and so on. Here again, it was not so much a question of establishing new party organizations within the army or other administrative bodies, but of ensuring that those which already existed were more responsive to centralized control.

THE DECLINE OF POLITICS AFTER 1949

After Liberation, however, the importance of political education was eclipsed by such new and pressing tasks as modernization, regularization, mechanization, and the many technical and structural innovations which were introduced with Soviet advice and on the Soviet model. This much can be inferred by mainly negative evidence—the noticeable lack of reference to

[42] Mao Tse-tung, 'The Tasks for 1945', ibid., 16 Dec. 1944.

political education and related subjects and the high priority attached to modernization.[43] A useful yardstick by which to measure this is the 'Order of the Day' issued by Chu Teh, in his capacity as commander-in-chief of the PLA, every year on National Day (1 October).

During the first year of the Korean war, when the extent of the Soviet commitment to China was still uncertain and the PLA was required, to some extent, to 'go it alone', the political factor in warfare continued to be stressed. In his speech on the eve of Army Day (1 August) 1951, Chu Teh called for modernization of the PLA, but placed such modernization within the context of the PLA's existing 'glorious tradition' and 'rich experience' in popular armed struggle. In stressing the need for 'revolutionary heroism' and 'a high fighting will', Chu Teh emphasized that

This requires of the whole army that it continue to conduct profound political training of officers and men, and ceaselessly raise the level of political consciousness of the whole army. The high morale and excellent political quality of the People's Liberation Army are always a basic factor for defeating any enemy.[44]

It was apparently during the following two months that a firm Soviet commitment was first made to assist the PLA in its modernization. Chu Teh's Order of the Day on 1 October reflects this change to such an extent that he does not even mention the role of political training.

I order you therefore to stand firm at your fighting posts with vigilance, to strengthen further the construction of national defences and consolidate the national defences of our Motherland, to study unconceitedly and in earnest so as to master new techniques and learn the skill of the co-ordinated operation of all arms, to raise the level of modern military science and the art of leading troops, to strengthen further the planning, organisation and precision of all aspects of work,

[43] Political officers were criticized for their lack of interest in technical matters. One pronouncement in 1953 criticized the conception that 'military training was the task of officers, and political personnel could just stand by and watch'. The main object of political work was 'to arouse the interest of officers and men in military training'. It was laid down that 'in company training, political instructors should be jointly responsible with the company commander in military training—they were cadres on the same level. They should diligently study military training; political work could not be carried out without good military knowledge' (Chungking radio, 2 Sept. 1953, summary of editorial in *Jen-min Chan-shih*, in *FE* 284).

[44] 'Chu Teh's speech at meeting of 24th anniversary of formation of PLA', NCNA, 31 July 1951 (*SCMP* 147).

to consolidate and raise the level of military discipline, and to strive to build up modernised internal defence forces.

In the equivalent order for National Day 1952, pride of place was given to the injunction to 'heighten your vigilance at all times, to hold your weapons in your hands and be on the alert to master your profession'. In that for 1953, the army was ordered to 'study hard from the advanced military science and technique of the Soviet Union'. Politics was merely bracketed with 'culture' as another item for study.

By 1954 the emphasis on modernization had begun to wane, and the theme of revolutionary heroism reappeared in the Order of the Day. In 1955 both modernizing and revolutionary concepts were evenly balanced. In addition to abiding by 'regulations, orders and systems', the PLA was urged to 'strengthen unity within and outside the armed forces' and 'carry forward the glorious tradition of revolutionary heroism'. Finally, in the Order of the Day for 1956, modern military science, technique, and training continued to be itemized, but the first two injunctions on the list were significantly concerned with matters which came within the political orbit: 'all officers and men must continue to strengthen unity between the armed forces and the people, [and] to give greater initiative free rein'.[45] The year 1956 saw a renewal of emphasis upon the standards of political education and loyalty which were felt to have deteriorated over the previous years. Since then the relative importance of political control has been elevated stage by stage until it now dominates every military policy and pronouncement, and probably occupies more attention than at any previous period in the history of the PLA.[46]

[45] For Orders of the Day see NCNA, 1 Oct. 1951; NCNA, 1 Oct. 1952 (*FE* 180); NCNA, 1 Oct. 1953 (*FE* 292); NCNA, 1 Oct. 1954 (*FE* 395); NCNA (London), 1 Oct. 1955. The above analysis based on these documents should not be taken to indicate precise chronological shifts in policy. It does however suggest a significant fluctuation over the years 1950–6 in the importance attached to the role of politics in the PLA.

[46] These developments are dealt with in chs 8 & 12.

6

Modernization and Sino-Soviet Relations 1950-5

The Chinese PLA deems it an unparalleled honour to stand alongside the powerful and invincible Soviet Army at the forefront of the defence of peace in the Far East and the rest of the world. The Chinese PLA is now enthusiastically studying the military science and all advanced military experience of the Soviet Union so as to hasten its modernization.[1]

THE objects of military reform were clearly outlined in the Common Programme adopted by the People's Political Consultative Conference in September 1949. This specified that China should build up a 'unified army', and should institute a 'unified system, unified organisation and unified discipline' (Art. 20). The land forces should be modernized and an air force and navy should be established to consolidate national defence (Art. 22). Finally, the people's militia should be expanded to 'prepare for the enforcement of an obligatory military service system at the appropriate moment' (Art. 23).[2]

But no serious attempt was made to start the modernization of the PLA before the Korean war, in spite of rumours of a secret Sino-Soviet military agreement which would include substantial retraining and re-equipment.[3] In the celebrations for Army Day in August 1950 modernization was hardly mentioned at all. The key to modernization was in the hands of the Soviet Union, and it was China's intervention in Korea which opened the floodgates of Soviet aid. Even so, this aid was not at first forthcoming on anything like a sufficient scale to satisfy the Chinese. Reading between the lines of Chinese statements in the first year of the Korean war, one can detect a degree of coolness towards the

[1] Chu Teh, message to Marshal Bulganin on Soviet Army Day, 23 Feb. 1954 (*FE* 332).
[2] Common Programme of the CPPCC (NCNA (London), Suppl. No. 29, 29 Sept. 1949).
[3] See the accounts of alleged secret agreements in *South China Morning Post*, 18 Oct. 1949 & 16 Feb. 1950.

Soviet Union which only diminished as Soviet aid became more available on a more generous scale. Since the modernization of the PLA itself was tied to the supply of Soviet aid, the policy of reorganization on the Soviet model was similarly delayed.

During the first phase (October 1950–June 1951) of the war, China's calculated risk of intervention had revealed both its strength and its weakness. The CPV's first fast-moving offensive took the UN forces by surprise, crossing the 38th parallel by the end of the year and capturing Seoul on 4 January 1951. But despite the second Chinese offensive in April–May, the UN forces' counter-offensives had driven the communist armies back to the north of the 38th parallel by mid-June 1951. The CPV had shown itself to be superior in mobility and in determination, but 'the course of the fighting showed that despite the large numbers of troops available to the Chinese, they were still inadequately supplied with modern weapons'.[4] The CPV lacked sufficient transport with which to service its extended lines of communication. It was also no match for the United Nations' superior strength in the air.

Between the opening of truce talks in Korea in July 1951 and the agreement on a line of demarcation in November, fighting along the front was heavy but ineffective, and United Nations gains amounted at the most to some 20 kilometres on the eastern section of the front. From the end of 1951 until the signing of the armistice on 27 July 1953, the front or 'Main Line of Resistance' remained practically unchanged, disturbed only by limited probing operations on both sides, often timed to coincide with political developments at the truce talks or elsewhere. Most dramatic of these was the Chinese advance of June–July 1953 across the Kumsong river against South Korean troops, which achieved its apparent objective of quelling President Syngman Rhee's opposition to the armistice. Even this advance made only a maximum gain of 10 kilometres. The main focus of the war throughout this period was in the air, with persistent attempts by the United Nations forces to cripple communist supply lines to the front and to prevent the building and strengthening of air bases in North Korea. On the ground, both sides concentrated upon reinforcing and digging in their armies. The North Korean and Chinese armies entrenched themselves behind a fourteen-

---

[4] Beloff, *Soviet Policy*, p. 204.

mile deep defensive network reminiscent of the Maginot Line which protected them for the remainder of the war. The piece-meal attempts at reinforcement and modernization undertaken in the first year of the war by the PLA and CPV now gave way to a systematic build-up and reorganization of their forces. Soviet aid had certainly been supplied throughout this first year, but it was only after the stalemate began in mid-1951 that the CPV's artillery heavy equipment and air strength was built up by the Russians on a scale comparable with that of the United Nations forces.

The pace and extent of re-equipment and modernization of the PLA was controlled principally by the development of Sino-Soviet relations. The inadequacy of Soviet military aid until the autumn of 1951 is reflected in signs of friction and coolness be-tween Moscow and Peking. Similarly, the quickening in the tempo of technical and structural modernization from 1952 on-wards coincided with the development of a more cordial and equal relationship between them.

This initial coolness in Sino-Soviet relations is revealed by a comparison of the way in which the Chinese government handled the anniversaries of the Soviet and Chinese 'Army Days' in 1950 and 1951 respectively. Soviet Army Day of 1950 (23 February) had been greeted by Chinese military leaders with speeches which glorified the Soviet Red Army, extolled Stalin's inspired leadership, and pledged the PLA to emulate strictly the Soviet example. The PLA's deputy chief of staff, Nieh Jung-chen, to quote one of the speakers, 'thanked the Soviet Army for the liberation of North-east China, and hoped that the PLA would model itself on it', while the commander-in-chief Chu Teh praised the invincible Soviet army with its superb organization 'under the direction of the most advanced military science as personified in Stalin'.[5]

On the Chinese Army Day (1 August) of 1950, a rally in Peking sent a telegram to Stalin thanking him for the 'friendly assistance' rendered to China by the Soviet Union and hailing him as 'the great leader of working people throughout the world'. Chu Teh ended his speech at the rally with the words 'Long Live Generalissimo Stalin, leader of the world camp of peace and democracy', and a similar slogan was included in the official list

[5] NCNA reports, 23 Feb. 1950.

of Army Day slogans published in Peking.[6] This should be contrasted with the treatment of the Chinese Army Day a year later. Stalin and the Soviet Union had disappeared from the slogans for 1951, as they had from the previous list of slogans for May Day of the same year. There was a conspicuous lack of references to the Soviet Union in speeches and articles by Chu Teh, Ch'en Yi, P'eng Teh-huai, and Ho Lung.[7]

Chu Teh referred once to 'the sympathetic support of our Soviet friends and progressive people throughout the world', and stated that the PLA would 'absorb the highly advanced military science of the Soviet Union', but these remarks stood alone in a speech which emphasized the 'correct leadership' of Chairman Mao, and the 'glorious tradition' of the PLA. Articles by Generals Ho Lung and Ch'en Yi dwelt at length upon Mao Tse-tung's 'creative leadership' in military affairs, and Ho Lung concluded that the army must regard itself as 'diligent school pupils' in studying 'the whole of Mao's military strategy and line'. Neither writer referred to the Soviet Union in any form.

One purpose of these remarks was perhaps to counter criticism of China's decision to intervene in Korea, in the light of heavy casualties and military setbacks which the CPV had suffered in the spring offensive of 1951. This was a decision which —it is generally believed—was reached only after long heart-searching and debate within the party leadership, and in which Mao himself had the final word.[8] In what reads as a rebuttal of this type of criticism, Ch'en Yi wrote that

> Mao had insisted on the political, social and revolutionary aspects of military problems; he had also refused to regard offensive or defensive actions in the usual narrow meaning attached to them: he knew that a retreat might be either a complete defeat or a kind of 'victorious offensive'—a possibility which military experts usually tended to overlook.[9]

Ho Lung's article was devoted to an account of how Mao's 'cor-

[6] Ibid., 29 July & 1 Aug. 1950. Slogans Nos 27 and 28 read: 'Support the bulwark of world peace, the Soviet Union'; 'Long Live Generalissimo Stalin, leader of the peoples of the world'.

[7] Speech by Chu Teh, NCNA, 31 July 1951; Ch'en Yi, 'Learn Chairman Mao's realistic working attitude concerning Marxism-Leninism', ibid.; P'eng Teh-huai, 'Tribute to the CPV', ibid.; Ho Lung, 'The Significance of the Nanchang Uprising', *JMJP*, 1 Aug. 1951.

[8] Cf. David J. Dallin, *Soviet Foreign Policy After Stalin* (Philadelphia, 1961), p. 88.

[9] Summary of Ch'en Yi's article in *FE* 121.

rect ideological line of leadership' had triumphed over right and left deviations during the past twenty years of revolution, and of how Mao's military doctrine was essential to 'the present great task of building up our national defences'.

Chu Teh's solitary reference to the Soviet Union's 'sympathetic support' recalls similar language used by the Chinese communists in 1946–7 when sympathy was all that Stalin had to offer them.[10] Chu Teh also referred briefly to the need for the PLA to undertake the 'great historical transformation' from a purely land force to one with all three services and 'modern technical equipment' of which the PLA already possessed 'a certain amount'. P'eng Teh-huai's tribute to the Chinese volunteers, published on the same day, revealed how little this equipment was. The CPV, according to P'eng, was fighting an enemy far better equipped with aircraft, tanks, and artillery. It was common knowledge that against these weapons the Chinese volunteers had to rely on 'light infantry weapons and a small amount of artillery'. The enemy enjoyed a superiority in modern equipment, although the CPV had begun to build up its artillery and air forces in considerable strength. P'eng paid tribute to the way in which the Chinese people were able to 'support the fighting of their volunteers in Korea with all the necessary manpower, materials and finance'. His remarks gave added weight to the nation-wide 'arms donation campaign', initiated the previous month, which itself conveyed an implicit criticism of the Soviet Union, both for not supplying enough equipment and for exacting payment in return.

Friction over the question of military aid was apparently mended very soon after the statements quoted above, and a massive reinforcement of the CPV in Korea began to take effect in the following months. The policy of modernization of the PLA

[10] In particular, the terse congratulatory message from Mao and Chu Teh to Stalin on the occasion of the 29th October Revolution anniversary (*CFJP*. 7 Nov. 1946), which read: 'Over the past 29 years the Soviet Union has consistently sympathized with China's accomplishments of national independence and people's liberation. The Chinese people from Sun Yat-sen onwards have consistently sympathized with the peaceful and progressive contributions of the Soviet Union towards mankind; and hope that our friendship will endure.' And the isolated reference by Lu Ting-yi, in his lengthy analysis of the post-war international situation (ibid., 4–5 Jan. 1947, text in *US Relations with China*, pp. 711–19), to the fact that the united democratic front in China 'will undoubtedly have the sympathy and moral support of the socialist Soviet Union'.

on the Soviet model was again publicly put forward in progressively warmer terms. The anniversary of V-J Day was celebrated by a cordial exchange of telegrams between Stalin and Mao, both of whom paid tribute to the other's efforts in defeating Japan and pledged unbreakable friendship.[11] Soviet Army Day the following February 1952 was welcomed in an article by General Nieh Jung-chen which stated categorically that the PLA should 'learn earnestly from the rich experience and brave example of the Soviet armed forces', and praised the Soviet army and Marshal Stalin as the 'powerful guarantor of world peace and security'. The Soviet army was the bastion of peace and independence and the PLA was proud to stand by its side.[12]

In congratulatory messages for China's Army Day in August 1952, both Stalin and Vyshinsky sent their 'sincere wishes' for further achievements in what they described as the 'highly successful task' of strengthening China's armed forces. It was on this occasion that General Hsiao Hua, deputy director of the PLA's Political Department, outlined for the first time in explicit detail the PLA's plans for modernization on the Soviet model, and it is possible that long-term plans to this effect were made during Liu Shao-ch'i's protracted and unpublicized visit to Moscow the following winter.[13] In February 1953 Mao Tse-tung called for 'a tidal wave of learning from the Soviet Union on a nation-wide scale', and the celebrations of the Soviet Army Day in the same month produced the most explicit statements to date of the PLA's intention to model itself exclusively on the Soviet pattern.[14]

[11] *Soviet News*, 3 Sept. 1951.   [12] Nieh Jung-chen in *JMJP*, 23 Feb. 1952.

[13] Liu Shao-ch'i arrived in Moscow in the first week of October, and delivered a personal message from the CCP CC to the Soviet party's 19th Congress, which acknowledged Soviet influence and guidance in the most forthright terms since Liberation. The CCP, he said, 'was formed under the direct influence of the Great October Revolution and modelled on the CPSU'. Stalin's 'brilliant teachings' had played a 'tremendous and invaluable part' in the success of the Chinese revolution. Liu stayed in Moscow until 11 January 1953. It was rumoured that he was accompanied by Ch'en Yi, Liu Ya-lou (the commander of the air force), and deputy chief of staff Nieh Jung-chen (NCNA, 15 Oct. 1952; *Manchester Guardian*, 27 Oct. 1952 & 5 Jan. 1953).

[14] In an eve of Soviet Army Day speech at Port Arthur, Chou En-lai said: 'The entire Army has firmly pledged to double its efforts to study from the Soviet Army, to strengthen national defence, streamline organisations, and raise the standards of training aimed at the building of a strong and modernised national defence army. I believe that, with the assistance of the Soviet Union and the example of Soviet advanced experiences, the national defence construction of China will . . . go forward day by day towards success' (NCNA, 22 Feb. 1953, in *FE* 229).

At home, long-term planning began to take over from the day-to-day improvisation which had characterized the PLA during the critical early period of the Korean war. In its editorial for 1952—'A Year of Still Greater Exertions'—the *People's Daily* took a look into the future. The history of American aggression in Taiwan and in Korea, it commented, had shown that 'if we do not possess a modernised and strong national defence, we shall be unable to protect ourselves, and all our construction work will be reduced to shambles under enemy bombardment'. China must build up a modernized army, air and naval forces, and 'all our construction work must revolve around national defence'.[15] One of the main themes of the third People's Political Consultative Conference in October 1951 had been the overriding priority of national defence. In his political report to the Conference, Chou En-lai insisted that 'production in our country must serve the purpose of strengthening our national defence forces', and the Minister of Heavy Industry, Ch'en Yun, revealed that funds which might otherwise have been used in the economic, cultural, and other fields would have to be diverted to the needs of defence. Li Fu-ch'un, the vice-chairman of the Finance and Economic Committee, described the consolidation of national defence as the nation's 'first task', and stated that heavy industries connected with defence would have to be reinforced before any others.[16]

As the prospects of a renewal of major hostilities in Korea receded during 1952–3, the lines of the PLA's development as a peacetime army began to develop more clearly. Although never very likely, it was in theory possible that China would reject the heavy economic burden involved in building up a modernized army, rely heavily upon her Soviet ally, and cease to concentrate upon national defence. This hypothetical alternative was firmly repudiated, although mention was later made of 'some people' who believed that 'it was not necessary to strengthen or support the armed forces while the country was engaged in peaceful construction'.[17] Peaceful construction itself, it was stressed, depended upon a 'peaceful international environment', and this in turn

[15] *JMJP* editorial, 1 Jan. 1952.
[16] Chou En-lai, speech of 23 Oct. 1951 (*FE* 133). Li Fu-ch'un & Ch'en Yun, speeches of 4 Nov. 1951 (*FE* 134).
[17] *JMJP* editorial, 4 Jan. 1955 (*FE* 424).

K

depended upon strong national defences. China was carrying out socialist construction 'under conditions of imperialist encirclement', and America fully intended to 'remain hostile to the people of China, to destroy peace in the Far East and the world and to launch an aggressive war'. If China was to be certain of victory in the case of aggression, then she must have a modernized army. This was essential because 'the USA was an industrialised nation and its forces possessed modern weapons'.[18] This view was to become heretical in later years when the doctrine of man's superiority to weapons was reasserted. At this stage, little more than lip-service was paid to the Maoist concept of the 'paper tiger' nature of American imperialism. As one army training manual, published in 1953, commented:

> The American army is politically a reactionary military organisation of the imperialists, and basically is a 'paper tiger'. But it is an army with modernised equipment and fighting power. Its training and equipment are very different from that of the reactionary nationalist [i.e. KMT] troops. To destroy thoroughly such enemy troops, it is necessary to build up a strong modernised national defence army, and responsible officers should give an all-out and correct understanding of the American army to every soldier of the PLA. . . .[19]

The discord between Moscow and Peking in 1951 had not been confined to the question of military supplies, although this has again been resurrected as a grievance by the Chinese in their recent polemics with the Soviet Union. They have complained that China shouldered heavy sacrifices and stood in the first line of defence in Korea 'so that the Soviet Union might stay in the second line'. They have also claimed that most of the Soviet loans to China were used for the purchase of war material 'the greatest part of which was used up in the war to resist U.S. aggression and aid Korea'. (According to the Soviet account, only one-quarter of total Soviet aid, or approximately 450 million new roubles, was granted during the Korean war.)[20] At the time of dispute,

[18] Peking radio, 9 Apr. 1955, political lecture for the armed forces (*FE* 449).
[19] Chungking radio, 30 July 1953, excerpts from army training manual entitled 'Build up a Strong and Modernised National Defence Army' (*FE* 275).
[20] See Central Committee of the CCP: Letter of 29 Feb. 1964 to the Central Committee of the CPSU, *PR*, 8 May 1964, p. 14; and Novosti press agency, 'Soviet Aid to the People's Republic of China, Facts and Figures', *Soviet News*, 14 Aug. 1964, p. 47.

however, the question of military supplies was only one aspect of a wider pattern of Sino-Soviet relations. This is an area which has still to be investigated in detail, and most of the theories regarding Sino-Soviet relations at this time remain unsubstantiated. What evidence there is suggests that China was reluctant to enter the Korean war in the first place, and that the Soviet Union delayed the armistice agreement which ended the war against the wishes of the Chinese government. Broader policy issues may have included the questions of the retrocession of the Changchun railway and Port Arthur, and China's admission to the United Nations—where Soviet behaviour was judged by some observers to be calculated more to keep China out than to secure her entry. There was also the question of ideology and doctrine, concerning China's original claim that her specific road to victory—the 'way of Mao Tse-tung'—was to be the path of revolution in all the underdeveloped colonial and semi-colonial countries. This belief led to initial Chinese hostility towards such nationalist leaders as U Nu, Sukarno, and Nehru. A more moderate Chinese attitude towards such newly independent 'bourgeois' nations as Burma, Indonesia, and India emerged during 1951–2 at about the same time as the consolidation of relations with the Soviet Union which has been described above.[21]

The sequence of events after Stalin's death suggests a growing ability on China's part to win military, political, and economic concessions from Moscow. The deadlock on the repatriation of

[21] For an example of the shift in China's attitude towards world-wide tactics against imperialism, compare the May Day article by Peng Chen, NCNA, 29 Apr. 1951 and the May Day *JMJP* editorial of 1 May 1952. P'eng claimed that the Chinese people's successful struggle against imperialism was indivisibly linked with the struggles of the USSR and of all working people. Armed struggle against the imperialist aggressors had begun to become the 'main struggle pattern' not only in China but in Korea, Indochina, the Philippines, and Malaya. Imperialism and the oppressed people 'could not exist side by side'.

The *JMJP* editorial for 1952 pointed to the growing strength of the peace camp and the increasing internal contradictions of the capitalist countries. It emphasized that the peaceful coexistence of capitalism and communism was possible, and pledged China to strive for lasting world peace and friendly co-operation between the peoples of all the countries. The existence of 'armed struggle' in some colonial and independent countries was referred to, but the general tone of the article was reflected in its title, 'Strive for lasting world peace to celebrate 1st May'.

On the transition of Chinese foreign policy from 'join with revolutionaries' to 'unite with all', see H. Arthur Steiner, *The International Position of Communist China* (New York, IPR, 1958), pp. 8–24.

prisoners-of-war in the Panmunjom negotiations was swiftly broken, and the Chinese trade delegation which had lingered in Moscow since November 1952 returned home with substantial Soviet aid commitments to the first five-year plan. In October 1954, during their visit to Peking, Marshal Bulganin and Premier Khrushchev made substantial concessions to China in a series of agreements which included the retrocession of Port Arthur, the return of which had previously been postponed by an arrangement made by Chou En-lai on his visit to Moscow in September 1952. This retrocession, apart from being a graceful gesture to Chinese desires to regain control of all concessions made under 'unequal treaties', also indicated that the Soviet Union was now satisfied with China's ability to assume defence responsibilities in the area. It was accompanied by the return of all installations in Port Arthur without compensation, and the transfer of 'a large quantity of (military) supplies . . . in the form of loan credits'.[22]

In this honeymoon period of Sino-Soviet relations, the Chinese leadership appeared confident that the Soviet Union would continue to help with the strengthening of the PLA, and that the military clauses of the Sino-Soviet alliance would remain in force indefinitely. This at any rate was the impression given in their public statements. The alliance was described as a 'mighty bulwark safeguarding peace and security in the Far East and the whole world'. In the event of war, it was said, the two armies would fight 'shoulder to shoulder'. One newspaper commented editorially:

> The Soviet army possessed all the weapons and the technique for fighting a modern war. If the imperialists started a war they would be completely destroyed by the Soviet army. If the growing power of the Chinese forces was taken into consideration, then the imperialist aggressors could have no hope at all.[23]

The Soviet army was accepted without question as the model for the PLA of the future. According to the *People's Daily*, 'The Soviet army provided the PLA with a great example; the future PLA would resemble the Soviet army of today'.[24]

Yet while China admitted that she had much to learn from the

[22] Li Hsien-nien, budget report for 1955 (*JMJP*, 7 July 1955).

[23] *Ta-kung Pao*, editorial, 23 Feb. 1955 (*FE* 435).

[24] *JMJP* editorial, 24 July 1954 (*FE* 376).

Soviet Union in matters of technique, she constantly implied an equality of role with the Soviet Union as a 'bulwark of peace' in international affairs, especially after the Bandung conference of Afro-Asian nations in 1955 when China began to claim that she spoke 'for the whole of Asia'. This sense of equality was reflected in military terms. Thus at the European Security conference held in Moscow in December 1954, the Chinese observer Chang Wen-t'ien suggested that China would be bound by the terms of the Sino-Soviet alliance to join in the defence of Europe if peace in Europe was threatened. The same theme of the 'indivisibility of peace' was repeated by Marshal P'eng Teh-huai at the Warsaw Pact conference in May 1955. The description of the struggle for peace in Asia as integral and indivisible with the struggle for peace in Europe implied a parallel commitment by the Soviet Union in the case of aggression against China.

The confidence of the Chinese leaders was probably genuinely felt. At this time the new Soviet leadership under Khrushchev, still seeking to establish itself at home and abroad, was perhaps more anxious to secure Chinese friendship than at any time before or since. The visit by Khrushchev and Bulganin to Peking in October 1954 had taken place in an atmosphere of great cordiality, and was repeatedly referred to in the Chinese press as an example of 'truly fraternal friendship'. The agreements reached in Peking on Soviet withdrawal from Port Arthur, the retrocession of Soviet rights in joint-stock companies, on further loans and technical aid, were undoubtedly popular. Khrushchev is reported to have later said that Sino-Soviet relations continued to be tense right up to the time of Stalin's death; that the main reason for his trip to China in 1954 was to remove causes of tension, and that this was done by the dissolution of the joint-owned stock companies and the surrendering of concessions. The sense if not the authenticity of these remarks may well be correct.[25]

We cannot be sure whether the Chinese leadership felt that their good relations with the Soviet Union were likely to persist into the indefinite future, or whether it was foreseen that they would at some time run into difficulties. The whole-hearted way

---

[25] Report by Sidney Gruson in *NYT*, 4 June 1956, and *Daily Telegraph*, 5 June 1956, of remarks alleged to have been made by Mr Khrushchev at a gathering of communist party leaders the previous March in Warsaw for the funeral of Boleslaw Bierut.

in which China elected to 'learn from the Soviet Union', and the bitterness of her reaction later to the difficulties which developed, does suggest that in the mid-1950s the leadership had become over-confident about the probable durability of the Sino-Soviet alliance. As the complex dispute between the two countries began to emerge into the open, it became clear that China's military strategy and capability would suffer adversely from a deterioration in relations with the Soviet Union. This is not to suggest that the previous policy of relying upon the Soviet Union for military aid was wrong; there was after all no alternative source of aid to which China could realistically turn. It became clear that military considerations were not only affected by the dispute; they also helped to bring it about and to broaden its scope. Even in 1954–5, at the time of the maximum Sino-Soviet unity, the seeds of discord were already present in military relations with the Soviet Union as well as in other aspects of China's foreign policy.

In the first place, it is very unlikely that the Soviet Union's military guarantee to China was open-ended. There is little doubt that it was felt to apply automatically to any acts of overt aggression against China. Whether it could be invoked in the case of military hostilities initiated by China herself was another matter. During the Taiwan straits crisis, in the autumn of 1954, when China began military operations against the offshore islands, the Soviet Union expressed her support in the most guarded of terms, and her actions made it clear that she was opposed to the use of force to settle the question of Taiwan.[26] This episode foreshadowed the very similar events during the second Taiwan straits crisis four years later in September 1958, when Soviet support again was extremely lukewarm, and contributed to China's growing dissatisfaction with her ally.

Secondly, by 1954 the PLA's modernization was well advanced in terms of basic re-equipment. The supply of Soviet

---

[26] Statements made by Khrushchev on his visit to Peking in September 1954 avoided explicit commitment either to the offshore islands operation or to the goal of 'liberating Taiwan'. See further: Alice Langley Hsieh, *Communist China's Strategy in the Nuclear Era* (1962), pp. 18–19. In the exchange of greetings between Soviet and Chinese leaders on the Fifth Anniversary of the Sino-Soviet alliance in February 1955, the Chinese message emphasized that 'The Chinese people's struggle to liberate their own territory of Taiwan is a righteous one'. The Soviet reply failed to mention the question of Taiwan (NCNA, 13 Feb. 1955).

modern weapons diminished in subsequent years, to some extent because China's military budget was being cut back but probably also because adequate levels in the three services had already been reached. The next stage in China's military development necessitated the building up of a modern defence industry. This could only be achieved with Soviet help, yet it was not necessarily in the Soviet Union's interest to assist the PLA beyond a certain point. Soviet assistance in building up China's national defence industry was later acknowledged by Peking with gratitude, but this does not rule out disagreement over the level to which it should be built up. Soviet help appears to have been given for the 'partial construction and assembly of jet fighters, complete construction of light piston aircraft, and construction of tanks and of submarine and small patrol craft'.[27] This suggests that aid was given mainly for defensive purposes. We do not know whether China asked or was refused assistance in—for instance—the construction of a heavy aircraft and warship capability. Disagreement emerges more clearly over the question of nuclear weapons—a further logical step if China really intended 'the PLA of tomorrow to be like the Soviet Army of today'. Discord over Soviet nuclear aid to China was a major factor in the Sino-Soviet dispute as it developed after 1958.

Finally, the close association of the PLA with the Soviet Union during its modernization and reorganization meant that many of the military policies formulated at that time became linked to the general question of Sino-Soviet relations. Thus they became casualties of any deterioration in the alliance, regardless of their intrinsic merits. The same appears to have been true to some extent of military personnel who had become closely involved with their Soviet counterparts during modernization.

[27] Raymond L. Garthoff, 'Sino-Soviet Military Relations', in *Annals of the American Academy of Political and Social Science*, spec. issue on communist China and the Soviet bloc, Sept. 1963, p. 86.

7
Modernization—Facts and Figures

*We must have unification in organization, armaments, training,
discipline and other fields, for the high degree of centralization of
command needed in modern warfare so as to advance the modernization of our army. Every member of our army must strictly obey
orders, self-consciously observe discipline, promote the sense of
accuracy, planning and organization, and oppose individualism.*[1]

THE steps by which the PLA would progress towards a professional and regular status were first spelt out in detail by the
deputy director of the General Political Department, General
Hsiao Hua, in a speech delivered on the occasion of Army Day,
1952. Hsiao Hua called for technical advances in the 'mastery
of modern techniques of military science, and the skillful use of
modern weapons and equipment'. More time and energy should
be devoted to military training 'in order to ensure continual ele-
vation of the tactical and technical levels of the army units'.
Hsiao Hua also called for the 'strict observance of military discipline' under a more precise 'unified command' and 'unified
organisation'. Thirdly, he emphasized the need for intensified
training of professional officers. It was 'necessary to prepare in a
planned manner and train cadres who can master military
science'. The level of education among the rank and file was also
to be raised by an intensive campaign for the elimination of
illiteracy.[2]

During the following year reforms were put in motion in every
category of modernization outlined by Hsiao Hua, so that by
1 August 1953 Chu Teh, the PLA's commander-in-chief, could
claim with some justification that 'the great historic transition of
the PLA from a lower stage to a higher stage has begun'.[3] By
1955, with the introduction of conscription, of a system of ranks
and awards for officers, a new mode of discipline, and the com-

[1] General Su Yü, deputy chief of staff, *JMJP*, 31 July 1954 (*FE* 378).
[2] Hsiao Hua, 'The Chinese PLA marching towards modernisation', NCNA,
(Peking), 31 July 1952 (*CB* 208).
[3] Chu Teh, speech at Army Day, NCNA, 1 Aug. 1953 (*FE* 274).

plete reorganization of the PLA's command structure, the process of modernization was basically completed.[4]

MODERNIZATION OF THE ARMY

The PLA claimed that it had captured a phenomenal amount of military equipment from the Nationalist forces during the civil war. Over the three years July 1946–June 1949 this amounted to 60,000 heavy and light artillery, more than a quarter of a million machine guns, and over 2 million rifles and small arms (not to mention 134 aircraft, 123 naval vessels, 582 tanks, and 361 armoured cars). The greater part of this haul of booty was claimed in the last year of the war, and in view of the mass surrenders and defections of KMT forces, the figures may well be correct.[5] However, these statistics meant very little in terms of effective fire-power. The equipment captured was a mixed bag of American, Japanese, and Russian material of widely varying age and efficiency, nor was there sufficient ammunition to keep even the best weapons in use. As early as May 1950 the Chinese government announced its intention of strengthening its munitions production in order to build up 'a modern munitions industry and unite all munitions workers in a drive for greater production. . .'.[6] Much of the armoured equipment was unserviceable, and the tanks, according to one observer, were 'mostly worn out'.[7]

During their first year in Korea, the CPV suffered from major deficiencies in logistics and ordnance. The first troops to enter Korea were particularly badly off; one document captured from the Twenty-sixth Army of the CPV during the Changjin Reservoir campaign in November 1950 revealed that

a shortage of transportation and escort personnel makes it impossible to accomplish the mission of supplying the troops. As a result, our soldiers frequently starve. From now on, the organisation of our rear service units should be improved.

The troops were hungry. They ate cold food, and some had only a few potatoes in two days. They were unable to maintain the physical

---

[4] This chapter deals with all aspects of modernization in the PLA, with the exception of the reform of the PLA's command and staff structure, which is discussed in ch. 13.

[5] PLA GHQ, 15 July 1949: Three Communiqués on achievements in the civil war (*FE* 14).

[6] *South China Morning Post*, 15 May 1950.   [7] Rigg, *Red China's Fighting Hordes*, p. 100.

strength for combat; the wounded personnel could not be evacuated. . . . The fire power of our entire army was basically inadequate. When we used our guns there were no shells and sometimes the shells were duds. [8]

More than 90 per cent of the Twenty-sixth Army suffered from frostbite; the Twenty-seventh Army suffered 10,000 noncombatant casualties out of a strength of four divisions. The Twentieth Army complained of poor communications:

Our signal communication was not up to standard. For example, it took more than two days to receive instructions from higher level units. Rapid changes of the enemy's situation and the slow motion of our signal communication caused us to lose our opportunities in combat and made the instructions of the high level units ineffective. . . . [9]

Captured Chinese prisoners-of-war also revealed that ex-KMT American weapons still constituted the bulk of the CPV's armament, and that American-type artillery shells were being mass-produced in Manchuria—'with a high proportion of duds'. [10]

The artillery battalion, supposed to be 'organic to every division', was considered 'theoretical rather than actual as far as Korean operations of 1950 are concerned'. POW interrogations revealed that in many cases each soldier was issued with only 80 rounds of small-arms ammunition on crossing the Yalu. It was not uncommon to find several different kinds of rifles of varying calibres in the same regiment—Russian, Japanese, American, German, etc. [11]

Throughout the major offensive of the first half of 1951, the CPV continued to be underequipped and poorly serviced, relying on superior numbers and tactics to compensate for its shortcomings in logistics and ordnance.

The Chinese soldier went into the offensive carrying enough rice, millet and soya bean for five to six days; withdrawal from the line for replenishment invariably precluded sustained offensives and time after time it was noticed that the momentum of Chinese attacks fell away in this period. Communications were primitive, the radio net only reached down to regimental level, with telephones down to company CPs. Below, whistles and flares were used. [12]

---

[8] Karig, *Battle Report*, p. 353.   [9] Ibid.   [10] *NYHT*, 18 Nov. 1950.
[11] Montrose & Canzona, *The Chosin Reservoir Campaign* (Washington, 1957), pp. 86–93.
[12] Rees, *Korea*, p. 138. See also the description of the CPV soldiers on p. 249 (quoted

Re-equipment began to take place on a major scale from the autumn of 1951 onwards. In March 1952 General Ridgway's headquarters reported that Soviet weapons in use included tanks, self-propelled armoured artillery, trucks, artillery, anti-aircraft guns, machine guns, and small arms. Some ordnance—small arms and ammunition—was manufactured by the Chinese arsenals in Manchuria and in North Korea, but the majority came from the Soviet Union or East European countries.[13] By June 1952 observers reported that there appeared to be no shortage of infantry weapons in front-line battalions, although ammunition was still often rationed, and the CPV continued to use captured UN weapons whenever possible. Soviet light and medium machine guns, sub-machine carbines, and anti-tank grenades were part of the regular infantry equipment. The lack of artillery had been remedied, and front-line troops were supported by a considerable number of active guns, including horse and lorry-drawn 105 mm. and 152 mm. guns, and at least one rocket-launcher regiment. Armoured units were equipped with the Soviet T34 medium tank of second world war vintage. The CPV had by now the resources to support offensive operations with accurate and heavy artillery fire, starting several hours before the infantry attack. Engineers and signal units, however, were still limited in number, and their operations tended to suffer from a lack of flexibility due to poor communications.[14]

After the Korean war China's production of infantry weapons and artillery increased steadily with Soviet assistance. By 1957 it was claimed that 'we are in possession of various types of China-made artillery pieces and supplies capable of all types of combats".[15] According to one recent Western estimate, China is basically self-sufficient in light and medium weaponry, but

---

from Farrar-Hockley: *The Edge of the Sword* (1954), p. 23), which described them as 'clad in khaki suit; plain, cheap cotton caps; rubber-soled canvass shoes upon their feet'; and armed with 'rifles, carbines, burp guns, and Tommy guns that we supplied to Chiang Kai-shek'. Their supply lines consisted of mules or ponies, and coolie carriers with bamboo poles.

[13] *Manchester Guardian*, 11 Mar. 1952.

[14] This account is based on Major R. C. W. Thomas: 'The Chinese Communist Forces in Korea', *Army Quarterly*, Oct. 1952.

[15] Ch'iu Ch'uang-ch'eng, Lt. General of Artillery, 'The Growth of the People's Artillery', *Kung-jen Jih-pao*, 14 Mar. 1957 (*SCMP* 1510).

suffers from shortages of heavy equipment of all kinds following the withdrawal of Soviet aid in 1960.

In respect to modern, standardised infantry weapons, i.e. automatic rifles, sub-machine-guns, and 'burp' guns, light and heavy machine-guns, light and medium (60-mm. and 122-mm.) mortars; 90-mm. rocket launchers; recoilless rifles (57-mm. and 76-mm.), and light and medium artillery (all of which are being produced by the Chinese), the Army is adequately equipped. Major shortages exist however in heavy and self-propelled artillery, lorries and other military vehicles, heavy engineers [*sic*] equipment (tractors, dozers, dump trucks, patrollers and other road and airfield construction machinery) and tanks other than the obsolete T-34.[16]

AIR FORCE

In June 1946 Captain Liu Shan-pan, a Nationalist pilot, flew his B-24 bomber from Chengtu to the communist capital of Yenan. It was chiefly through the defection of Liu and other Nationalist pilots that the PLA acquired its first planes and trained personnel. (These defectors formed the nucleus of the new communist air force—Liu himself was identified in September 1956 as deputy director of the Air Force Training Department.) A few ex-Japanese fighter aircraft were also allowed by the Soviet occupying forces in Manchuria to pass into communist hands. Some 200 young men were reported to have been sent to the Soviet Union for flight and combat training, and in spring 1948 the first aviation training school was set up in Manchuria.[17]

The People's Air Force was officially inaugurated after Liberation in 1949 under the command of Liu Ya-lou, then chief of staff of the Fourth Field Army, with the most modest of capabilities. In early 1950 its total strength was about 100, including commercial planes. As Liu Ya-lou later related, the building of the air force was a 'most difficult task'.

The new China was just established, our national economy was in rags, our industrial foundation was very weak and there was no aviation industry at all. The Kuomintang airforce, which was also in a miserable state, almost wholly fled to Taiwan on the eve of the

---

[16] Samuel B. Griffith, 'The Military Potential of China', in Alastair Buchan, ed., *China and the Peace of Asia* (London, 1965), p. 73.

[17] S. M. Chiu, 'The Chinese Communist Army in Transition', *Far Eastern Survey*, Nov. 1958, p. 171.

liberation of the mainland, only a small number of the personnel came over to our side and reported for work.[18]

The air force was naturally the most dependent of all three services upon Soviet aid. According to Liu Ya-lou, the Soviet Union has

not only given us a first-class modern equipment, but also sent here a large number of very learned and experienced experts to teach us aviation science, superior aviation techniques and airforce tactics, and all kinds of advanced experience.[19]

But as in the case of the land forces, this aid did not materialize until the Korean war was well under way. The supply of Soviet planes before the war was limited to a number of LA-7 and LA-9 propeller fighters and a few twin-engined Tupolev light bombers, with perhaps a very few jet fighters.

It was not until late 1951—after the campaign to purchase planes for the CPV was launched on a nation-wide basis in China—that the CPV air strength reached proportions where it could begin to contain that of the United Nations forces. According to General Vandenberg, the US Air Force chief of staff, in November 1951 'almost overnight China has become one of the major air powers of the world', and monthly sightings of MIG fighters over Korea stepped up from 300–400 in spring 1951 to 1,400 in September and 3,000 in October.[20] The greater part of Soviet reinforcements consisted of modern jet aircraft, mainly MIG-15 jet fighters but also including a smaller number of IL-28 twin-jet bombers. Unofficial estimates vary widely, but it seems clear that the total air strength of the communist forces in Korea roughly tripled in size during the year 1951, with most of the increase consisting of jets. At the end of 1950 it is doubtful whether there were more than some 500 communist planes in Korea, of which the majority were propeller fighters, with only a few MIG jets. By the end of 1951 the effective strength had risen to between 1,200 and 1,500, of which at least half were jets. A less dramatic increase took place over the following year, producing a total in 1953–4 of some 2,000, of which again over half were jets. The great majority (700–850) of the jets were fighters, and esti-

[18] Liu Ya-lou, 'The Young Airforce of the Chinese PLA', *JMJP*, 31 July 1957 (*SCMP* 1596).
[19] Ibid.   [20] Rees, *Korea*, pp. 370–8.

mates of China's jet bomber strength in 1953–4 never exceeded 100 IL-28 light bombers.[21]

Both during the Korean war and later, the Soviet Union appeared to be willing to build up the Chinese air force on defensive lines, but not to supply it with anything like a major offensive capability. It was revealing that at no stage did the Soviet Union provide China with either medium or long-range jet bombers. This may in part be explained by China's preoccupation with the defence of her air space against enemy attack, and the probable irrelevance of even contingency planning for any offensive operations involving the use of air bombing. It is also extremely likely that the Soviet Union was reluctant to provide China with a viable offensive aerial capability which might at a later date be considered as a potential threat to Soviet security. Some measure of conscious restraint on the part both of China and of the Soviet Union in building up the Chinese air force may have been dictated by a consideration of its effect upon American deployment in the Far East, and the danger that any increase in China's offensive strength would produce a disproportionately larger increase in American commitments to the area. One example of this kind of self-imposed limitation is the fact that while United States planes from South Korea, Japan, and from aircraft carriers regularly bombed targets in North Korea during the Korean war, virtually no bombing raids were carried out by the communist side south of the 38th parallel. (For its own part the United States may be said to have exercised self-restraint in refraining from bombing Chinese airfields or supply routes in Manchuria north of the Yalu.)[22]

After the Korean war, 1954 saw a shift in the attentions of the Chinese air force back to the South China coastal provinces opposite Formosa. A major programme of airfield construction began, to supplement the existing bases at Shanghai, Canton, Ningpo, and Hangchow. In 1955 Nationalist sources claimed that a huge jet base was being completed at Luchiao, 220 miles due north from Formosa, together with a dozen other subsidiary bases in the same province. Redeployment of the air force was

---

[21] Estimates in *NYT*, 8 July 1951 & 30 Sept. 1952; *NYHT*, 30 Sept. 1953; *Combat*, 30 May 1954; *Manchester Guardian*, 23 Oct. 1951; *Daily Telegraph*, 6 July 1954.
[22] See further Morton H. Halperin, 'The Limiting Process in the Korean War', *Political Science Quarterly*, Mar. 1963.

reported from North China to the South, where half of the total air strength of some 2,000 was said to be located, including a large proportion of the 850 MIG fighters and 100 Ilyushin light bombers believed to be in Chinese possession. The possibility of a full-scale aerial engagement by the Chinese to win control over the Formosa straits air space was seriously contemplated in the West, and the renewed bombardment of the offshore islands in September 1954, leading to the crisis which persisted throughout the winter, encouraged expectations that Chinese air power would be used at least to capture those islands. It was no doubt China's intention to secure diplomatic and political gains by a display of air power, and to deter any thought by the United States or Taiwan of hostile action against the mainland. China was indeed able to demonstrate to the satisfaction of General Earle Partridge, commander of the United States Far East Air Forces, that she now possessed about the same number of planes, which were also equivalent in type and performance, to those under his own command.[23] However, the actual use of the Chinese air force was cautious in the extreme, and it was not employed—as it could well have been—to make the Nationalist position on Quemoy and Matsu untenable. Speeches by air force leaders suggested that they were more concerned with the long-term development of the People's Air Force than with its immediate use for the purpose of 'liberating' Taiwan. The need for improved technical performance and for closer co-operation with the army and navy were stressed at a meeting of model air-force representatives held in Peking between 22 and 29 March 1955. The air force was called upon to be ready at all times 'for co-ordination with the brother services in liberating Formosa and defending the territorial waters and skies of the Fatherland', and it was told by its commander-in-chief, Liu Ya-lou, 'to avoid complacency and impetuosity, to co-operate closely with military and naval units'.[24] A *People's Daily* editorial commented that

... our Airforce is still very young. We still do not have enough knowledge and experience in command, combat, navigation and other matters concerning the expansion of the Airforce. With a view to making one further step in establishing a powerful People's Airforce, all flying personnel must redouble their effort to study and master advanced and complicated aeronautic techniques and to improve air

[23] *NYT*, 27 Feb. 1955.   [24] *Scotsman*, 24 May 1955.

combat tactics, so that they will be able to carry out combat assignments under any kind of weather. . . . Our Airforce has a short history. Therefore, we still have shortcomings in organisation, execution of duties, discipline and accuracy. . . .[25]

In 1955 China began to take delivery from the Soviet Union of the later MIG-17 model, and in the following year started to manufacture these under licence in her Manchurian factories, with Soviet equipment and under the direction of Soviet engineers. No effort was apparently made to undertake independent research on aircraft production, or to produce Chinese-designed aircraft. This was a field where China lagged so far behind that even the assemblage of Soviet planes posed major problems. According to an interview with Ch'ien Hsueh-sen in 1956, who was then director of the Peking Institute of Mechanics, and had been entrusted with the task of laying the scientific foundation for China's aircraft industry, China was not yet thinking of trying to produce planes of her own design. She did not even have a design section at the factory assembling MIGs or at his own institute. Current efforts were concentrated on improving existing production processes, and reserves of research workers were woefully inadequate.[26]

Soviet assistance to the Chinese air force continued until the withdrawal of all Soviet aid and technicians in 1960, with the same emphasis on the provision of fighter defence as hitherto. Intelligence estimates in 1960 placed China's air strength at between 2,500 and 3,000 planes, of which between 2,000 and 2,500 were jets. At least four-fifths of the jet air strength was composed of fighters—mostly MIG-15s and 17s with a few of the more recent 19s—and the remainder of IL-28 light bombers.[27] According to some reports, China also possesses one squadron of TU-4 heavy bombers.

Although it was frequently stated during the Great Leap Forward that China was now producing her own aircraft,[28] the air-

[25] *JMJP*, 29 Mar. 1955 (*FE* 445).

[26] Interview with Ossian Goulding in *Daily Telegraph*, 26 Oct. 1956.

[27] *Japan Times*, 3 June 1960; *Sunday Times*, 5 June 1960; *NYT*, 1 Mar. 1964.

[28] 'The forces began to be equipped in 1956 with the newest types of jet fighters produced by ourselves. Following the Great Leap Forward of socialist construction, production of other new types of aircraft is also expanding by leaps and bounds. This is the important material and technological basis for the rapid development of our military and civilian aviation' (Liu Shan-pen, 'Swift Expansion of Our Airforce', *Wen Hui Pao* (Hong Kong), 1 Aug. 1958 in *CB* 514).

craft in question were those manufactured under Soviet licence and with Soviet aid, and were not independently produced. Since 1960 the shortage of spares and replacements has reduced the air force's total strength by perhaps as much as one-third. According to Western intelligence estimates in 1964, about 500 planes were grounded or dismantled since 1960, including about 200 in 1963 alone. The total was down from nearly 3,000 to approximately 2,000, and grounded planes had been 'cannibalized' in order to maintain the remainder in serviceable condition.[29]

In spite of the withdrawal of Soviet aid, there is as yet no evidence of the sort of crash programme for China's aircraft industry which would be necessary if she were to replace her existing air strength with more modern and advanced models. Production capacity seems to be limited to the renovation and replacement of the existing jet fighters and light bombers. (This in itself would be a considerable achievement, and Western reports in 1964–5 suggest that China may be capable of producing her own MIG-19s and possibly even the more advanced MIG-21s.) As for the airborne means of delivery for China's nuclear capability, a deliberate decision appears to have been taken to by-pass altogether the manned bomber stage, and to concentrate upon the development of a missile delivery system. (There is in fact no sign of a Chinese-designed bomber.) As of 1965, China is believed to have under way a vigorous missile research programme, headed by Dr Ch'ien Hsueh-Sen and other experts in jet propulsion who had previously been associated with rocket development in the United States before returning to China. A missile range has been reported in Sinkiang province, and China is believed to be working on the development of short- and medium-range ballistic missiles.[30]

NAVY

The origins of the People's Navy were as modest as those of the air force, and it encountered the same problems which were created by building up from scratch with a high proportion of

[29] *NYT*, 1 Mar. 1964; *NYHT*, 6 Mar. 1964.
[30] See further Halperin, *China and the Bomb* (London, 1965), pp. 77–78; Alice Langley Hsieh, 'China's Secret Military Papers: Military Doctrine and Strategy', *CQ*, Apr.–June 1964, pp. 92–93.

L

ex-KMT personnel. Its official birth occurred when the Yangtze was crossed in April 1949 and a number of KMT vessels were captured. As was later recalled, 'in the early days of building the People's Navy, it had only a small number of ships, some of which had come over from the enemy side, others had been captured from the enemy, and still others salvaged from the rivers or the sea and rebuilt'.[31] One early naval battle was fought between an 'enemy fleet of warships' and 'a [communist] fleet of small gun-boats and wooden sailing junks'.[32]

The purpose of the navy was clearly defined by Mao Tse-tung in 1949 when he said that 'we must build a navy, which will be capable of defending our territorial seas and effectively preventing any possible imperialist aggression'.[33] Its duties were therefore primarily those of coastal defence, including the patrolling of China's territorial waters, the interception of enemy infiltration by sea, and the provision of escorts for mercantile convoys and fishing fleets.

> From time immemorial [it was observed] our people have been closely connected with the sea in their productive activities and every day life. But in the past hundred years, as a result of our complete lack of coastal defence, imperialist aggression against us has come mostly from the sea.[34]

The navy's defensive role was reflected in the nature of its development after Liberation. Estimates of its total tonnage have never exceeded 200,000 tons since 1949 to the present day, and the greater part of this has always been made up of small, light but fast, torpedo or patrol boats. The largest craft whose existence has been reported is a 5,000-ton light cruiser.

In spite of the United Nations forces' strong naval presence in Korean waters, very little development of the Chinese navy occurred between 1949 and 1954. Its strength appeared to consist of the 1 light cruiser, some 10–20 escort frigates or destroyers —including ex-Japanese destroyers—a number of landing craft, and several hundred fast gunboats and speedboats. A few pre-

---

[31] Teng Chao-hsiang, 'The People's Navy in a leap forward', *Wen Hui Pao* (Hong Kong), 1 Aug. 1958 (*CB* 514).
[32] Ibid.
[33] Quoted by Chou Hsi-han, 'Let us inherit and uphold the glorious tradition of our army and strengthen the building of our navy', *JMJP*, 30 July 1957 (*SCMP* 1596).
[34] Ibid.

war ex-Soviet submarines, between 4 and 6 according to different accounts, were also reported. Production at the Kiangnan naval shipyards in Shanghai was said to be confined to gunboats under 500 tons, and it was noted that Chinese illustrated journals only published pictures of auxiliary vessels and rarely those of combat warships.[35]

During these years maritime security in the Far East was the responsibility of the Soviet Union, and with the transfer of the Soviet naval base at Port Arthur to China in 1955, part of this responsibility was also transferred to the Chinese. The agreement to this effect of October 1954 was explicitly described in a *People's Daily* editorial as an agreement for 'the withdrawal of the Soviet armed forces from the Port Arthur naval base and for the [Chinese] PLA to undertake the coastal defence itself'.[36] The same editorial also stated that 'Our coastal defence units have greatly improved in training and in mastering advanced military science', and it commented more cautiously that 'improvement is also seen in equipment. . .'. The Soviet equipment which accompanied the transfer of Port Arthur was thought to include a number of submarines and destroyers. According to one account, the Chinese navy received over 80 warships of various kinds, including 2 fast destroyers of 1,600 tons and 5 submarines of which 2 were ocean-going.[37] Soviet 'W' class medium-range submarines began to be constructed under Soviet licence and supervision in the Kiangnan shipyards, and between 10 and 15 of these were constructed in the following years.

No major naval construction has been reported since the Great Leap Forward and the withdrawal of Soviet aid. In 1962 the British Institute for Strategic Studies reported that China has no operational ships heavier than destroyers, of which there are 4, and placed China's submarine strength at 30, of which half are 'W' class. In addition there are frigates, MTBs, gunboats, and patrol craft. The Institute's report commented that 'the Navy is not an offensive force and is ineffective except for inshore defence'.[38] In the words of Admiral Burke, Chief of US Naval Operations in 1958, 'China is incapable of operating in distant

---

[35] *South China Morning Post*, 30 Mar. 1954.   [36] *JMJP*, 23 Feb. 1955 (*FE* 435).
[37] *The Times*, 25 Feb. 1955.
[38] London Inst. for Strategic Studies, *The Communist Bloc and the Western Alliances, the Military Balance 1962–3* (London, Nov. 1962), p. 8.

waters or engaging in large-scale combat with any modern deep-water navy'.[39] There has been no significant development of the People's Navy since then.

SOVIET ADVISERS

A large number of Soviet technical advisers accompanied the supply of Soviet military equipment both to the Korean armies and to the PLA, and Chinese officers were sent for training to military academies in the Soviet Union. As far as we know, their status was strictly technical and advisory rather than political. Soviet advisers in Korea may have played a more influential role in policy formulation, and there were a number of reports of a joint Sino-Soviet–North Korean command, but these must all be considered speculation.

No reliable estimate of the number of Soviet military advisers exists, and many of those often quoted may be exaggerated. According to Soviet sources, in the entire period 1950–60 the Soviet Union sent to China a total of 8,500 economic specialists and 1,500 experts in science, education, public health, and culture.[40] The number of military advisers is not specified, but by comparison Western estimates ranging between 15,000 and 25,000 seem excessive.[41] United Nations reports of Soviet advisers in Korea suggest a figure of 7,000–8,000, but while there was 'incontrovertible' evidence of the existence of technical advisers, there was none that any of these played a direct combat role.[42] The number of military advisers in China must in any case have declined considerably after the Korean war, since the number of technical experts withdrawn in 1960 by the Soviet Union—which amounted to all the experts in China—was, according to Chinese claims, only 1,390 in all.[43]

---

[39] Testimony to the House of Representatives Appropriations Committee, in *The Hindu*, 7 Mar. 1958.

[40] Novosti press agency, 'Soviet Aid to the People's Republic of China—Facts and Figures', *Soviet News*, 14 Aug. 1964.

[41] See Dallin, *Soviet Foreign Policy*, pp. 83–85. The most commonly quoted estimates are the following: 1950–2—army, 5,000; navy, 1,000; air force, 1,000, to be increased by 1954 to army, 10,000; navy, 2,500; air force, 1,500 (*NYT*, 30 Sept. 1952; Dallin, p. 84 n. 29).

[42] *Daily Telegraph, Manchester Guardian*, 1 Oct. 1952.

[43] 'Carrying on the struggle for building an independent, comprehensive and modern national economic system', *JMJP* editorial, 4 Dec. 1963 (*PR*, 6 Dec. 1963).

EDUCATION, TRAINING, AND DISCIPLINE

Instinct and initiative may be at a premium in guerrilla warfare, but modern weapons systems call for a degree of acquired technical training and a general level of education of which the PLA at the time of Liberation was almost totally devoid. In 1949 'young people' formed nearly 80 per cent of the PLA, and most of these were of peasant origin, with little or no education. Before soldiers could begin to understand the complicated and un-Chinese terms for weapons, military techniques, and logistics, or read training manuals, they had to be literate.[44]

Starting in late 1951, campaigns against illiteracy were launched among PLA units throughout China, with the aim of raising the rank-and-file's educational standard at least to the level of a primary school graduate, in other words to acquire a knowledge of something like 2,000 Chinese characters. A simplified method of learning characters, named after its inventor, a PLA teacher by the name of Chi Chien-hua, was used, and it was claimed that by this method between 1,500 and 2,000 characters could be learnt within fifteen days. Simplified courses in elementary mathematics and in calligraphy were also organized among the rank and file. When these experimental systems had been successfully tested in the army, they were then practised on a wider scale among the civilian population. By mid-1953 it was claimed that the overall majority of rank-and-file PLA had reached primary school standard, and were able to read texts on military technique and to take notes at lectures. There had been much talk of mass education campaigns in the PLA ever since Liberation, but it was not until 1952–3 that the problem appears to have been tackled energetically. In August 1952, when other plans for modernization were first systematically expounded, a cultural study programme was launched in the PLA, and a year later it was said to have not only eliminated illiteracy, but to have brought about a complete change of attitude towards education on the part of the rank and file.

[44] One analysis of captured Chinese soldiers in Korea produced the following estimate: about 30 per cent were almost illiterate, being only able to read numbers, road signs, and essential characters needed for shopping and following simple directions; a second 30 per cent had a reading vocabulary of about 200 characters; a further 30 per cent knew approximately 500 characters; the remaining 10 per cent had a knowledge of about 1,500 characters (Roy A. Gallant, 'Why Red Troops Surrender in Korea', *The Reporter*, 5 Aug. 1952).

The rank and file of the Army [it was claimed] now do not limit their leisure time activities to singing and dancing only as they did before. They attend forums, lectures and reading groups. They rehearse and perform plays written by themselves. . . . The raising of the cultural level of the PLA men makes it easier for them to master modern military technique.[45]

Mass education provided the essential foundation for raising the technical standards of the PLA, and on Army Day of 1953 Chu Teh announced that a 'unified regular training programme' had begun throughout the PLA. This programme covered the fields of weapon training and manœuvres, of organization and planning, and of military discipline. All these were to be co-ordinated and centralized on a uniform basis. Formal military training was accorded a degree of importance which it had never possessed during the civil war, and which was to become heretical at the time of the Great Leap Forward. The following typical extract from an army manual in use in South-west China evaluated the importance of training and equipment in these terms:

The situation has changed since the liberation of China, and our nation is able to arm our troops with the most modern weapons. Modern equipment is the material foundation of a regular modern army. Soldiers should be taught that an army's equipment can be improved gradually, and is only a matter of time. The use of weapons of various services in combat must be co-ordinated. This requires that every soldier should know how to use the weapon in his hand and to master modern military techniques. . . . The implementation of a highly centralised system requires every soldier to display organisation, planning, accuracy and discipline. . . . Every soldier, therefore, must be urged to acquire assiduously military, political, literary and scientific knowledge, to elevate his political-scientific knowledge and political consciousness, study the use of the weapon in his hands and improve organisation and discipline.[46]

Military training sought to give the rank-and-file soldier an all-round knowledge of the various component arms of the PLA,

---

[45] Report by Mo Wen-hua, director of North-east PLA Political Dept, NCNA, 2 July 1953 (*FE* 267). See also the special feature on the Chi Chien-hua simplified method in *Chieh-fang-clün Hua-pao*, Jan. 1952. For mass-education campaigns in 1949–50, see Rigg, *Red China's Fighting Hordes*, pp. 143–7.

[46] 30 July 1953, Chungking radio, excerpts from training manual entitled 'Build up a Strong and Modernized National Defence Army' (*FE* 275).

and it emphasized that they should be thoroughly co-ordinated in combat. The infantry was the 'main arm' of the PLA, but it could only function successfully with the full co-operation of its sister units. These included artillery—described as 'the god of modern warfare'—as well as the armoured, engineering, anti-aircraft, signal, and railway corps. The navy was essential for coastal defence, while success in modern warfare was 'unimaginable' without co-operation from the air force. Finally, the supply difficulties of the Korean war were cited to show that adequate logistics were an important factor in winning a war.[47]

It was not suggested that the PLA should turn its back upon the past, or reject the experience which it had gained during the revolutionary wars, although soldiers were warned not to grow conceited or complacent about their achievements in the past. But as the *People's Daily* also pointed out, new techniques in training were called for in the age of modernization. The army had acquired 'rich and valuable experience during the revolutionary war, but this experience did not suffice to meet modern requirements'. Military training should be intensified, and the PLA should redouble its efforts to strengthen its 'highly centralised and united organizational disciplinary qualities'.[48]

The loose, informal discipline which had characterized the revolutionary PLA was also eroded by the progress of modernization. (It should be added that this very informality had sometimes led to exploitation of the rank and file by their officers, and in this respect a stricter disciplinary code may have been an improvement.) New regulations on discipline, formulated on the basis of the future requirements of the PLA and from the example of the Soviet army, were promulgated in July 1953. Their purpose was to ensure unified leadership in the PLA, and to secure 'smooth progress in regular troop training and the building up of the army'. Soldiers were reminded of Stalin's saying that without discipline and military knowledge there could be no successful military training and education, and they were told the story of how a Soviet army hero had explained to Stalin that heroism was 'just a matter of discipline'. The keynote of the new regulations was that of strict obedience to all laws and regulations, to be

[47] 13–14 Aug. 1953, Chungking radio, instructions on how to lecture on the training manual cited above (*FE* 278).

[48] *JMJP*, 24 July 1954, editorial on the tasks of the PLA.

observed by officers as well as by the rank and file. Army discipline, it was stated,

requires that each soldier should correctly execute the stipulations of the army organisations, the order and instruction of senior officers, and the glorious disciplinary tradition of the Liberation Army. [The Regulations] exhort the rank and file to perform their duties properly, resolutely surmount all difficulties and hardships, protect the nation's territories, diligently study military science, and thoroughly familiarise themselves with their assigned tasks.[49]

Strict obedience to all laws and regulations was 'the primary duty of revolutionary soldiers', and it was incumbent upon officers and Youth League members to set a good example in this respect. Discipline was the key to modernization, and to the creation of a unified and centralized army capable of 'matching powerful imperialist forces in case of war'. The model soldier should be a well-disciplined soldier: 'A good fighter in a modernised army for national defence must be brave and skilful in using his weapons, and must study scientific knowledge, obey orders, observe discipline, and cultivate a uniform style of work'.[50]

This new emphasis on discipline was sharply at variance with the revolutionary tradition of unity between officers and men, however much it may have been abused in practice. The concept that heroism was simply a function of discipline also ran counter to the old ideals of initiative and self-sacrifice. It was of course explained that 'the discipline of the Chinese PLA is vastly different from that of the armies of capitalist nations or the Kuomintang reactionary government', since the PLA was a people's army and its discipline was 'formulated on the basis of every soldier's consciousness of safeguarding the fatherland'.[51] Yet in practice the disciplinary code appears to have been similar to that of any professional army.

CONSCRIPTION

In March 1953 the PRMC set up a Military Service Law Drafting Committee to prepare a system of compulsory conscription. On 9 September 1954 the SAC approved a conscrip-

---

[49] Chungking radio, 2–3 July 1953, reference material on army discipline regulations (*FE* 267).
[50] Chungking radio, 8 & 10 July 1953, commentary on the importance of a 'high sense of discipline' (*FE* 269).
[51] As n. 49.

tion order which provided for the recruitment of 450,000 men during the winter to take the place of demobilized soldiers. This was regarded as a trial scheme, and it was carried out on a 'tentative basis' in twenty-five provinces and the Inner Mongolia Autonomous Region. Tentative or otherwise, it resulted in a net recruitment of 830,000 men, or almost twice the original figure, and it was claimed that these had been selected out of a total voluntary registration of 10,032,000. Somewhat belatedly, a draft conscription law was put before and approved by the Standing Committee of the National People's Congress (NPC) on 7 February 1955, and then referred to people's committees at all levels for 'nation-wide discussion'. Finally, the law was resubmitted to the NPC by the Minister of Defence, P'eng Teh-huai, with some minor amendments, and was approved in July 1955.

According to the new law, conscription was carried out during the months November 1955–February 1956 for the year 1955, and it is believed that a total of about half a million conscripts were enlisted. As far as we know, approximately the same number have been enlisted by the same process in subsequent years. In 1958 500,000 out of the original 1954 draft of 830,000 were demobilized. (The remainder presumably either had their service extended or had been attached to the air force and navy, where the terms of service (4 and 5 years respectively) are longer than those of the army (3 years).) This suggests that approximately three-fifths of the PLA since 1958 has been composed of conscripts.[52]

[52] In the aftermath of the Great Leap Forward, recruitment was severely cut back. 'Very few soldiers were drafted throughout the nation' in 1960, and in July 1961 the Ministry of National Defence published provisional regulations for the 'extended service by noncommissioned officers and soldiers of the Chinese PLA'. These regulations provided that between 20 and 25 per cent of the PLA's total strength would be required to render extended active service for periods varying from one to three years (*KTTH*, 11 Jan. & 29 July 1961 (Cheng, pp. 124, 712–17)).

One reason for these changes was to avoid further social dislocation by recruitment at a time of unrest and natural disasters. Another reason may have been that the original term of service proved to be too short for the effective use of recruits after training. Chief of Staff Lo Jui-ch'ing reported after an inspection of army units that 'The term of service for soldiers with technical skill is too short. An automobile driver who has just learned to drive is soon entitled to be discharged from the service. That is why many automobiles cannot move' (ibid. 2 Mar. 1961 (Cheng, p. 282)).

In January 1965, an order was issued in the name of Chairman Mao to extend the length of active service of all noncommissioned officers and privates (NCNA, 19 Jan. 1965). This will not necessarily increase the overall size of the PLA, since

The conscription law might more properly be termed a law for selective service coupled with a universal reserve. All able-bodied men aged 18–20 are required to register for conscription at the appropriate time. The only automatic exceptions are for criminals, those who have been deprived by law of their political rights, or those who are physically incapable. An only son, or the only bread-winner of a family, can apply for exemption, as can students at senior secondary school level or above. The latter receive military training at their place of study, which in the case of university students entitles them to a commission in the reserve. After registration and a preliminary physical examination, the local authorities select a number of those registered for active service according to a fixed quota previously decided on a provincial basis by the State Council, and then apportioned out by the provincial and lower authorities. In times of hardship, some districts or even provinces may be exempted from their requirement to fulfil the quota.

Conscript soldiers and n.c.o.'s serve their term of office, which can be extended for as long as the 'needs of the forces' require, and are then demobilized into 'class one reserve service', where they undergo regular training and remain enrolled until the age of 40. Here they may be promoted to the ranks of reserve n.c.o.'s, or in the case of former active n.c.o.'s, to that of reserve second lieutenant. Local cadres and officials tend to be drawn from this class of reserve. The much larger number of potential conscripts, who have registered for conscription but have not been enlisted, are enrolled in the 'second-class reserve service', in which they too serve until the age of 40. They are liable for military service at any time within five years of initial registration. If national mobilization is declared, they are to hold themselves ready for conscription however long they have been in the reserve.[53]

---

the size of the draft may be proportionately reduced. Terms of service have been extended as follows:

		1955 (years)	1965 (years)
Army:	Infantry	3	4
	Special Arms	3	5
	Public Security Forces	3	5
Air force:		4	5
Navy:	Shore Arms	5	5
	Fleet	5	6

[53] The reserve system described here was merged with the people's militia in 1957. The two reserve categories then corresponded to the 'hard-core' and 'basic-level' militia. See further below, pp. 207–8.

The introduction of conscription in 1955 was justified on the following grounds. First, while the previous voluntary system had been 'necessary and correct' during the revolutionary wars, it was illogical and unfair to expect a relatively small number of regular soldiers to shoulder the burden of defence while the majority of the population had no part in it. Short-term conscription would spread the load more evenly, avoid permanent hardship to army dependants and their consequent economic drain to the state, and would also help to create an army which would 'always be young and healthy'.

Secondly, a modernized defence system required higher standards of education and military training. These would be provided for the pick of the nation's youth, which would then pass into the reserve where they would be readily available in times of emergency. This strong and well-trained reserve force would allow the army to 'maintain fewer troops in peacetime and produce more troops in time of war'. A further advantage was that conscript soldiers would, as well as acquiring military technique, also raise their political and cultural levels. On demobilization they would become 'positive elements in the work of construction' and their special skills and knowledge would help the country to advance towards socialism.

Thirdly, now that the country had entered into the stage of peaceful reconstruction, economies were called for in military expenditure. Conscription helped to cut down costs, and it also helped to conserve manpower for production purposes. Without conscription, demobilization to the new 'low' figure of approximately 2½ million soldiers, which was achieved by 1956, would not have been possible. Finally, the existence of a large secondary reserve would provide a vast source of manpower for immediate call in times of crisis.

Conscription did not come into being without resistance from those most immediately affected. Although the small proportion selected for active service knew that it would be for a limited period, they also knew that they had been chosen from many who were more fortunate in being rejected, and that their term of service could be extended indefinitely. There were references to 'vicious rumours and sabotage' which had been spread against conscription by alleged counter-revolutionaries and to the need to avoid 'simple and rash compulsory measures' in enlisting recruits, and to eliminate 'misunderstanding'. The policy of exemption for the only son or only working member of a family was to be strictly observed. In view of the Chinese people's peculiar and well-justified antipathy to military service, it was also felt necessary to emphasize that conscription was a much superior article in the new China. As the Minister of Defence said, 'The so-called conscription law under the reactionary rule of the Kuomintang was . . . an instrument for use against the people and consequently the Kuomintang still had to resort to pressganging and outright kidnapping.' But under the new regime, the Chinese people, he claimed, regarded military service 'as their glorious obligation and sacred right'.[54]

Veteran soldiers still serving in the PLA also had to be reminded that the introduction of conscription did not mean that they would all be demobilized on the spot. It would take time for them to be completely replaced by rotation, and meanwhile their fear of 'being a soldier for life' should not lead them to be impatient. Demobilization was in fact spread over the next three years 1955–7, with roughly 800,000 men demobilized each year.

THE PROFESSIONAL OFFICER

During the revolutionary period a party cadre needed above all to be versatile. He might be simultaneously a member of the local government, and of the local party committee, and an army officer with both military and political responsibilities. Although many cadres continued to be jacks-of-all-trades after Liberation, especially those attached to the regional or provincial MACs, the growing need for full-time experts in all areas of administration and government meant that there was a constant tendency towards specialization, and this was equally true in the PLA. The regulations on officers' service which were published in February 1955, and the conferment of awards and medals on leading PLA officers towards the end of the same year, amounted

---

[54] For the conscription law and discussion on it see further 'Introduce compulsory military service to increase our country's defence strength', *JMJP* editorial, 1 Nov. 1954 (*SCMP* 921); 'Draft Conscription Law', NCNA, 15 Feb. 1955 (*FE* 433); 'A major reform in China's military system', *JMJP* editorial, 15 Feb. 1955 (*FE* 433); 'Fu Ch'iu-t'ao on the advantages of conscription', ibid. 9 Mar. 1955 (*FE* 441); P'eng Teh-huai (Minister of Defence), 'Report to National People's Congress of 16 July 1955 on draft conscription law', *SCMP* 1090.

to formal recognition that the character of the officer corps had by now been totally transformed.

The stated purpose of the regulations on officers' service[55] was 'to change the voluntary military service system into a compulsory military service system and to strengthen the regularised and modernised construction of the Chinese PLA'. Entry into the officer corps was to be confined in the main to graduates of military schools and academies, on the basis of the individual's 'scholastic standing'. N.c.o.'s and soldiers who had displayed special military merit could also seek commissions by enrolling in special training courses sponsored by the Ministry of Defence. Once commissioned, officers would be promoted from one grade to the next according to a fixed time schedule, varying between two and four years according to the particular grade. Promotion to the rank of colonel, for instance, would take place after three years service as major. Promotion could be deferred for a period of between six months to two years but if the officer concerned was still unable to meet the requirements for promotion after such deferment, he would be removed from his post and transferred into the reserve. Upper age-limits were stipulated for each rank in active service, and these limits might only be extended by a maximum of five years.[56] The regulations also prescribed in detail the exact designations of officers in sixteen different arms or branches of the PLA, ranging from the cavalry corps to the medical branch.

The authority for granting commissions was carefully centralized. Initial commissions would be conferred by the Ministry

[55] 'Regulations on the Service of Officers of the Chinese PLA', NCNA (Peking), 9 Feb. 1955 (*FE* 431, *CB* 312).
[56] Upper age-limit for active officers in all services except the navy:

2nd Lieutenant	Shao-wei	30
Lieutenant	Chung-wei	30
Captain	Shang-wei	35
Senior Captain	Ta-wei	35
Major	Shao-hsiao	40
Lieut.-Colonel	Chung-hsiao	45
Colonel	Shang-hsiao	50
Senior Colonel	Ta-hsiao	50
Brig.-General	Shao-chiang	55
Major-General	Chung-chiang	60

No age-limit was prescribed for the superior ranks of Lieut.-General (Shang-chiang), General (Ta-chiang), Marshal (Yuan-shuai) and Supreme Marshal (Ta-yuan-shuai). Naval age-limits were five to ten years higher.

of Defence; promotion to the rank of lieutenant or captain could be granted by a leading officer at army or military district level. From senior captain to colonel, authority was again confined to the Ministry of Defence, and all ranks above colonel were conferred by the State Council itself (except for that of marshal which was conferred by the Standing Committee of the NPC). The State Council or the Standing Committee of the NPC also appointed officers to all positions at divisional staff level or above.

The same centralized authority applied to the dismissal or retirement of officers. All officers who were retired through reaching a stipulated age limit, or for any other reason such as ill health or redundancy, would be transferred to one of the two categories of reserve service set up by the conscription law. Reserve officers were subject to a similar, but longer, timetable for promotion and tenure of rank, and could rise to the post of major-general with an upper age limit of 65 in the 2nd Class Reserve. They were expected to take part in regular training and could be recalled at any time by the state. Also designated as reserve officers were graduates of institutes of higher learning who had been commissioned into the reserve by virtue of their particular technical qualifications. Some idea of the scope of this provision, and of the PLA's anxiety to recruit technical experts into the reserve, is given by the specified list of eligible qualifications. These included knowledge in the fields of aviation, shipbuilding, mechanics, civil engineering, meteorology, telecommunication, electrical engineering, medicine, veterinary science, study of liquid fuel, physics and chemistry, economics and finance, law and political science, foreign languages, and transportation and communication.[57]

The officer corps' new professional status was also enhanced by the introduction of ranks, decorations, and awards. According to Article 24 of the regulations, all officers were required to wear shoulder badges and other insignia appropriate to their rank, thus breaking with the long revolutionary tradition of the PLA that there should be no formal distinction between officers and men. The system of ranks itself was a reversal of previous practice.[58] Later this was extended to include insignia which would

[57] 'More questions and answers on the Regulations on the Service Officers of the Chinese PLA', *JMJP*, 15 Jan. 1956 (*SCMP* 1222).
[58] During the revolutionary period there was no system of formal ranks. Officers

indicate the particular branch of the armed forces to which the officer in question belonged. In September 1955 the NPC conferred Orders of Merit in three categories on a total of nearly 500 leading PLA officers. Lesser awards and decorations were bestowed on a much larger number of officers at various provincial ceremonies in the following three months. At the same time the title of Marshal of the People's Republic of China was conferred on Chu Teh and nine of the senior revolutionary generals.[59]

RESISTANCE TO MODERNIZATION

The introduction of a standard procedure for the service of officers was a natural consequence of the army's progress towards modernization. With any other army than the PLA, it might have passed without excessive comment. But such was the legacy of the past in the PLA's image in China, that it was felt necessary to justify the reform, and others like it, in what sometimes amounted to apologetic tones. The *People's Daily* insisted that the new distinctions set up between officers and men would 'definitely not affect unity in the least'. On the contrary, the new burden of rank would cause officers to feel an even greater responsibility towards their men and take greater care of them. In the past, when there was no unified command, military titles

---

were given functional designations corresponding to their responsibilities; e.g. 'commander of XX unit', 'head of political department of XX division', etc. One observer wrote in 1940 that '[The Eighth Route Army] has discarded the idea which prevails in Occidental armies that a leader, in order to be effective, must be accorded privileges and be set on a pedestal. Leadership is based entirely on merit. Even the customary labels by which military categories are known in Western armies have been discarded. The group which is customarily known as "officers" is called "leaders". The balance of the men of the army are known as "fighters". Leaders who command a unit the size of a brigade, or larger, are referred to as "commanders" ' (Carlson, *The Chinese Army*, p. 35). In May 1965, ten years after the introduction of military ranks, the system was again abolished, and the categories of 'leaders' and 'fighters' were restored. See further ch. 12, p. 251.

[59] On 27 September 1955 Mao Tse-tung personally conferred the title of Marshal of the People's Republic of China on Chu Teh and on nine other leading generals or ex-generals of the PLA. These were: P'eng Teh-huai, Lin Piao, Liu Po-ch'eng, Ho Lung, Ch'en Yi, Lo Jung-huan, Hsü Hsiang-chien, Nieh Jung-chen, Yeh Chien-ying.

Three separate Orders of Merit were created for those who had performed meritorious service in one of the three periods of revolution; Order of August 1st (1927–1937), Order of Independence and Freedom (1937–1945), Order of Liberation (1945–1950). Each Order was subdivided into three classes—1st, 2nd, & 3rd.

had not been necessary, but the improvement in equipment, organization, and control of the PLA had created the need for stricter systems, regulations, and ranks. Officers, it was argued, would in fact be encouraged to make greater efforts, since promotion would act as a material incentive to them.[60]

The strength of the old-style traditions in at least some sections of the PLA is indicated by the amount of resistance with which the modernizing measures apparently met. Such opposition was described as emanating from two different quarters: first, the political officers who tended to look down upon purely military matters; and secondly, those veteran military officers who failed to appreciate the profound changes necessitated by China's new strategic requirement of preparedness against a hypothetical 'US imperialist' attack, and who were somewhat sceptical of the importance of technological progress in the military sciences.

The political officers were criticized not only because they failed to keep in touch with both everyday military affairs and technological developments in the armed forces, but because by this omission they tended to weaken party control and influence in the PLA. As an editorial in the army's newspaper complained, many military officers did not bother to include their political colleagues in training and study programmes, while the political officers often avoided such activities on the grounds that they were 'too busy'. Nor did they show sufficient interest in the everyday life of the ordinary soldier and in his training. The result was that while the technical standards of the great majority of officers and men were rising fast, those of the political officers were falling behind. Unless this trend was speedily reversed, political work itself would inevitably suffer. To avoid this happening, the General Political Department decided in February 1956 that all political officers must become familiar with the military training requirements of their units within the next two years.[61]

Some veteran military officers also looked askance at the new reforms which they were expected to help carry out. This was especially true of those who had not been to the new military

---

[60] 'Major measures for the modernisation and regularisation of the armed forces of our country', *JMJP* editorial, 28 Sept. 1955 (*SCMP* 1147).

[61] 'Political officers must strive to study military affairs', *CFCP* editorial, 29 Mar. 1956.

colleges set up after Liberation, and who clung to the old revolutionary traditions. P'eng Teh-huai, the Minister of Defence, referred to those who 'fail to realize that past revolutionary experience, even experience of the Korean war, has a definitely limited value', and again to 'some officers' who were 'only satisfied with our past battle experience, and are not sufficiently enthusiastic about the study of modernized military knowledge'.[62] There was also opposition to the new disciplinary measures. These were regarded by some as amounting to 'formalism' which could degenerate into 'bureaucratism and warlordism'. In their opinion, the practice of saluting, and rules concerning wearing uniform, and suchlike, were 'small matters' which did not deserve serious consideration. These officers were criticized for 'wearing old clothes, refusing to be saluted', and other breaches of good discipline.[63] Officers had to be asked to set a personal example in carrying out the various disciplinary rules and regulations, and were exhorted to observe the precept that 'an officer of a modernized revolutionary army must not only have a high level of military and political knowledge, but must also have a strong professional ability'.[64]

---

[62] P'eng Teh-huai, speech of Nov. 1955, ibid. 28 Jan 1956; editorial, 'Strengthen party committee leadership over battle training', ibid. 24 Mar. 1956.

[63] Editorial, 'Strictly regulate army uniform discipline', ibid. 13 Dec. 1955; editorial, 'Carry out existing disciplinary rules until new code is promulgated', ibid. 19 Mar. 1957.

[64] Editorial, 'A lofty honour', ibid. 28 Sept. 1955; article by Chang Ai-p'ing, ibid. 21 Feb. 1956.

M

8

The Reaction against Professionalism, 1956–8

Deviations in the PLA

1. *Neglecting the tradition of unity of officers and men and unity of the higher levels and lower levels.*
2. *Neglecting democracy.*
3. *Method of leadership is often characterized by stress of administrative orders, neglect of ideological work and departure from the mass line.*
4. *Doctrinairism and formalism divorced from reality exist in school education and army training.*
5. *The army is estranged from the people and local Party and Government organs.*[1]

THE major technical and structural reforms which took place in the PLA during and after the Korean war had brought about rapid changes in its role and composition. Although these reforms were a necessary part of the army's conversion to a peacetime footing, they created a degree of estrangement in its relations with both the party and the civilian population. In the space of some five years the PLA had changed from a largely guerrilla force of volunteers to a conscript army staffed by professional career officers. The rise of this new professional caste, many of whom were recent graduates of the new military academies set up during the Korean war, and the progressive replacement of volunteers by untrained conscripts had weakened the traditional comradeship between officers and other ranks; there were complaints of 'Big Bossism', of excessively harsh discipline, and of arrogation of privileges. The incentives towards close cooperation between army and people which existed before Liberation no longer applied to the same extent; the bulk of the

---

[1] Summarized from T'an Cheng, 'Questions of political work at the new stage of army-building', speech of 23 September 1956 to the Eighth Party Congress, *JMJP*, 24 Sept. 1956 (*CB* 422).

army was now a garrison force, making no direct military or economic contribution to the livelihood of the local civilian populace. Lastly, the emphasis on the role of technology and on professionalism had produced a sense of impatience with the system of party control and education, expressed by the attitude that 'technology comes first', and that 'we military men are too busy to study'.

These developments do not, however, wholly explain the much more critical attitude adopted towards the PLA by the party leadership from 1956 onwards. It is very probable that many of the PLA's 'deviations' which were now criticized had been allowed to exist without too much concern for their effects in previous years. A fuller explanation must be sought in the shift in national priorities as envisaged by the party leadership under peacetime conditions, and by parallel shifts in strategic thinking. (There was also a growing disenchantment with the Soviet model in both the military and economic spheres.) With the ending of the Korean war and the consequent reduction in tension, purely military considerations were increasingly subordinated to those of national reconstruction. The army was now expected to play its part in the restoration of the economy, and no immunity was granted from nation-wide campaigns which might conflict with military requirements. This was made clear by the then Minister of Defence, P'eng Teh-huai, at the Eighth National Congress of the Chinese Communist Party in September 1956:

> The Chinese people need an environment of lasting peace for their socialist construction and they also need a modernized revolutionary army to cope with any possible accident and safeguard the nation's socialist construction. Our responsibility is to adequately unify the two and we must, therefore, in the course of modernizing our army, cope with the needs of economic construction of the State, exercise every economy possible, oppose waste, take into consideration the people's interests both in production and living whenever measures are taken for military construction, maintain a close tie between our army and the people, and promote the frugal style of work of the people's revolutionary army.[2]

This policy led to the PLA's intensive participation in pro-

[2] P'eng Teh-huai, 'The Chinese People's Liberation Army', NCNA, 19 Sept. 1956 (*CB* 422).

duction, in economy campaigns, and the institution of reforms designed to improve officer-men and army-people unity. The harmful effects of these campaigns on military morale and efficiency will be analysed in the next chapter. This chapter will be concerned rather with the question of party-army relations and with the attempts made to strengthen party control over the army, at first in order to prosecute the above-mentioned policies more efficiently, and later in order to rectify the harmful effects produced by these very same policies.

MODERNIZATION AND 'REVOLUTIONIZATION'

Although the effect of the communist party's increasing interference in military matters from 1956 onwards was undoubtedly to diminish the PLA's technical efficiency and to impair its professional *esprit de corps*, this was not necessarily the original intention. The extreme preoccupation with modernization and with professionalism which the party itself had shown earlier became heterodox during the Great Leap Forward, but it does not follow that it ever became opposed to modernization or professionalism *per se*. Although the party leadership has in recent years increasingly emphasized the spiritual and political factors in its military doctrine at the expense of its technical and material components, it has at no stage denied the need for a modernized PLA with a professional officer corps. In this sense, the line of analysis which postulates a sharp dichotomy between 'professionalism' and 'guerrilla-ism' in Chinese military doctrine overstates the degree of cleavage between the differing schools of thought which became apparent during this time. It is true that at the height of the Great Leap Forward, modernization and professionalism were devalued to a much greater extent than before or afterwards. What was at issue, however, was not so much the intrinsic value of these attributes of a regular army, but the forms which they had assumed and the political context in which they should be set. The central issue throughout was not the desirability of a modernized army as such, but the nature of its relationship with civilian society and with the political arm of government.[3]

---

[3] For a lucid and balanced account of the sources of conflict between party and army since 1949, and especially during the period under discussion, see further Joffe, *Party and Army*.

In the official view, the need for a highly modernized army, equipped and trained to the highest possible standards, was self-evident. 'From now on,' commented a *Liberation Army Newspaper* editorial of August 1958, 'our most important enemy is the aggressive armed forces of American imperialism which is highly modernized. . . . Any viewpoint which tends to neglect or overlook modernization is completely mistaken.'[4] Over the years 1956–7, while the tempo of political activity in the PLA increased, editorials in the same paper continued to call loudly for improvements in such technical matters as artillery training and night exercises, anti-aircraft defence, mechanization, scientific research, naval forces, anti-atomic, bacteriological and chemical warfare training, logistics, etc., etc.[5] One such editorial in November 1956 frankly recognized the deterrent nature of modern weaponry. The possession of nuclear weapons, and modern jet aircraft by the Western powers, it admitted, gave them a so-called 'massive superiority', but the Soviet military strength deterred them and was in some respects superior. In the past the PLA had suffered serious losses through 'lack of good equipment, and could do nothing about enemy bombing raids'— a clear allusion to the early phase of the Korean war—but the situation had now improved. The PLA now possessed planes and heavy artillery, as well as the greater part of its requirements of tanks, warships, and other modernized equipment. The Soviet Union was assisting in this, and China would soon be able to produce such weaponry herself.[6]

It was felt, however, that the value of modernization would be entirely negated unless built upon a firm political foundation. As T'an Cheng, deputy director of the General Political Department, observed in a speech to the Party Congress of September 1956:

It must be noted that modernization itself bears no class character; there are modernized people's armies as well as modernized bourgeois armies. So-far-as equipment and organisation are concerned, the people's army is not much different from the bourgeois army. Outwardly, many systems and command relations within the army are

---

[4] 'Oppose one-sided emphasis on modernization', *CFCP*, editorial, 17 Aug. 1958.
[5] Ibid. editorials of 12 June, 7 July, 12 July, 7 Aug., 27 Oct. & 15 Nov. 1956; 7, 14, & 26 Feb., 7 Mar. & 20 Apr. 1957.
[6] 'Advance the army's military scientific skills', ibid., editorial, 15 Nov. 1956.

generally the same. What are different are the different contents of these systems and forms and the different political relations. Take our army for instance. Its main characteristics are the education in the revolutionary spirit of Marxism-Leninism, the principle of unity of officers and men, unity of army and people and unity of our friends and ourselves, and the Party leadership and the revolutionary political work, etc.[7]

The process of modernization, it was explained, would itself suffer if divorced from the army's revolutionary traditions.

Revolutionization is the army's basis and essence; modernization is its special tendency, and is dependent upon revolutionization. Not only can we not weaken the latter for the sake of the former, but we should not place them on the same level or regard them as co-extensive. If we overlook revolutionization, and concentrate excessively on modernization, not only will we not raise our army's fighting strength, but on the contrary we shall enfeeble our army's revolutionary characteristics, and even make it become a 'fake tiger'.[8]

INADEQUACIES OF THE SOVIET MODEL

The question must be asked whether this renewed emphasis upon the 'revolutionary' components of the PLA's tradition was simply an abstract reformulation of Maoist doctrine, unrelated to the actual circumstances of 1956–8, or whether specific developments in the PLA necessitated such a reassertion of 'revolutionization'. Two developments in particular appear to have worried the party leadership at this time. First, they were concerned at the growing division between party and army, and the worsening of relations both within the armed forces between officers and men, and externally between the PLA and the 'people'. But secondly and of equal importance—at least in the earlier period of greater emphasis on political control—they were concerned at deficiencies in the actual implementation of the modernization programme itself, and viewed improvements in the role of the party committee and its leadership over military affairs primarily as a remedy for such deficiencies. In the early months of 1956 the 'right-wingers' and 'dogmatists' were not so much those who exaggerated the importance of technical

---

[7] T'an Cheng, 'Questions of political work at the new stage of army building', 18 Sept. 1956 (*CB* 422).

[8] 'Oppose one-sided emphasis on modernization', *CFCP*, editorial, 17 Aug. 1958.

modernization as those who hindered its progress. This point was succinctly made in the slogan 'Oppose right-wing conservative thought, and speed up our army's modernized construction'.[9] It had become apparent that in the military sphere, as in other fields of technological development, the pace of modernization could not be sustained by theoretical study alone—often based uncritically upon Soviet models. Officers and cadres of the PLA tended to lack the skill to integrate theory with practice, producing a situation where book learning and field manoeuvres were divorced from each other. The combination of a formalistic approach to military science by some officers and the 'guerrilla-type' rejection of its value by others had led to a point where the PLA's technical proficiency lagged far behind the standards required of a 'modernized' army. This was the phenomenon described by T'an Cheng as 'doctrinairism and formalism', in which

cramming education pursues only contents regardless of the results; lessons are read according to books; stress is laid on memory and not understanding in examination; training systems and methods are not practical and foreign experience is mechanically applied etc.[10]

and which, according to P'eng Teh-huai, had 'weakened the excellent tradition of our army and affected its internal and external unity'.[11]

Officers of middle and lower ranks were said to lack the know-how to train their troops adequately, while many of their superiors failed to exercise supervision over their work, and limited their leadership over training activities to the putting out of slogans and material, passing on all the real work to be carried out by subordinate training departments. They tended to be unfamiliar with even the basic techniques, and some had 'no intention of going and studying them'. They were too easily put off by complaints from below that 'time is too short, contents [of training programmes] too much, speed too quick'.[12] Reference was made to the 'contradiction between old-style officers and new'; too many party commissars and military unit leaders had not been to military college and lacked sufficient technical train-

---

[9] See features under this slogan in *CFCP*, 3, 15, & 20 Mar. 1956.
[10] T'an Cheng, 'Questions of political work . . .', *CB* 422.
[11] P'eng Teh-huai, 'The Chinese People's Liberation Army', ibid.
[12] 'Strengthen party committee leadership over battle training', *CFCP*, editorial, 24 Mar. 1956.

ing.[13] There were also complaints about the over-theoretical nature of college training, and the failure to link the 'classics of Marxism-Leninism' with the 'actual experience of the Chinese revolution'.[14] Staff commanders were accused of having become 'divorced from the company level', of being overwhelmed by pointless paper work and failing to inspect—or only making the most superficial inspection of—their subordinate units, of issuing orders without specifying how they were to be carried out or relating them to practical experience. They were often only interested in results, so that cadres at lower levels felt obliged to satisfy them by fictitious reports of training achievements.[15]

Other complaints were made about the way in which many officers carried out the new disciplinary code, and it was admitted that the code, as well as other recent rules and regulations, was 'in certain instances not in keeping with the historical characteristics and present conditions in our army'.[16] Some officers applied the regulations dogmatically and even exceeded them; others went so far as to make up their own rules and to say that they were part of the code, while yet others ignored the code entirely on the grounds that it was 'formalistic'. T'an Cheng described this situation as one where 'foreign experience' had been 'mechanically applied', and it was promised that these and other regulations would be suitably modified to accord more closely with the PLA's traditions.[17]

---

[13] Ibid., editorial, 15 May 1956.

[14] Kan Szu-ch'i, 'Several important questions on opposing dogmatism', ibid., 21 Aug. 1956.

[15] 'Overcome subjectivism, dogmatism, commandism, thoroughly carry out the mass line', ibid., editorial, 4 Oct. 1956. Incorrect 'work-style' was criticized by T'an Cheng as being marked by 'subjectivism, bureaucratism and commandism'.

'Specialisation is inappropriately stressed with the result that the business of departments is separated from the immediate tasks and central work and turned into a purely technical and professional business devoid of ideas and clear political direction. . . . In carrying out a task and organising work, no attention is given to ideological fermentation and cadres are not aroused to express their opinions and carry on full discussions but simply the directives of the higher levels are transmitted, tasks are assigned, figures are apportioned and time-table is arranged, thereby reducing the relations between the higher level and lower level into simple relations between one who assigns the task and who who accepts the task' (T'an Cheng, 'Questions of political work . . .', *CB* 422).

[16] P'eng Teh-huai, 'The Chinese People's Liberation Army', ibid. p. 12.

[17] 'Carry out existing disciplinary rules until new code is drawn up', *CFCP*, editorial, 19 Mar. 1957. This editorial criticizes sections of the existing code as incompatible with the PLA's democratic traditions. For instance:

The problem which the army faced in 1956 was part of the more general problem shared by China's industrial and agricultural sectors at this stage of 'national reconstruction'; namely, how to assimilate modern technology, imported for the most part exclusively from the Soviet Union, to specific Chinese conditions where the educational and technical basis was still largely deficient. There was a growing realization that it was not enough to follow simply from the book, or in Mao's phrase, to indulge in the eight-legged essay style—*pa-ku-chu-yi*—and also that the Soviet model itself was inadequate. As Marshal Yeh Chien-ying told the sixth Military Colleges Conference in May 1956,

the study of Soviet advanced experience must be well combined with the development of our own army's excellent traditions. We must also learn from the fraternal [socialist] countries, and study their useful experience. Apart from this, we must also study the military doctrine of the capitalist countries. This must be studied both from the point of view of learning their doctrine and techniques, and from that of understanding how to prevent aggression, in order that we may know our enemy.[18]

---

(1) 'A soldier may only voice criticism on his personal matters. He may not criticise other people's affairs'.

(2) 'Unless a commander exceeds his disciplinary powers, he may not be accused of excessive harshness in discipline'.

It commented that 'these clearly lack the democratic spirit', and complained that the system of democratic meetings were not even included in the regulations. Comrades were asked to carry out the existing regulations until they were modified, but to report any criticisms to their superior organs.

[18] Yeh Chien-ying, address to 6th Military Colleges' Conference, 3 May 1956, *CFCP*, 5 May 1956. The importance of Soviet aid was not denied, both in strengthening the PLA and in overcoming 'guerrilla-ism' among its cadres. T'an Cheng told the Eighth Party Congress that 'It should be noted that the above success [the 'transition from the old stage to the new stage'] is inseparable from our study of the advanced experience of the Soviet Union. We conducted much education among some cadres who grew conceited, stuck to the old rut, rejected new things and did not learn from the Soviet Union with an open mind. This was entirely necessary. Without doing this, conservatism, dispersionism and the habit of guerrilla warfare could not be overcome in time, identity of idea and understanding on the question of transition could not be smoothly effected.' But the mechanical implementation of foreign models was criticized by P'eng Teh-huai at the same Congress, and he stressed the importance of the PLA's own experiences. 'We should combine in our study the historical experience of our army and the advanced military experience of foreign nations.

'In learning the military experiences of foreign nations, we must adopt the scientific attitude of analysing them, criticizing them and learning them in a matter-of-fact manner. We must not be superstitious and follow them blindly, nor should we use them without any flexibility. Because any experience, whether our

In military affairs, as in other departments of Chinese life, there was an increasingly eclectic and pragmatic approach towards the usefulness of Western models, which was summed up in the catch-phrase 'integration of theory with practice'. As the inadequacies of these imported models became clearer, there was also the same tendency to revert to the traditional 'revolutionary' models which had been successfully tested before Liberation and which the leadership was predisposed in any case to favour. This tendency was further accentuated by the growing 'contradictions' within the army and between the army and society, whose emergence was unfavourably compared with the more harmonious relationships which existed in these fields during the revolution.

For the PLA, the 'revolutionary' models to be revived included such concepts as the 'mass line', the 'three military democracies' (political, economic, and financial), the Soldiers' Committee, the collective leadership of the party committee, the PLA's intensive participation in production and economy campaigns, and the movement for officers to leave their offices (*hsia hsi*) and mix with the ranks. The initial purpose, it must be emphasized, was not to eliminate professionalism or bring to a halt the army's modernization, but to encourage them to flourish in a more proper, revolutionary, and specifically Chinese context. The whole campaign was motivated by a sense of urgency, for, as the *Liberation Army Newspaper* commented editorially, 'Modern military science and techniques are developing very rapidly, and if we don't raise our heads and catch up, we may get left behind, and left behind can mean being beaten.'[19] This was the same spirit which motivated the Great Leap Forward, when it was felt that in order to 'catch up' with the advanced Western powers, only the revolutionary principles of self-reliance and struggle could succeed where more conventional techniques had proved inadequate.

Just as the ideal behind the Great Leap Forward was that China should advance simultaneously on the three fronts of

---

own or of foreign nations, has its time, place, and other elements; it may be correct in foreign countries but not correct or entirely correct under the concrete conditions of China. Even our own experience which, in future, may not be correct or not entirely correct under changed conditions. We simply cannot forcibly apply it without analysing or criticizing it in a realistic manner, otherwise there will be serious errors in our study, no matter how much we have done.'

[19] 'Strengthen party committee leadership over battle training', *CFCP*, editorial, 24 Mar. 1956.

social progress, industrial, and economic development, so in the case of the PLA it was hoped to achieve successes in three totally different spheres of activity at one and the same time. First in the military sphere, for the goal of a modernized army was not to be abandoned. Secondly in the non-military sphere of production work and the fostering of 'army-people unity', and thirdly in the political sphere of intensified theoretical learning and party control. In 1956 these three goals were accorded roughly equal priority, but by 1958 the latter two, and especially that of politics, had begun to submerge the first. This was perhaps inevitable, since the policy of pressing ahead on all fronts created its own contradictions in the PLA as well as in other fields where it was applied. Greater emphasis upon the non-military and political roles of the army aroused resistance and encouraged those tendencies which it was designed to check. This in turn produced an even greater preoccupation with those roles which forced the military role further into the background. The crisis of confidence in the PLA at the height of the Great Leap Forward was in large measure caused by this ever-widening circle of party control and interference, as well as by the somewhat mechanical and clumsy methods which were adopted in order to resurrect the 'revolutionary' ideals of former years.

THEORETICAL EDUCATION

The remedial measures which began to be put into effect in the PLA during 1956 can be summarized under three separate categories: (1) theoretical education, with special emphasis upon a knowledge of the history of the CCP and an understanding of the principles of Marxism-Leninism; (2) pursuit of the 'mass line', involving greater internal democracy, more contact between officers and men, improvements in civilian relations, participation in production campaigns etc.; (3) stronger party leadership through the army party committees and in co-ordination with local civilian party authorities. Within the framework of these measures, vigorous programmes of military training continued to be put into operation.

In January 1956 the PLA General Political Department issued a directive on a new system of education in political theory for all military cadres. It was explained that in the past, the ideological knowledge of military cadres had fallen far short of the masses' requirements. The new programme specified that all officers of the rank of major and above should complete by 1961 the study of the following five subjects: history of the Chinese Communist Party, history of the Soviet Communist Party, political economy, dialectical materialism, party constitution. Officers of the rank of senior captain and below were to take a three-year course covering political, ideological, and basic party knowledge. There were to be no exceptions; examinations in these subjects were to be taken annually, and officers could miss promotion or be demoted if they failed to pass.[20] In order to make time for the new curriculum, unit commands were encouraged to set up 'political night-schools' at which officers could study, and over 1,300 had been established by the end of the year.[21]

Although it was reported in the public press that 'enthusiasm for study of theory is mounting high among the officers throughout the entire Chinese People's Liberation Army',[22] the *Liberation Army Newspaper* revealed a certain amount of 'right conservative' opposition to the new scheme. The General Political Department had trained 3,000 instructors in the past few years, but some officers ignored or obstructed them, prevented their subordinates from attending night school, or even from fulfilling the stipulated half-day a week of theoretical study. Some leading officers echoed the remarks 'we're too busy to engage in study', 'Wait a couple of years, and then we'll be ready', and so on. 'As a result', we are told, 'the common phenomenon is that learners are bound up hand and foot and cherish numerous worries.'[23] Possibly disturbed by this recalcitrance among even senior officers, the General Political Department called in July for all officers of regimental rank and above to rectify their outlook and work-style by carefully perusing five key documents by Chairman Mao himself, by October at the latest. Study of these five documents at a slower pace was also organized at lower officer levels.[24]

[20] *CFCP*, 21 Jan. 1956.
[21] Ibid., editorials, 6 Feb. & 19 June 1956; 'Good results of PLA officers in theoretical studies', NCNA, 28 Dec. 1956 (*SCMP* 1455).
[22] 'Entire PLA officer corps takes up theoretical study', ibid. 21 Feb. 1956 (*SCMP* 1241).
[23] Wen Shan (head of education bureau of GPD Propaganda Department), 'Overcome right conservative thought about theoretical education', *CFCP*, 7 Feb. 1956.
[24] 'General Political Department notification on need for study of five documents', *CFCP*, 19 July 1956; ibid. editorial 24 July 1956.

The implication behind these moves was one which was to become familiar in many fields of party activity in the army. Attempts to raise the level of ideological knowledge among cadres had revealed that their existing level of knowledge was lower than previously thought. The party's perfectionist instinct therefore led to an intensification of such attempts. These in turn aroused opposition, which had previously been absent or at least dormant, within the army to party interference. By September 1957 the campaign for 'socialist education' was no longer confined to cadres but had spread throughout the army.[25] As 'mistaken viewpoints and muddled thoughts' emerged in the course of education within the army, it became increasingly clear to the party that '. . . the enhancement of the Marxist-Leninist knowledge of the cadres is a task of immediate importance for our Army. Only when the Marxist-Leninist knowledge of our cadres is enhanced can our work become really effective.'[26] From this it was but a short step to a fully-fledged campaign to 'study Mao's military theories', launched by the Military Affairs Committee in March 1958.[27] This last development was accentuated by shifts in Chinese strategic thinking which will be examined further on,[28] but the cumulative effect of the previous two years of party initiatives and army resistance to ideological education must be considered as an important contributory factor.

THE 'MASS LINE'

The concept of the 'mass line' concerns itself with the techniques by which the party and government ensures that it is not alienated from the people whom it leads and controls. It also seeks to canalize the enthusiasm and energies of the 'masses', and to associate them more closely with the process of policy formulation and government. The importance of this was especially

[25] 'PLA General Political Department orders socialist education in army companies', NCNA, 5 Sept. 1957 (*SCMP* 1611). All soldiers and cadres were required to participate in 'group debates' on the following themes: (1) superiority of cooperatives; (2) unified purchase and unified sales of foodgrains and other farm produce; (3) relations between workers and peasants; (4) observation of discipline and improvement of service attitude; (5) relations between officers and men.

[26] 'Party leadership is decisive factor which leads our army to victory', *CFCP* editorial, 30 July 1957 (*SCMP* 1588).

[27] Liu Ya-lou, 'Seriously study Mao Tse-tung's military thinking', ibid. 23 May 1958 (*SCMP* 1900).

[28] See further ch. 11.

emphasized during the Great Leap Forward. The belief that, as Mao expressed it, 'the tremendous energy of the masses' provided a foundation on which 'it is possible to accomplish any task whatsoever' was central to the whole philosophy behind the Great Leap.[29] The 'mass line' embodies three basic principles: that 'the party must represent the masses' interests', that 'one must trust in the masses' viewpoint and strength', and that 'one must use correct methods to lead the masses'. It was felt to be as relevant in the army as in civilian life, notwithstanding the army's more formal disciplinary structure and tighter organization. The view of some army officers that 'the mass line was only suited to the requirements of our army at a lower stage, and not to its structure at a higher stage' was firmly rejected.[30] The partial alienation of officers from men and the PLA from the civilian population would be rectified by the mass line, and the same techniques would ensure that military theory and science was more closely integrated with the actual reality and requirements of the situation.

The part which the 'mass line' played in the PLA's participation in production and economy campaigns, in measures to improve relations between the army and the people and between officers and men will be discussed below. Its effect upon military training was equally marked. The object of military training remained unchanged:

> to continue improving modern military techniques, and to learn the co-ordination of the various branches of the army in combat under the modern conditions of atom bombs, chemical warfare and guided missiles as well as in other complicated situations, so that the army may be ready at all times to deal with any emergency.[31]

But its methods were characterized by a greater degree of flexibility, improvisation, sinification, and rejection of conventional procedures. Textbooks, training manuals, and schedules were rewritten and revised in a more popular style to conform with the PLA's individual requirements. Training manœuvres discarded the Soviet-style emphasis upon classic positional warfare,

[29] Mao Tse-tung, statement to a reporter of the Hsinhua agency, 29 Sept. 1958, quoted in Schram, *Political Thought of Mao Tse-tung*, pp. 253–4.

[30] Ch'ao Hua, 'What is the mass line?' *CFCP*, 3 July 1956.

[31] 'New training program promulgated by General Department of Supervision of Training', *CFCP*, 16 Jan. 1958 (*SCMP* 1786).

and concentrated upon light but fast mobile warfare on more traditional revolutionary lines, taking into account the specific peculiarities of Chinese terrain and climate. It had, for instance, been observed that although most of China south of the Yangtze was composed of paddy, training manœuvres from the textbook had failed to appreciate the special features which this required. Greater importance was now attached to the need to prepare against surprise attack from the air, whether conventional or in the form of atomic or chemical warfare. Troops were therefore taught to operate in smaller units, to take fast evasive action, and to become adept at hand-to-hand fighting and guerrilla tactics. The principle of 'military democracy' required officers to take part at first hand in manœuvres, and all ranks to discuss and criticize tactics at group training meetings. Suggestions for improvements and innovations were also encouraged from the rank and file. Physical education was also popularized among officers and men, 'so as to improve their physical fitness, improve their combat skill, and foster courage, agility, cleverness and other desirable qualities'.[32]

While these ideas were perfectly sound in themselves, they seem to have been carried to excess, like many other innovations of the Great Leap period. It was, for instance, a sensible move to persuade officers to leave their desks and carry out inspections at company level to see whether their instructions matched requirements. The wisdom of making officers spend one month or more a year 'in the ranks', practising arms drill, growing vegetables, and polishing uniforms, was more questionable. The demands imposed by economy, production, and political-thought campaigns also conflicted with training programmes. Nevertheless, a high premium continued to be placed upon professionalism, and at the end of 1957 a 'Five-Year Training Programme' was launched, which called for all army officers to be transformed into professionals or basically professionals within five years. During the Great Leap, emphasis was again placed on raising

---

[32] Ibid. See also 'General P'eng Shao-hui on scientific advancement in military units', *Chung-kuo Ch'ing-nien Pao*, 3 Nov. 1956 (*SCMP* 1416); 'Good results in PLA training last year', NCNA, 11 Jan. 1957 (*SCMP* 1458); '1957 training of PLA starts', ibid. 15 Mar. 1957 (*SCMP* 1497); 'Many major improvements introduced in army training work', *CFCP*, 8 Aug. 1957 (*SCMP* 1692); 'To consummate training, we must first consummate training of army officers', ibid. 24 Jan. 1958 (*SCMP* 1743).

the standard of modern military techniques, on co-ordination of fighting under conditions of atomic, chemical, and missile warfare, and on technical education of field commanders and headquarters personnel. But in 1959 the time spent in training was shortened by two months, although the number of training courses was greatly increased, while in the military colleges and academies the proportion of political to military study was raised at the expense of the latter. These contradictory moves, coupled with the other non-military demands made on the PLA, only helped to increase confusion.[33]

ARMY OPPOSITION TO PARTY CONTROL

The moving force behind the multitude of reforms and campaigns with which the PLA was deluged was naturally the communist party, operating through its party committees, both within the army and in the localities where army units were stationed. It was necessary first of all to reorganize the party committees themselves in the PLA, which had grown accustomed to meet irregularly and to leave important decisions to the leading officers. In 1956 over 80 per cent of party branches at company level were said to have been reorganized, eliminating 'disunity between the party branches and the army companies'. Collective leadership was strengthened and criticism and self-criticism at general meetings of the party members also encouraged.[34] Army authorities were also required to co-operate more closely with local party authorities. As early as January 1954 the General Political Department had required army commands to delegate representatives to serve on local party committees and to ensure a regular exchange of information with them, but this had not been universally carried out. Liaison was now required not only over questions of good relations with the people, but also over the methods and extent of recruitment. In Chekiang Military Region, for instance, the provincial party committee was asked to 'strengthen leadership' over the military authorities, and to integrate military work into the province's annual plan.[35]

[33] This paragraph is based on the account of training during the Great Leap, in *Communist China 1949–59*, i. 222–4.
[34] 'Great achievements of party building in PLA in 1956', *CFCP*, 12 Jan. 1957 (*SCMP* 1616).
[35] T'an Cheng, 'Questions of political work . . .', *CB* 422, p. 20: 'Although the command of our army is highly centralized, since the modernization of our army, all

When Marshal P'eng and General T'an told the Party Congress in September 1956 about the serious deviations which needed to be rectified in the PLA, one was missing from the list. There was no suggestion that any element in the army was hostile to party leadership as such, although it was admitted that the effectiveness of such leadership had been allowed to lapse. But the cumulative effect of the numerous demands made on the PLA in the next two years appears either to have brought into the open opposition which was already latent, or to have created it anew. In 1957 the PLA, like all other sections of Chinese society, underwent the Hundred Flowers campaign and the 'rectification' which followed it. 'Poisonous anti-party weeds' were discovered in the PLA as elsewhere, although they were not given so much publicity. During the rectification movement, reference was made to those who took advantage of the method of criticism 'to attack us with the object of weakening our Party leadership and army discipline and of sabotaging our unity'.[36] Officers and men were called on to 'distinguish between right and wrong' and to hit back at the rightists who 'have published anti-Party, anti-socialist statements and are conducting anti-Party, anti-socialist activities in a vain attempt to usurp the leadership and overthrow the people's democratic dictatorship'.[37] By mid-1958, it was being alleged that

. . . purely military views, warlordism, and doctrinairism have revived among a part of the personnel. They assert that collective leadership of Party committees is not adapted to the requirements of modernization and regularization. One-sidedly stressing the suddenness and complexity of modern warfare, they assert that the system of Party committees will impede the better judgement and concentration of command. They even openly advocate liquidation of the system of Party committee leadership. Further, they liquidated and restricted the activities of Party committees in leadership and political work. While these views have not predominated in the whole army,

---

parts of our army are still required, as in the past, to accept the supervision of local party organization, government and people's organizations and must not reject such supervision on the plea of centralization of command'. See also 'Report of Chekiang Military Region on relations with local party and government officials', *CFCP*, 4 Dec. 1956.

[36] 'Party leadership is decisive factor which leads our army to victory' (*SCMP* 1588).

[37] Su Yü, 'Strengthen national defence, consolidate the fruits of victory of the revolution', *JMJP*, 1 Aug. 1957 (*SCMP* 1596).

N

they have caused certain ideological confusion and weakened the fine tradition of our army in practical work.[38]

It would be a mistake to conclude from this that there was ever open opposition in the PLA to the party as such. It seems in fact that both the criticism encouraged by the Hundred Flowers and its subsequent rectification was much smaller in scale than outside the army among students and the democratic parties.[39] Other statements make it clear that what was being objected to was not party control itself, but the policies which the party was trying to popularize within the PLA, and the time-consuming demands which these entailed, especially in the field of theoretical study. Politics was fine, as long as it did not get in their way.

There are those who concentrate excessively on modernization, and advocate the weakening of party leadership, and try to weaken political work. . . . They pay lip-service to political leadership, but they believe that modernization is not related to and is in a different class from politics. . . .

Some comrades often think: Politics in command; that means party committee leadership, officer/men unity, army/people unity, doing political theory education . . . in short, it's the business of the political organs.[40]

But by the beginning of the Great Leap in the summer of 1958, a dichotomy had begun to materialize between the party and some sections of the officer corps which was previously absent. The delicate balance between the military, social, and political roles of the PLA had begun to break down, with the party on the one hand emphasizing the political role, and opposition within the PLA emphasizing the military role. The party's point of view was summed up by Marshal Chu Teh, in an article written to commemorate Army Day 1958:

There are people who advocate an exclusively military viewpoint,

---

[38] 'Hold aloft the banner of the party committee system' (*SCMP* 1881).

[39] Only one rightist critic was identified by name in the senior ranks of the PLA. The director of the GPD's Cultural Dept was denounced as a 'bogus left-winger and a genuine right-winger' by the GPD's party committee ('True identity of Ch'en Yi revealed', *JMJP*, 1 Mar. 1958 (*SCMP* 1729)). It is clear that much of his case revolved around the decision to merge his department with the Propaganda Department. Ch'en was alleged to have complained that the Hundred Flowers movement was not allowed to flourish in the PLA.

[40] 'Oppose one-sided emphasis on modernisation', *CFCP*, editorial, 17 Aug. 1958.

who have a one-sided regard for military affairs and look down upon politics, have a one-sided high regard for vocation and technique and look down upon ideology, have a one-sided high regard for the role of individuals and neglect the collective strength of the Party and the masses. They only deal with tactics and technique, but not strategy; they only want the army but neglect the function of masses of the people; they only pay attention to national defence, but not to the significance of economic construction to national defence. In essence this is a kind of manifestation of bourgeois military ideas. This is contrary to Marxism-Leninism. They are of the opinion that politics should not take the lead.[41]

This was a serious indictment of the PLA, and it reflected the extent to which the PLA's relationship with the party had deteriorated during the past three years, in spite of—or perhaps because of—the numerous attempts which had been made to strengthen political control and restore 'revolutionary' practices.

[41] Chu Teh, 'People's Army, People's War', NCNA, 31 July 1958 (*CB* 514).

9
The PLA and Society

Since our Army is the army of the people, it must regularly maintain close relations with the masses, and nourish itself with what is acquired from the struggles waged by the masses. Unless this is done, the Army will be like a tree that has no root, a stream whose source has dried up, and will lose its vitality and combat strength.[1]

BY 1956 the communist party had become concerned at the number of 'contradictions' which were identified within the PLA and which were already felt to be threatening both the armed forces' traditional internal unity and its good relations with the people. In order to rectify these contradictions, the party turned to the revolutionary model established before 1949, and sought to revive the procedures and practices by which the army's internal and external social behaviour had been regulated in the past. This chapter will deal with the way in which these practices were revived, the mistakes and excesses to which they led, and will consider the extent to which they were still relevant to the PLA under the vastly changed circumstances of the mid-1950s. The revolutionary practices under discussion are the movement for PLA participation in production work, the economy campaign, the rectification of civilian grievances against the PLA, and the 'officers to the ranks' and other democratic measures introduced into the army's administration and structure.

PLA PRODUCTION WORK

The attempts made in 1950 to involve the PLA in large-scale production work had been abandoned as soon as China intervened in the Korean war, except for Sinkiang province where the PLA continued to expand its productive operations. The PLA Production and Construction Corps was only officially constituted in 1954, when it was estimated to number 140,000 men,

[1] Hsiao Hua, 'Participation in national construction is a glorious task of the People's Liberation Army', *Hung Ch'i*, 1 Aug. 1959 (*ECMM* 182).

but as early as March 1950 the North-west Military Region had detached 80,000–85,000 men from combat duty to work exclusively on production. These were mostly composed of units from General T'ao Chih-yüeh's Nationalist army, and from the Sinkiang Nationalities Army or 'Ili rebels', which had been reorganized into the PLA's First Field Army on their surrender. The PLA in Sinkiang launched an ambitious five-year irrigation plan in 1950, and its cadres personally supervised land reform, and later led the movements for mutual-aid teams and cooperatives. The majority of Sinkiang's state farms were started by the PLA, and by 1958 their acreage amounted to 30 per cent of the total arable land in the province or 20 per cent of the sown area. The Production Corps was divided into three sections: agriculture, industry, and mines. Impressive (though sometimes conflicting) statistics were given for the agriculture section's achievements in crops (cotton and grain), afforestation and irrigation, and soil conservation. The industrial section built a number of factories which were later turned over to the state. The mining section was responsible for the extraction of strategic minerals such as petroleum and coal and possibly uranium, of which the province had important reserves. Sinkiang was, however, a special case. From the first it had been regarded as an area of special economic significance. As General P'eng Teh-huai had reported to the Chinese People's Government Council in January 1950, it included at least one-third of China's territory while possessing only 5 per cent of her population. It contained petroleum and other mineral reserves which were ripe for development, as well as large areas of uncultivated land and a possible source of hydro-electric power in the upper Yellow river. He described Sinkiang as 'one of the industrial and defence bases for the construction of the new China'. Moreover the establishment of the PLA Production Corps, and the considerable migration of Chinese civilian labour to Sinkiang which took place, was partly intended as a measure of defence, in order to counterbalance and control the province's indigenous population of national minorities.[2]

[2] General P'eng Teh-huai (commander-in-chief of the North-west Military Region), report to Central People's Government Council, 8 Jan. 1950 (*FE*39). See further on the Sinkiang Production and Construction Corps *Chung-kung Wen-t'i*, iii. 50 ff.; 'The magnificent service rendered by PLA in Sinkiang cannot be obliterated by local nationalists', *Hsin-chiang Jih-pao*, 10 Jan. 1958 (*SCMP* 1750); Saifudin,

The concept of PLA production work in the country at large was not revived until the Korean war had come to an end. While the main emphasis continued to be placed upon the army's technical modernization, it was realized that this did not exempt the PLA from production work and from observing the same need for economy and restraint which was imposed upon the civilian sector of the country. In an article published on the eve of Army Day 1954, Su Yü, deputy chief of general staff, had made the point that modernization in itself was not enough under peacetime conditions.

To step up the modernization of our army it is necessary to be responsive to every need—that is to participate in the socialist construction of the fatherland, to carry out a strict economy drive, to eliminate waste, to care properly for weapons and equipment and to conserve materials and supplies. We should use our limited military funds only for the most urgent needs, for things that would directly raise our fighting power so as to conserve manpower, materials and capital for the industrial construction of the State.[3]

For the following year, however, the PLA continued to be chiefly preoccupied with its reorganization, the inauguration of conscription, and mass demobilization. Apart from the PLA Production and Construction Corps in Sinkiang, the army's contribution to non-military construction was only made in specific areas at times of flood, drought, or other emergencies. During the widespread floods of autumn 1954, for instance, troops in East China were reported to have saved 10,000 lives and to have contributed 1,300,000 man-days to the work of digging earth, repairing breaches in the dykes, and draining water from the land. In the North-west army units received special instructions to co-operate with the local authorities in flood prevention and control, and each soldier was asked to save one *liang* (1 oz.) of food daily for flood relief.[4]

The army first became involved in production on a systematic basis in 1956, as the tempo of agricultural collectivization in-

---

'Sinkiang's great achievements in agriculture in 10 years', *Chung-kuo Nung-pao*, 8 Oct. 1959 (*ECMM* 193); 'Production and reconstruction army corps in Sinkiang', *JMJP*, 31 July 1960 (*SCMP* 2318).

[3] *JMJP*, 31 July 1954 (*FE* 378).

[4] Nanking radio, 19 Oct. 1954; Sian radio 6 Sept. 1954: in *FE*, Econ. Supplements 136 & 130.

creased and China began to gather momentum for the Great Leap Forward. Following Mao Tse-tung's call for a speedy advance on the road to collectivization in his report *On Agricultural Co-operation* of July 1955, the party's Central Committee set new targets for the setting up of agricultural producer co-operatives (APC's). In January 1956 the Draft 12-Year National Programme for Agricultural Development was published, which raised the targets and demanded that collectivization should in the main be completed by 1958. In response to this, the PLA's Political Department drew up the 'Programme for Participation and Support by Army Units in the Agricultural Co-operative Movement and Agricultural Production', which enumerated twenty separate ways in which the army could 'support with practical actions' the Draft Programme. A summary of the Programme's twenty points reveals the wide variety of ways in which the PLA was called upon to support the collectivization programme. Moreover the Programme's scope is wider than the straightforward promotion of agricultural production. Its measures can be divided into two categories: those designed to make a specific PLA contribution to production, and those which were clearly aimed at improving relations with the local populace.[5]

---

[5] The following summary is taken from the text of the 'Programme for Participation and Support by Army Units in the Agricultural Co-operative Movement and Agricultural Production', NCNA, 8 Feb. 1956 (*SCMP* 1234):

1. Soldiers should persuade their dependants, relatives and friends to take the road of socialism, to join co-operatives, to increase production and efficiency.

2. 'In areas where army cadres are required to take part in construction and re-organisation of co-operatives (particularly in late liberated areas, border regions, islands along the coast and minority nationality areas), work teams of officers and men should be placed under the leadership of the local party committee to help in agricultural work. Officers should be specifically assigned to these areas to support socialist construction.

3. An economy drive will be launched throughout the army, to oppose extravagance and to conserve equipment. Soldiers will be encouraged to contribute to a 'patriotic savings campaign'.

4. Within the three years 1956–8 the army will raise the funds to establish 30 tractor stations to support agricultural production. Trained personnel for these stations will also be provided from the ranks of demobilized servicemen.

5. 'A system of contributing free labour in support of socialist construction shall be adopted.' Army units will, in conjunction with the local party committees, arrange a system of labour-days on which soldiers will take part in local construction. 'On the average each person should contribute from 5 to 7 free labour-days.'

6. The entire PLA will be mobilized during its spare time and holidays to elimin-

In addition, a third objective which was associated with the PLA's production movement soon received much greater emphasis, namely participation in production as a therapeutic method of combating erroneous attitudes within the PLA itself. As General T'an Cheng, deputy director of the General Political Department, told the Eighth Party Congress in September 1956,

for the army to help the people in production and take part in some social activities at their leisure hours will primarily do good to the army itself; because it will strengthen the mass outlook and labour outlook of the army personnel and will build closer relations with the people and strengthen the unity of the army and the people.[6]

ate the Four Pests (rats, sparrows, flies, and mosquitos). The militia will be organized on occasion to hunt down dangerous wild animals.

7. All military buildings and works are to be landscaped with trees, and the PLA will assist in afforestation schemes throughout the country.

8. Army units will make their human manure available for the use of local co-operatives (as fertilizer).

9. Military barracks are to be kept clean. The army medical corps should treat civilians and help to prevent epidemics.

10. Army units will protect and breed livestock, and avoid the slaughter of draft animals and calves. All army units stationed in the country or in small towns will raise hogs at the rate of one hog per fifty persons.

11. In times of flood, drought, tempest, or insect plague, local army units will be mobilized to fight the disaster and provide relief.

12. The army will help local co-operatives to set up primary schools and evening classes to combat illiteracy. Within the army all servicemen should on demobilization have reached junior primary school standard and have been taught to speak Mandarin.

13. Film projector units and cultural groups will tour the neighbouring district and put on shows according to a regular schedule.

14. Army signal units will help to set up broadcasting and telephone networks in rural districts. The army will allow civilian use of their communications poles and will service equipment and train maintenance personnel.

15. Military engineering workshops will help co-operatives to repair agricultural tools and machines.

16. The building of military electric power stations will be co-ordinated with local requirements.

17. Excessive requisition of land for building or training purposes is to be avoided.

18. Soldiers to be demobilized will be educated to prepare them for active participation in socialist construction. The army will liaise with local authorities to ensure that technical personnel are demobilized to areas where they are most needed.

19. Army officers should teach those dependants who are with them about 'the honour of performing labour', and should encourage them to join local co-operatives or take part in other productive labour.

20. Every army unit, office or school except those in the cities should be associated with a specific co-operative, and should maintain regular social and cultural contact with it.

[6] T'an Cheng, 'Questions of political work. . . .' (*CB* 422).

Once the principle of PLA production work as a social duty rather than as an economic contribution had been accepted, the way was open for a massive increase in the amount of time devoted to this work, which in turn met with opposition in the PLA. Already in 1956, according to T'an Cheng, 'a number of people take the view that for the army to help the people in production and take part in certain social activities in leisure hours will hinder training',[7] and their view was doubtless strengthened by the increasing demands made on the PLA by production work.

The standard method used to calculate the PLA's direct contribution to 'socialist reconstruction' since 1956 has been the number of man-days per annum devoted by PLA personnel to production work 'without compensation' or 'freely'. This, according to Article 5 of the Draft Programme, should be provided on fixed days by mutual arrangement between army units and local party authorities. The Draft Programme laid down that there should be an average contribution of 5–7 work-days per person. This would have meant a total contribution by the 2½ million strong PLA of between 12½ and 17½ million man-days for 1956. In fact, the published figure for 1956 was only just over 4 million man-days, which suggests that there was a considerable volume of resistance to the production programme. The figure rose sharply to 20 million in 1957, and almost unbelievably to 59 million in 1958. This last figure meant an average contribution by every PLA soldier and officer of almost one month's 'free' labour. It is of course possible that this was one of the many statistics inflated by the Great Leap Forward, and that the original target figure of 30 million set for 1958 is nearer the mark.

In 1959 the target was raised to a minimum of half a month's 'free' labour in socialist construction. A directive of the PLA's Political Department called on officers and men to spend 'one to two months a year' in production, of which half the time should be used for production for army purposes, and the other half for civilian production.[8] If the official figure of 44 million man-days for 1959 is accurate, then the PLA achieved the minimum total consistent with this directive (i.e. an average of just under 15 man-days per PLA person of civilian production work). Pro-

---

[7] Ibid. See further Joffe, *Party and Army*, pp. 84–87.

[8] 'PLA programme for armed forces to join in construction', NCNA, 25 Feb. 1959 (*SCMP* 1963).

duction in 1960 was maintained at about the same level, but it fell by almost exactly half in 1961. Three years later, it had declined to a little above the 1956 total. Thus the army's direct participation in production had described a curve which paralleled almost exactly the rise and fall of the Great Leap Forward.

PLA 'Uncompensated' Participation in Production Work

1956	4,050,000[a]
1957	20,000,000[b]
1958 (projected)	30,000,000[b]
(completed)	59,000,000[c]
1959	44,000,000[d]
1960	46,000,000[e]
1961	22,780,000[f]
1962	—
1963	8,500,000[g]
1964	5,410,000[h]*

* Agricultural production only

Sources:

[a] NCNA, 25 Dec. 1956 (*SCMP* 1443).

[b] NCNA, 18 Feb. 1958 (*SCMP* 1724).

[c] Hsiao Hua, 'Participation in national construction is a glorious task of the PLA', *Hung Ch'i*, 1 Aug. 1959 (*ECMM* 182).

[d] Fu Chung, 'Achievements made by armed forces in support of socialist construction', *JMJP*, 6 Apr. 1960 (*CB* 624).

[e] 'Chinese armymen active in production work', NCNA, 27 Jan. 1961 (*SCMP* 2430).

[f] NCNA, 3 Feb. 1962 (*SCMP* 2682).

[g] NCNA, 30 Jan. 1964 (*FE*(2) Weekly Suppl. No. 250).

[h] Peking radio, 28 Jan. 1965 (*FE*(2) Weekly Suppl. No. 302).

Army support for production until the Great Leap Forward of 1958 consisted in the main of providing manpower and technical assistance to the agricultural co-operatives. In 1956 large numbers of men were reported to have assisted the co-operatives in 'reclaiming wasteland, sowing, hoeing and reaping'. Others built reservoirs, helped with afforestation work, sponsored evening classes and health clinics, serviced tractors and other farm tools. Army transport was lent to civil construction sites, while engineers helped to build water-conservancy works. Similar activities were reported on an increasing scale in 1957 and 1958. In the latter year it was claimed that the PLA had built over 20,000 water-conservancy projects, contributed nearly 16,000 million catties of natural fertilizer to local agriculture, loaned 8,800 trucks to assist in steel production, harvested 460,000,000 catties of vegetables, kept over 480,000 pigs, donated over 3,000 tractors and power units, and serviced almost half a million machine tools and parts. The air force created artificial rain over 40,000 hectares of land, sprayed crops with 50,000 kg. of insecticide, and flew 1,510,000 ton-km. in support of production in two months alone.

During 1958–9 the emphasis shifted to support for industrial construction. In Nanking alone, 82 large factories were built or extended with PLA aid. 3,000 officers and men helped to build Canton's General Railway Station. In 1959 the railway corps worked on 25 different railway lines; other units laid 415 km. of railway track and built 11,600 km. of motor roads. In September 1958 the Military Affairs Committee issued a special directive to the army, calling for their all-out support in the campaign to increase iron and steel production. Four thousand army trucks were to be seconded to the Ministry of Metallurgy. Army units were to organize the collection of scrap metal, and to prepare inventories of obsolete aeroplanes and engines for disposal. It was claimed that the army collected over 100,000 tons of scrap metal, and produced in its own furnaces 154,000 tons of steel, in the last three months of 1958 alone.

During the natural disasters of floods and droughts in 1960–1, PLA voluntary labour was mainly devoted to relief work and agriculture. In the busy farming seasons, when peasants were working against the clock and the weather to sow or reap in time, 'most armed forces units had their training discontinued temporarily, and all soldiers, horses and carts were mobilized to work together'. A total of 24,000 army technicians went 'deep into the country' to repair and service over 100,000 farm implements. By 1963 the pressure and the publicity for army production work had been relaxed, and it was now described as a 'spare-time activity', to be engaged in during off-duty hours as long as it did not interfere with training and other duties. [9]

[9] For annual accounts of the PLA's achievements in production, see 'Liberation Armymen give great support to agricultural cooperativization', NCNA, 25 Dec.

Less well publicized than the activities quoted above, but probably of greater value to agricultural production, was the transfer of army cadres and work teams to co-operatives as specified in point 2 of the 1956 Draft Programme. The transfer of military cadres to play a 'spearhead' role in social and economic reform had been a regular practice since Liberation, especially in the 'new liberated areas' in the North-west and South-west where reforms met with most resistance. This was in addition to demobilized servicemen who were also expected to take the lead in land reform and other mass movements. In Hunan, for instance, 100,000 servicemen were 'scattered over the villages to defend and take part in land reform', while 'land reform work teams' totalling 24,000 soldiers in all were sent into the countryside. One account tells us that

> After studying the main course and policy of land reform, they directly took part in the work of land reform. Soldiers swelled the ranks of reformers and expanded the propaganda teams. Comrades of the land reform teams ate and lived and worked with the poor peasants, shed tears of class hostility together with the peasants, and waged merciless struggles against the landlord class.[10]

During the first year of liberation many army cadres had been transferred to work in local administration. These were known as 'cadres transferred to civilian occupation' and were registered as reserve officers. The conscription law of 1955 also provided for 'detached' officers. These were active officers who were assigned by the Ministry of Defence to take up 'work of a military character in a non-military department', for instance military instructors in schools or militia organizers in the country co-operatives. This practice of assigning military officers to civilian occupations, whether 'transferred' or 'detached', in other words whether shifted to the reserve or remaining on active service, was

---

1956 (*SCMP* 1443); 'PLA units make great contributions in aid of national construction', ibid. 12 Feb. 1958 (*SCMP* 1724); 'Officers and men of armed forces establish reputation on economic front', *JMJP*, 13 Jan. 1959 (*SCMP* 1944); 'Chinese PLA active in national construction', NCNA, 4 Jan. 1960 (*SCMP* 2174); 'Chinese armymen active in productive work', ibid. 27 Jan. 1961 (*SCMP* 2430); 'PLA renders great help to agricultural production', ibid. 3 Feb. 1962 (*SCMP* 2682); 'PLA armymen help people's communes win good harvests', ibid. 30 July 1963 (*SCMP* 3032).

[10] 'Eight years of the Chinese PLA in Hunan', *Chang-sha hsin Hu-nan Pao*, 1 Aug. 1957 (*SCMP* 1619).

widespread during land reform and co-operativization. It is also the only feature of the PLA's production campaign of the middle 1950s to survive unmodified to this day. Since 1963 army cadres have been seconded in large numbers to commercial and industrial enterprises, as part of the nation-wide movement to 'learn from the PLA'.[11] The more publicized but probably less useful aspects of the production campaign have meanwhile been drastically curtailed.

PLA ECONOMY CAMPAIGN

Attempts to cut down the military budget had been halted by the Korean war. As Liu Shao-ch'i told the Eighth Party Congress:

> One important way of increasing our fund for construction is to economize more on military and administrative expenses. The Central Committee of the Party had already decided on this policy in 1950. But with the outbreak of the Korean . . . war, it has not been carried out earlier.[12]

While military expenditure in 1955 as a percentage of the annual budget had steadily declined since 1950 (from 41·53 per cent in 1950 to 24·30 per cent in 1955), it had more than doubled in absolute terms (from 2,827 to 6,500 million yuan). This was due both to inflation and to the combined effects of expenditure on the Korean war and on modernization. From 1955 to 1958 not only did the military proportion of budgetary expenditure continue to decline (to 15·12 per cent) but for the first time the actual figure fell by almost one-quarter (to 5,000 million yuan).[13] Since the end of the Korean war the army had already been frequently urged to cut down expenditure and practise economy. In autumn 1953, for instance, a patriotic economy campaign was launched throughout the PLA. In the South-west Military Region army units were called on 'to carry out an extensive propaganda drive to oppose the detrimental capitalist concept and way of administering affairs'. Financial departments were ordered to curtail excess expenditure and retrench unnecessary personnel. In the navy an austerity campaign was launched to

---

[11] See further ch. 12, p. 257.

[12] Quoted in 'Building the army with industry and thrift', *CFCP* editorial, 16 Dec. 1956 (*SCMP* 1476).

[13] For detailed figures, see Table 7 (p. 309).

improve techniques and reduce accidents, economize on materials, and save money for the purchase of national bonds.[14] It was later claimed that in the four years 1953–6 the PLA had 'saved over 1,400 million yuan for the state by means of cutting down their budgets and checking their stores'—over 6 per cent of total expenditure in that period.[15] But this was clearly not enough for the frugal spirit of 1956, and the PLA increasingly found itself called on to join in the nation-wide 'Production Increase and Austerity campaign', which had been launched with the purpose of increasing the rate of capital accumulation in order to speed the process of 'socialist construction'.

In March 1956 all PLA army units were called on to plan their budgets systematically and with an eye to economy. The old attitude of 'the more money the more we do, the less money the less we do' was to be liquidated. In future the military commander of a unit would personally sign the unit's budget, which should be drawn up on the basis of sound and reliable statistics. Units should cut down on unnecessary expenses, even if such expenses did not cause the budget to be exceeded. The new scheme would require the closest co-operation between the financial departments and the working units, and officers should cease to regard questions of finance as 'too troublesome'.[16] In the winter of 1956 attention to economy in the PLA was renewed, since defence expenditure was due to be cut by 600 million yuan in 1957, and results of economy campaigns in the previous year were judged disappointing.

In an editorial of 15 December 1956, the *Liberation Army Newspaper* admitted that 'there does exist a contradiction between the demand to spend less of the state's funds and the demand to definitely ensure the needs of national defence construction'. The way to solve this contradiction, it continued, 'is to resolutely carry out the rigid practice of economy'. The editorial complained that the significance of economy was not yet fully understood, and it listed various instances of waste and carelessness: 43 million yuan had been wasted on engineering projects for frontier defence posts in the last year; there had been

---

[14] Chungking radio, 29 Sept. 1953 (*FE*, Econ. Suppl. No. 82); Peking radio, 24 Jan. 1954 (*FE* 334).

[15] 'Great achievements of PLA's practice of economy to aid construction during past few years', NCNA, 26 July 1957 (*SCMP* 1588).

[16] *CFCP*, editorial, 22 Mar. 1956.

'alarming' losses of arms and equipment. Some units 'expanded their establishments at will', and in Peking alone there were 3,085 extra-establishment personnel. Oil and grain had been wasted, and there were cases of theft of state property. It criticized the habit of paying lip-service to the economy campaigns, so that the situation would improve for a short time and then rapidly decline again. In future, it insisted, 'the spirit of economy must permeate all concrete tasks'. It specified in detail the types of activities and equipment where economy should be practised, and called for the drawing up of economy plans and stricter supervision by financial departments.[17]

Economies which were initiated varied from the most trivial to ones with serious implications for military efficiency and morale, ranging from 'the pouring out of every drop of the remaining oil from empty tins' to cuts in salary. Major economies were effected in the three fields of commissariat, logistics, and training. Rations were cut by one *liang* of grain per day in 1957, and again in 1958. A special directive was issued to encourage army units to raise hogs and livestock. The consumption of coal for various purposes was cut by between 10 and 20 per cent. The quality of uniforms was lowered, and their period of use was extended. By the end of 1957 it was claimed that the PLA had saved 50,000 tons of coal and 60 million catties of grain, and had raised 200,000 hogs and 110,000 head of cattle.

More important economies were effected in logistics and supplies. Expenditure by the army's Rear Services Department was to be cut by one-third in 1957, and further 'drastic cuts' were decided upon for 1958. It was admitted by General Hung Hsueh-chih, the Department's director, that because of this 'supply of some military supplies cannot fully satisfy the needs of the army units', but he still believed that the army could devise 'ways and means' to do the same things with less money. Some at least of these ways and means must have had adverse repercussions upon the army's efficiency. Fuel economies were described as 'startling', amounting to as much as 25 per cent among many units. In order to achieve this, the army had to 'strictly limit the use of motor cars and . . . transport supplies as far as possible by horse carts, boats and railway trains'. The life of barrack-room equip-

---

[17] 'Building the army with industry and thrift', ibid. editorial, 15 Dec. 1956 (*SCMP* 1476).

ment was arbitrarily extended by one year, and in 1957 building plans were drastically cut. In the construction of one barracks, economies were effected by cutting down on 'clubs, crêches and reception centres for servicemen's families'. By 1958 it had been decided that the construction of military barracks should be 'basically stopped'. Building construction of all descriptions was to be reduced by 10 per cent. The army's chief of staff, General Su Yü, celebrated Army Day for 1957 in an article which specifically singled out 'building projects such as sanitoriums, auditoriums, crêches and primary schools for the children of military personnel' as projects which should be 'shelved'. This was hardly language calculated to raise the morale of serving officers.[18]

Perhaps the most serious economies were those carried out in the field of training, under the new slogan of 'drill troops industriously and thriftily'. It was made clear that where necessary the economy plan should take precedence over training requirements. Some economies can only have had an adverse effect on safety standards—for instance, the practice of cutting down the ground testing of aircraft engines before take-off; or of prolonging the life of equipment. Others must have directly affected the quality of training. Military schools reduced the number of live ammunition exercises as well as the number of units taking part and the amount of ammunition consumed on the exercise. Officers and men were required to make many of their own training implements with their own hands. Straw ropes were used for assault courses instead of barbed wire. Criticism was voiced against young officers, fresh from training school, who rejoined their units and brought a 'bad influence' to them by asking for 'big quantities of materials and equipment'.[19]

RECTIFICATION OF CIVILIAN GRIEVANCES

The production and economy campaigns were not regarded as

[18] Su Yü, 'Strengthen national defence, consolidate the fruits of victory of the revolution' (*SCMP* 1596).
[19] The above is drawn from: Gen. Hung Hsueh-chih, 'Industrious and thrifty army-building measures', NCNA, 24 Feb. 1957 (*SCMP* 1481); 'PLA units tap economy potentiality', ibid. 23 Feb. 1957 (*SCMP* 1486); 'PLA directive on movement for production increase and economy', ibid. 13 Apr. 1957 (*SCMP* 1518); 'Great achievements of PLA's practice of economy to aid construction during past few years', ibid. 26 July 1957 (*SCMP* 1568); Kan Szu-ch'i, 'Army building with diligence and thrift and participation of servicemen in national production', ibid. 6 Feb. 1958 (*SCMP* 1724); *CFCP* editorial, 24 Jan. 1958 (*SCMP* 1743).

sufficient in themselves to bring about the improvement in relations between the PLA and the people which was felt to be so necessary in 1956. It was felt that in its new role as a garrison army, exclusively concerned with national defence, the PLA had allowed the traditional links between it and the people to become dissipated, and that specific popular grievances against the armed forces had been created which called for urgent attention. As the *People's Daily* observed in an editorial:

> With the progress of defence construction, the army will concentrate its forces to strengthen modern military construction and raise the level of military science and technology. It is also necessary to concentrate the garrisoning and training. Because of this, inevitably the army will have less direct contact with the masses. But on account of this, some army units do not show the same concern for the interests of the people as they did in the past, do not maintain the same close connections with local Party and Government organs as in the past, and do little or no mass work.[20]

Lo Jung-huan, director of the PLA's Political Department, complained that some officers had reached the conclusion that 'there is now no need for the tradition of unanimity of army men and civilians, and support of the government and love of the people', and he listed some of the grievances held by civilians against the army—over the requisition of land, luxurious standards of living, disregard of road safety by army vehicles, etc. He claimed that some officers were totally indifferent to the well-being and needs of the civilian population.[21]

Strenuous efforts were made to settle these grievances. To correct what was quaintly described as the 'irrational' tendency of occupying civilian houses, 72,400 such houses were returned to their original owners in 1957; rent was paid up where it was overdue, and compensation made for damages inflicted over the past years. Local provincial authorities found it necessary to draw up regulations on army rentals, which suggests that previously accommodation had been requisitioned without payment. The army also returned 175,000 mow of land (28,875 acres); much of this had originally been appropriated in the

---

[20] 'Support the army and honour the dependants! support the government and love the people!', *JMJP* editorial, 17 Jan. 1957 (*SCMP* 1459).

[21] Lo Jung-huan, 'Continue to promote the glorious tradition of the Chinese PLA', ibid. 1 Aug. 1955 (*SCMP* 1106).

Korean war, and was now in excess to requirements.[22] Meetings were held with local authorities to clear up disagreements over the supply of grain to army units, and in some cases army rations were cut in order to ease the burden on the local population. Army delegates were sent to sit on local party and administrative committees; civilian authorities and ordinary people were 'invited' to visit army units and make 'criticisms and suggestions'. A variety of minor grievances were also ironed out; officers stopped using army vehicles on private business or to transport their children to and from school. The practice of reserving theatre and cinema tickets for commanding officers was abolished. There was even a suggestion that some army officers had attempted to exert a *droit de seigneur*. According to General T'an Cheng,

> The officers of some units sought too many spouses in one area to the dissatisfaction of the local populace. It has been suggested that the officers must observe the following three points in seeking wives. First, they must not seek wives in schools. Second, they must not use money or other material goods as their means in getting wives. Third, they must not interfere with other people's marriages.[23]

More seriously, General T'an observed that in some companies 'the contradiction within the ranks of the people' was solved by 'the methods of solving contradictions with the enemies'—a remark which implies the improper use of force and violence against the civilian population.

One important source of friction was the wide differential between the living standards of officers' families and of the remainder of the civilian population. Since 1955, when PLA had adopted the salary system instead of paying wages in kind, the number of officers' dependants who joined them at their stations had increased by 150 per cent—from 330,000 in 1956 to over 780,000 in 1957. This created a demand for housing, schools, and supplies which naturally gave rise to resentment among the civilian population on whom the burden fell. In November 1957

---

[22] In July 1961 the Rear Services Dept reported that 300,000 mow of land (49,500 acres) had been returned to the people's communes. The army still retained 1,660,000 mow (*c.* 250,000 acres) of land, of which nearly half was waste land which it had reclaimed in 1960. The remainder is presumably largely accounted for by PLA holdings in Sinkiang (*KTTH*, 26 Aug. 1961 (Cheng, p. 744)).

[23] 'General T'an Cheng on question of rectification in army', NCNA, 12 May 1957 (*SCMP* 1547).

the Political Department of the PLA issued a special notification to deal with this 'very abnormal phenomenon'. All dependants except those with nowhere to go were to return to their place of origin. Since 80 per cent of them were 'working women from rural villages', it was hoped that this would not only normalize the situation at military establishments but also assist production at home. Meanwhile the local authorities were ordered by the State Council to be prepared to integrate army dependants and to welcome them home.[24] For the future, it was decided, 'in principle, dependants are not supposed to stay together with members of the armed forces'. Those few who stayed should be provided for by the officers concerned. Normally, officers would only be allowed to see their families during their annual leave. Within a very short time it was claimed that one-third of the army's dependants had left for home. By March of the following year 633,000 dependants were scheduled to have left the army for the rural areas to do productive work.[25] There was, however, a hard core of malcontents 'who hanker after the urban life or are unwilling to part with their husbands, thereby creating a conflicting sentiment'.[26]

The disparity between the army and civilian standards of living was lessened in other ways. Some officers' salaries were reduced—those of divisional level and above from 1957 onwards—although those of regimental level and below were not revised because of 'the numerous problems which are yet to be looked into'.[27] Ostentatious spending was also discouraged, and before the Spring Festival of 1957, the army newspaper called on all officers to

refrain from purchasing meat during the Spring Festival, and also to make less purchases of other supplies needed for the festive season, so that more supplies of meat and other festive needs may be made available to the people and ranks of the army.[28]

[24] NCNA, 27 Nov. 1957, various reports (*SCMP* 1668).
[25] 'PLA units effect tremendous achievements in penetrative rectification and improvement', ibid. 20 Feb. 1958 (*SCMP* 1724).
[26] 'A measure of important revolutionary significance', *JMJP*, 28 Nov. 1957 (*SCMP* 1668).
[27] 'Officers of regimental level and below not to have salary revision this year', ibid., 26 Feb. 1957 (*SCMP* 1625).
[28] 'Army paper calls on officers to refrain from meat purchases during spring festival', NCNA, 12 Jan. 1957 (*SCMP* 1460).

'MILITARY DEMOCRACY'

In the same speech at the Party Congress of September 1956 in which General T'an Cheng discussed the 'deviation' of estrangement between the army and the people, he also listed three other 'deviations' which affected the PLA's internal cohesion. These were:

1. Neglecting the tradition of unity of officers and men and unity of the higher and lower levels.
2. Neglecting democracy.
3. Method of leadership often characterized by stress of administrative orders, neglect of ideological work and departure from the mass line.

According to T'an, relations between officers and men and between the higher and lower levels were not so intimate as they had been. Officers tended to show no concern for the enlisted men, to abuse their powers over them, and to substitute punishment for education. The 'three-point democracy' (political, military, and economic democracy) had been 'pigeonholed' in many cases. The rank and file and junior officers were given no chance to voice their opinions. The methods of leadership had become increasingly 'divorced from reality and from the masses'. There was a prevalent attitude that 'the decisions of the superiors always leave nothing to be desired and that all that is required is to carry them out'. Much of the blame for this development was attributed to an excessive preoccupation on the part of the army cadres with technical training and modernization, and the growth of tendencies, enhanced by the new systems of ranks and honours, towards conceit and arrogance. It was said that

the conception of honour and position is slowly gaining prominence, and some people become very particular over the question of ranks and grades, and over the question of personal treatment. Some people exhibit the habits of a 'big boss', giving themselves away to pomp and splendour, asking to live in big mansions and not willing to live in huts and simple dwellings, looking for space and comfort in their offices and living quarters. Such ideological trends and working style are incompatible with the traditional working style of industry and simplicity of the PLA.[29]

---

[29] 'General Su Yü on contradictions within army in report to Chungking armymen', NCNA (Chungking), 22 May 1957 (*SCMP* 1539).

T'an Cheng criticized the erroneous view that 'political work should guarantee the prestige of officers', and that public criticism would damage their prestige. On the contrary, he emphasized, prestige could only be gained through hard work and approval by the masses, not through the efforts of others or by artificial means. Discipline must be observed and enforced, but it too could only be maintained through the voluntary efforts of the rank and file, by practising self-criticism and by raising their level of political consciousness. It could not be maintained solely by 'the control and supervision of the lower level by the upper level'.[30]

In the rectification movement which followed the Hundred Flowers of early 1957, and in which the PLA was as much involved as was the civilian population, the question of relations between officers and men was high on the list. Officers' privileges were curtailed, and some disciplinary regulations—for instance, 'certain salutation addresses in classrooms'—were abolished. Officers and cadres, especially those described as 'intellectuals' who came under fire during the rectification movement, were said to have enthusiastically 'volunteered' for transfer to lower army levels, or service on remote frontiers and in combat areas. One of the decisions of the PLA's political work conference, convened by the General Political Department in January 1958, was the 'transfer of cadres to lower levels', according to the theory that 'it is the characteristic of a revolutionist that he be equally at home in a high position or in a low position, as the governor or as the governed'. The problem of relations between officers and men would be solved by cadres 'living with the companies and marching on foot with the infantrymen'. Commanders of armies, divisions, and regiments, it was said, 'generally drill, labour, sweep away snow, fetch firewood together with their subordinates and help the work in the kitchen'.[31]

The participation of senior officers in military training was widely publicized. 'They wore the uniform, colour badges and steel helmet and other paraphernalia of the ordinary soldier.' They personally took part in rugged field manœuvres known as 'groping, crawling, rolling, fist-fighting, grabbing and sneak-

---

[30] P'eng Teh-huai, 'The Chinese PLA' (*CB* 422).
[31] 'PLA units effect tremendous achievements in penetrative rectification and improvement' (*SCMP* 1742).

ing'. All officers were required to take part in the course, which would last for two weeks.[32] Experimental companies were promoted, in which cadres served as enlisted men, or 'exercise the duties of an officer in daily work but . . . treat themselves as enlisted men in all drills'.[33] As a result of those and other hectic exercises, it was claimed that 'the somewhat estranged relations between officers and men, the result of the regularising and modernising construction of the armed forces, have . . . improved'. The rank and file were inspired by their officers, in whom they saw 'the old spirit of the Eighth Route Army'. They commented: 'Formerly, cadres only made gestures, now they do the actual work'. And those who used to grumble in the past now changed their minds, saying 'it is really not easy to be a cadre . . .'.[34]

As the Great Leap Forward got under way, this practice of temporary demotion received fresh impetus with the 'Officers to the Ranks' movement, announced by the Political Department on 20 September 1958. All cadres were required to spend a month annually in the ranks as ordinary soldiers, except for the aged, infirm, and sick. Young cadres who had not been ordinary soldiers or had not worked at the basic levels would begin by spending six months or even the whole of their first year in the ranks.[35] By February 1959 over 150,000 officers had 'gone to the ranks' including more than 70 generals.

Once sent to the company level, they eat, live, work, do manual labour, and pass their leisure moments together with the ordinary enlisted men regardless of the rank they hold. They have to obey the orders of the commanders of the platoons or sections, just as if they were ordinary privates, strictly observe the various rules and regulations of the companies, ask for leave of absence when they want to go out and cancel their leave when they return, observe the codes of etiquette, and try to excel in everything. They have to do with eagerness all chores in the companies, including the drawing of water, sweeping of floors and grounds, cleaning spitoons, cleaning the lavatories, and so forth. These appear to be trivial matters; but the

---

[32] Reports in *CFCP*, 24 Jan. 1958 (*SCMP* 1743).

[33] 'PLA "experimental companies" worthwhile', NCNA, 28 Mar. 1958 (*SCMP* 1750).

[34] 'Traditional unity between PLA officers and men further promoted', *JMJP*, 4 June 1958 (*SCMP* 1792); 'Working style of PLA officers undergoes great changes during rectification campaign', ibid. 24 June 1958 (*SCMP* 1812).

[35] ' "Serve in the ranks" system for all PLA cadres', NCNA, 21 Sept. 1958 (*SCMP* 1861).

cadres would have to thoroughly abandon their superior and bureaucratic airs if they are to perform their duties well.[36]

REAPPRAISAL OF PLA MASS MOVEMENTS

The value of the mass campaigns outlined above in which the PLA was involved from 1956 onwards and during the Great Leap Forward must be regarded as equivocal. The wholesale application of techniques which had been evolved during the revolutionary period without regard for their current relevance appears only to have intensified mistrust within the army towards the party's policies. We know that one of the contributory factors in the dismissal of the Minister of Defence, Marshal P'eng Teh-huai, in September 1959, was his opposition to the extent to which these measures were carried.[37] While the fundamental idea behind these campaigns—the need for closer association between the armed forces and the people—was still valid, the somewhat indiscriminate way in which they were carried out may be presumed to have largely negated their value. It was openly admitted that the non-military demands made on the PLA during the Great Leap Forward had created some difficulties. General Hsiao Hua wrote in August 1959 that:

There is a definite conflict between participation in national construction and training in their respective demands for time. . . . Needless to say, as the Army is an armed combat organization, it must carry out its task as a 'work force' in such a way that its task as a 'combat force' is not affected. . . . It is obviously wrong to think that, as no war is going on at present, the Army should exert itself mainly in the direction of production construction, or to set too high requirements concerning the Army's participation in construction and labour production. Anything that may weaken war preparations and training tasks is impermissible.[38]

In line with this more realistic attitude, army production work in 1961 was cut, as we have seen, to half the 1959 level, and has since continued to decline. The methods by which the PLA economized on its expenditure became more modest in scale and more compatible with military requirements. While training and

---

[36] Ch'en Tsai-tao, 'Army officers, upholding their fine tradition, go to the companies to serve as privates', *JMJP*, 27 Apr. 1959 (*CB* 579).

[37] See further below, pp. 225.

[38] Hsiao Hua, 'Participation in national construction is a glorious task of the PLA', *Hung Ch'i*, 1 Aug. 1959 (*ECMM* 182).

equipment levels were badly affected during the years of hard-ship in 1960–1 by shortages in production and the cessation of Soviet aid, they no longer suffered from mass economy drives. Thrift and productive work were now encouraged only in limited areas where they would personally benefit those involved. Instead of cultivating other people's land, the PLA now culti-vated its own. In one division visited by Edgar Snow in 1960, 1,700 acres of land were cultivated, enabling the guaranteed ration to be fixed at one-third more than the civilian ration. No doubt this form of agricultural work was more acceptable to the armed forces than the haphazard and uncompensated work per-formed for the benefit of the civilian population in previous years.[39] The scale of economy was shifted from the level of equipment and major expenditure to the personal level. 'Per-sonal frugality' was popularized by the story of the now legend-ary 'Good Eighth Company on Nanking Road', a Shanghai PLA company whose parsimonious habits were widely broadcast throughout the mass media. Once again this kind of personal economy (switching lights off, mending clothes, etc.) was more easily comprehensible to the individual involved than the major economies which previous campaigns had called for.[40]

[39] *The Other Side of the River* (1963), pp. 288–9. Available issues of the *KTTH* for Jan.–Aug. 1961 reveal a marked lack of emphasis on army production assistance to civilians. Such assistance appears to be mainly confined to emergency help for 'disaster areas', where apart from helping in production, the army is called upon to 'spread relief, and cure disease; assist the local government to maintain social order and pay serious attention to maintaining cordial relations between the soldiers and the people' (directive of the Military Affairs Committee and the General Political Dept for 1961, *KTTH*, 1 Jan. 1961 (Cheng, p. 5)). A rather per-functory reference to production work in 1960 merely claims that 'many work hours' were contributed by the army (ibid. 19 Apr. 1961 (Cheng, p. 440)).

The major emphasis is placed upon army production for internal purposes as a means towards partial army economic self-sufficiency. According to a report of the Rear Services Dept, in 1960 the army opened over 700 farms of its own, 'thus improving life and reducing its dependence upon supplies from the market'. 'Sideline production' resulted in the raising of nearly 3 million domestic fowls, 300,000 sheep, 50,000 cows, and well over a million hogs, all of which were con-sumed by the army (ibid. 1 Jan. 1961 (Cheng, pp. 19–25)). The Department hoped in 1961 'to supply all the meat and vegetables we need ourselves, and a part of the grain and oil we shall need'. Large-scale production of substitute foods was encouraged. By July 1961, it was reported that living conditions in most army units were much better than in the previous winter, physical health had im-proved and outbreaks of oedema had been basically cured (ibid., 1 Feb. & 26 Aug. 1961 (Cheng, pp. 194–9, 743–50)).

[40] 'An account of the "Good Eighth" Company on Nanking road', *Chung-kuo Ch'ing-nien Pao* (Chinese Youth Paper), 30 Mar. 1963 (*SCMP* 2965). Members of

The tempo of the 'Officers to the Ranks' movement slackened from 1960 onwards, although this practice has not been altogether discarded. Indeed, by December 1962 it was claimed that more than 771,000 army officers had served as privates in the ranks 'at one time or another'.[41] The absence of reference to the movement in the previous two years does, however, suggest that this figure is exaggerated, or that the definition of 'to the ranks' is somewhat elastic. During these years officers continued to be urged to 'go to the basic level', but with a different purpose in mind from that of the 'Officers to the Ranks' movement. The latter had been intended to purify the officer corps itself of tendencies towards 'élitism' and 'bourgeois military thinking'. The new measures instituted in 1960 and later were essentially designed to strengthen leadership over the basic-level companies. PLA officers, we are told, established 'base points at lower levels', whose purpose was 'to transmit the orders of the higher authorities to the lower levels promptly and to reflect the conditions at the lower levels to the upper levels quickly'.[42] Again we are told that 'PLA leadership organs at the regimental level turn to the companies, strike root at the basic level, and exercise dynamic leadership'.[43] In other words, the purpose behind bringing officers and men 'face to face' at the company level was no longer to discipline and reform the officers, but to enable them to exercise more effective leadership over the rank and file. With this very different purpose in mind, one may wonder whether the demotion of officers to the ranks continued to be as thoroughgoing as it had been during the Great Leap Forward. Certainly, it receives much less prominence in reports and policy statements, and it is probable that like other PLA mass movements it was carried out less rigorously from 1960 onwards.

---

the Good Eighth Company carried needle and thread to keep their clothes in repair; they wore sandals to economize on shoe leather; they made brooms out of reeds and dustpans out of scrap metal. They cut each other's hair, and mended each other's clothes. Their motto was 'Save for the state a grain of rice, a drop of water, a unit of electricity, one cent of money and one inch of cloth'. Their achievements are narrated at length in *Nan-ching lu-shang hao-pa-lien* (Peking, 1963).

[41] Kan Wei-han, 'A talk on the practice of army cadres going to companies to serve as privates', *JMJP*, 29 July 1963 (*SCMP* 3042).

[42] 'PLA leading cadres establish base points at lower levels', ibid. 22 July 1961 (*SCMP* 2552).

[43] Ibid. 25 Mar. 1962 (*SCMP* 2719).

On the evidence of official statements, therefore, 'deviations' emerged within the PLA sometime in 1955, leading to a succession of vigorous measures in order to rectify them. These deviations had basically disappeared by 1959, and the measures were correspondingly reduced. The official time-span of deviations dates roughly from August 1955, when Marshal Lo Jung-huan, in an article already referred to, complained that the traditions of the PLA had been gravely weakened, to August 1959, when General Hsiao Hua stated that as a result of the PLA's participation in mass construction all the erroneous views of the past had been corrected.[44]

This is almost certainly an over-simplified picture. No doubt the pace of technical modernization and the institution of ranks and of conscription helped to widen the gaps between officers and men and between army and people, and no doubt these gaps were partly bridged by such measures as the production and economy movements and the 'Officers to the Ranks' campaign. Yet it is unlikely that either the deterioration or the subsequent recovery in army-people-party relations was as dramatic and swift as presented in official accounts.

The complexity of these relationships created, after all, perennial and recurring problems in the management of the PLA which of their very nature could not easily be solved once and for all. In spite of Hsiao Hua's optimistic remarks in August 1959, we find that officer-men relations were again causing concern in 1960–1. Hsiao later admitted that 'some individual cadres are likely to beat and insult the soldiers, impose indirect physical punishment upon them, and abuse the authority in their hands'. He also criticized cadres for showing 'contempt and sarcasm' to soldiers, allowing bias to influence their judgement, discriminating against soldiers who were ill, obstructing visits from soldiers' families, and ignoring the needs and preferences of soldiers from minority groups.[45] An important campaign for 'improving the methods of supervisory education' in the army was initiated in January 1961 by Lin Piao. The basic purpose of this campaign was to ensure that the supervision of the rank and file by cadres

[44] Lo Jung-huan, 'Continue to promote the glorious tradition of the Chinese PLA' (*SCMP* 1106); Hsiao Hua, 'Participation in national construction is a glorious task of the PLA' (*ECMM* 182).

[45] Hsiao Hua, 'On strengthening the work of supervisory education in the company', *KTTH*, 18 June 1961 (Cheng, pp. 617–31).

was effective without being excessively severe. As one military region had reported, 'because the new cadres were many and the ways of management few, there has not yet been built up a feeling of comradeship between officers and men'.[46] Treatment of civilians also came in for some criticism, although apparently it was not such a serious problem.[47]

One should not exaggerate the gravity of these continuing 'deviations' within the PLA. The disciplinary relationship between officers and men creates problems in most armies— although it is not always so frankly recognized as it is in the PLA. Many of the instances of victimization condemned by PLA leaders would pass unremarked in, for instance, the British army. The PLA's tradition of 'military democracy', and its refusal to sacrifice this tradition entirely to the interests of good discipline, helps in itself to create areas of ambiguity in the relationship between officers and men, which a rigid system of discipline would avoid. Similarly, the standards set up by the PLA leadership for relations with the civilian population are based upon the close working relationship which existed during the revolution. The kind of bad feeling and friction which is bound to arise from time to time between soldiers and the population amongst whom they are garrisoned is therefore treated with more concern than it might be thought to warrant elsewhere. The use of the term 'warlordism' to describe comparatively petty incidents is symptomatic of an almost obsessive determination by the PLA leadership not to inherit the legacy of hostility between the military and civilians which existed before 1949 under Nationalist rule.

The apparent outbreak of major 'deviations' in the PLA during the mid-1950s and their subsequent rectification is therefore only part of the picture. Changes in official policy towards the PLA's role and status during this period were probably as important as the changes which took place within the PLA itself. In 1949–50, before the Korean war, when plans were under way

[46] Canton Military Region CCP committee, 'Regulations for improving the methods of supervisory education in army units', ibid. 1 Feb. 1961 (Cheng, pp. 204–9).

[47] An object lesson in how not to treat civilians was publicized by the General Political Dept in January 1961. The soldiers in question had 'used the Kuomintang way of dealing with people and chose to use the most wicked method of injuring the people bodily, damaging the relationship between the Army and the people and tarnishing the reputation of our Army', ibid. 17 Jan. 1961 (Cheng, p. 145).

to convert the PLA to a peacetime footing, frequent mention was made of the need for better discipline and strict non-interference with civilian life.[48] Less attention was paid to these aspects during the Korean war itself, when the PLA's status and prestige rose to exceptional heights. It was allowed to concentrate upon its technical modernization at the expense of political education, to acquire privileges and to expect unconditional popular support. After the war, as China found herself at peace for the first time in many years, the order of priorities was reversed, and the PLA was expected increasingly to defer to party and popular pressure. The implications of growing professionalism within the PLA began to cause alarm to the party, while shortcomings in discipline and in relations with the civilian population gave further grounds for concern.[49] In order to 'rectify' the 'deviations' which were now officially admitted to exist, the party turned to the well-tried techniques of its revolutionary past—production work, the practice of economy, popular co-operation, and 'military democracy', which had proved so successful during the anti-Japanese and civil wars. (Similar revolutionary techniques were also revived in the fields of social and economic policy.) Yet the exaggerated form in which many of these techniques were now prescribed created an atmosphere of make-believe and unreality about them, and led to a worsening of relations between the PLA and the party authorities. In the more rational

[48] After the communist victory, Lin Piao and Liu Po-ch'eng on several occasions publicly reprimanded their men for malpractices (*South China Morning Post*, 9 Jan. 1950). The CCP CC of the South China Military Region called for 'thought education for the overwhelming number of fighters' in order to 'create a new atmosphere in the army units', and establish 'perfect unity' between officers and men, troops and civilians, and military and civil administrations (Wuhan radio, 10 July 1950, in *FE* 65). The 2nd Field Army was criticized for 'extravagant habits prevailing among certain political and army sections' (NCNA, 10 Aug. 1949, in *FE* 17). These and other criticisms ceased after intervention in Korea.

[49] Lack of discipline and bad public relations began to cause overt concern in 1953–4. In, for instance, the South-west Military Region, the Political Department ordered all army units to form inspection teams to 'solicit opinions of local governments and people about the troops, and apologise and provide indemnity for any damage done', stressing that 'all serious violations of policy or discipline would be severely dealt with and reported to the authorities' (Chungking radio, 30 Dec. 1953, in *FE* 317). A later directive from the same region called on its troops to '. . . overcome the lethargy—currently prevalent in certain units as a result of victory in the war to resist America and aid Korea, and the entrance of our country into the stage of large-scale economic construction—and especially to eliminate pride, arrogance, pursuit of personal enjoyment and complacency among certain personnel' (Chungking radio, 15 Mar. 1954, in *FE* 338).

mood which prevailed as the tempo of the Great Leap Forward began to slacken at the end of 1959, a more sober approach was adopted towards the PLA. Some of the more flamboyant movements which had been launched within its ranks were now curtailed. Instead, a conscious and systematic attempt was now made to restore the essential element which had continued to be lacking—effective political control and education—by reconstructing the party apparatus and by enlarging the content of political education at the basic company level of the PLA. The story of the PLA since then is largely the story of this new approach.[50]

[50] See further ch. 12.

10

The People's Militia

*If the enemy dares attack us, they will be drowned in the great sea
of the people's armed forces, and there will be no place to bury
them.*[1]

THE 'Everyone a Soldier' movement (*ch'üan-min chieh-ping*)
which was launched in the autumn of 1958 during the first
months of the Great Leap Forward represents on paper perhaps
the most ambitious military enterprise in the history of mankind:
220 million men and women of a predominantly agricultural
population were to be transformed into an 'ocean of soldiers',
equipped and prepared to defend their homeland against the
invader. The militia in its expanded form was to be both an all-
inclusive mass movement and a permanent feature of society.
Thus it differed in extent and in conception from previous
militia movements under the Chinese communists. These had
always comprised a relatively small percentage of the population
and had been assigned specific and short-term tasks which varied
according to the military and political conditions of the time.
Furthermore the 'mass' nature of the 'Everyone a Soldier' movement was a departure from traditional Chinese caution in putting
military fire-power into the hands of the civilian population.

Was the militia campaign primarily only a symptom of the
commune movement, intended to force the pace in the early
stages of that movement? Was it rather a sign of increasing dissatisfaction with the PLA, an attempt to counterbalance the
army's strength and influence? Or did it reflect a more fundamental reappraisal of China's military strategy in the nuclear
age? 'Everyone a Soldier' appears to have been influenced in
varying degrees by all three factors. In more general terms, the
militia movement is an example in the military field of the
systematic attempt during the Great Leap Forward to devise
specifically indigenous Chinese solutions to the problems of
administration and government. As in the case of the PLA's

[1] Liu Hsien-sheng, 'Let the whole people be armed to defend the homeland',
Kiangsu Ch'un-chung, 1 Oct. 1959 (*ECMM* 150).

production and economy campaign, it is also an example of the way in which 'revolutionary' models were revived, and put into effect in exaggerated form. The rise and fall of the militia during the Great Leap, and its subsequent partial revival, provides a useful case study of this return to the revolutionary model.

The militia is defined as a popular military organization, recruited on a voluntary and democratic basis, whose members are 'not divorced from production' and 'do not quit their civilian occupation'. It is thus distinct from both the guerrilla and regular forces, who may participate in production on occasion, but who perform either a part-time or full-time military role. It is a home-based defence force which is activated in the interests of the local community, although its members may be called upon for service in the regular forces.[2]

THE MILITIA IN THE REVOLUTION

From the Kiangsi Soviet period right up until 1958 an important distinction must be drawn between the militia's mass *character* as a popular volunteer force, and its élite *composition* as a carefully hand-picked minority. During the Kiangsi Soviet period and before, the Red Army and the guerrilla forces were the main elements in the party's strategy. The militia (Red Guards) was an élite local force originally set up to oppose the 'white' home guard (*min-t'uan*), and it was not a mass organization. One estimate puts the number of Red Guards in the Kiangsi–Fukien area at 200,000 in 1934.[3] The figure of 2,560,000 given by Liu Yun-cheng, a Chinese writer on the subject, in a recent account appears to be wildly exaggerated.[4]

The militia (*min-ping*) was first established on a regular basis

[2] Liu Yun-cheng in 'The Militia in Chinese People's Revolutionary Wars' (*PR*, 21 Aug. 1964), gives the following definition of the militia:

'(1) It is the military force of the masses, whose members are not disengaged from their civilian employments. Its units are made up of producers—the working people—bearing arms; and its organization, combining labour power with armed strength is at once military and civilian in character.

'(2) It is organized on a voluntary and democratic basis, its daily life is ordered on the principle of democratic centralism; its leading members at all levels are, in general, elected democratically.

'(3) It is an armed organization which has the character of the entire people. It is a vast organization whose many members are scattered widely throughout the villages and cities and engage in various occupations.'

[3] *Peabody Report*, p. 2325.

[4] 'The Militia in Chinese People's Revolutionary Wars' (*PR*, 21 Aug. 1964). Liu Yun-cheng also claims that the 'role of the militia was belittled' during the second

during the Sino-Japanese war. The existence of scattered communist bases behind enemy lines created the need for a localized defence force which could supplement the mobile activities of the Red Army and guerrilla units. It was still an élite force, which comprised at the most 8 per cent of the population 'in places with a dense population where political work had been done thoroughly', and it functioned most effectively in areas behind enemy lines.[5] By April 1945 its numbers were estimated at 2,200,000. The militia was composed of the 'crack members' of the People's Anti-Japanese Self-Defence Corps[6] which, as its name implies, was a popular organization more concerned with civil defence than with fighting. By April 1945 the Self-Defence Corps itself had expanded to some 10 million, out of a total population in the liberated areas of $95\frac{1}{2}$ million.[7]

It was on the basis of these existing militia units that the communist army was greatly expanded during 1945. Chu Teh told the Seventh Party Congress in April 1945 that 'the enormous force of militia corps in the liberated areas is something we never had before. We have now learned the technique of organizing militia corps. The significance and importance of this accomplishment are beyond imagination', and announced that in future the militia would be incorporated into the same organizational structure as the guerrilla and regular units, thus facilitating recruitment from one to the other.[8] The success of the militia in providing local defence against the Japanese was also acknowledged at the Party Congress by Mao Tse-tung, who said that 'without the co-operation of these armed forces of the masses, it would be impossible to defeat the enemy'.[9]

---

revolutionary war after the rise of 'Leftist' opportunism in the party and the Li Li-san line of 'Every gun to the Red Army'. There is, however, no indication in Mao's writings of this period that the expansion of the militia or Red Guards was a point at issue. The military debate in the party at this time was concerned with the relative merits of positional and guerrilla warfare.

[5] Ho Kan-chih, *Hist. Modern Chinese Revolution*, p. 397. Yeh Chien-ying, in his report of 22 June 1944 to the Chinese and foreign correspondents at Yenan, gives detailed figures on the location of 'more than two million People's Militia organised behind enemy lines' (Gelder, *Chinese Communists*, pp. 73–102).

[6] *MAO III*, p. 265.

[7] Statistics in Ho Kan-chih, *Hist. Modern Chinese Revolution*, p. 425.

[8] Ting Li, *Militia*, pp. 51, 79–80.

[9] *MAO III*, p. 265. For details of the militia's activities during the anti-Japanese war, see further Ting Li, pp. 49–79 and Mu Hsin, *Chin-Sui Chieh-fang ch'u min-ping k'ang-Jih chan-tou san-chi* (1959), *passim*.

THE MILITIA DURING MODERNIZATION

As the area under communist control expanded during the third revolutionary war, so did the number of militia. By 1950 they were estimated at $5\frac{1}{2}$ million, together with 'many more millions' of the People's Self-Defence Corps.[10] The local population would in addition be mobilized when necessary to support a specific military campaign. Many militiamen, members of the Self-Defence Corps, and ordinary peasants were drafted away from home and employed in servicing transport, building defence works, maintaining supply and communications lines to the front, and providing first-aid and stretcher-bearing squads. Under such names as 'auxiliary service volunteers', 'field army militia corps', and 'brethren's squads', they would accompany a field army until the end of its campaign.[11] The Shantung campaign alone was supported by nearly 6 million 'civilian war service workers'.[12] This kind of labour corps would be led and organized by the militia. Next to captured or surrendered Nationalist troops, the militia was also the main source of reinforcements for the regular army.

After Liberation, the militia was again allotted tasks which were both short-term and tactical in nature. Article 23 of the Common Programme stated that:

> The Chinese People's Republic shall enforce the system of people's militia to maintain local order, lay the foundation for national mobilization and prepare for the enforcement of an obligatory military service system at the appropriate moment.

Thus the expansion of the militia was directly linked to plans for conscription and for maintaining law and order in the countryside, while social measures such as land reform were introduced and the remaining 'bandits' and 'counter-revolutionaries' were eliminated.

As in every other field of military activity, plans for expansion only began to be put into effect once the Korean war had started.

[10] Liu Yun-cheng, 'The Militia in Chinese People's Revolutionary Wars', *PR*, 21 Aug. 1964.
[11] Ting Li, *Militia*, pp. 98–102.
[12] Report by NCNA (Tsinan), 23 July 1949. The civilian workers helped 'in transport work, taking charge of prisoners, carrying the wounded and other services'. 'Women and children ground flour, sewed uniforms and made shoes for troops, and helped to build railways, roads and bridges to ensure a continuous flow of supplies to the front.'

P

Following a national conference of militia cadres held in Peking during October 1950, a plan was adopted 'to weld this mighty force . . . into a more efficient fighting force, by raising its combat and political level to a higher plane'.[13] It was soon reported that 'several hundred thousand' militiamen, including PLA veterans, guerrillas, and stretcher-bearers, were guarding the Northeastern frontier with Korea, while others had left for service as volunteers or transport workers in Korea itself.[14] In Manchuria, in North and East China, and in the coastal provinces militiamen were said to have been organized into joint defence networks with local military units to protect frontiers and vital installations. In the towns, 'winter vigilance corps' were set up to carry out fire-prevention work, to report special agents and help to investigate anti-government propaganda or rumours.

In spite of this increase in militia activity, the actual numbers involved were still relatively small, as was the targeted militia strength to be achieved within three years—23,750,000 militia or 5 per cent of the population—according to the new plan.[15] Chu Teh had told the militia cadres' conference in October that militia expansion would be 'a time-consuming delicate and onerous job', and attempts at over-hasty recruitment were severely frowned upon. There was no suggestion that this should be a mass movement for 'arming the people'. In fact it was stressed that the militia's 'compositional purity' should be maintained, that expansion should proceed at a cautious pace, and that political training should take priority over military training.[16] Besides their military functions, the militia were intended to be activists in the campaign for social reform, playing a key role in the land reform movement, and were assigned such duties as suppressing 'bandits' and protecting crops and communications.

So the militia was still seen as an élite organization, acting both as a 'spearhead' in social reform and as a reservoir of trained manpower for the Liberation Army, rather than as a mass movement. Militia organization was para-military, with detachments, battalions, and companies at the appropriate civil level, and the highest command at all times was the PLA. Im-

---

[13] NCNA, 28 Oct. 1950 (*SCMP* 1).   [14] Ibid. 28 Nov. 1950 (*FE* 85).
[15] *JMJP*, 25 Nov. 1950, summarized in Ting Li, *Militia*, pp. 103–6.
[16] See Chang Ching-wu, 'Strengthening our militia work', NCNA, 21 Nov. 1950.

plicit in this structure was the militia's subordination to the PLA. The slogans of this time included 'Learn from the PLA', 'the PLA is your elder Brother', and the militia was subject to the army disciplinary code. It provided a large number of volunteers for Korea, and in critical defensive areas such as Fukien militiamen were detached altogether from production and formed into regiments.

Apparently the target set for militia expansion was never reached, perhaps due to the demands of the Korean war or perhaps to popular resistance to serving in the force. Another factor, frequently referred to, was the reluctance of army and party cadres to put arms into the hands of civilians, and their excessive caution in accepting new recruits into the militia. The last official estimate of its strength was given in September 1951 (12,800,000 men),[17] but completion of the target figure of 23,750,000 was never announced. When conscription was introduced at the end of 1954, it was not linked to the militia as previously planned. An initial draft of over 830,000 men was chosen from more than 10 million volunteers, but there was no indication that these were militiamen.[18] The reserves were not integrated into the militia system, as might have been expected if the militia was to be the major source for conscription and reserve. The Military Service Law merely specified that 'militiamen will continue to maintain local security and protect production and construction, after the Military Service Law goes into force'.[19] From 1954–7 there is almost no information about the militia, except for isolated reports of militia activities on the Fukien coast.[20] Non-Chinese estimates of its strength range from only 6–12 million.[21] The prevailing military policy of that time was the 'reorganization and modernization' of the regular armed forces on Soviet lines, and militia work suffered through lack of attention.

An important upgrading of the militia's role took place in 1957, when the militia and the reserve were finally merged

---

[17] Chou En-lai, report of 23 Oct. 1951 to the People's Political Consultative Conference, NCNA, 2 Nov. 1951.
[18] P'eng Teh-huai, 'Report to National People's Council on Draft Military Service Law', 16 July 1955 (*SCMP* 1090).
[19] 'National People's Council adopts Military Service Law', NCNA, 2 Aug. 1955.
[20] For instance, reports in *SCMP* 1389 & 1494.
[21] *Manchester Guardian*, 18 June 1955; *The Times*, 7 June 1956.

through the adoption of a universal reserve system. This meant that all those who were eligible for conscription but who were not chosen would henceforward join the militia instead of, as previously, a separate reserve category. Ex-conscripts would in future be discharged into the militia as cadres or hard-core members. This was described as a 'cyclical military conscription system', and produced a sharp increase in the militia's nominal strength, which was unofficially estimated at 30 million by the end of 1957.[22]

This was followed by a significant editorial in the *Liberation Army Newspaper* of 26 June 1958, which revealed that remedial measures had been under way during the past year, and hinted at the forthcoming mass movement.

For a certain time after our country was liberated [the editorial noted] the glorious tradition of the unity of labour and arms was neglected by people and lost. Some comrades mistakenly believed that in the modernized war against imperialism, the usefulness of the militia was no longer very great. Therefore in practical work, they allowed their leadership of the militia to lapse, with the result that the work of the people's armed forces was weakened and the militia's organization became dissipated.[23]

In previous months the militia's organization in the various production units had been overhauled; the editorial claimed that 'the masses welcome it, the government is satisfied, and the militia themselves are happy'. Such attitudes as 'in peacetime

[22] *Communist China 1949–59*, i. 226–7. See also 'State Council promulgates provisional regulations on handling of recruits discharged from obligatory military service', NCNA, 18 May 1955 (*SCMP* 1780), which comments that 'since basically they [the recruits] have been incorporated in the militia forces for reserve service, they constitute a valuable force for defending the motherland and safeguarding socialist construction'. Another sign of increased interest in the militia was shown in May 1958 by Liu Shao-ch'i, who, in his speech to the party National Congress, called on the CC and all local party committees to devote more attention to militia work, as well as to political work in the army and to military training (Liu Shao-ch'i, 'The present situation, the party's general line for socialist construction and its future tasks', NCNA, 26 May 1958, in *CB* 507, p. 20).

[23] 'Develop the glorious tradition of the unity of arms and labour', *CFCP* editorial, 26 June 1958. The general tone of this editorial was, however, more restrained than that of the subsequent mass movement. In particular, it stressed that production should remain 'at the heart' of all militia work, pointing out that except on the frontiers and border areas, the 'armed' aspect of the militia was less important than it had been during the revolution. A news story in the same issue also emphasized the financial economies effected by the merger of the reserve and the militia, implying that this was a major reason for the merger.

militia work cannot be developed' and 'to do militia work can hinder production' were being proved wrong.

'EVERYONE A SOLDIER', 1958

With the official launching of the 'Everyone a Soldier' movement in August 1958, the militia came into the limelight with a new and enhanced status. It was not just a question of the enormous size envisaged for the militia, but of the crucial and unprecedented role it was expected to play. Far from being in any way transitional or short-term in nature, it was now to be a permanent feature of society, a 'proletarian revolutionary militarization'. It would act as the 'spearhead' in the commune movement and as the 'vital factor' in national defence. Moreover the militia was not described simply in terms of whatever tactical advantages it might bring. It was, on the contrary, supposed to be a strategic innovation of the utmost significance. It was 'a new development of Comrade Mao Tse-tung's strategic thinking on the people's war and has a profound political and strategic significance. . . .'[24]

'Everyone a Soldier', like the people's communes, was said to have originated as a spontaneous popular movement. The stimulus for its birth in August 1958 was supposed to have come from 'widespread indignation' at 'US imperialist armed provocation' in the Lebanon and Jordan. It soon received overt party sanction when, at the end of September, on returning from a tour of the Yangtze provinces, Mao Tse-tung called for the 'all-out organisation of militia divisions',[25] and in October the PLA convened a national militia work conference in Peking to co-ordinate the movement.[26] One province after another reported that all eligible people had enrolled in the militia. By January 1959 it was claimed that the grand total of 220 million militia men and women had been reached.

In one sense the militia was simply a logical extension of the concept of the people's commune. This was seen as 'the basic unit of the socialist social structure of our country, which combines industry, agriculture, trade, education and military

---

[24] Fu Ch'iu-t'ao, 'Everybody is a Soldier', *Hung Ch'i*, 16 Oct. 1958 (*ECMM* 150).
[25] 'Important statement by Chairman Mao following provincial tour', NCNA, 1 Oct. 1958.
[26] 'National Conference discusses militia work', ibid. 19 Oct. 1958.

affairs',[27] in which the militia formed an integral part. Yet the creation of a nation-wide militia could not fail to have important implications for China's social structure, relations between the army and the party, and for her national defence strategy, and we must assume that the merits of 'Everyone a Soldier' in these fields were considered before the launching of the campaign.

In the context of the reassessment of China's defence strategy in the nuclear age, which took place at the same time as the Great Leap Forward, the militia was seen as playing an important role in deterring foreign invasion. This aspect was emphasized by Mao in his call for building up the militia at the end of September.

> Chairman Mao Tse-tung pointed out that the imperialists were pushing China around in such a way that China must deal with them seriously. He declared that China required, in addition to mighty regular armed forces, a tremendous number of militia divisions. Thus, when imperialists invaded China, they would find difficulty in moving a single step.[28]

It was argued, first, that in view of China's geographical size and her relatively dispersed industry, she could survive a nuclear attack; secondly, that a conventional 'follow-up' would encounter popular resistance of massive proportions. The militia would solve the 'contradiction between a small-sized army in peacetime and a large-sized army required in wartime' by forming an inexhaustible reserve for the Liberation Army. It was a question of military training as well as of sheer numbers:

> The moment the state is attacked by the imperialists, the militia organizations become the reserves of the regular army. . . . Everybody should be able to handle guns and take advantage of geographical positions and local materials, air-defence and anti-poisoning measures.[29]

The Chinese communist movement had always placed a high value on popular mobilization; what was new was the application of this concept in the military field. In his lecture *On Protracted War* in May 1938, Mao Tse-tung had said that 'the mobilization of the common people throughout the country

[27] 'Party resolution on questions concerning people's communes', 10 Dec. 1958 (*CB* 542).

[28] 'Important statement by Chairman Mao', NCNA, 1 Oct. 1958.

[29] Liu Hsien-sheng, 'Let the whole people be armed to defend the homeland', *Kiangsu Ch'un-chung*, 1 Oct. 1958 (*ECMM* 150).

will create a vast sea in which to drown the enemy. . . .'.[30] Here he was talking exclusively about *political* mobilization. The same metaphor was to be widely used in a *military* sense during 'Everyone a Soldier', leading to the conclusion that 'a sea formed by several hundred million militiamen is something that no modern weapon can destroy'.

The expansion of the militia was naturally resisted by those in the army who were already antagonistic to excessive party control. Military opposition to the militia was expressed by the view that 'fighting is the business of the army, and the masses must not be mobilised and relied upon'.[31] It was said that:

some comrades . . . take a purely military view of the militia organizations and overlook the part played by militia organizations in promoting socialist construction; or else they take the view that the war for national defence and against aggression is the business of the army, not of the whole people.[32]

On the contrary, the army was no longer the militia's elder brother, but an equal partner in national defence, and the militia was regarded as vital to its success. Thus it was claimed that 'if we detach ourselves from the militia forces, we can no longer talk about the growth of the people's army'.[33] Henceforth, according to the slogan, the army would come from the militia and return to the militia. In other words, the militia would both supply the annual draft and act as a permanent reserve. (This was the role envisaged for the militia before 1955, and there was therefore presumably no objection in military quarters to the merging of the reserve with the militia in 1957. But the need for conscription could have equally well been satisfied by a much smaller militia than that envisaged in the 'Everyone a Soldier' movement of 1958.)

One need not suggest that the expansion of the militia was intended to counterbalance the PLA or as an answer to any symptoms of political unreliability in the regular army. But the party leaders' dissatisfaction with the PLA was to some extent symptomatic of the rejection of conventional techniques and institu-

---

[30] *MAO II*, p. 154.   [31] As n. 29.

[22] Fu Ch'iu-t'ao, 'People's militia—Favourite system of our people', *Che-hsueh Yen-chiu*, 1959, No. 1 (*ECMM* 159).

[33] Huang Huo-ch'ing, 'Strengthen party leadership and create an upsurge in militia build-up', *Liao-ning Jih-pao*, 27 Feb. 1960 (*SCMP* 2236).

tions which characterized the Great Leap Forward. The militia movement presented in theory an attractive improvement upon the established military structure. One should not however interpret 'Everyone a Soldier'—even in its initial stage —as a move towards a citizen army on Jaurèsist lines,[34] or as the replacement of the standing army by a proletarian militia which both Marx and Engels had envisaged. Lenin had at times advocated merging the police, the army, and the bureaucracy with the 'universally armed people',[35] but here the Chinese have departed from orthodox Leninism (as Lenin did himself when faced with the realities of the civil war). They are at pains to point out that—unlike the armies of capitalist countries—the Chinese army is *not* opposed to the interests of the people; those contradictions which are admitted to exist in the armed forces can and will be peacefully resolved. The militia therefore is intended to supplement but not to replace the regular army.

The close relationship between the militia and the commune movement was emphasized from the beginning of the 'Everyone a Soldier' campaign. According to Mao:

> The establishment of militia divisions on a large scale is not purely a question of mobilization of manpower, collective action, and fulfilment of production tasks. It is a question of having the masses militarize and collectivize their life.[36]

The militia was intended to inject an element of 'army-style' organization into the commune system, so that work would be done like a military operation. In Szechwan for instance:

> The habit of unified 'rising, eating, sleeping, setting out to work and returning from work' was fostered. This greatly strengthened the collectivization of life and the organizational discipline, and nurtured the fighting style in production and work.[37]

---

[34] In his *L'armée nouvelle*, published in Paris in 1911, the French Socialist Jean Jaurès advocated a citizen army for France. Trotsky was influenced by Jaurès's arguments while Minister of War in 1918–20 (see Isaac Deutscher, *The Prophet Armed* (London, 1954), pp. 477–81).

[35] 'A real people's militia [is] one that consists of the entire population, of all the adult citizens of both sexes; secondly, one that combines the functions of a people's army with those of the police. . .' (V. I. Lenin, *Letters from Afar* (London, 1933), No. 3, 'On Proletarian Militia', Mar. 1917).

[36] Quoted in 'Report by Teng K'o-ning to Kiangsi's Militia Work Conference', Dec. 1959 (*SCMP* 2196).

[37] 'Szechwan has 30 million militiamen', NCNA, 5 Oct. 1958.

As with previous militia movements, it was also supposed to help promote social reform. It was to: 'increase the organization, discipline, and militancy of the people and change the disunity and backwardness left over from the old society'.[38] Within the militia structure itself, the distinction between 'ordinary' and 'hard-core' militia was maintained. The ordinary militia was to include all able-bodied citizens of both sexes between the ages of 15 and 50. A smaller number of those between 16 and 30 were assigned to the hard core or 'basic-level backbone' units, and supplemented by demobilized servicemen and veterans. This élite was organized into 'shock-corps' to act as the spearhead in production, leading the masses in such tasks as spring ploughing, drought fighting, and production of iron and steel.

The militia structure closely paralleled that of the people's commune. At the lowest level the production team formed a militia company, while the commune was classified according to size as a militia battalion, regiment, or division. There is evidence that in the early days of the movement the assumption of military authority went to the heads of some local cadres. (These cadres were chosen from the regular army reserves by the local party committee.) At the end of 1958 there were admissions that 'formalism' and 'despotism' had occurred in some regions. Cadres were warned not to imitate army uniforms and ranks, and to use reason rather than compulsion in militia recruitment.[39] Apparently in order to check excessive local power, the December plenum of the Central Committee laid down that militia cadres should not hold commune offices concurrently, and that the militia system must not 'in the least infringe on democratic life in the commune and in the militia organisations'.[40]

Ultimate leadership of the militia was to be shared equally between the commune and the 'superior commanding organisation of the militia'.[41] The latter was a PLA organ but, possibly in view of the army's apathy towards the militia, there were repeated calls to strengthen party control over the militia, which was described as being under the *leadership* of the party and *aided* by the army. This contrasts with the militia structure in previous

[38] Fu Ch'iu-t'ao (see n. 32).
[39] Fu Ch'iu-t'ao, 'Everybody is a Soldier' (*ECMM* 150), and Yen Fu-sheng, speech of 14 Dec. 1959, in *SCMP* 2188.
[40] Party resolution of 10 Dec. 1958 (*CB* 542).   [41] Ibid.

years, where ultimate authority had always been vested in the Liberation Army. Towards the end of 1959 there were renewed attempts to establish 'absolute party control' over the militia.

It is hardly surprising that the grandiose claims made for the militia in the first flush of enthusiasm turned out to be greatly exaggerated. A 'proletarian militarization' was carried out, but only on the most superficial level. Of the 220 million militiamen officially enrolled by the end of 1959, only a small proportion—15 per cent at the most in some provinces—belonged to the hard core, and only the hard core appears to have been systematically drilled and instructed in the use of fire-arms. In Honan, for instance, which boasted 20 million militiamen in October 1958, only 200,000 had been trained as hard core by the following summer, of whom 100,000 had 'practised with the firing of loaded guns'.[42] A very small number of so-called 'tactical' troops had received special training in such techniques as anti-aircraft and anti-gas defence, but these were admitted to be few in number and inadequately trained.

A major reason for these shortcomings was undoubtedly apathy among local party or military cadres. Agricultural disasters also hindered militia work from 1960 onwards, and created doubts about the wisdom of 'arming the people'. But the root of the problem was perhaps the paradoxical position of the militia in the commune movement, which becomes clear in the reports of various provincial militia conferences held during the winter of 1959–60. Either the militia was efficiently organized to the detriment of production, or it existed only on paper and was superfluous from a military point of view. The blame for this state of affairs was, of course, placed solely on the cadres. Some cadres had feared that militia training would interfere with production, and had merely created an 'empty structure, with no role to play'. In other places cadres had shown excessive zeal. 'Complex and stereotyped systems' had been devised, which cut across the commune structure, interfered with production, and gave rise to 'defects of arrogance and slackness'.[43]

The provincial militia work conferences of winter 1959–60, regardless of the difficulties encountered during the past year,

[42] NCNA, 17 Oct. 1958, and *Ho-nan Jih-pao*, 27 Oct. 1959 (*CB* 530 & *SCMP* 2173).
[43] For a good example, reported at length, of a provincial militia work conference see items on the Kiangsi conference in *SCMP* 2196.

called for 'a new high tide in militia building'. Four points were emphasized: stronger party leadership, training of militia cadres, more political work for the hard core, and strengthening of 'tactical' troops. Following the provincial conferences, a national militia work conference was held in Peking in early February 1960, at which it was 'unequivocally decided to continue the policy of further intensifying militia construction and the large-scale organization of militia units in the future'.[44]

A SHIFT IN POLICY, 1960

The line shifted abruptly during the next two months, and in April yet another national conference was held in Peking. The call for a large-scale militia build-up was quietly dropped, while military training and production work for the militia were no longer placed upon an equal footing. The new slogan was that 'Production is the Keynote in Militia Work', and the point was driven home by a series of speakers that included Lin Piao, Lo Jung-huan, Lo Jui-ch'ing, Chu Teh, and Teng Hsiao-p'ing. 'All activities of the people's militia should centre on the development of production', said Lo Jung-huan, and an editorial in the *People's Daily* declared that 'the first and foremost task is to concentrate forces for production and construction, and to whip up a high tide to make greater leaping progress at the various fronts'.[45] At the closing session of the conference Lin Piao stated once again the new order of priorities:

Socialist economic construction is the material foundation for defence construction. . . . The current central task of the people's militia throughout the country is to exert full efforts for socialist construction.[46]

The delegates adopted ten proposals, the first of which was to 'take an active part in socialist construction'. Militia-building came way down the list after a call for support of the patriotic health campaign.[47]

There were obvious economic reasons for the shift to a policy

[44] 'National militia conference decides to strengthen militia organization', NCNA, 8 Feb. 1960 (*SCMP* 2195).
[45] 'For the construction and defence of socialism', 19 Apr. 1960 (*SCMP* 2247).
[46] NCNA, 27 Apr. 1960 (*SCMP* 2252).
[47] 'Delegates to national militia conference make proposals to all militiamen in China', NCNA, 27 Apr. 1960.

with production as the keynote for militia work, and this shift only anticipated by a few months the new line in economic policy of 'taking agriculture as the foundation'. The stress on production increased throughout 1960–2 as natural disasters grew worse, and militia work and training were relegated to 'spare-time' activities or even suspended altogether. Following Lin Piao's appointment as Minister of Defence in September 1959, a new Military Affairs Committee of the party Central Committee had been set up. It was under this new leadership that the shift in militia policy was carried out. The aims and policies governing militia activities were redefined, and the Military Affairs Committee, at Lin Piao's suggestion, drew up a nine-point plan for the militia. It was on the basis of this plan that the new and more moderate line of April 1960 was evolved.[48]

As conditions in the countryside grew worse during 1960, the militia structure also deteriorated. At the end of the year an investigation was carried out by Fu Ch'iu-t'ao[49] into the state of the militia in Honan, one of the two provinces (the other was Shantung) worst hit by natural disasters. Fu's report revealed a 'serious situation', which the Military Affairs Committee described as throwing light upon 'several widespread and important problems about the building up of the present militia'. For the first time, so it seems, the party's military leaders were informed of the divergence in practice of 'Everyone a Soldier' from its theoretical model, and were alarmed by what they learnt.

Fu quoted examples of communes where the militia organization had completely disintegrated. The common explanation was simply that 'in 1958 I was a militia man, but now I am not'. The position regarding militia cadres was also disturbing. In some cases rich peasant or rightist elements held cadre office, and in 'backward places' they had incited the rank and file to commit rape and robbery. Militia records had been falsified; some

[48] Information on military policy under Lin Piao's leadership in 1959–61 is derived from reports in the *Kung-tso T'ung-hsün* (Bulletin of Activities), 1 Jan.–26 Aug. 1961. This journal was published by the PLA General Political Department and distributed only to party cadres of regimental level or above. The first issue was that of 1 Jan. 1961. The 29 issues which are available were secured by undisclosed means, and released in Aug. 1963 by the US Dept of State through the Library of Congress. A full translation has been published by the Hoover Institution on War, Revolution and Peace (*KTTH* (Cheng)).

[49] Fu Ch'iu-t'ao was head of the PLA's mobilization dept, with special responsibility for militia work.

people did not even know that they were cadres. The control of weapons was chaotic; there were serious losses and many weapons were destroyed. Some had been stolen by 'bad elements', and in one place were used for highway robbery. In the first half of 1960 training had been given to only 400,000 militiamen out of the nominal provincial total of nearly 20 million. There were cases of cadres misappropriating funds and falsifying statistics.

On the basis of this and of other reports, the Military Affairs Committee took immediate action. On 12 January 1961 it communicated 'Five Requirements on Militia Work' to leading PLA organs throughout the country. These requirements were to be fulfilled not later than March 1961, before the start of the spring season. The analysis by the Committee called for a complete reassessment and overhaul of the militia; the situation was said to be unsatisfactory in approximately one-third of all communes and districts. There was to be a thorough investigation of all militia cadres. Those who were incompetent should be dismissed democratically, and bad elements should be driven out by mass movement methods. Top priority should be given to militia work at strategic points: around towns, railways, communications, major bridges, granaries, in coastal positions, and on frontiers. Control should be strengthened over the militia's weapons to ensure that every gun was in reliable hands. An investigation and census should be carried out before March, and a system of regular checks set up. All automatic weapons should be withdrawn and kept by military authorities. Rifles might be retained by reliable militiamen after approval by the local party and military committees. In bad areas they should be withdrawn altogether.

The Military Affairs Committee was especially concerned with the use of the militia for unauthorized purposes. Some cadres had failed to distinguish between friend and foe, and had used the militia to abuse the people, and to commit acts of robbery and violence. The militia should be used to subdue internal and external class enemies, but on no account should it attempt to repress the people's internal contradictions. It should not be used against petty criminals and disturbers of the peace, and might only co-operate with the public security forces subject to prior approval. Only in dealing with counter-revolutionaries and parachuted spies, or in protecting strategic points, might it take action without previous authorization. Cadres who used the militia to detain people forcibly or to search their homes would be dealt with by law.

In April 1961 a number of discussion meetings on militia work were held in Peking, and were attended by the heads of all military regions and provincial military districts. These were addressed by General Lo Jui-ch'ing, chief of staff of the PLA, who reiterated the policy of retrenchment which had been laid down by the Military Affairs Committee and stressed the need to concentrate on strategic points, on the militia's 'purity', on the hard-core element and cadres, and on retaining control of the militia's weapons. He also acknowledged the current difficulties in militia training. 'To concentrate on military training is to depart from reality; it will also be unpopular.' In the hard-hit provinces training should be dropped altogether, and 'if there are contradictions between production and militia work, militia work should give way'. In the reorganization of the militia one should follow a cautious policy of 'finding the seams in order to stitch them up' (i.e. of putting existing units into good order before attempting to expand elsewhere). Overall control and supervision of the militia should be placed in the hands of the provincial military districts and sub-districts. These should become 'the real leaders of the militia'. A rather vague and unspecific target was set—to raise the standard of militia building within three years.

In effect, the militia was now reverting to its original auxiliary role, and was again expected to perform those functions usually associated with such a body—guarding strategic points, maintaining law and order, and assisting the security forces. Its effective strength (in terms of hard core plus cadres) can only have been a very small proportion of the total working population. The decision to restore control of the militia to the PLA was particularly significant, since both in Fu Ch'iu-t'ao's report and in the Military Affairs Committee directive of January 1961, the provincial PLA military districts had been criticized for their lack of interest in the militia. Although the PLA could not fail to be lukewarm towards the concept of militia expansion, the shortcomings of the rural cadres in this field had been so great that there was apparently no alternative but to renew the PLA's control of the militia. This move may also have been intended to encourage the PLA to take a greater interest in the militia. There is a parallel here with the role of the rural party cadre in the communes, and his inability to provide effective leadership which led to the gradual dilution of his authority.

Yet in spite of the pragmatic approach now adopted towards the militia by the party leaders, there was no admission of second thoughts on its theoretical importance. Lo Jui-ch'ing emphasized that in spite of recent setbacks:

> The Central Committee and Chairman Mao are unanimous in regarding militia work as of great importance. . . . Since 1958 they have raised the strategic slogan of 'Everyone a Soldier', and they look on the militia as a strategic question. . . . Everybody must fully realize the importance of doing good militia work. The militia is the foundation of the people's war; and an inexhaustible source of strength. . . . If militia work is done well, then, as Chairman Mao has observed, when imperialism commits aggression against our country it will be unable to move an inch.[50]

One wonders how far this view was still held outside Mao's intimate circle, especially within the army. In any case, as far as one can tell from the scanty publicity given to the militia during 1961–2, militia policy continued in a minor key. Almost all news items during this period were concerned only with its organization in the coastal provinces and with its successes in dealing with Chiang Kai-shek's spies. Priority was given to political education and to militia hard core and cadres, and military training was only to be carried out 'at odd moments' and as a 'spare-time activity'. A cautious note was frequently struck, with references to the 'long-term, arduous, and complicated nature' of militia work. The role of the PLA and of army veterans in militia training was emphasized.[51] There were some complaints of militiamen who violated the law and abused their positions.[52]

REVIVAL OF THE MILITIA, 1962

The year 1962 saw the beginning of an upward trend in militia-building which has subsequently continued without in-

[50] *KTTH*, 26 May 1961.
[51] See further editorials of *Nanfang Jih-pao*, 3 Oct. 1961 (*SCMP* 2802) and of *Chieh-fang-chün Hua-pao*, 16 Mar. 1962 (*SCMP* 316); also reports in *SCMP* 2796, 2800–1, 2803.
[52] Wenchow radio, 13 Aug. & 9 Sept. 1962, in *Extracts from China Mainland Publications* (Hong Kong, US Consulate General), No. 72.

terruption. In June a major theoretical statement on the subject was published, which reiterated all the essential principles of 'Comrade Mao Tse-tung's thought concerning the people's war' without conceding any modification. It praised the role of the militia in the past, claimed that militia divisions were 'universally established' in rural villages, cities, and towns, people's communes, industrial factories and mines, enterprises, public organs, and schools, and repeated the prediction that 'in a modern war, the role to be played by the militia will be even greater instead of being weakened'.[53]

There was, however, no repetition of the uncontrolled and disorganized militia expansion which had taken place in 1958–9, and stress was laid upon the need for a qualitative rather than quantitative increase in the militia's strength. Sometime during 1962 Mao Tse-tung issued a personal directive calling for militia work to be put on 'a solid basis organisationally, politically and militarily',[54] and subsequent expositions of these 'three bases' made it clear that development would be firmly grounded upon strong political control and education, a well-defined organizational structure, and regular military training under supervision. The lesson had been learnt from the slap-dash and haphazard expansion of previous years.

The political basis, it was explained, took first place.

A solid political basis means strengthening the people's militia politically according to the Party's class line, making sure that the organizations and the armed forces of the militia are entirely in the hands of the most reliable class brothers who are loyal to the Party, the people, the revolution and the cause of socialism.

Militia organizations were now to have political cadres attached to them, and to carry out political and ideological education. The organizational basis required that the militia should be 'purified and improved in conformity with the principles and policies of militia building by the party Central Committee and Comrade Mao Tse-tung', with clearly defined groupings from squad to divisional level. The military basis involved regular military training of the hard-core militia in order that everyone of them should be able 'to use a rifle, throw hand grenades, utilise terrain

[53] Liu Yun-cheng, 'The Militia in Chinese People's Revolutionary Wars', *PR*, 21 Aug. 1962.
[54] Liu Yun-cheng, 'The Role of the People's Militia', *PR*, 5 Feb. 1965.

features, stand on guard, go on sentry, and guard themselves against air raids and poisonous gas'.[55]

Yet caution continued to be the keynote in militia work, and the preamble to the militia's Three Major Duties and Ten Requirements, also published in 1962, stated explicitly that 'during the present period of peaceful construction, militiamen must subordinate all their other activities to their participation in production and construction'.[56] Production continued to take priority over military training throughout 1962–4. Even in Sinkiang the militia were said to play a 'spearhead role' on all production fronts, only indulging in military training during their 'leisure'.[57] In times of emergency, as in Hunan during the 1964 spring ploughing season, the militia were ordered to 'temporarily suspend' their training, to reduce the number of 'unnecessary meetings', and to send their cadres to 'reinforce the frontline of agricultural production'.[58]

More attention appears to have been devoted to the militia in frontier provinces—both along the coast (Fukien, Kiangsi, and Kwangtung) and on the Sino-Soviet border (Sinkiang) than elsewhere. In early 1962 Peking had been 'obviously worried that the Nationalists, supported by the United States, would launch an invasion to take advantage of an internal crisis before conditions could be stabilised', while as early as January 1961 a secret directive from the Military Affairs Committee had 'noted the need to preserve the tranquility and safety of both the southwestern and northwestern frontiers' and had called for border defences to be gradually strengthened.[59] (China later claimed that in April and May 1962, the Soviet Union had carried out 'large-scale subversive activities in the Ili region and enticed and coerced several tens of thousands into going to the Soviet Union', while the Soviet Union alleged that in 1962 alone there had been 'more than 5,000 violations of the Soviet frontier from the Chinese side'.)[60] 'Hundreds of thousands' of militiamen in

---

[55] 'Strengthen the building of the people's militia movement in the socialist education movement', *JMJP* editorial, 17 Nov. 1964 (*FE*(2) 1713).
[56] *Chieh-fang-chün Hua-pao*, 16 Mar. 1962 (*ECMM* 316).
[57] Urumchi radio, 2 Oct. 1964 (*FE*(2) 1693).
[58] Changsha radio, 12 Mar. 1964 (*FE*(2) 1529).
[59] Powell, 'Communist China's Mass Militia', *Current Scene*, 15 Nov. & 1 Dec. 1964, pt 2, p. 2.
[60] Quoted in the author's *The Sino-Soviet Dispute 1956–63; Extracts from Recent Documents* (RIIA, Feb. 1964), pp. 66–67.

Sinkiang were said to have given active support both in the campaign against India on the Ladakh frontier and in maintaining social order within the province itself,[61] and 'brilliant results' were reported on the Fukien front in the struggle against American-Chiang Kai-shek secret agents. In 1963 it was revealed that the people's public security forces were training militia to act as their 'assistants' in 'defending the coastal and border regions and maintaining railway communications'.[62]

From 1963 onwards a more optimistic tone appeared in reports on militia activities. In June Kwangtung held its second provincial militia conference (the first had been held, as in other provinces, during the winter of 1959). It was said at the conference that the Kwangtung militia was now ready for 'a higher stage of development', and that great achievements had been made in reconstructing the militia's organization. It was implied that the process of 'cleansing' and reforming the militia had begun to produce results—at least in Kwangtung—and that the improving economic situation allowed more time for military training. Great progress was reported to have been made, and 'important instructions' were given for militia work in 1964. Other provinces subsequently held their own second militia conference, indicating that a similar stage of reorganization had been reached, and that they too had received 'important instructions' for the future. But there was a considerable time-lag between one province and another in reaching this stage, which suggests that the task of militia reconstruction did not prove easy.

In the autumn of 1964 another 'new stage' was reached in militia-building with the holding of a national militia political work conference in Peking—the first of its kind since 1960. Organized by the PLA's General Political Department, it was attended by leading cadres both from the army and the party organs responsible for the organization of local people's armed forces. Apart from reaffirming the strategic importance of the militia at a time when China had just exploded her first atomic bomb, this conference revealed a new and most significant emphasis upon the militia's role in maintaining internal security and law and order. This aspect of its functions, which had not

---

[61] Urumchi radio, 2 Oct. 1964 (*FE*(2) 1693).
[62] 'Public security men eagerly help militiamen raise their political and military levels', *JMJP*, 21 Mar. 1963 (*SCMP* 2958).

been highlighted since the early 1950's when the militia played an important part in backing up law enforcement by the army and the police, was reasserted at a time when—by the Chinese leadership's own admission—the 'class struggle' in China had intensified and the danger of a 'capitalist restoration' was very real. The militia was now defined, for the first time explicitly, as 'an important instrument for safeguarding the people's democratic dictatorship' at home, as well as in the more customary terms of its value as a 'powerful reserve for national defence'.[63] The national militia political work conference declared that the socialist education movement and the 'class struggle' should be the means in future by which the militia was built up, since 'the militia is an instrument used by our country to resist imperialist aggression from abroad and to carry out the people's democratic dictatorship at home'.[64] Top priority was to be given to militia work in the field of politics, and special attention was to be given to the placing of weapons in the hands of the poor and lower-middle peasants and of the 'politically reliable workers'. The *People's Daily*, in an editorial on the conference, stressed the importance of continuing 'the glorious tradition of exerting firm control of military affairs by the Party'. Party committees at all local levels were called upon to strengthen their leadership over militia work, to include such work in their regular schedules for discussion and study, and to consolidate and develop the militia organizations. All local military districts, subdistricts, and county and city people's armed forces departments were to devote their major effort in the forthcoming winter to militia work under the leadership of the party committees.[65]

Although this is likely to lead to a further increase in the size of the militia, it will be a very different organization from that envisaged at the time of the Great Leap Forward. The original ambitious concept has been modified in the light of experience, and the emphasis upon strict party control, high political standards, and 'hard-core' components is unlikely to be reversed in favour of unplanned 'ordinary' expansion. Training of all except the hard core is confined to occasional drill, physical

[63] Marshal Yeh Chien-ying, speech in Hunan on 1 Oct. 1964 (Tsinan radio, 11 Oct. 1964, in *FE*(2) 1694).
[64] NCNA, 10 Nov. 1964, report on militia political work conference (*FE*(2) 1707).
[65] 'Strengthen the building of the people's militia in the socialist education movement' (*FE*(2) 1713).

sports, and summer camping activities. More fundamentally, there has been a change in doctrinal approach towards the militia, which means in practical terms that it is once again regarded as an élite force, a well-honed tool of the people's democratic dictatorship, rather than as a mass organization. Although lip-service is still paid to the principle of 'turning all the people into soldiers', the people in question are a minority, to be carefully selected on the basis of class origin and of political reliability. A distinction is now drawn between the 'militia masses' and the 'great masses' in society. The former 'helps the Government to maintain social order and protect the interests' of the latter, and it possesses a mass *character* rather than a mass *composition*. It is explained that

because the militia masses come from among the workers, poor and lower-middle peasants and revolutionary intellectuals, they are not only highly revolutionary, but also possess the broadest mass character. Since militia organizations are found in every corner of the country, no counter-revolutionary activity of the landlords, rich peasants, counter-revolutionaries and bad elements can escape the eyes of the people's militia; as soon as a counter-revolutionary spark appears, it will immediately be put out by the militia. . . . The militia masses also help the Government to maintain social order and protect the interests of the great masses. At the same time, the organizing and training of the people's militia, the policy of turning all the people into soldiers is also an important measure to guarantee that the guns will be for ever in the hands of the Party and the people, and will never become tools of careerists. With this and the thorough going work of socialist education and other measures, we can effectively prevent capitalism from making a come-back, and we can consolidate and carry the cause of socialism to final victory.[66]

The new order of priorities has elevated the role of the militia as a 'class weapon' over its role in production and even over its military role in national defence. The concept of the militia as a mass organization, primarily concerned with defence and production, performing 'spearhead' social roles, has been very largely reversed in favour of an organization which, while still relatively large, is constructed on a carefully selective basis, is mainly concerned with maintaining law and order, and allows its 'spearhead' operations to be used as a weapon in the class struggle under the close supervision of the party.

[66] Liu Yun-cheng, 'The Role of the People's Militia', *PR*, 5 Feb. 1965.

11

Return to the Revolutionary Model
1959–65

Weapons are an important factor in war but not the decisive one; it is man and not material that is decisive. The contest of forces is not only a contest of military and economic power, but also one of the power and morale of man. Military and economic power must be controlled by man.[1]

DISMISSAL OF MARSHAL P'ENG TEH-HUAI

AT the end of September 1959 Marshal P'eng Teh-huai was dismissed from his post as Minister of Defence, to be replaced by Marshal Lin Piao. His chief of staff, Huang K'o-ch'eng, was also dismissed, giving way to Lo Jui-ch'ing, then Minister of Public Security. Three senior officers who had served on P'eng's command during the Korean war were also removed from office. These were Hung Hsueh-chih (rear services director), Li Ta (a Deputy Minister of Defence), and Teng Hua (commander of Shen-yang Military Region). Although not specifically associated with P'eng's downfall, three other leading officers—Su Yü, T'an Cheng, and Hsiao K'o—also fell from favour during the first year of the Great Leap Forward.[2]

It is difficult to assess accurately the scanty evidence concerning the dismissal of P'eng and his colleagues. Some analyses of P'eng's dismissal have explained it mainly in terms of a major

[1] Mao Tse-tung, 'On the Protracted War', quoted in *People's Daily* Editorial Dept, *Comrade Mao Tse-tung on 'Imperialism and All Reactionaries are Paper Tigers'* (Peking, 1958), p. 14.

[2] Hung Hsueh-chih served on P'eng's staff in Korea as rear services director, Li Ta as chief of staff, and Teng Hua as deputy commander.

Hsiao K'o, Li Ta, and Huang K'o-ch'eng were Deputy Ministers of the Ministry of National Defence under P'eng Teh-huai as Minister until their dismissal in September 1959.

Su Yü and T'an Cheng were not so closely associated with P'eng. Su was dismissed as chief of staff in September 1958, but became a Deputy Minister of Defence in September 1959, when P'eng was dismissed. T'an was replaced as director of the Political Department sometime in 1960, but remained a Deputy Minister of Defence until March 1965.

intra-party dispute over the economic policies of the Great Leap Forward. P'eng is said to have submitted a memorandum to the Central Committee's plenum at Lushan in August 1959, attacking the shortcomings of the Great Leap Forward which he described as 'petty bourgeois fanaticism'. P'eng is also supposed to have made his attack with the fore-knowledge of the Soviet Union, having been in personal contact with Khrushchev himself. The evidence for this analysis comes from secret briefings later given to party members and revealed by refugees from China, and from the vociferous campaign against 'right opportunists' which broke out in the party and the army at the time of P'eng's dismissal.[3] There is little doubt that P'eng and his colleagues were dissatisfied with the economic policies behind the Great Leap. The new Minister of Defence, Lin Piao, referred obliquely to P'eng's and other 'right opportunists'' opposition to the Great Leap in a major speech immediately after his appointment: 'Confronted by the mass movement, they are only interested in picking faults and exaggerating them so as to spread slackness, despondency, dissatisfaction and pessimism, to negate our achievements and the Party's general line.'[4] Other references, however, in conjunction with the evidence contained in the secret PLA Bulletin of Activities, make it clear that the main dispute was over military policies. Charges laid obliquely or directly against P'eng, Huang, and their supporters include allegations that they represent 'the military line of the propertied class', that they advocate an 'erroneous military line' and oppose army participation in production, that they favour 'unreasonable military systems and formalities' and have committed the sins of 'dogmatism', 'warlordism', and 'feudalism'. They are also accused of preferring foreign military theory (i.e. Soviet) to Mao's own military doctrines, and of advancing the theory that 'weapons decide everything'.[5]

Many of these allegations are likely to have been exaggerated in order to present P'eng and his supporters as scapegoats for the worsening of relations between army and party during the Great Leap. They were, after all, without exception veterans of the

[3] For a detailed analysis on these lines, see further David A. Charles, 'The Dismissal of Marshal P'eng Teh-huai', *CQ*, Oct.–Dec. 1961.

[4] Lin Piao, 'March ahead under the Red Flag of the party's general line and Mao Tse-tung's military thinking', NCNA, 29 Sept. 1959.

[5] *Kung-tso T'ung-hsün*, summarized in Powell, *Politico-Military Relationships*, pp. 2–3.

revolutionary wars and senior party members, who had pursued the greater part of their military careers in the context of Mao's political and strategic theories. It is probable that they objected not to those theories in themselves, but to the unbalanced way in which they were implemented during the Great Leap. More radical opposition to Mao's military strategy is likely to have materialized at lower levels of the officer corps among younger professional elements with less experience of the PLA's revolutionary traditions, and to these officers the dismissal of P'eng Teh-huai would serve as a salutary warning.

Opposition to the 'Everyone a Soldier' movement, to the more extreme manifestations of military democracy such as the 'Officers to the Ranks' movement, and to the excessive time spent by the PLA in production work, doubtless played some part in P'eng Teh-huai's dismissal, but these are hardly sufficient reasons in themselves for such a major upheaval in the top-level military leadership at a critical time in China's domestic political scene. The major difference of opinion appears to have concerned the 'weapons versus man' debate and the closely related subject of policy towards the Soviet Union.

Military policy after the Korean war had been predicated on the assumption that the Soviet Union would remain a reliable ally, both as a supplier of military hardware and as a potential nuclear guarantor. Based upon this assumption, it was reasonable to reduce the size of the regular armed forces, to effect economies in defence expenditure, and even to involve the army in production on at least the limited scale of 1956–7. There is no reason to believe that P'eng or any other leading officers took serious exception to these policies.

Soviet military aid in 1955 allowed China to take the first steps in nuclear research, with a Soviet-supplied experimental reactor installed in Peking, and the training of Chinese atomic scientists at the Joint Institute for Nuclear Research at Dubna in the Soviet Union. Although these were officially intended for peaceful purposes, it may be supposed that research was also conducted with nuclear weaponry in mind.[6] Soviet aid also provided new

[6] In January 1955 the Soviet Union offered to supply China, along with Poland, Rumania, Czechoslovakia, and East Germany, with a research reactor and accelerator and fissionable material. Agreement was reached in April and China's first atomic research centre was opened in June under Soviet supervision. The Chinese government's State Council 'warmly welcomed' the Soviet offer,

equipment for the PLA and the rudiments of a national defence industry. Although China was still dependent on the Soviet Union for most heavy-armour arms, and aircraft, it was hoped eventually to produce this kind of advanced weaponry in China under Soviet licence. In the autumn of 1957 China attempted with apparent success to secure a larger Soviet commitment of military aid. An agreement 'on new technology for national defence' was signed on 15 October 1957. China has since claimed—and the Soviet Union does not deny—that this included Soviet agreement to 'provide China with a sample of an atomic bomb and technical data concerning its manufacture'. The signing of this agreement came immediately before the Moscow Meeting of Communist and Workers' Parties of November 1957, at which Mao Tse-tung strongly supported the Soviet Union as leader of the socialist bloc against East European demands for greater equality, and there may be an element of *quid pro quo* in this coincidence.

It is reasonable to suppose that P'eng Teh-huai and his staff had developed close contacts with Soviet military authorities, both while directing the Korean war with Soviet advisers and military equipment, and later at the Ministry of National Defence. P'eng accompanied Mao Tse-tung to Moscow in 1957, and while there he acted as head of a separate Chinese top-level military mission which arrived shortly afterwards. (The mission's deputy head was Marshal Yeh Chien-ying, and its two leading staff members were Su Yü and T'an Cheng.) It seems certain therefore that P'eng was personally in charge of the subsequent negotiations on how to implement the military agreement of 15 October.

The military agreement was only one illustration of a short-lived honeymoon in Sino-Soviet relations which followed the Moscow Meeting. As the *People's Daily* editorial of 14 February 1958 commemorating the 1950 Sino-Soviet treaty commented,

---

but commented ambiguously that 'an atomic pile can produce electric power to serve peace. It can also produce dangerous fissionable substances for the manufacture of atomic weapons to serve war' (resolution of 31 Jan. 1955, *People's China*, No. 4, 1955).

In September 1956, Chou En-lai told the Eighth Party Congress that the peaceful use of atomic energy was one of the 'weak links' in heavy industry. It would be given special attention in the five-year plan and would have the status of a 'major project' (NCNA, 20 Sept. 1956).

friendly relations between the two countries were strengthened and their unity consolidated 'especially in 1957'. Other agreements reached at the same time included a five-year scientific co-operation protocol concluded between China and the Soviet Union—this too may have had military implications.[7] It is impossible to say whether or not the Chinese leadership was fully united in this attempt to secure greater Soviet backing for China's military and technological development, but in any case P'eng was in charge of the most sensitive area of negotiations. These negotiations ran into difficulties during 1958 and finally broke down just two months before P'eng's dismissal in the following year.

It was common ground among the Chinese leadership that the PLA should aim for a higher level of technical modernization— not excluding nuclear weapons. What may well have been at issue was firstly the relationship of this aim to the political and economic demands made on the PLA, and secondly how far the Soviet Union could be relied upon to provide material assistance. Statements made by military leaders—especially by P'eng Teh-huai—around the time of the Moscow Meeting implied a high degree of confidence that Soviet aid would be forthcoming, but subsequent negotiations not only proved complex in themselves but also suffered from the general deterioration in Sino-Soviet relations.[8]

Negotiations probably centred on the difficult questions of control and command. It is likely that the Soviet Union favoured increased integration of communist bloc defences, including those of China, and would not supply nuclear weapons or technology to China without retaining effective control. This is confirmed in exaggerated form by the later Chinese allegation that

[7] The protocol, signed on 18 January 1958, provided for joint research by the two countries in the period 1958–62 on 122 scientific and technological items of great significance to China. The exchange of scientists and experts was agreed on, and other agreements were signed between ministries of higher education and academies of agricultural science and of science.

[8] In his Army Day speech of 31 July 1957, P'eng stressed the 'primary' role of the Soviet Union as a model for the PLA. He also linked the 'fraternal aid of the Soviet Union and the People's Democracies' to the forecast that the technical level of the army's equipment would rise and, in particular, that China would produce 'more and better aircraft' during the second five-year plan (NCNA, 31 July 1957, in *SCMP* 1584). See also P'eng's eulogy on the Soviet army, delivered during his visit to Moscow—'Learn from the Heroic Soviet Army', ibid. 4 Nov. 1957 (*SCMP* 1649).

'. . . in 1958 the leadership of the CPSU put forward unreasonable demands designed to bring China under military control. These unreasonable demands were rightly and firmly rejected by the Chinese government. . . '.[9] It is not known precisely when such demands were made and rejected. Soviet Army Day in February 1958 was celebrated with effusive demonstrations of solidarity on the part of China, but China's own Army Day in August was distinguished by a notable lack of reference to her Soviet ally. It is possible that negotiations reached an impasse during Khrushchev's surprise visit of that period to China (31 July–3 August) on which he was accompanied by his own Defence Minister, Marshal Malinovsky. China's position in these negotiations may have amounted to a refusal to surrender her right to undertake independent military initiatives; whilst the Soviet Union probably required assurances that such initiatives would not be taken before committing nuclear aid to China. The Taiwan straits crisis which was inspired by China immediately after Khrushchev's visit had the effect, and perhaps the intention, of clarifying the Soviet attitude. Soviet expressions of support for China in the crisis were only made at a late stage, and as China later commented:

Although at that time the situation in the Taiwan Straits was tense, there was no possibility that a nuclear war would break out and no need for the Soviet Union to support China with its nuclear weapons. It was only when they were clear that this was the situation that the Soviet leaders expressed their support for China. . . .[10]

This coupled with Soviet criticism of the Great Leap Forward and mounting disagreement over the desirability of peaceful co-existence and the correct communist-bloc tactics to be pursued towards the West, led to increasing and well-documented Sino-Soviet friction during the following year. It is interesting to note, therefore, that negotiations on mutual defence arrangements continued during the first half of 1959, and there were indica-

---

[9] Editorial Depts of *JMJP* & *Hung Ch'i*: 'The Origin and Development of the Differences Between the Leadership of the CPSU and Ourselves', 6 Sept. 1963 (*PR*, 13 Sept. 1963).

[10] 1 Sept. 1963, 'Statement by the Spokesman of the Chinese Government: a Comment on the Soviet Government's Statement of 21 August', ibid. 6 Sept. 1963. For an extended discussion of this question, see John R. Thomas, 'Soviet Behaviour in the Quemoy Crisis of 1958', *Orbis*, Spring 1962.

tions that China still hoped to secure nuclear aid from the Soviet Union.[11] It was not until 20 June 1959 that, according to the Chinese,

> the Soviet Government unilaterally tore up the agreement on new technology for national defence concluded between China and the Soviet Union on 15 October 1957, and refused to provide China with a sample of an atomic bomb and technical data concerning its manufacture.[12]

The continuation of negotiations until this time is also indirectly confirmed by a number of unofficial reports from Eastern European capitals regarding Sino-Soviet negotiations and rumoured agreements on Soviet nuclear sharing, joint command, and the remodelling of the Chinese army on lines capable of being equipped with nuclear weapons. These reports may well reflect the nature of the Soviet proposals rather than the Chinese reaction to them.[13] It is even possible that the Soviet Union made a limited goodwill gesture by supplying China with a number of ground-to-air missiles during the course of negotiations.[14]

The final rupture of 20 June came only a week after the return of a Chinese 'military goodwill mission', led by P'eng Teh-huai in person, which had spent seven weeks (24 April–13 June) touring the socialist countries of Eastern Europe. Passing through Moscow on the way out and back, P'eng had met Soviet military leaders including Marshal Malinovsky. The delegation's visit to Poland coincided with a meeting in Warsaw of the Foreign Ministers of the Warsaw Pact countries, and whilst in Albania, P'eng was said to have had a cordial meeting with Premier Khrushchev. He returned from Moscow to Peking on 13 June, accompanied as far as Ulan Bator by Marshal Koniev.[15] It seems probable, therefore, that the movements of this mission were at least partly connected with continuing negotiations with the

[11] Cf. Garthoff, 'Sino-Soviet Military Relations', *Ann. Amer. Acad. Pol. & Soc. Sci.*, Sept. 1963, pp. 89–90.

[12] As n. 9.

[13] e.g. reports in *NYT*, 18 Aug. 1958; *Sunday Times*, 22 Feb. 1959; *CSM*, 10 Oct. 1960; *Observer*, 12 Feb. 1961.

[14] In June 1959 Averell Harriman was told by Khrushchev that Russia had sent missiles to protect China against attacks from Taiwan (*Life*, 13 July 1959). Diplomatic sources in Moscow confirm that these are anti-aircraft ground-to-air missiles. It is possible that these have since been used to shoot down American high-altitude spy planes.

[15] Charles, 'Dismissal of Marshal P'eng. . . .', *CQ*, Oct.–Dec. 1961.

Soviet Union and the Warsaw Pact countries. It would not be surprising if the Eastern European governments urged China to accept closer defence co-ordination with the Warsaw Pact in return for increased military aid, on the same lines that the Soviet Union was urging. A probable exception was Albania— for even at this stage the tone of the Chinese mission's visit to Tirana was notably more cordial and 'anti-revisionist' than elsewhere.[16]

It is significant that the Warsaw Pact meeting was attended by Chang Wen-t'ien, Deputy Minister of Foreign Affairs, in an observer capacity. Chang, formerly a Comintern representative and ambassador to Moscow, was dismissed from office at the same time as P'eng Teh-huai in September. Immediately after the Warsaw Pact meeting it was reported that Huang K'o-ch'eng—also subsequently dismissed with P'eng from his post as chief of staff—delivered a report to one of the infrequent meetings of the National Defence Council in Peking.[17] After the return of the Chinese military mission from abroad—and exactly three days after the rupture of 20 June in negotiations with the Soviet Union—it was Hsiao Hua, the up-and-coming deputy director of the Political Department, and not P'eng Teh-huai, who delivered a report on the mission to a mass meeting of senior officers.[18]

P'eng was therefore responsible for negotiations concerning closer defence integration with China's allies at a time when the general trend in Chinese foreign policy was in the opposite direction—towards greater 'self-reliance' in the Great Leap style. These negotiations failed, perhaps against his own inclination and efforts, and P'eng may well have felt that this was the result of mistaken domestic policies and their effect upon foreign policy, and particularly upon Sino-Soviet relations. By moving farther away instead of closer to the Soviet Union, China was depriving herself of a redoubtable military ally and a potential supplier of

[16] 'Tirana reception for Chinese Military Goodwill Mission', NCNA, 29 May 1959 (*SCMP* 2026); 'Welcome meeting in Northern Albania for Marshal P'eng Teh-huai', ibid. 31 May 1959 (*SCMP* 2028).

[17] 'China's National Defence Council meets', NCNA, 5 May 1959 (*SCMP* 2010).

[18] 'Chinese military delegation reports back to PLA Officers', ibid. 23 June 1959 (*SCMP* 2044). Hsiao Hua reported on the visit to 'more than 5,000 officers', at this meeting. This may have been an Enlarged Conference of the Military Affairs Committee.

nuclear equipment. The safety of China, and of the whole socialist world, P'eng may have argued, lay in interdependency and not in going it alone in the spirit of 'self-reliance', as the Defence Ministers of the 'fraternal countries' had hinted at in their customary Army Day messages of August 1959.[19]

If this analysis is correct, an important element in P'eng's 'anti-party' activities for which he was dismissed was a fundamental disagreement over policy towards the Soviet Union with special military implications. Should China sacrifice some measure of control over her military affairs for the sake of continued, and possibly nuclear, support from the Soviet Union? Or should she do what in fact was done, accept a transitional period of military inferiority in which the Soviet guarantee was of dubious value, and meanwhile go all out to acquire an independent military capability? This latter policy was another example of the way in which military considerations were subordinated to the doctrinal requirements of Maoist theory which had been redefined during the Great Leap to cover every aspect of Chinese life. It also reflected a growing mistrust of Soviet willingness to seek a *détente* with the West, and disillusion with the effectiveness of her aid and overall support. On the other hand the rightist viewpoint, with which P'eng was identified, may have feared that Chinese military isolation would place her in an extremely vulnerable position *vis-à-vis* America's superior military strength, and may have regarded Mao's 'revolutionary' strategy—with its emphasis on the primacy of spiritual and political over technical factors—as an inadequate substitute for more conventional means of defence. Their position was distorted and exaggerated by official rebuttals to make it appear as if they were opposed to the Maoist doctrine as such.

They say that modern warfare is a war of technique, of steel and machinery, and that in the face of these things, man's role has to be relegated to a secondary place. They attach importance only to machinery and want to turn revolutionary soldiers into robots devoid of revolutionary initiative.[20]

---

[19] 'Minister of Defence of fraternal countries send messages of greetings on China's Army Day', NCNA, 1 Aug. 1959 (*SCMP* 2574). Their messages, according to this NCNA summary, 'pointed out that the unity of the socialist camp was the strongest guarantee for the defence and consolidation of world peace'.

[20] Lin Piao, 'March ahead under the Red Flag. . . .', NCNA, 29 Sept. 1959.

Yet the strength of the PLA's revolutionary tradition is such that it is doubtful if even the younger officer class took such an extreme view as was attributed to the rightist opposition. A more plausible form of opposition would be one which accepted that 'weapons' and 'man' are interrelated factors, but argued that the extreme policies of the Great Leap had led to an unacceptable imbalance in favour of the latter, which affected not only the domestic status of the PLA in political and economic terms, but its military preparedness for defence and its reliance upon external allies to render its defence posture credible. Although the question of the relevance of Mao's military strategy is presented in official pronouncements simply as a matter of theory and class outlook, it is inextricably connected with China's strategic position in the late 1950s and with the progress of the Sino-Soviet dispute.

STRATEGIC REAPPRAISAL

It is indeed not easy to talk about China's military strategy as such, since it is so intimately related to, and part of, the overall Maoist concept of China's place in the world which covers the entire range both of domestic and foreign policy. China's defence posture is based as much upon doctrinal predictions about the inevitable outcome of the struggle between socialism and imperialism as upon military forecasts as to the nature of any contingent threat to China's security. The same doctrinal predictions are also held to be valid in anticipating the outcome of the class struggle on the domestic scene. The military aspect of this doctrine is, however, disproportionately important, since analogies with the wartime experience of the Chinese communists play such a large part in their assessment of the contemporary situation at home and abroad. The writings of Mao Tse-tung—the doctrinal canon for the solution of all problems— are themselves largely concerned with military questions, and the great majority of those in print were written during the long pre-1949 revolutionary period.

This Maoist *weltanschauung*, although always implicit in his writings, only began to be clearly formulated and defined during the Great Leap Forward and the early phase of the Sino-Soviet dispute in 1958–9. This process of clarification was advanced by the publication in October 1958 of 'Imperialists and All Reactionaries are Paper Tigers'.[21] This was a hastily compiled collection of extracts from Mao's writings and speeches, ranging in date from *On Protracted War* (May 1958) to Mao's Yangtze tour of September 1958. It linked together three fundamental principles which provided theoretical justification for the militant and self-reliant policy underlying the Great Leap and the dispute with the Soviet Union over the correct tactics to be adopted towards the imperialist West. These were that imperialism is a 'paper tiger', that the east wind of socialism and national revolution now prevails over the west wind of imperialism and its running dogs, and that 'men, not materials are the determining factor in war'.

This publication was followed two years later, in October 1960, by the long-expected fourth volume of Mao's *Selected Works*, which covers the civil war period of 1945–9. Although this volume is of great historical value, in that it reproduces a large number of Mao's writings and speeches which had never before seen the light of day, the principle behind its selection is clearly biased in favour of those aspects of communist policy in the civil war which are felt to be relevant today. Its publication was accompanied by a number of much fuller and more coherent analyses of the contemporary meaning of Mao's military doctrine. While 'All Imperialists and Reactionaries Are Paper Tigers' had appeared to be intended mainly for a domestic audience—perhaps the 'rightists' like P'eng Teh-huai and others who were dubious about the new policies—the *Selected Works* was regarded as equally relevant abroad for those who were fighting for national independence and might otherwise be corrupted by Soviet 'modern revisionism'. It was described by Lin Piao as

. . . an event of great importance in the political life of the Chinese people. At the same time, it is a great event in the international working class movement because this work is a reflection of the victory of Marxism-Leninism in a big country which has the largest population in the world. Comrade Mao Tse-tung's ideas about daring to win and skill in waging struggle, his ideas about the use of dual revolutionary tactics to counter those of the counter-revolution, his ideas about imperialism and all reactionaries being paper tigers, his ideas about scorning the enemy strategically and taking full account of him tactically, his ideas about the people's revolutionary forces, inferior

---

[21] NCNA, 31 Oct. 1958 (*CB* 534).

numerically and in equipment, defeating the counter-revolutionary forces which are superior in these respects, and other ideas and theories will retain their great vitality in the long, historical period to come.[22]

More recent statements, especially in 1965, at the height of the war in Vietnam, have continued to elaborate upon the international significance of Maoist doctrine as 'a great contribution to the revolutionary struggles of the oppressed nations and peoples throughout the world'.[23] Emphasis upon this doctrine has become increasingly pronounced as China emerges more clearly as the champion of the national liberation struggle, as the Sino-Soviet rupture becomes irreconcilable, and potential conflict with the United States more likely. The intensification of these causes of tension, far from producing any modification or softening in the Chinese leadership's doctrinal analysis, has made it more rigid and defiant in tone. Significantly, the phrase 'Mao Tse-tung's military doctrine' has now been replaced by the more vivid description 'Mao Tse-tung's Theory of People's War'. This theory is regarded as being

. . . of vital practical importance for the Chinese people and for the people of the whole world in their struggle against U.S. imperialism and its lackeys and, in particular, for the oppressed nations in Asia, Africa, and Latin America in their struggle for liberation.[24]

Close analogies are drawn between the communist position during the civil war and that of today. First, there is the same confidence that, in the long run, their cause is invincible, and that the enemy is beset by innumerable internal contradictions. Although in terms of short-term tactics, imperialism is an adversary who must be taken seriously, in terms of long-range strategy it can and should be despised as a 'paper tiger'. At home there is the same confidence that, while the struggle between the bourgeois and socialist paths may be protracted and complicated, ultimately the right cause will prevail. Second, there is the same willingness to 'go it alone', if necessary, rather than accept compromise. To compromise with imperialism today on its own terms would be as disastrous as if the communists had accepted an un-

[22] Lin Piao, 'The victory of the Chinese people's revolutionary war is the victory of the thought of Mao Tse-tung', *Hung Ch'i*, 1 Oct. 1960 (*ECMM* 231).
[23] Lin Piao, 'Long live the victory of people's war', *PR*, 3 Sept. 1965.
[24] *Hung Ch'i* editorial note, 21 Aug. 1965 (ibid. 27 Aug. 1965).

equal compromise with the KMT in 1946. If a refusal to compromise means forfeiting Soviet support, as it did in 1946, this again is a price which has to be paid. The counterpart of this in domestic economic terms is the policy of 'self-reliance' or 'reliance upon one's own resources', which was the keynote of the Great Leap Forward and was retrospectively justified by the withdrawal of Soviet aid in 1960. Third, morale and class consciousness are the decisive factors in determining one's strength and potentiality. Material possessions are common to both sides in any struggle, or they may even place one's adversary in a position of technical advantage. But human endeavour and the pursuit of a just cause not only compensate for any disadvantage in the material field, but provide the decisive edge over one's adversary which will enable one to be victorious. Just as a numerically inferior communist army triumphed over its KMT opponents in the civil war by virtue of its superior morale and class consciousness, so in the atomic age a numerically superior Chinese people will triumph over a nuclear enemy with sophisticated modern weapons for the same reasons. By the same argument, economic progress at home is important, but it takes second place to, and indeed is determined by, political progress in creating a national spirit of revolutionary endeavour and class consciousness.

These doctrinal concepts have important consequences for China's military posture and strategy. The first and most important question which dominates Chinese thinking is that of the possibility of war being 'unleashed' by the United States against them. They take it for granted that such a war would involve the use of nuclear weapons. In 1957, when the Sino-Soviet alliance was still regarded as valid, in a military sense, China appeared to believe that the Soviet Union's attainment of nuclear parity with the United States would effectively inhibit the latter from aggressive action. Just as the achievement of numerical parity by the PLA in the autumn of 1948 with the Nationalist forces had created a 'momentous turning-point' which opened the way to victory, so—as Mao Tse-tung told the Moscow Meeting of Communist and Workers' Parties in November 1957—the East–West nuclear stalemate had created a 'new turning-point' in which 'the east wind prevails over the west wind, that is, the strength of socialism exceeds the strength of imperialism'. Unlike the Soviet leaders, Mao did not regard the nuclear stalemate

R

as imposing inhibitions on the conduct of communist bloc policy; on the contrary, it created a new situation in which more dynamic policies could be pursued. This was the crux of the Sino-Soviet debate over the correct tactics to be adopted towards the imperialist West. Mao did not altogether rule out the possibility of nuclear war, and he claimed that if the worst came to the worst the socialist world could survive it. But he argued—and the same argument has been consistently put forward since 1957 by China—that appeasement of or compromise with the imperialist camp was more likely to encourage its aggressive appetite—and therefore lead even to nuclear war—than the reverse.

As Sino-Soviet discord developed over the next two years, it became clear to China first that the Soviet Union was more interested in reaching a rapprochement with the West—even at China's own expense—and secondly that China herself could no longer rely upon the Soviet nuclear umbrella to protect her from attack. China was not prepared to accept Soviet nuclear aid on the terms on which it was offered, nor to grant acquiescence in Soviet foreign policy which the acceptance of her nuclear aid would have involved. By refusing to compromise with the Soviet Union, China deliberately accepted that she would render herself temporarily more vulnerable to the danger of enemy attack which, if it came, would in all probability be directed exclusively against her rather than against the communist bloc as a whole. While China's own nuclear programme was pushed ahead with all possible speed, the risk of enemy attack was accepted with open eyes. Even since the explosion of China's own first nuclear weapons, she has made it clear that she does not regard her present primitive nuclear capability as sufficient to automatically deter the United States, although as it grows stronger it will be an increasingly credible deterrent.

The *Kung-tso T'ung-hsün* documents reveal that contingency planning to cope with a possible enemy attack was a constant preoccupation in 1960–1. It is true that such an attack was not felt to be very likely; the internal contradictions which were seen to beset American foreign policy and the strength of the 'peace forces' in the world were felt to be in all probability sufficient to deter such an attack. Yet the possibility that the United States would 'lose its sanity' and embark upon nuclear war could not be ruled out. If such a war took place, it was expected to take the form of a surprise nuclear air attack against urban and industrial centres on the Chinese mainland, followed by a conventional invasion with ground forces, and ultimately by the use of chemical and biological weapons.

This contingency was accepted, and the plans which were made to assimilate its possible effects were based on a mixture of shrewd strategic analysis and of a doctrinal belief in the superiority of 'man' over 'weapons'. The consequences of a surprise nuclear attack could be minimized in the first place by better anti-air defence and communications in the PLA—improvements in these sectors were frequently called for in the *Kung-tso T'ung-hsün*. It was also decided to build all new military installations well away from main urban and industrial centres, in order to decrease their vulnerability to nuclear attack. It was recognized that China's cities and industries would be badly hit, but on the other hand China's vast territory and population meant that outright victory could not be secured by a nuclear strike alone. Such a strike would have to be followed by a protracted war on China's own territory, involving a massive commitment of enemy manpower. It was here that China would demonstrate both her numerical and moral superiority. The role of her regular forces would be to engage the enemy at close quarters, thus inhibiting any further use of nuclear weapons once the initial strike had been made. Military training, according to the *Kung-tso T'ung-hsün*, of PLA ground forces emphasized the importance of close combat. This was another area where the PLA's revolutionary experience in tactical manœuvring and in combat at close quarters was felt to be of continued relevance. The PLA would be reinforced in case of war by the militia, which would both replenish its ranks and provide defence in depth against enemy invasion.

Paradoxically to the West, but not to the Chinese, this essentially cautious and defensive strategy does not preclude support, moral or material, for wars of national liberation elsewhere. On the contrary, viewed from a world perspective, such wars supplement China's own security, by inducing the United States to over-extend its military commitments abroad, and by widening the area in which it is confronted by the forces of 'democracy'. Just as in the anti-Japanese and civil wars, the 'towns' occupied by the enemy were eventually encircled by the 'countryside' in which the communist strength was located, so on a world-wide scale, the capitalist countries of Europe and North America are seen as the towns which the vast countryside of the peoples of Asia, Africa, and Latin America will eventually surround and overwhelm. There is no reason to doubt that when Chinese spokesmen say that they are 'grateful' and 'indebted' to the revolutionary struggles of the people of Vietnam and elsewhere, they do not genuinely see such movements as assisting China herself to ward off the forces of imperialism.

Three points need to be emphasized about the strategic outlook which has emerged in China since 1958. First, it is essentially defensive, concentrating upon preparations to meet the contingency of enemy invasion which, while unlikely, cannot be altogether ruled out. Training for offensive warfare appears to be confined to the sort of limited operations which have been carried out in Tibet and on the Sino-Indian and Sino-Soviet borders. There is no indication that even the 'liberation' of Taiwan in a military sense is considered to be a realistic objective. Secondly, a relatively low priority is placed upon technological progress for offensive purposes, with the notable exception of the development of nuclear weapons and a missile delivery system. The navy is barely mentioned in the *Kung-tso T'ung-hsün*, the air force appears to receive no special priorities in the allocation of resources. Although the production of weapons, munitions, and related items was said to have fallen a long way behind requirements, nevertheless the PLA was expected to 'firmly respect' the reduced budget for 1961 for national defence. There is no evidence to show since then that any major effort has been made in improving the PLA's firepower or logistics in order to acquire a sophisticated military machine rivalling that of either the United States or the Soviet Union. The emphasis appears to be on the replacement of existing Soviet-supplied weapons systems by similar systems of Chinese manufacture. Thirdly, political calculations play an unusually important part in determining military strategy, and fill many gaps which would otherwise have to be filled by increased military expenditure. The essence of Mao's military strategy is indeed precisely this: that it is only a component part of a wider doctrinal analysis of the situation in which China finds herself, and that military requirements alone are not allowed to be the sole determinant of policy decisions. The most obvious example of this is, of course, the question of relations with the Soviet Union. Finally, while many of the strategic arguments which are advanced may well be correct and appropriate in China's particular situation, they stem from a unitary doctrinal approach which covers the entire range of domestic and foreign policy, and which is specifically based upon the experience and analogy of the revolutionary period, and especially of the civil war. Mao Tse-tung's military dialectics are regarded as 'objective' laws which will continue to be as relevant in the future as they were in the past. As one panegyric concludes:

> Comrade Mao Tse-tung's military dialectics is broad and profound. . . . Comrade Mao Tse-tung's military dialectics is practical philosophy. It was born in the revolutionary wars and demonstrated infinite fighting power in them. It radiates dazzling rays of victory like the sun and the moon in the sky. It will live for ever.[25]

This brief summary of Maoist doctrine and strategy cannot do justice to the very complex issues concerning both foreign and domestic policy, and the relationship of ideological theory to practice, which are raised by it. It is intended only to illustrate the profound changes in the outlook of the Chinese leadership over recent years, which have radically affected their attitude and approach towards the PLA as towards every other aspect of policy. Against this background of the revolutionization of foreign and domestic policy, the PLA itself has been subjected to a similar process, especially in the vital field of political control and education.[26]

[25] Fu Chung, 'Great victory for Mao Tse-tung's military dialectics', *JMJP*, 6–7 Oct. 1960 (*SCMP* 2360).

[26] For further reading on recent Chinese military doctrine and strategy, see especially Hsieh, 'China's Secret Military Papers; Military Doctrine and Strategy'. *CQ*, Apr.–June 1964; Halperin, *China and the Bomb*.

12

Restoration of Political Control

Only by actually arming ourselves mentally with Mao's thoughts can we be good and do good ceaselessly. The countless model heroes were able to perform heroic deeds of various kinds under dissimilar circumstances because they had attained a revolutionary world outlook devoted to a struggle to the finish for communism. . . . Come ghosts or ghouls, imperialism or revisionists, they have no fear for any enemy and they hold hardship and adversity in contempt. They can weather any kind of political storm and withstand the ravages of a force 12 typhoon.[1]

THE replacement in September 1959 of Marshal P'eng Teh-huai as Minister of Defence by Marshal Lin Piao meant that the PLA had once again an effective leader and spokesman. P'eng, as a 'rightist' and an opponent of the Great Leap policy, could hardly have represented their interests effectively. Lin, closer in spirit to the party leadership, and also personally popular with the rank and file of the army, was in a better position to modify the more extreme policies which had affected the PLA. The major task facing Lin and the Military Affairs Committee, which was reorganized at the time of his appointment, was to restore the PLA's political morale, to strengthen party control over it, and to resolve the 'struggle between bourgeois and working-class ideology' which resulted from military concern about the effect of the Great Leap policies upon its own position. In his first major policy speech Lin called for intensified political education, stricter party control, and more contact with the masses, yet in a more conciliatory tone than had recently been shown towards the PLA. In criticizing those elements within the army who had rejected the mass movements, he admitted that there had been 'shortcomings' in setting up the people's communes. And in attacking those who took a 'materialistic' view of modern warfare, he nevertheless emphasized the importance of technique and modernization.

[1] *CFCP* editorial, 23 Nov. 1965 (*FE(2)* 2022).

Some comrades take the view that modern warfare differs from warfare in the past, that since the weapons and equipment available to our army in the past were inferior we had to emphasize dependence on man, on his bravery and wisdom, in order to win victories. They say that modern warfare is a war of technique, of steel and machinery, and that in the face of these things, man's role has to be relegated to a secondary place. They attach importance only to machinery and want to turn revolutionary soldiers into robots devoid of revolutionary initiative. Contrary to these people, we believe that while equipment and technique are important, the human factor is even more so. Technique also has to be mastered by man. Men and material must form a unity with men as the leading factor.

This was a subtle but significant modification of the theory that 'men are superior to material', which had placed 'man' in a position of unqualified primacy. While endorsing the importance of 'military democracy', Lin again defined the concept in terms which were more acceptable to the professional mind.

The democracy which we practise is democracy under centralized guidance and it is carried out under leadership. We are at all times opposed to anarchism and equalitarianism. While carrying forward democratic life in the army, we also consider and take into account the special features of an army at all times and places. We take democracy as a means whereas our end is to increase the army's unity, strengthen its discipline and raise its fighting strength.[2]

---

[2] Lin Piao, 'March ahead under the Red Flag. . .', NCNA, 29 Sept. 1959 (Foreign Languages Press trans., pp. 16–17, 21–22). See also Lin Piao's speech of 27 Apr. 1960 to the national militia work conference, in which he again spoke of 'the important role modern technology plays in war' (*SCMP* 2252). The same point was made by Fu Chung, 'Great victory for Mao Tse-tung's military dialectics', *JMJP*, 6–7 Oct. 1960 (*SCMP* 2360).

'Stressing the role of man does not at all signify that the role of weapons is no longer important. Following the development of science and technology, obviously more powerful modern weapons have been invented. It is military conservatism to close one's eyes to the development of the military techniques or to attach no importance to the role of modern weapons. Conservatism will only make the technical equipment of the army backward, and backwardness means receiving blows without being able to strike back.'

The importance of military training was also re-emphasized. Previously, it was said, 'dogmatism and empiricism swung either to the right or to the left' on this question (*KTTH*, 6 Feb. 1961 (Cheng, p. 217)). It was now to be clearly understood that while political training was the 'commander-in-chief' and the essential basis for all other work, 'in terms of time, military training must be given first priority . . . we must make sure that at least 60 to 70 per cent of our time is given over to military training' (speech by Liu Ya-lou in *KTTH*, 20 Feb. 1961 (Cheng, pp. 264–5)).

The task of the new military leadership was complicated by the severe economic crisis which hit China in 1960–1, and which had serious repercussions on army morale, health, and political responsibility. The secret *Kung-tso T'ung-hsün* (Bulletin of Activities) documents, which are available to us for the first half of 1961,[3] make this abundantly clear. The PLA's peasant conscripts were perturbed by reports coming from their homes of malnutrition, widespread shortages, and economic hardship, and even of victimization of their families by corrupt local cadres. One of the problems frequently discussed in the *Kung-tso T'ung-hsün* is that of how to handle letters and visits from soldiers' families in the worst hit 'disaster areas', and of how to prevent such soldiers losing faith in the party's leadership and its policies.

Although living conditions in the PLA were maintained at a higher level than those of the civilian population, they were not immune from major cuts and shortages. Rations were cut in September 1960, and troops were urged to increase production of their own food. The winter of 1960–1 saw a serious decline in health standards in the PLA, and it was reported that about 5 per cent of all personnel suffered from body swelling due to malnutrition. Cases of contagious disease rose sharply by 30 per cent over the same period of the previous year. Another symptom of the PLA's general malaise was the way in which equipment was carelessly maintained and stored, or even lost. This aggravated the already serious shortages created by the withdrawal of Soviet aid in 1960. There were also complaints of alarmingly high accident rates, especially in the air force.

Most of these shortcomings appear to have been solved by 1962, when the economic situation had greatly improved and various remedial measures had had time to take effect. Yet although the Military Affairs Committee took them very seriously at the time, and expended a great deal of personal attention in putting them right, the *Kung-tso T'ung-hsün* reveals that, even during the worst period of economic crisis, the military leadership was chiefly concerned with political education in the PLA and the reassertion of party control.

The year 1960 onwards has seen a determined and uninterrupted drive, under the close supervision of Minister of Defence

[3] For details of the *Kung-tso T'ung-hsün*, see above, p. 216 n. 48.

Lin Piao, the Military Affairs Committee, and Mao Tse-tung himself, to raise the PLA's political loyalty and ideological commitment from the low level to which it had sunk at the time of the dismissal of Marshal P'eng Teh-huai. The methods used to raise political standards are not new, and they owe much to past experience. What is, however, new is the intensity with which they are applied, and the thorough attention to organizational detail which distinguishes them from previous efforts of a similar nature. Politics is seen to be 'the soul and the supreme command'. It is 'the lifeline of the Liberation Army as well as the fundamental guarantee of all kinds of work'.[4] Every single aspect of military life is subsumed within the framework of political control and education, and scarcely a month goes by without a major pronouncement or editorial in the *People's Daily* or *Liberation Army Newspaper* on the subject.

This continuous campaign to raise the political and ideological standards of the PLA dates back to an extraordinary meeting of an enlarged session of the party's Military Affairs Committee, held from 14 September to 20 October 1960. It was at this meeting that Marshal Lin Piao called for a 'breakthrough' in ideological work. 'It is impossible to fight other battles well', he said, 'if the ideological battle is not fought victoriously.' He propounded four basic principles—subsequently known as the 'Four Firsts'—which provided the theoretical foundation for the renewed emphasis upon political work. The 'human factor' came first in the relationship between weapons and men; politics came first in the relationship between political work and other kinds of military work; ideology came first in the relationship between routine and ideological political education; and 'living thought' came first in the relationship between book learning and its practical application. Implicit in Lin Piao's formulation is an attempt to overcome the weakness which had characterized previous political campaigns—the tendency for the content of political education to become stereotyped, and for its application to become a formal ritual with only a superficial impact upon military thinking. The previous military leadership was blamed by implication for having allowed political work to become a formality, and we are told that the 'Four Firsts' were formulated

---

[4] 'Marshal Lin Piao on political work in the Chinese PLA', NCNA, 8 Oct. 1960 (*SCMP* 2358).

by Lin Piao after criticism of the 'capitalistic military road' of P'eng Teh-huai and his chief of staff Huang K'o-ch'eng. The new political drive was endorsed in a resolution of the Military Affairs Committee on 'The Strengthening of Political and Ideological Work among the Armed Forces', which called for a radical overhaul both of the content and of the machinery of political education in the PLA. This resolution drew attention to the continuing importance of Mao Tse-tung's Kutien speech of December 1929 as the 'basis for political work', and stated that Mao Tse-tung's thought was the 'basis for our army in the past present and future'. The detailed measures which were laid down in the resolution amount to a reaffirmation of the all-inclusive nature of political work as formulated by Mao at Kutien.[5] Since the enlarged session of the Military Affairs Committee, political work conferences have been held by the General Political Department of the PLA approximately once a year, which have assessed the progress of the movement and called for greater efforts.[6] A series of slogans and campaigns have been popularized, of which the most important are the 'Five-Good' campaign for the rank-and-file soldier, the parallel 'Four-Good' campaign for army companies, the 'Three-Eight' working style, the 'seven measures in improving leadership over companies', the 'twelve basic experiences in company building', and the 'company management and education' campaign.[7]

POLITICAL WORK AT COMPANY LEVEL

Behind these slogans and campaigns, one can detect two distinct but complementary approaches to the problem of political control and education; firstly the emphasis placed upon the company as the basic unit of army organization, and secondly the attention devoted to political education of the ordinary rank-and-file soldier. During the period of modernization political education at the company level had been allowed to lapse, just as in terms of strategy the importance of the battalion and regiment was enhanced at the expense of the company. By 1960,

[5] The text of this resolution and of Lin Piao's speech on the 'Four Firsts' is found in *KTTH*, 7 Jan. 1961.
[6] PLA political work conferences have been held in Mar. 1961, 18 Oct.–11 Nov. 1961, Feb. 1963, Jan. 1964 and Jan. 1966.
[7] For the text of these and other formulae, see 'Terms of PLA political work', *CFCP*, 22 Jan. 1964 (*CB* 732).

according to the resolution of the enlarged Military Affairs Committee, there were no party branch committees in approximately one-third of all PLA companies. Party control was even faultier below company level, where most platoons had no party cells, and most squads had no party members.[8]

The company was now seen as the fulcrum on which the whole apparatus of political control was balanced. As General Hsiao Hua described it:

> The company is the basic combat unit. It must be tough in the battlefield. It cannot do this if it does not have the strong leadership of the Party or the practical work of a Party branch. . . . The quality of the work of a company depends on the work of its Party branch and on the role played by its Party members. The Party branch is the nucleus of leadership and unity of the company and is the company's fortress.[9]

In April 1961, after thorough investigation, the party branch had been restored to all companies, 80 per cent of the platoons had organized party cells, and over half of the squads had party members. About 2,000 unreliable regular and probationary party members in the PLA had been dismissed and 229,000 new party members had been recruited.[10]

Once the party's membership had been reconstituted, attention turned to the company-level political organizations, which had also been allowed to become ineffective. The PLA political work conference of November 1961 adopted four sets of regulations governing political work, which re-defined and re-emphasized the importance of the company political instructor, the party branch, the Revolutionary Servicemen's Committee, and the Young Communist League branch. The first three of these, it will be recalled, were all institutions which had been encouraged or revived during the third revolutionary war, and were now once again reinvigorated for the same purpose of strengthening party liaison with the company level. The party branch was now described as 'the basic-level organization(s) of the Party in the armed forces, the basic transmission belt(s) between the Party and the masses, and the core of unified leader-

---

[8] *KTTH*, 7 Jan. & 13 June 1961.
[9] Hsiao Hua, 'Basic experiences of the past two years concerning the creation of Four-Good Companies in the army', *JMJP*, 1 Apr. 1963 (*SCMP* 2971).
[10] See further Powell, *Politico-Military Relationships*, pp. 7–8.

ship and unity of companies'.[11] It is reported to have extensive powers 'over not only political indoctrination, but also promotions, punishments, training and even operational matters'.[12] The Revolutionary Servicemen's Committee was the elected committee of the Soldiers' Club, an institution which itself had lapsed and had to be revived. In a predominantly youthful army, the main burden of party recruitment fell upon the branches of the YCL (successor to the NDYL, which had performed the same function during the Korean war).[13] YCL members were regarded as the party's 'storm-troopers' in the army; they were required to be 'models of the 3–8 work-style, special-grade marksmen and technical experts of distinction . . . pace setters in the technical innovation movement and . . . backbone elements in the armed forces'.[14]

EDUCATION OF RANK AND FILE

The second approach towards the problem of political control and education was through efforts to secure the loyalty of the individual rank-and-file soldier, and in particular the younger element in the PLA. Thus the problem was attacked at its weakest point—the young, conscript soldier who is deficient both in battle experience and in revolutionary zeal. For as one military spokesman observed:

Since the revolutionary military service system was put into practice, all privates in our Army have been youths, and a considerable portion of its basic-level cadres have also been youths. . . . Youths between the ages of 18 and 19 especially have never experienced in person the great calamity of class exploitation and national oppression. . . . Individual youths even forget what they are and cannot adopt a correct attitude towards certain temporary difficulties encountered in the advancement of the revolution, and are frequently susceptible to the corruptive influences of bourgeois ideology.[15]

---

[11] 'Four sets of regulations on political work in company-level units of PLA promulgated for enforcement', NCNA, 21 Nov. 1961 (*SCMP* 2630).

[12] Powell, p. 9.

[13] 40 per cent of new recruits to the PLA in 1960 joined the YCL, and over 95 per cent of the new party members enrolled from the PLA in the 1961 enrolment drive were already YCL members (*Chung-kuo Ch'ing-nien Pao*, 11 Feb. & 3 May 1961 (*SCMP* 2460 & 2503)).

[14] 'Regulations on the work of YCL branches', ibid. 24 Nov. 1961 (*SCMP* 2632).

[15] Liu Chih-chien, 'Strengthen ideological and political work among youths in the army, bring them up as "Red and Expert" successors', ibid. 3 May 1961 (*SCMP* 2503).

Young soldiers were encouraged to join their local branch of the YCL, or the Soldiers' Club, and to compete in the Five-Good movement, which calls for good performance in political thinking, military training, style of work, fulfilment of tasks, and physical education. This movement, initiated in its present form by the enlarged session of the Military Affairs Committee in 1960 (a previous version had been introduced in May 1958),[16] extolled all the simple virtues and basic principles by which the personal behaviour of the individual soldier should be governed if he was to be truly 'revolutionary'. He should study Chairman Mao's writings, adroitly use and protect his weapons and equipment, obey orders promptly and agilely, acquire good habits of cleanliness and hygiene, etc., etc. In accordance with the precept of Lin Piao that 'One who knows nothing about exploitation knows nothing about revolution',[17] young soldiers were invited to re-create in their imaginations the bitter days of pre-Liberation—a process known as the 'recollection of past bitterness and appreciation of present sweetness'. They sang revolutionary songs, interviewed veterans, visited exhibitions of revolutionary relics, and read the memoirs of wartime heroes.

By the end of 1963 the intensive efforts made over the previous three years to inculcate the PLA with the revolutionary traditions of the past and to ensure obedience to party control had apparently been very successful. The *People's Daily* wrote that

a great change has been brought about in the ideological aspect of the troops, the viewpoint of class and class struggle has become even more definite, the proletarian fighting will has become stronger, the concept of combat readiness has been strengthened, the revolutionary spirit of working hard and the fine communist quality has been further developed, and more and more heroes, models, good persons and good deeds have emerged.[18]

---

[16] The 1958 movement called for good performance in study, care of weapons, prevention of accidents, practice of economy, and production and physical training ('PLA General Political Department issues directive on practice of "Five-Good" campaign in all army companies', NCNA, 14 May 1958, in (*SCMP* 1777)).

[17] Quoted in 'Comrade Hsiao Hua dwells on important work of company-building at PLA political work conference', *JMJP*, 15 Nov. 1961 (*SCMP* 2626).

[18] 'Raise still higher the Great Banner of Mao Tse-tung's thinking, perform the tasks of creating "Four-Good" companies in a still better manner', *JMJP* editorial, 1 Jan. 1964 (*FE(2)* 1448).

1963 POLITICAL WORK REGULATIONS

In February 1963 the party leadership appeared sufficiently confident in the PLA's receptiveness to radical and 'revolutionary' measures to draw up a new code of Political Work Regulations which raised the status of the political commissar to a level which he had not possessed since before Liberation. The greater part of these new regulations consisted of a reformulation of the traditional political control structure through party committees and political departments down to regimental level, but their most significant provisions concerned the political commissar. As before, the political commissar was responsible for carrying out decisions relating to political work, while the military commander of the same unit was responsible for decisions relating to military work. Yet in effect the scope of the former had been extended to cover the latter; and both fighting and training now came within the ambit of politics. The regulations defined the role of the commissars in the PLA in the following wide terms:

The political commissars are in charge of the daily affairs of the Party committees, whose main job it is to carry out leadership over Party work and political work in the army. They must devote their main efforts to matters dealing with guiding principles and to politico-ideological work in order to ensure the successful implementation of the lines and policies of the Party and the laws and decrees of the State, and to guarantee the resolute execution of orders and directives at higher levels and the fulfilment of tasks pertaining to fighting, training and so forth.

In addition to this, it was also laid down that

Political commissars and military commanders are army unit leaders and both are responsible for the work of their unit. . . . By instituting the system of making both the political commissars and military commanders army unit leaders, we shall . . . guard against the tendency of unilaterally pursuing a purely military view point and leaning towards militarism.[19]

While appearing simply to place the commissar and commander

---

[19] The Regulations governing PLA Political Work are summarized in 'Raise aloft the Great Red Banner of the Thought of Mao Tse-tung, resolutely implement regulations governing political work', *JMJP*, 10 May 1963 (*SCMP* 2984). The original text has not been made public.

on an equal level, this measure was clearly intended to ensure that the commissar's control extended to even those functions of the commander which had been regarded as 'military' and therefore within his own sphere.

The Political Work Regulations may mark the high-water mark in the party's efforts to re-establish its influence in the PLA. Nor did it apparently arouse sufficient objection within the ranks of the PLA to warrant rebuttal and argument of the kind which had accompanied all previous attempts by the party in the 1956–9 period to assert its control. A similar and more recent measure which also suggests that the PLA officer corps has been conditioned to accept the most 'revolutionary' of measures is the outright abolition of the system of ranks, awards, and insignia which had been first introduced in 1955. These were abolished in May 1965 by decision of the State Council. All distinctions in rank and uniform were to be done away with, in order to 'carry forward the glorious traditions of our army and promote the revolutionisation of it'. The PLA would revert to the practice whereby officers were simply known as 'commanders', and the men as 'fighters'. The Western style of military dress worn by officers of field rank and above would be dispensed with. Epaulettes would be abolished, and every single member of the PLA would wear the same red star on his hat and red badge on his collar.[20] It was explained that the system introduced in 1955 had proved to be 'not in conformity with our army's glorious tradition, with the close relations between the officers and men, between the higher and lower levels, and between the army and the people'. Its abolition would

help to eliminate certain objective factors contributing to breed rank consciousness and ideas to gain fame and wealth; it will also help us more consciously to place ourselves in the position of ordinary soldiers and ordinary workers, remould ourselves ideologically, and go further in establishing the idea of wholehearted service to the people.[21]

[20] 'State Council decision on abolition of military ranks', NCNA, 24 May 1965 (*FE(2)* 1868).
[21] 'An important measure in promoting further the revolutionisation of our army', *CFCP* editorial, 25 May 1965 (*FE(2)* 1868). The abolition of ranks does appear to have met with some opposition. Ho Lung's speech of 1 Aug. 1965 is clearly intended to rebut criticism of this measure (see below p. 260).

ALL-INCLUSIVE NATURE OF PARTY CONTROL

The apparent success of the political campaign in the PLA since 1960, and of the improved receptiveness to party control which it has induced, stems from the thoroughness with which it has been carried out and its universal applicability to every aspect of army life. No individual person, function, or unit is exempt from its operations. As the Political Work Regulations of 1963 emphasized,

political work is not only to be carried out by the political cadres, but also by military cadres, administrative cadres, and technical cadres; not only to be carried out by cadres, but also to be carried out by combatants; not only to be carried out by a few advanced elements, but also to be carried out by the masses.

What in effect has been sought after is a total *rapport* between the party leadership and the rank and file which is all-inclusive in character. It should extend beyond the cadres into the grass-roots of the masses. It should embrace not only the broad principles but also the year-to-year shifts of policy. It should ensure a two-way continuity between ruling and ruled, with no awkward breaks in the transmission system. As Marshal Lin Piao described it, 'the function of political work was to communicate the ideas of the leadership to the masses and vice versa and clear away any possible obstacles'.[22]

If the slogans of the 'Five-Good' and other political education movements seem at times to be repetitious and statements of the obvious, they must also be seen in the light of the comparative youth of those for whom such movements are intended, and of the lack of a well-established military tradition, which makes it necessary to emphasize the most elementary of instructions. Although the study of Chairman Mao's writings occupies the prime position in this and every other movement, the lessons learnt from this study are translated into practical action in every field of army life, however mundane or commonplace. Maoism provides a substitute for the traditions and *esprit de corps* which had begun to develop during the modernizing period, and which were deliberately thwarted by the party. The thought of Mao Tse-tung is the fabric which holds and binds together the complex relationships and functions of a regular army. It is a uni-

[22] 'Marshal Lin Piao on political work in the Chinese PLA' (*SCMP* 2358).

versal framework which covers the entire spectrum of army life, and from which nothing is excluded. Bodily cleanliness is regarded as important and as significant as ideological purity. Even the PLA 'sanitation campaign' is said to have an inner significance for the soldiers taking part, for, 'when carrying out sanitation work, they also pay attention to doing well in man's ideological work'.[23]

The most famous 'Five-Good' soldier of them all was Comrade Lei Feng, who was posthumously celebrated as a model soldier and student of Chairman Mao's thought after his death in a road accident. Extracts from his diary were published to show how the ordinary soldier could apply the lessons learnt from Chairman Mao to the most mundane of circumstances, and Mao himself called upon the entire youth of China to 'learn from Lei Feng'. As one commentator explained:

In order to become Chairman Mao's good fighter, one should learn the ordinary and yet great communist spirit of Lei Feng. . . . In our socialist construction, the bulk of our work is ordinary, routine work in which the morality and style of every youth will necessarily be expressed. By demonstrating 'the most enduring, the most dogged, and the most praise-worthy' revolutionary spirit in all aspects of routine work, one's utterance and action will naturally shine with the brilliance of greatness. Lei Feng was just like that.[24]

This wide scope and attention to detail of political work, and its application to the most ordinary situations, was emphasized by Hsiao Hua:

Our ideological work must be done with increasing care and must be ever more alive. It must be carried out on every single person. In doing ideological work, it is necessary to pay special attention to opportune moments. Such moments include, for instance, the time when a major change has occurred in the national or international situation; the time when the Party or the State has promulgated a major policy; the time when the tasks of the forces have changed; the time when estrangement has occurred between veterans and new recruits; the time when old warriors have retired or new warriors have joined the Army; the time when influences are exerted by difficulties in family life or by problems of marriage or bereavement; the

---

[23] NCNA, 6 Mar. 1964 (*FE(2)*, Weekly Suppl. No. 255).
[24] Hu Yao-pang, 'Raise the proletarian consciousness of young people to a new height', *JMJP*, 28 Apr. 1963 (*SCMP* 2985).

s

time when applications for Party or Young Communist League membership are not approved; the time when promotions in rank or position are not granted [etc., etc.].[25]

The purpose of the political campaign in the PLA has therefore much in common with the nation-wide 'socialist education' movement, which is also concerned to bring politics and the thought of Chairman Mao into every aspect of ordinary life, to raise the revolutionary standards and to find 'revolutionary successors' among the younger generation. Significantly, the PLA's political campaign antedates by three years the national 'socialist education' movement (which started in 1963). In a sense, the PLA was used from 1960 onwards as a test-bed for political work methods, before their application to the nation at large. If political loyalties could not be strengthened in the army, it may have been thought, with all the advantages of military discipline and total control of personnel, what hope was there in the far more difficult conditions of civilian life? If on the other hand the techniques evolved since 1960 were successful, they could then be extended more widely. The original key resolution of the enlarged session of the Military Affairs Committee of October 1960 was endorsed by the party Central Committee in words which explicitly underlined its relevance to party activities in the civilian sphere.

This resolution is not only the right direction and the basic principle for the reconstruction and political work of army units, but it can also be of use to all levels of party organizations, government organs and schools, enterprises, etc., and should be distributed to all organizations of district committee level and above.[26]

1964 'LEARN FROM THE PLA' CAMPAIGN

Just over three years later the entire nation was publicly called upon to 'Learn from the Experience of the PLA in Political Education and Ideological Work'. This emulation movement extolled the 'rich experience and great achievements' of the PLA's political work, and made it a model for the whole nation to 'learn from, study and compare with'. It followed a year of renewed efforts to raise political standards and devotion to the thought of Mao Tse-tung in all strata of society. It also came at a

[25] Hsiao Hua, 'Basic experiences of the past two years . . .' (*SCMP* 2971).
[26] *KTTH*, 7 Jan. 1961.

time when military leaders spoke with exceptional warmth of the PLA's achievements in the political field. In January 1964, one month before the 'Learn from the PLA' campaign was launched, the PLA's political work conference had been told that 1963 was a 'bumper year' for the PLA, in which the class consciousness of officers and men had been greatly elevated, and the army's ideological and organizational work greatly improved.[27] In a lengthy report to the conference, Hsiao Hua called for further efforts on all fronts, but at the same time expressed satisfaction with the 'remarkable successes' which had been recently achieved.[28]

The 'Learn from the PLA' campaign was launched by the *People's Daily* in an editorial of 1 February 1964 which described the PLA in laudatory terms as 'an army of extremely high proletarian and combat character' which had gained 'valuable . . . experiences in political-ideological work' in recent years. The PLA was praised in language which would have been unthinkable only three years previously, and which is reminiscent of the idealized concept of the *'Pa-lu Chün'* (Eighth Route Army) during the anti-Japanese war.

The PLA ardently loves the country, the people, and socialism and is boundlessly loyal to the cause of the proletariat. The combatants maintain vigilance day and night to safeguard the socialist fatherland and defend world peace. Where they are needed by the Party and the country, they enthusiastically go without delay. They love the localities in which they are stationed. They not only protect the localities whole-heartedly but also build them up with their full efforts. They are impartial and selfless. They always render service to others without considering their own interests. They even sacrifice their valuable time and life for the sake of socialism.[29]

The PLA appears to have been regarded with especial favour at this time because its intensive political studies had enabled it to avoid contamination by the 'poisonous weeds' of modern revisionism, bourgeois thinking, and other undesirable trends which were making themselves felt in civilian life.

---

[27] Peking radio, 17 Jan. 1964 (*FE(2)* 1461).
[28] Hsiao Hua, 'Several questions on the present political work in the armed forces', *JMJP*, 22 Jan. 1964 (*SCMP* 3154).
[29] 'The whole country must learn from the PLA', ibid. editorial, 1 Feb. 1964 (*SCMP* 3164). The progress of the 'Learn from the PLA' campaign is analysed in Powell, 'Commissars in the Economy: "Learn from the PLA" Movement in China', *Asian Survey*, Mar. 1965.

The 'Learn from the PLA' campaign sought to publicize throughout the country the techniques and activities of political education and control which had been practised in the PLA since 1960—the army's 'proper handling' of the 'four first' relationships, its 'revolutionary work-style', the emulation campaigns and the five-good soldier and four-good movements. Within a short time industries, commercial enterprises, government departments, trade unions, rural work cadres, and other important sections of the community were reported to have responded to the call to study the 'advanced political work' of the PLA. If this were all that the 'Learn from the PLA' campaign involved, it could be simply regarded as yet another well-publicized mass movement, more concerned with slogans and propaganda than with practical results. The campaign's distinctive feature, however, was the way in which it inspired the creation of a new political apparatus in industry, commerce, and government which was directly modelled on the PLA's own political control system.

On the direct analogy of the PLA's company party branch, workshops and departments in industry and commerce were directed to reorganize existing party branches or to set up new ones. 'In the PLA', it was explained, 'the basic-level combat unit is the company. In the industrial enterprise, the basic-level production unit is the workshop.'[30] Politics were seen to be the key to productivity and, as in the PLA, the vital link where politics could be transformed into political awareness and productive efficiency was held to be the basic-level party branch and its cadres.

Meanwhile all units above the basic level in industrial and communication enterprises were required to organize political departments, with a director and political staff, again on the analogy of the PLA's Political Department structure, down to regimental level. Top-level organs—government ministries and bureaus—in the fields of industry and communications—were also supposed to establish new political departments. Within the party Central Committee itself, two new bodies—an Industrial Communications Political Department and a Trade and Finance Department—were established, and these were subsequently ex-

---

[30] See further 'To create a Five-Good workshop, efforts must first be made to establish a firm and efficient party branch', *JMJP* editorial, 18 Mar. 1964 (*CB* 732).

tended to regional bureaux of the Central Committee and to provincial party committees. This attempt to extend the PLA's political control system into the very different field of commerce and industry emanated from the highest authority; it was described as

a new development of Mao Tse-tung's thinking concerning socialist construction, an innovation relating to the construction and mangement of modern enterprises, and a fundamental question regarding the orientation of China's socialist construction.[31]

An important and inevitable consequence of the 'Learn from PLA' campaign and the selection of the PLA as a national 'model' was to enhance its influence and prestige, both in the public press and in private life. Army cadres were called in for consultation on methods of political work by a variety of commercial and industrial organs. Demobilized officers were drafted in at least one province (Shantung) to work in stores, warehouses, and supply and marketing co-operatives, bringing with them 'many of the fine traditions of the PLA'.[32] Already in 1963 a 'considerable number' of active serving officers had been transferred to business and financial enterprises, and many more were transferred during the 'Learn from the PLA' campaign. It was implied that the principal task of these cadres, who worked under direct party leadership, was to prevent corruption and waste in the departments to which they were assigned. 'They adhere to principle, firmly resist the bourgeois influence and combat various undesirable practices.'[33] These transfers were part of a two-way process, for many civilian economic officials and political cadres were sent for political refresher courses to PLA units and training schools.

Like many similar nation-wide campaigns in China, the 'Learn from the PLA' campaign dropped out of the news after some four to five months of intensive publicity, and it is difficult to gauge its long-term effect upon the industrial sector of society. Again following a familiar pattern, the exaltation of a particular section of the community—in this case the PLA—as a flawless

---

[31] 'Industrial and transport departments must learn well from the good experiences of the PLA', ibid. 4 Apr. 1964 (*FE*(*2*) Weekly Suppl. No. 259).

[32] Peking radio, 28 Feb. 1964 (*FE*(*2*) Weekly Suppl. No. 254).

[33] *JMJP*, 20 Feb. 1964 (*FE*(*2*) Weekly Suppl. No. 253); *Ta-kung Pao* editorial, 29 Feb. 1965 (*SCMP* 3183).

'model' only served to reveal defects in the model itself. As the campaign died away, the PLA began to be reminded that it, too, was not perfect. Lo Jui-ch'ing, the chief of staff, warned the PLA that

> Acclamations from the outside have promoted self-assurance, complacency and stagnancy among some of our comrades. As a result, they fail to see their own short-comings and to heed the criticism by others, thereby deteriorating their progress and achievements. . . .
>
> The more successful is our work and the more we are acclaimed for it, the more humble, careful and prudent we should be. . . .[34]

The PLA's return to favour and to political grace since 1960 may appear to be at least a qualified success story, culminating in the 'Learn from the PLA' campaign. The party has, so it seems, managed to reconcile the position of a professional and modernized army with the rigid requirements of political control. In marked contrast with the haphazard and hasty efforts of 1956–9 to resurrect the revolutionary model, since 1960 it has been employed selectively but thoroughly, concentrating more on the vital sector of politics than on public relations. At the same time as this intensive grass-roots political drive was mounted, the more extreme policies of the Great Leap were abandoned, the disgraced P'eng Teh-huai section of the leadership was allowed to become a scapegoat for previous mistakes, and the PLA's military role was accorded greater respect and public esteem. In this way, it was claimed during the 'Learn from the PLA' campaign, the PLA has at last attained the 'Red and Expert' goal which it is hoped the whole of China will emulate; in other words, it combines at the same time a high level of political awareness with an equally high level of technical sophistication.

RECURRENCE OF POLITICAL DEVIATIONS

Nevertheless, the 'Red and Expert' formula does impose definite limitations upon the expertness of the PLA, while more recent developments have cast some doubt upon the durability of its redness. One drawback in a prolonged and intensive campaign of political education is its very length and intensity; it cannot be relaxed for even a short time, and yet it can easily be-

---

[34] Peking radio, 31 Dec. 1964 (*FE(2)* 1778).

come stereotyped and a meaningless chore for those taking part. Since the 'Learn from the PLA' campaign, it has again been felt necessary to intensify political work and the study of the works of Chairman Mao. Even senior officers are said to suffer from 'serious shortcomings' in their theoretical knowledge, and from a failure to appreciate the relevance of their revolutionary experience to the current situation. According to Li Chih-min, political commissar at a PLA military academy:

All senior cadres of the PLA have been brought up under the personal guidance of Comrade Mao and the Party Centre. They have a wealth of experience in revolutionary struggle. However, owing to the long period of leading the revolutionary war in the past and to the subsequent pressure of work which prevented them from devoting much time to serious study, some comrades have become conscious of their relative deficiency in theoretical training and of their lack of skill in summing up their rich experience in struggle and to elevate it to a higher plane. In the past few years in particular, rapid developments in the objective situation have impressed upon them the need to set aside a definite amount of time for serious study.[35]

Difficulties in relating political theory to practice have also been mentioned by the chief of staff, Lo Jui-ch'ing:

. . . we should realize that there are still many shortcomings and weaker links in the chain of our operations. On many occasions we have been unrealistic, very unrealistic sometimes, in not carrying out complete sets of principles and measures outlined by Marshal Lin Piao, Vice-Chairman of the Military Commission [Military Affairs Committee].[36]

As the attempt to explain the international scene in terms of the communist party's own revolutionary history becomes increasingly comprehensive in 1965, some signs have emerged within the PLA of confusion or doubt about the continued relevance of this militant revolutionary approach to the present day. A provincial report of PLA activists in Kwangtung revealed that 'some cadres and fighters in the armed forces are not very clear about the current situation and current tasks and have thus developed the benumbed thinking of being in the midst of a peaceful environment'.[37] A defensive note has reappeared in the speeches

---

[35] Li Chih-min, 'Experience gained in organizing senior cadres for study of Marxism-Leninism', *JMJP*, 6 May 1964 (*SCMP* 3229).
[36] Ibid.   [37] *Nan-fang Jih-pao*, 30 July 1964 (*SCMP* 3289).

of those expounding Mao's military line, carrying with it the implication that the line is not accepted without question in the PLA. At the National People's Congress in January 1965, Marshal Lin Piao gave what was described as an 'important' speech on the theme of 'Comrade Mao Tse-tung's great thinking on people's warfare is, as always, the guiding principle in building the national defence of our country', in which he was reported to have 'scathingly denounced the revisionist military line' (i.e. probably that of the Soviet Union).[38] Later that year, in a speech defending 'the Democratic Traditions of the PLA', and attributing to that tradition all the past and present successes of the PLA, Ho Lung took pains to refute the arguments of 'those whose heads are crammed full of foreign doctrines', and of those who persisted in 'bourgeois military thought'.[39] Also in 1965, renewed emphasis was placed upon the study of Mao's works, which, according to the *Liberation Army Newspaper*, 'still fails to meet the high requirements which are imposed upon us in order to deal with the current situation and to fulfil the present tasks'.[40] For 1966 as well, according to the Minister of Defence, Lin Piao, the PLA's primary requisite would be 'continued emphasis on politics', and especially upon the 'creative study' of the works of Chairman Mao.[41]

In spite of the degree of party confidence in the PLA which the 'Learn from the PLA' campaign indicated, these more recent expressions of dissatisfaction—although still in a relatively minor key—must raise some doubts about the party's overall success.[42]

[38] NCNA, 3 Jan. 1965 (*FE(2)* 1750).

[39] Ho Lung, 'The Democratic Traditions of the Chinese PLA', *JMJP*, 1 Aug. 1965 (*FE(2)* 1926): 'Indeed, from the very first day of the founding of our army, people infected with the habits of the old type of army and those clinging to bourgeois thinking on military affairs have stubbornly opposed Comrade Mao Tse-tung's line on army building. At the same time as they have opposed the strengthening of absolute leadership by the Party over the army, they have used one reason or another, one pretext or another, for opposing the movement for democracy and resisting the mass line. Clearly, the system of democracy and the democratic tradition, characteristic of a revolutionary army of the proletariat, cannot possibly be established, and still less consolidated and developed, unless this influence of bourgeois thinking on military affairs is again and again knocked down and the resistance of conventional notions and habits overcome.'

[40] *CFCP*, editorial, 17 Mar. 1965 (*FE(2)* 1819).

[41] NCNA, 26 Nov. 1965 (*FE(2)* 2024).

[42] A much more serious critique of the PLA's political outlook was made by Hsiao Hua, director of the PLA General Political Department, in his report to the PLA political work conference in January 1966. He told the conference that the class

One disadvantage, apparently, of the type of political education carried out since 1960, is that it cannot afford to be relaxed. The kind of break caused by the 'Learn from the PLA' campaign causes an immediate deterioration. Can it be maintained indefinitely at an intense enough pitch? Secondly, does not this very intensity of political education produce its own reaction, or lead to the mechanical application of political formulae without producing any real effect upon those involved? Thirdly, it must be considered possible that, if the 'revolutionization' of the PLA is pushed to extreme lengths, this will again produce a deterioration in army morale, on similar lines to that which occurred in 1956–9. These questions, as yet unanswered, make necessary some qualification of the undoubtedly high esteem and favour in which the PLA is still held at the time of writing. They are, of course, questions which also apply to the whole of Chinese society, where the movement to establish 'revolutionary successors' to the present leadership, and to combat 'modern revisionism' by means of class struggle, is being carried out as assiduously as in the PLA. As in the case of the immediate post-Great Leap period, however, the PLA can be seen as the test-bed in which the party's policies must be proved if they are to succeed in a wider social context.

Another consideration for the future of the PLA concerns the way in which both its equipment and strategy affect and are affected by foreign and economic policy. At present the Chinese leadership appears to have decided to go all out to acquire an efficient nuclear deterrent and its (missile) means of delivery. There is no indication that any increase in the PLA's conventional offensive capability is planned, i.e. bombers or heavy warships, nor is it yet entirely clear how far it is intended to keep abreast with world technological advance in defensive weapons, e.g. more sophisticated supersonic jet fighters. At some time in

struggle still existed within the PLA, and its outcome would 'resolve the question of whether the gun will direct the Party or the Party will direct the gun'. He referred to people who said that 'military affairs and politics are of equal importance', and attacked this as an 'absolutely wrong' view which would only serve to 'substitute military affairs for politics'. He also warned that 'the class enemy at home and abroad always regards our Army as a sworn enemy, and invariably seeks ways and means to undermine and corrode us in a futile attempt to cause us to degenerate' ('Report by Director of PLA General Political Department', Peking radio, 24 Jan. 1966, in *FE(2)* 2071, 2073).

the future, the PLA may ask for some or all of these conventional weapons. Yet they could only be supplied either by a radical shift in foreign policy back towards closer relations with the Soviet Union, or by a major transfer of economic resources to the defence industry.

It may indeed be true that the kind of tight political control which the party seeks to establish over the PLA can only be compatible with a defensive strategy, and one which is limited in terms of capability at that. At the moment ideology is to some extent a substitute for advanced technology—the 'thought of Mao Tse-tung' is intended to make good deficiencies in material equipment. Would a PLA which was equipped to the hilt with the most modern and sophisticated weapons systems be prepared to devote much attention to the works of Chairman Mao? The obsession with defence which pervades Chinese military strategy—its overriding concern with the defence of China's frontiers against what is believed to be the possible contingency of 'imperialist aggression'—also helps to reinforce party control. Again, it may be doubted whether a PLA which had been inculcated with an offensive and aggressive military ethos would be so inclined to defer to centralized political control. If a change did occur in Chinese thinking towards a more outward-going type of strategy, this might also in the long run weaken the party's grip over the PLA.

In addition to these problems, there remains the question of possible changes in the leadership of the PLA itself, as present incumbents die or retire and are replaced by successors with less 'revolutionary' experience. This is perhaps less of a problem than it might be thought, since both the uppermost and second échelons of military leadership are still relatively homogeneous and free from major internal discord. The final section of this book will examine this question in more detail.

13
The Military Leadership
1949–54

THE imposition of communist authority at the end of the civil war meant that PLA officers were extensively used in positions of administration and control, especially in the 'new liberated areas'. Although a large number of ex-KMT officials were absorbed into the administration at lower levels or in supernumerary positions of prestige, most of the highest offices in the liberated areas were held by army officers with concurrent military duties. Military control, as laid down in the Common Programme, was to be a short-term means of establishing effective control throughout the country, and was to yield to civil government as soon as social conditions were satisfactory and local popular democracy had been given time to stand on its feet.[1] To those who objected that military control stood in the way of democracy, Liu Shao-ch'i replied that

far from restraining the people or causing them inconvenience this sort of military control only protects the people, helps to free the people from the oppression and bondage of old influences, gives the people all kinds of facilities and encourages them to be their own masters. . . .[2]

It was, said P'eng Chen, the chairman of Peking's Military Control Committee (MCC) and concurrently secretary of the Peking Committee of the CCP, 'only imperialist, feudal, bureaucratic and capitalist elements' who were afraid of his MCC, and he singled out speculators who manipulated prices and disrupted finance for severe punishment.[3]

[1] Art. 14 of the Common Programme stipulated that: 'The duration of military control shall be determined by the Chinese People's Government in accordance with military and political conditions of the locality. In all places where military operations have ended, agrarian reform has been thoroughly completed, and peoples of all circles have been fully organised, elections through universal suffrage shall immediately be held to convene local people's congresses.'
[2] Liu Shao-ch'i, 'On the System of People's Representatives' Conferences and the Transition to Elected Peoples Congresses,' 28 Sept. 1951, in H. Arthur Steiner, *Chinese Communism in Action* (California Univ., 1953), pt 2, p. 97.
[3] NCNA, 30 Aug. 1949 (*FE* 20).

There are some similarities between the communist concept of military control leading in the course of time to democratic government, and the three-stage theory of revolutionary process as propounded by Sun Yat-sen (i.e. military rule followed by political tutelage followed by constitutional government). These, wrote Sun, were the

inevitable stages leading from malgovernment to good government, and none of them should be overlooked. China cannot be a true republic unless she undergoes such a transition. It was a matter of deep regret that the revolution of 1911 neglected the revolutionary fundamentals: they were shelved and obstructed.[4]

The communists disagreed with this in theory. The prominent theoretician Ch'en Po-ta wrote that 'from a Marxist's point of view, a revolution, if expected to succeed, requires a revolutionary people's democratic dictatorship', and he argued that the stages of military rule and political tutelage would only hinder this and would be used by the counter-revolutionaries to 'oppress the people'.[5] They also denied that the communist revolution was taking place in stages at all, and claimed that the people's democratic dictatorship had been realized in one fell swoop. Liu Shao-ch'i argued that military control and the realization of democracy were simply two different facets of the same system of people's democratic dictatorship, and that 'these two phases of work have always complemented and strengthened each other. This has been made possible by the fact that our military control is the military control of the people, and that the PLA is the armed force of the people.'[6]

Nevertheless the fact remained that both Sun Yat-sen and Mao Tse-tung realized the necessity for a gradual period of transition from civil war to normal peacetime. The communist period of military control can be compared to the Nationalist 'military rule' and 'political tutelage' combined into one, since under their rule both processes occurred simultaneously between 1949 and 1954. Mao Tse-tung had said that there were two aspects of the people's democratic dictatorship—'democracy among the

---

[4] Sun Yat-sen, *Fundamentals of National Reconstruction* (Chungking, 1945), p. 46, quoted in Shao Chuan Leng & Norman D. Palmer, *Sun Yat-sen and Communism* (London, 1961), p. 37.

[5] Quoted in Shao and Palmer, p. 117.

[6] Liu Shao-ch'i, in Steiner, *Chinese Communism*.

people and dictatorship over the reactionaries'. It was the second aspect which had to be realized by military control before the first could properly be established. Military control, it was explained,

> was the first step in the dictatorship. It turned over its power to various people's governmental institutions step by step. It would be completely replaced by people's governments at all levels 'when the reactionaries were wiped out, land reform completed, the majority of the people organized, and when the people's conferences and people's governments were able to exercise their functions'.[7]

This was the process in which the PLA played a prominent and influential part and which was not finally completed until the promulgation of the constitution and the convening of the National People's Congress in September 1954, five years after Liberation.

MILITARY CONTROL COMMITTEE

Military control began at the local level as soon as a town or county had been liberated. The first action of the officer in command of the newly-arrived PLA units would be to set up an MCC as the supreme administrative organ of the state. The chairman of the MCC, who usually held the concurrent post of mayor, was invariably the senior ranking military officer in the locality, as in the cases of Yeh Chien-ying (Peking), Huang Ching (Tientsin), Liu Po-ch'eng (Nanking), and Ch'en Yi (Shanghai). The MCC was appointed directly from Peking by the PRMC, and in turn made appointments to the local 'people's government' which was usually set up shortly afterwards. So-called 'Take-Over Committees' were organized by the MCC to assume control of government offices, major utilities, communications, schools, and military installations. There were four of these— Financial and Economic, Educational and Cultural, Administrative, and Military—and their first task was to take over all former KMT bureaux, staff, and property with the maximum speed. In Shanghai, where the take-over was particularly complex and lasted from the end of May till August, the Educational and Cultural Take-Over Committee assumed control of '26 universities and colleges with over 8,000 students, over 500 public

---

[7] NCNA, 14 Mar. 1951 (summarized in *FE* 100).

schools and educational institutions with 176,000 students, and 58 publishing houses and newspapers', whilst the Financial and Economic Take-Over Committee accounted for 'all organisations, including banks, factories and warehouses belonging to the Municipal and Central Governments' and large quantities of money, fuel, grain, and motor vehicles. The Military Take-Over Committee took charge of several military academies, 116 other military institutions, and nearly 37,000 military personnel. All local and central government bureaux were taken over by the Administrative Committee, but it was stated that 'nearly all the Kuomintang employees had been left in their former positions'.[8]

As in the case of reorganizing the Nationalist armies, it was felt to be politically undesirable to allow mass unemployment among the KMT civil service. The shortage of trained communist cadres made it all the more imperative to retain their services. All ex-KMT officials were required to register with the MCC, and the great majority were allowed to remain in employment. All key positions in administration were of course taken over by communist cadres, however inexperienced or unskilled they might be. As the independent English-language *Monthly Report* (30 June 1949) guardedly observed a month after Shanghai's liberation:

> About the only adverse comment made of this taking over procedure has been in the form of criticism of the lack of experience of the officials. It has been stated that some of the take-over officials have impeded the day to day functioning of some organizations because sometimes relatively simple business or commercial procedures have had to be explained in detail. The suspicion of the take-over officials has made them question all activities with which they are unfamiliar.

The occupation of urban centres raised new problems of totally different dimensions from those which the PLA had faced in the countryside. Before the troops moved in, they were carefully instructed in the communist party's urban policy, and were warned that exemplary discipline would be enforced on them. They were required to protect existing shops and industries, and to encourage business to carry on normally. They were not to harass or to arrest ex-KMT officials, such as teachers, civil servants, technicians, or police, but were to allow them to carry on

[8] Survey by General Ch'en Yi of the take-over, NCNA (Shanghai), 17 Aug. 1949 (*FE* 18).

at their posts. Looting was strictly prohibited, and any stocks of munitions or supplies found in the towns were to be put under guard but not requisitioned. Billeting in factories, churches, or schools was forbidden, and all PLA troops except for a garrison detachment were to withdraw from the town as soon as fighting had ceased. In public proclamations and posters, the PLA's Eight Rules of Conduct were advertised throughout the locality, even before the arrival of troops. Other announcements guaranteed protection of lives, property, industry, and commerce, including those of foreign nationals and KMT officials.

Military discipline was rigorous—a Shanghai report that a soldier who stole a torch from a foreign resident was shot dead by his commanding officer was only one of many which contrasted the PLA's behaviour with that of former KMT occupying troops. Soldiers were unobtrusive as well as being well disciplined. This was helped by the practice of stationing them outside the town, and of allowing ex-KMT personnel to continue day-to-day administration. PLA units were forbidden to occupy houses, to accept gifts or hospitality, and were not allowed to deal with breaches of law upon their own responsibility, but were to report such breaches to a higher authority. Western observers in Peking, Tientsin, and Shanghai were almost without exception impressed by the PLA's politeness and discipline during the take-over, and reported only minor lapses.[9]

In spite of the MCC's extensive powers, it would be an exaggeration to say that after Liberation China's local government administration passed into military hands, or that the entire country came under martial rule. Once the take-over had been completed, effective control began to be transferred to local

[9] Directive of the North-east Bureau of the CCP,CC on 'How to Administer Occupied Cities', 10 June 1948, in Vidya Prakash Dutt, *Select Documents on Asian Affairs, East Asia, China, Korea, Japan, 1947–50* (Delhi, 1958), pp. 145–7. 'Liberation army guarantees protection to life and property in Peiping, Tientsin', NCNA (N. Shensi), 24 Dec. 1948. The PLA authorities were extremely anxious that its soldiers should not be corrupted by what were regarded as the 'sugar-coated bullets of the bourgeoisie'. Thus the Garrison Political Dept in Shanghai warned against such corrupting practices as 'gathering in the streets to see performances of street acrobats, visiting amusement resorts without getting permission from their superiors beforehand, ... ignoring the direction of traffic cops and violating traffic regulations while driving army vehicles', and it warned that the misconduct of a 'minority' of troops might be repeated on a larger scale unless efforts to educate them in urban discipline were redoubled (*Chieh-fang Jih-pao* (Shanghai), 1 July 1949, in *Chinese Press Review*, 924).

people's government and party committees out of purely military hands. The MCCs continued to exist in the big cities until at least 1951; by that time they appear to be concerned mainly with military matters and security (many of the mass trials in the Suppression of Counter-revolutionaries movement were organized and carried out by the MCC).

Paradoxically enough, the fact that in 1949 there was virtually no distinction between 'political' and 'military' communist cadres helped to prevent military domination of the civil administration, since cadres transferred from the army to local government also transferred their allegiances without difficulty. In many cases such transfers of cadres had been planned in advance. Thus before the capture of Tsinan in September 1948, 7,000 cadres were said to have undergone two months' training to prepare for their future jobs, and were moved in with the advance troops, already equipped with regulations and plans for the city's administration.[10] This was the policy put forward by Mao Tse-tung in his report of March 1949 to the Central Committee, in which he said that

we must prepare to turn all the field armies, 2,100,000 strong, into a working force. In that event, there will be enough cadres and the work can develop over large areas. We must look upon the field armies with their 2,100,000 men as a gigantic school for cadres.[11]

In this area of policy, as in others, the accelerated rate of victory in 1949 upset calculations, and there was a serious shortage of cadres;[12] this shortage encouraged the use of ex-KMT personnel, which in turn also helped to dilute the effects of military control.

REGIONAL MILITARY CONTROL

In December 1949 China was divided into six major administrative regions (North-west, South-west, Central-South, East, North, North-east), each modelled exactly on the structure of the central government and intended to act as middlemen between Peking and the provinces, municipalities, and counties. For

[10] 'How liberation comes to a Chinese city', NCNA, 4 Jan. 1949.
[11] *MAO IV*, p. 363.
[12] In September 1948 the CC had envisaged the training of 30,000–40,000 cadres during 1949, so that in 1950 'when the army marches they can march with it and bring orderly administration to newly liberated areas with a population of some 50 to 100 million' (ibid., p. 274).

military purposes, the country was also divided into the same six regions, so that in each case a military region controlled the same territory as an administrative region. The four regions which had most recently come under communist control were each garrisoned by a Field Army, and the highest organ of government in these regions was designated as an MAC (North-west, South-west, Central-South, and East).[13] The senior officials of the MAC, the military region, and the Field Army HQ, were in most cases identical. Furthermore, each province within these regions was also a military district under the control of the military region.[14]

Outside observers at the time were tempted to regard this arrangement as a *de facto* division of China into military satrapies. In spite of Mao Tse-tung's reported claim that this was out of the question, since 'the historical conditions giving rise to past feudal partitioning of the country have been eliminated',[15] large regional units posed a traditional threat to the stability of the central government, and this system could hardly fail to place a great deal of power in the hands of the army. Centralized control of the PLA from Peking was provided by the PRMC and its General Headquarters. The PRMC was the highest authority, in military affairs, equal in status to the State Administrative Council (SAC) and responsible only to the Central People's Government Council, thus effectively divorcing direct control over the military from the civil authorities. Among its twenty-eight members were such leading party officials as Mao himself (Chairman), Liu Shao-ch'i and Chou En-lai (vice-chairmen), the commanders and political commissars of each of the six military regions, and the Minister of Public Security. Thus in theory military control was centralized at the highest party level, but in practice the lines of communication leading down to Field Army level were not fully developed. The General Headquarters of the PLA had only been set up since 1946 and was still understaffed. The great majority of leading army officers were still attached to the Field Armies, which possessed their own self-contained headquarters and staff departments. In the final analysis, the subordination of the PLA to centralized party con-

[13] MACs were set up on the following dates: North-west, 19 Jan. 1950; East, 27 Jan. 1950; Central-South, 5 Feb. 1950; South-west, July 1950.
[14] See Table 5 (p. 307).
[15] *China Digest*, 14 Dec. 1949, p. 28, quoted in S. B. Thomas, *Government and Administration in Communist China* (New York, IPR, 1953), p. 83.

T

trol depended largely on the loyalty of the individual commands at Field Army level.

A closer examination of regional military control shows, however, that it was a highly selective instrument, and that its precise degree varied from region to region and from province to province, according to the actual political conditions prevailing. Military control was most extensive in the North-west and the South-west, where unfinished military business was still on hand. The North-west was largely populated by ethnic minorities with a tradition of anti-Chinese activity, and it was also of great strategic and economic significance in the Chinese view. Strong military forces and control were needed there, both to pacify the national minorities and to counterbalance the former Ili rebels and KMT troops who had been absorbed into the First Field Army. In the South-west, the last stronghold of the KMT, it was reported that 80,000 'secret agents' and 'several hundred thousands of bandits' were left over when the region was first liberated.[16] Furthermore, the military advance on Tibet was mounted both from Sinkiang in the North-west and from Yunnan in the South-west. In addition to the customary correspondence of chairman and vice-chairman of the MAC, and commander and political commissar of the military region, provincial government in both these two regions was heavily dominated by the military. Either the chairman or the vice-chairman of the people's government in each of the nine provinces in the Northwest and South-west was a leading army officer, and at least one ranking officer from army units stationed in the province was also a member of the provincial administration. The mayor or deputy mayor in the major provincial cities was also in most cases an officer of the appropriate Field Army.

Military control in the remaining two regions administered by MACs was from the outset less rigorous. In Central-South, the chairman and two vice-chairmen of the MAC, as well as the director of the People's Supervisory Committee, were officers of the military region headquarters, and 17 out of the 71 members of the MAC were also Field Army or military region officers. But only two out of the five provinces in the region (Kwangtung and Kwangsi) were dominated by the army, as was the island of

[16] Urumchi radio, 16 Mar. 1954 (*FE* 338); Shih Ch'eng-chih, *People's Resistance*, p. 48.

Hainan and the city of Canton. In East China military control was even more slender. The chairman and vice-chairman of the MAC were as usual also commander and political commissar of the military region. The region's deputy political commissar headed the MAC's land reform department and was chairman of the Chekiang provincial government. The MAC chairman (Ch'en Yi) was also mayor of Shanghai. But apart from Chekiang, the four remaining provinces in the region were predominantly under civilian control, and only 7 out of the 68 MAC members were army officers.

Among major office-holders in North China, where a people's government had functioned since mid-1948 and was absorbed in October 1949 into the central government as a Ministry of North China Affairs, only the mayor of Peking and the chairman of Shansi province held concurrent military posts. In the Northeast, where local government had progressively been established since 1946 and a fully-fledged people's government had existed since 27 August 1949, only three major officials held ranking posts in the military region. Finally, the Autonomous Region of Inner Mongolia formed a separate military region of its own, and its party, army, and administrative offices have been closely linked from 1949 to the present day. The province of Suiyuan, where the voluntary surrender of General Fu Tso-yi created special problems, was controlled by an MAC operating under the Ministry of North China Affairs until June 1954, when it was merged into Inner Mongolia.

To summarize, the North-west and South-west of China, and Inner Mongolia (including Suiyuan) were from the start heavily garrisoned and controlled by the army. In Central-South and East China, control was less pronounced, and was mainly confined to the major cities and the seaboard provinces. In North and North-east China there was apparently no further need for a strong military presence.

DISSOLUTION OF MILITARY CONTROL

The dissolution of military control took place over the years 1952–4, without any of the dire consequences which foreign observers had predicted. In November 1952 the concept of 'people's government' at regional level (of which only one, the North-east, actually existed) was abandoned. Both the people's government and the regional MAC were replaced by 'Administrative Committees', which were responsible solely to the central government for carrying out national policy at the regional level. The MAC's departments were reduced to the status of bureaux or offices, with the prospect of being absorbed in time into existing ministries of the Central People's Government.[17] In January 1953 the Central People's Government Council adopted a resolution calling for the election that year of people's congresses at all levels up to that of province, to be followed by the convening of the National People's Congress and the drafting of a constitution—thus setting in motion the process which led to the first National People's Congress and the promulgation of the constitution the following year.

This process of centralization was accompanied by the steady transfer of authority and of high-ranking PLA personnel from regional commands to the General Headquarters in Peking. In 1949 these headquarters had consisted of only three departments —Political, Staff, and Rear Services. By 1954 they had been reorganized to include an additional five—Training, Cadres, Ordnance, Finance, and Inspectorate of Armed Forces. Expansion also took place in the specialized service arms—the air force, navy, engineers, artillery, etc. Many leading officers in the regions were transferred to the headquarters or service arms during this period. Finally, in June 1954, at the end of the transitional stage of government, both the six military regions and the corresponding administrative regions were abolished, to be replaced respectively by thirteen military regions under PLA Headquarters control and by provincial governments responsible directly to the People's Government. The four massive Field Armies were broken up, and the component armies, now known themselves as Field Armies, were directly controlled by PLA Headquarters. The PRMC was dissolved and replaced by a National Defence Council numbering almost 100 members. Executive authority passed to the new Ministry of Defence, which was set up under the State Council on a par with other ministries, unlike the PRMC which had functioned independently and equal in status to the former State Administrative Council.

These moves appeared to many outside observers to indicate

[17] See further Steiner, *Chinese Communism*, p. 105.

a determined attempt to deprive the PLA of its political influence and authority. 'The stripping of political power from the Military', commented the *Far Eastern Economic Review*, 'has been pushed to extremes as effective as Stalin's purge of the Red armies before the war—except that the Red hierarchy in China has executed none.'[18] Yet the dissolution of the MACs was an integral part of the progress towards 'democratic centralism' which had been developing since 1949, while the Field Armies, originally the four spearheads of the communist advance in 1949, had clearly become redundant under peacetime conditions. If military representation on the regional administrations during 1949–54 did ever pose an actual threat to the régime's stability, this threat was liquidated with remarkable ease, and the great majority of PLA officers in the regions were promoted in the usual way to influential command posts or to the PLA General Headquarters.

This may be illustrated by an analysis of the subsequent careers of 57 PLA officers who were identified in military region or Field Army commands between the years 1950 and 1954. By at least 1960 or in most cases later, they could be identified in the following positions.

Military Affairs Committee	6
PLA General Headquarters Depts	10
Military region command	7
Garrison command	2
Major party and/or civil office	14
Known dead	3
Position doubtful	8
Demoted or removed	7

Excluding those known to have been demoted and those in the doubtful category (some of whom may be dead or in bad health), this represents a proportion of over 75 per cent who have continued to climb the promotion ladder without incident. The majority of these officers were transferred from field command to the general staff or to non-military posts before 1954. Most transfers were made in 1953, following the replacement of the MACs by Administrative Committees in November 1952, and in many cases command posts on the military regions continued to be held only in name.

[18] 9 Dec. 1954, p. 737.

The ease with which this change-over was made may simply indicate a high degree of party loyalty among the top PLA personnel. It may also have been facilitated by the transfer of some armies and their commanding officers to the Korean war, which tended to break up the Field Armies' cohesion. No discrimination in promotion appears to have been practised against the officers of any one military region or Field Army, with the possible exception of the North-east, whose commander, Kao Kang, together with Jao Shu-shih, the political commissar of the East China Military Region, fell from power in 1954 as leaders of the notorious 'Kao-Jao clique'. While the political ramifications of this purge lie outside the scope of the present study, it is still relevant to examine whether it represented in any sense a military revolt or manifestation of 'warlordism' against the régime.

THE CASE OF KAO KANG

The Kao Kang case is one of the only two major inner-party conflicts leading to the expulsion and dismissal of members of the top military hierarchy since 1949.[19] The first intimation of it came at the fourth plenary session of the Central Committee in February 1954, when Liu Shao-ch'i, in discussing 'the fight to strengthen party unity', criticized 'some cadres' who, he alleged,

exaggerate the role of the individual and emphasize individual prestige. They think there is no one equal to them in the wide world. . . . They even regard the region or department under their leadership as their individual inheritance or independent kingdom.[20]

This was followed by a campaign to strengthen party solidarity and democratic centralism, and party conferences, notably in the North-east and in East China, at which the 'conceit' of high-ranking cadres was criticized. In June 1954 a large number of lower officials were dismissed from organs of the North-east and East regional governments, and all five regional governments and the North China Administrative Committee

---

[19] The other case was the dismissal of P'eng Teh-huai and Huang K'o-ch'eng from their posts as Minister of Defence and chief of staff in September 1959; see further ch. 11.

[20] Report by Liu Shao-ch'i to the 4th plenary session of the CCP (NCNA, 19 Feb. 1954).

were dissolved. In the following months the regional bureaux of the Central Committee were also dissolved.

Suspicion that the object of these moves was Kao Kang and other leaders was confirmed by a resolution of the party's National Conference in March 1955 which, for the first time in public, discussed the 'Kao-Jao anti-Party alliance'. According to this resolution, Kao's anti-party activities had come to a head in 1953. After a serious warning was given by the fourth plenary session of the Central Committee in February 1954, 'Kao Kang not only did not admit his guilt to the Party, but committed suicide as an ultimate expression of his betrayal of the Party'. The resolution claimed that he had 'made the North-east area the independent kingdom of Kao Kang', and that his anti-party activities had intensified after he was transferred to the newly-formed State Planning Committee in 1953.

> He even tried to instigate Party members in the army to support his conspiracy against the Central Committee of the Party. For this purpose he invented the utterly absurd 'theory' that our Party consisted of two parties—one, the so-called party of the revolutionary bases and the army, the other, the so-called party of the white areas—and that the Party was created by the army.

Kao was alleged to have claimed leadership of the 'party of the revolutionary bases and the army' and to have sought the posts of Premier of the State Council and general secretary or vice-chairman of the Central Committee. Kao's chief ally was said to be Jao Shu-shih, who adopted a rightist policy and protected counter-revolutionaries while in control of East China, and, after his transfer to the Central Committee and the State Planning Committee in 1953, attempted to start a struggle on Kao's behalf in order to 'split the Party'.[21]

It is generally agreed that the Kao–Jao 'conspiracy' was in part an attempt to defend regional authority against the central government, although it does not follow that the abolition of the regions was directly aimed at Kao and Jao. As in the case of the dissolution of the military regions, this was an overdue move towards normal peacetime government. One convincing theory also suggests that this intra-party struggle was closely linked to

---

[21] 'National Conference of the CCP: Resolution on the Anti-Party Alliance of Kao Kang and Jao Shu-shih, 31 March 1955', *People's China*, 16 Apr. 1955.

disputes over economic policy. Kao, according to this interpretation, deviated to the 'left' in advocating increased industrialization, both in his capacity as chairman of the industrial North-east base, and as a member of the State Planning Committee, charged with drawing up the first five-year plan.[22] He also deviated to the 'right' in opposing a higher rate of agricultural co-operativization as urged by Mao, Liu Shao-ch'i, and other party leaders. It is also suggested that Kao's special position in the North-east since 1946 had enabled him to establish close connexions with the Soviet Union, and that after the death of Stalin this made him suspect to the party leadership and vulnerable to criticism. Another theory identifies Liu Shao-ch'i as the principal target of Kao's 'anti-party alliance'. According to this theory, Kao and Jao's real offence was 'failure to give sufficient weight to the position of the other top leaders, especially Liu Shao-ch'i and Chou En-lai. . .'.[23] The true explanation may incorporate aspects of all three theories, in addition to unknown factors of personal jealousy and rivalry within the Central Committee.[24]

How far was the PLA involved in this 'conspiracy'? The National CCP Conference resolution alleged that Kao 'tried' to enlist army support, but not that he succeeded. If Kao ever advocated the theory that he was the leader of the 'party of the revolutionary bases and the army', this can only have had a limited appeal to the army. Kao had been a guerrilla leader in Shensi since 1928-9 and did not take part in the Long March. During the Yenan period he held important party posts, including the secretaryship of the Shenkanning party committee, and was especially concerned with economic mobilization and cadre

[22] For this argument, see Harold C. Hinton, *The 'Unprincipled Dispute' within the Chinese Communist Top Leadership*, U.S. Information Agency, IRI Intelligence Summary, No. LS-98-55, July 1955.

[23] Peter S. H. Tang, 'Power Struggle in the Chinese CP, the Kao-Jao Purge', *Problems of Communism*, Nov.–Dec. 1955.

[24] As chairman of the North-east people's government, Kao had negotiated a separate trade agreement with the Soviet Union in July 1949. He was present with Mao Tse-tung's delegation in the winter of 1949. According to one report, at the concluding banquet of this mission he was given precedence over the Chinese ambassador and remained in Moscow after the mission's departure (Beloff, *Soviet Policy*, p. 137). At the Bucharest Conference of June 1960, Khrushchev is alleged to have defended the memory of Kao Kang, 'whose only offence was that he opposed the incorrect policies of the Chinese Party towards the Soviet Union' (Charles, 'Dismissal of Marshal P'eng Teh-huai', *CQ*, Oct.–Dec. 1961, p. 75).

training, but did not hold military office until 1946, when he became both commander and political commissar of the North-east Military Region. His appeal to the army, if it was made, could thus only be directed towards his former guerrilla associates in Shensi or towards his colleagues in the North-east Military Region. Jao Shu-shih was a veteran party member, having joined in 1925, when he worked on behalf of the party in the labour movement. Like Kao Kang, he did not take part in the Long March, having gone abroad both to the United States and Eastern Europe. He returned in 1939 and served as political commissar of the New Fourth Army in Central China during the war.[25] In 1946 he was the communist representative on the North-east Truce Committee, and this may have been his first opportunity for close contact with Kao Kang. He returned to his post as political commissar of the New Fourth Army, subsequently the East China PLA and then the Third Field Army, and in 1949 also became political commissar of the East China Military Region. Both Kao and to a lesser extent Jao were therefore not in the first rank of army leaders, and are unlikely to have won particular loyalty outside the units and staff under their own command.

Some evidence as to possible military involvement with Kao and Jao is provided by the subsequent careers of the PLA officers in their military commands. In the North-east Chang Hsiu-shan, deputy political commissar of the military region, was identified at the time as a member of the Kao faction. Chang was the director of the North-east People's Supervisory Committee, the key watch-dog organ which supervised the execution of their duties by the government and its officials.[26] Kao's deputy commander, Ho Chin-p'ing, and the chief of staff, Tuan Szu-chuan, appear briefly in 1953 and then disappear from sight. The deputy chief of staff, Wu Hsin-chüan, has remained in the army until at least 1956. Apart from Wu Hsin-chüan, only the head of the Political Department, Chou Huan, who replaced Chang Hsiu-shan as deputy political commissar in 1953, and his own

---

[25] Jao became political commissar of the New Fourth Army after the South Anhwei incident of January 1941.

[26] According to Art. 19 of the Common Programme, people's supervisory organs 'supervise the execution of duties by the various levels of State organs and public functionaries, and indict organs and functionaries who violate the law or are derelict in the performance of their duties'.

replacement as political head, Mo Wen-hua, retained positions of authority in the PLA after Kao's downfall.[27]

There is, therefore, some indication that some leading officers of the North-east military command fell from favour at the same time as Kao. However, the command was in itself the least important of the six regional commands. Apart from local forces, it possessed no armies of its own. As of March 1954, only one army group was stationed in the North-east (headquarters at Changchun), and two of its four armies were in Kwangtung province. This Army Group, the Fourteenth, formed part of the Fourth Field Army with its headquarters and staff in Canton. The North-east was also a staging post for the Korean war, and armies in transit or in reserve presumably came under the jurisdiction either of the CPV command or of the Field Armies whence they originated.

Kao and his command were therefore not in control of major army units. The positions held by the seven officials named with Kao as implicated in the plot suggest that his power depended on party rather than military support. These included the two deputy directors of the North-east People's Supervisory Committee and subordinates of Chang Hsiu-shan (Ch'en Po-ts'un and Chang Ming-yuan), the chairman of the Heilungkiang provincial government (Chao Te-ts'un), a departmental head of the North-east government (Kuo Feng), a former guerrilla associate of Kao's and now vice-chairman of Shantung province (Hsiang Ming), and the deputy secretary-general of the North-east Central Committee bureau (Ma Hung). Since Chang Hsiu-shan was secretary-general of the bureau in 1951–2, and Chang Ming-yuan was secretary-general of the North-east government in the same period, while Ma Hung was a colleague of Kao Kang's on the State Planning Committee, it appears that the clique was very closely centred around Kao and Chang Hsiu-shan as individuals, and the North-east party bureau and government as organizations.

Jao Shu-shih, on the other hand, was political commissar of a military region and a Field Army (the Third) which controlled 5 army groups comprising 16 armies. Yet there is no evidence

[27] Chou Huan became an alternate member of the CC in September 1956. From then until 1959, he was Political Commissar of the Shenyang Military Region. Mo Wen-hua was deputy commander of the PLA Political Academy in August 1956.

that he was supported by the army. All the leading officers on the region and Field Army command were subsequently promoted, as were the eight army commanders who were members of the East China MAC.[28]

One may conclude that the army played no significant or identifiable part in the Kao Kang case. Indeed, it is worth noting that this episode, the only major case of its kind during the period of consolidation of power, originated in the North-east, the region which had been longest free from military control. It was supported by a party leader in East China, which of the four regions garrisoned by Field Armies was the one with the smallest military influence on its government and the longest history of party control. If naked warlordism was not the threat which had been prophesied for the new China, the Kao Kang case was an indication that disputes over economic policy might be as damaging in their effects as any dissident army leader.

[28] Chou Chün-ming, a former commander in the New Fourth Army and deputy chief of staff in East China, and Chang K'ai, deputy head of the Political Department, have since 1954 been respectively Deputy Ministers of Forestry and of Health. This may constitute a mild form of demotion.

14
The Military Leadership
1954–65

ANY discussion of the PLA leadership over the past fifteen years is inevitably hampered by lack of information. No 'Army List' is published in China, and while major appointments are usually announced, dismissals are almost always left to be inferred. The names of military office-holders have to be correlated from isolated attributions in the Chinese press, with the proviso that the protracted non-appearance of an individual's name does not necessarily indicate his absence from active duty or his demotion.[1]

It is necessary first of all to define what constitutes a 'military' leader in China. Before 1949 it was difficult to distinguish between party and military leaders, in view of the frequent practice of holding concurrent military, party, and administrative office. After 1949, this practice continued in the MACs, but many leading officers had already begun to specialize in the service arms—navy, air force, etc.—which were created at this time, and the strengthening of the General Headquarters in Peking accentuated this tendency towards specialization. Many important officials in the MACs began to devote their time exclusively to government affairs. Prominent among these were such senior officers as Ch'en Yi, Teng Hsiao-p'ing, Teng Tzu-hui, Li Hsien-nien, and Hsi Chung-hsün. The watershed of the process of

---

[1] The biographical material for this analysis is drawn from the following sources: (1) *Gendai Chugoku Jinmen Jiten* (A Who's Who of Contemporary Chinese), ed. by the Kasumigaseki Ass. (Tokyo, 1962), an invaluable reference work containing brief biographical notes on over 7,000 names. (2) *Directory of Party and Government Officials of Communist China* (Dept of State, Bureau of Intelligence and Research, Washington, 20 July 1960, 2 vols.). (3) Anne B. Clark, *Selected Biographies of Chinese Communist Military Leaders*, Harvard Univ., East Asian Research Centre, July 1964. (4) Biographical Service, Union Research Service, Hong Kong, separate biographies published seriatim). (5) Shen Sung-fang, *I-chiu-wu-ling jen-min nien-chien* (Yearbook for 1950) (Hong Kong, 1950). (6) Chin Ta-k'ai & Chang Ta-chun, *Chung-kung chün-shih p'ou-shih*, ch. 9, detailed but not always reliable information on army personnel down to divisional command. (7) *Communist China: Ruthless Enemy or Paper Tiger? a Bibliographic Survey* (Dept. of the Army, Washington 1962) DA PAM-20/61, App. G: 'Chinese Communist Military Organisation'.

specialization can be fixed, with a few exceptions, to the year 1954, when China's administration and government was finally converted to a peacetime footing with the convening of the NPC and the promulgation of the Constitution. There was now a clear separation between military and civilian administration. With a very few exceptions, no active serving officer held concurrent civilian office, although veteran officers of the revolutionary army could of course be found in almost every ministry and people's government. Where dual tenure did take place, it was invariably a case of a *party* official assuming control over *military* affairs, and not the other way round as had been customary before 1954.

It would be a mistake either to believe that there is no distinction between China's military and civilian élites, or to exaggerate the gap between them. For the purposes of definition, one may describe a 'military' leader in China today as one who has held important military office since 1954, as well as before.

Since 1954 the real command structure, in terms of effective power, of the PLA has been as follows:

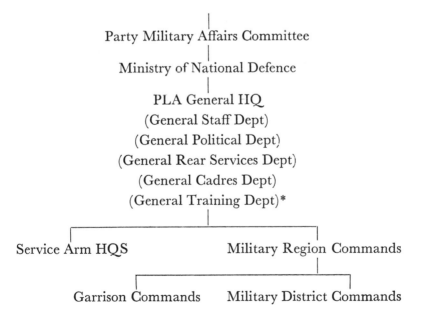

Party Military Affairs Committee

Ministry of National Defence

PLA General HQ
(General Staff Dept)
(General Political Dept)
(General Rear Services Dept)
(General Cadres Dept)
(General Training Dept)*

Service Arm HQS   Military Region Commands

Garrison Commands   Military District Commands

* Cadres and Training Depts abolished in 1959–60.

Based on a study of the promotion, seniority, and activities of the officers in this command structure, one can approximately subdivide the PLA leadership into the following échelons:

First échelon: Military Affairs Committee, Minister of National Defence. Chief of General Staff and Directors of General HQ Departments.[2]

Second échelon: General HQ departmental deputy directors and heads of sub-departments, military region and service arm commands.[3]

Third échelon: Military district and garrison commands.

I. FIRST ÉCHELON LEADERSHIP—MILITARY AFFAIRS COMMITTEE

Ultimate authority for military affairs rests with the handful of party veterans who make up the Military Affairs Committee.[4] This body has existed since the end of 1931 under one name or another, when its formation was called for by the first All-China Soviet Congress.

Only strictly centralized leadership (embracing the whole of the Red Army) the execution of the plans of the supreme leading bodies and the centralization of the activities of the Red Army will enable it to conquer the armies of the warlords and imperialists, will enable it to extend the territorial base of the Soviet regions

resolved the Congress, instructing the Central Committee to 'appoint as the supreme military body the Revolutionary Military Council and the chief of staff of the Chinese Red Army to guide the organization, provide for the supply and military training of the Red Army, and lead its military operations'.[5]

Since then the party's Military Affairs Committee has remained constantly in operation, although for considerable periods of time its activities and membership have been con-

---

[2] Including the Inspector-General of the Inspectorate of the Armed Forces.

[3] Including the deputy inspectors and directors of military academies where known.

[4] *Chung-kung chung-yang chün-shih wei-yuan-hui*, usually abbreviated to *Chün-wei* or 'military committee'. The Military Affairs Committee has been analysed in detail by Professor Powell, in 'The Military Affairs Committee and Party Control of the Military in China' (*Asian Survey*, July 1963), and *Politico-Military Relationships in Communist China* (US Dept of State, October 1963), pp. 5–7.

[5] 'Resolution of the All-China Congress of Soviets Concerning the Red Army', Bela Kun, ed., *Fundamental Laws of the Chinese Soviet Republic* (New York, 1934), p. 36.

cealed or unpublicized. Technically, it is a department of the Central Committee, provided for in Article 34 of the party constitution of 1945, which operates under the direction and supervision of the Politburo and of the Central Committee's chairman. In practice it appears to carry sufficient weight to operate on its own initiative. During the Yenan period it was composed of Mao Tse-tung as chairman, at least three vice-chairmen (Chu Teh, Chou En-lai, and P'eng Teh-huai), the directors of the general staff departments, the Inspector-General of Armed Forces and his two deputies.[6] During the civil war, still under the chairmanship of Mao, it was known as the Revolutionary Military Commission, and issued orders for operations to and through the headquarters of the PLA. Important proclamations were signed concurrently by Mao as its chairman and by Chu Teh as commander-in-chief of the PLA.

After Liberation, it was supposedly replaced by the PRMC. This body included all the leading military commanders, as well as Mao (chairman), Chu Teh, Liu Shao-ch'i, Chou En-lai, and P'eng Teh-huai (vice-chairmen). However, it also included two ex-KMT generals (Cheng Chien and Fu Tso-yi), and four representatives of democratic parties (Chang Chih-chung, Tsai T'ing-k'ai, Lung Yun, and Liu Fei). It seems likely therefore that major policy decisions were taken by the Military Affairs Committee operating as a party caucus within the PRMC, while the apparatus of a 'United Front' approach to military control was maintained, just as it was in other areas of government. The presence in the PRMC of generals like Fu Tso-yi, whose troops still remained intact in Suiyuan, no doubt facilitated military planning.[7]

Throughout the years 1949–58 references to the Military Affairs Committee are exceedingly scanty, but we are told that on 15 April 1954 (while the PRMC was still operating), the Central Committee and the Military Affairs Committee approved the 'Draft Regulations on the Political Work of the PLA', which confirms the supposition that major decisions con-

---

[6] *Peabody Report*, p. 2435.
[7] Non-party members of the PRMC were not left entirely idle; at its first meeting a sub-committee was set up with Chang Chih-chung as Chairman, to 'study and plan national defence'. Members included Fu Tso-yi, Tsai T'ing-k'ai, and Liu Fei (ex-KMT deputy chief of general staff, 1946–9) (NCNA 21 Oct. 1949). The results of its deliberations were not reported.

tinued to be taken by the Military Affairs Committee, acting
under the party Central Committee.[8]

In September 1954 the PRMC was replaced by the National
Defence Council, a body of over 100 members directly subordinate to the State Council, whose membership includes 30 former
Kuomintang generals, and a number of PLA officers who are no
longer directly concerned with military affairs. Between 1954
and 1958 the NDC only met four times; its functions are nowhere clearly defined, and all the evidence suggests that they are
purely symbolic, providing in expanded form the United Front
apparatus previously supplied by the PRMC.[9]

The real responsibility for military policy continued to rest,
behind the scenes, with the Military Affairs Committee. Very
little is known about its operations in 1954–7; it was not until
1958 that it began to be mentioned with any frequency. It is possible that during the hey-day of modernization its powers were
to some extent eroded by the Ministry of Defence and PLA
Headquarters, or simply that it was then less concerned with
detailed administration than it later became.[10] If this was so, it
had resumed its leading role at least by 1956, when the party

[8] Liu Ya-lou, 'Seriously study Mao Tse-tung's military thinking', *CFCP*, 23 May
1958 (the trans. in *SCMP* 1900 omits the words 'Central Committee'). Liu also
states that 'during the period [of modernization] our army carried out with great
results the guiding principles laid down by the Central Committee, Military Affairs
Committee, and Chairman Mao concerning army building', thus implying that the
Military Affairs Committee was operative during this period.

[9] See further Joffe, 'The Communist Party and the Army', *Contemporary China* (1961),
iv. 55–67.

[10] The Ministry of Defence was mentioned more frequently in the period 1954–9
than subsequently. It appears to be the administrative channel by which policy
decisions are transmitted to the appropriate army authorities. Orders affecting
the whole PLA—e.g. regulations on pay, recruitment, rank, etc.—are issued in its
name. The qualifications of its deputy ministers suggest that the Ministry to some
extent provides a channel for liaison between the major branches of the PLA.

Deputy ministers of defence

appointed *Nov. 1954*	appointed *Sept. 1959*
Hsiao Ching-kuang	Ch'en Keng
Hsiao K'o	Hsiao Ching-kuang
Huang K'o-ch'eng	Hsu Kuang-ta
Li Ta	Hsu Shih-yu
Liao Han-sheng	Liao Han-sheng
T'an Cheng	Liu Ya-lou
Wang Shu-sheng	Lo Jui-ch'ing
	Su Yü
	T'an Cheng
	Wang Shu-sheng

began to devote more attention to the question of the political control and education of the PLA. In March 1956 the Military Affairs Committee held an enlarged conference of leading cadres to discuss the need for rectification of various undesirable tendencies in the PLA, and to decide on new measures to improve the quality of political work. The decisions of this meeting provided the basis for the rectification campaign in the PLA which subsequently gathered way, and which was emphasized by P'eng Teh-huai and T'an Cheng at the Party Congress in September.[11]

Similarly, a second Enlarged Conference of the Military Affairs Committee, held between 27 May and 22 July 1958 and attended by more than 1,000 high-ranking cadres, preceded the radical shifts in military policy which took place later that year. Decisions were presumably reached by the Military Affairs Committee itself, and then communicated to the Enlarged Conference for extensive discussion and criticism. According to the official communiqué, the conference

reviewed the over-all strengthening of the PLA since the founding of the People's Republic, and defined the lines of policy for the future. At the same time, taking cognisance of the present world situation, it discussed the country's national defence and made decisions accordingly.

Self-criticism was also indulged in at the conference, to judge from the same communiqué's reference to the fact that it had employed 'the methods of the current rectification campaign'. Marshal Lo Jung-huan, in a speech to the conference, criticized 'the backwardness of the army' in political and ideological work. 'Dogmatism' and excessive reliance upon 'foreign thought' in military training was also criticized, and Mao Tse-tung himself instructed the army to draw up a new set of operational manuals and systems specifically based upon the PLA's own revolutionary experience.[12]

[11] 'Overcome subjectivism, dogmatism, commandism, thoroughly carry out the mass line', *Pa-yi Tsa-chih* editorial (*CFCP*, 4 Oct. 1956). Another reference to the Military Affairs Committee reports that in spring 1957 it took the decision to amalgamate the PLA Cultural and Propaganda Departments ('True identity of Ch'en Yi revealed', *JMJP*, 1 Mar. 1958, in *SCMP* 1729).

[12] 'CCP Military Committee hold Enlarged Conference', NCNA (Peking), 25 July 1958. See also *KTTH*, 6 Feb. & 13 July 1961 (Cheng, pp. 227, 651), for references to speeches by Mao and Lo.

U

The dismissal in September 1959 of the Minister of Defence, P'eng Teh-huai, and of his chief of staff Huang K'o-ch'eng, led to the establishment of a 'new' Military Affairs Committee. This body held another Enlarged Conference in September, at which the new Minister of Defence Lin Piao put forward a plan 'to build China into one of the strongest Socialist countries in the world'. This conference condemned the previous leadership of P'eng and Huang, and inaugurated the new lines of policy which have since governed the PLA's internal role and defence strategy. Three further Enlarged Conferences were held in 1960. At the third (14 September–20 October 1960), a comprehensive blueprint for the reassertion of party control down to company level and the restoration of army morale was decided upon. Since then the Military Affairs Committee has abandoned its former secrecy, frequently claiming open responsibility and credit for the improvements which are presented as having taken place in the PLA 'under the leadership of Chairman Mao, Lin Piao, and the Military Affairs Committee'.[13]

At present the Military Affairs Committee is a powerful body which not only formulates military policy but personally supervises its implementation. Mao Tse-tung is probably *ex officio* chairman, but the *de facto* head and initiator of policy is Lin Piao, the Minister of Defence. On the basis of his close study of the workings of the Military Affairs Committee as revealed in the *Kung-tso T'ung-hsün*, Professor Powell has reported that:

The [Military Affairs Committee] has designated strategic aims for the PLA. It issues directives regarding political ideology and indoctrination, promulgates training doctrine, lays down principles of military expenditures, and publishes orders regarding national defense reconstruction work. The Committee puts out instructions regarding the reorganisation and strengthening of the militia. It reviews regulations, supervises the writing of military history and ordinances, and holds conferences on subjects of military interest to

---

[13] *KTTH*, 20 Feb. & 5 Apr. 1961 (Cheng, pp. 263, 419). See ibid. 7 Jan. 1961 (Cheng, pp. 66–94), for the September 1960 Enlarged Conference's resolution 'on strengthening political and ideological work in the army'. According to an endorsement by the 'central authorities' of the CCP (Cheng, p. 65), this resolution 'unequivocally pointed out the direction of ideological work in the Army in the new historical period that has begun for us, presented suitable measures for consideration, and hit upon key points for emphasis'. As late as 1965 this resolution was still regarded as the primary source for all subsequent policy.

the Party. It receives reports from the military departments and regions and comments on general directives issued to the PLA.

Members of the Standing Committee of the [Military Affairs Committee] have conducted inspections, investigations, and studies in the field throughout Communist China. Investigations have included such problems as political reliability of the troops, indoctrination, and relations between the troops and the people and between officers and men. The [Military Affairs Committee] has also investigated morale, combat operations, troop dispositions, military units, schools, and factories. While on inspection trips, Committee members conduct conferences for cadres, provide guidance, issue directives, and write reports to the [Military Affairs Committee].

And he concludes that the Committee 'appears to combine most of the functions of the United States offices of the Secretary of Defense and Joint Chiefs of Staff'.[14]

In addition to Hsiao Hua and Lo Jui-ch'ing, the Military Affairs Committee Standing Committee comprises all the most senior PLA generals who have continued to specialize in military affairs. Apart from the disgraced P'eng Teh-huai, all except two of the ten marshals of the PLA are represented (Chu Teh has retired from active office and Ch'en Yi is Minister for Foreign Affairs). This small group has dominated the Chinese communist army for the past thirty years or more. It includes the commanders of the three Front Armies of the Long March, those of the three Eighth Route Army divisions in 1937, and those of the First, Second, and Fourth Field Armies in 1949.[15]

With the possible exception of Hsu Hsiang-chien, and of course P'eng Teh-huai, all have survived with unscathed careers. It used to be believed that after 1954 Ho Lung, Lin Piao, and Nieh Jung-chen had been quietly pensioned upstairs, and that Lo Jung-huan, who resigned as political director in December 1956, and Liu Po-ch'eng, who also resigned as training director in

---

[14] *Politico-Military Relationships*, pp. 5–6.

[15] The members of the Standing Committee of the 'new' Military Affairs Committee are identified in *KTTH*, 19 Apr. 1961 (Cheng, p. 437). They comprise Marshals Ho Lung, Hsu Hsiang-chien, Liu Po-ch'eng, Lo Jung-huan, Nieh Jung-chen, and Yeh Chien-ying, together with the Minister of Defence, Lin Piao, the deputy director of the General Political Dept, Hsiao Hua, and chief of staff Lo Jui-ch'ing.

Hsu Hsiang-chien's position is obscure. He did not speak at the Enlarged Conference of 1958, and does not feature prominently in the pages of the *KTTH*. In earlier years (1949–54), when he was nominally PLA chief of staff, it was rumoured that he had refused to take up office and remained in retirement (*South China Morning Post*, 29 Dec. 1953, 23 Feb. 1954).

November 1957, followed the same path. This was seen as the culmination of a consistent effort by Mao to strip his military hierarchy of actual power. It is still arguable that they only resumed control of military affairs after P'eng's dismissal and the collapse of army morale in 1959, and that Lin Piao himself was in retirement until he replaced P'eng. However, all of these leaders except Hsu Hsiang-chien addressed the Enlarged Conference of the Military Affairs Committee in summer 1958, which suggests at least that they were still directly concerned with military matters, and probably Military Affairs Committee members. In view of their continuity of control since the early 1930s, it seems improbable that it was allowed to lapse to any significant extent during the years 1954–8.

THE EXECUTIVE OFFICES

There was nevertheless a certain shift of authority in these years towards a small group of General Staff officers. These were Hsiao Hua, Su Yü, Hsiao K'o, Huang K'o-ch'eng, T'an Cheng, and Hung Hsueh-chih. All became departmental directors or chiefs of staff during this period, and all except Hsiao Hua have subsequently fallen from favour. This is the only stratum of army leadership with a high 'mortality rate', but it is also of particular significance for the future. The chief of staff and the directors of the four key departments—Political, Cadres, Training, and Rear Services—hold primary responsibility for the execution of policy as formulated by the Military Affairs Committee and Central Committee. They are also directly subject to army pressure from beneath, as well as having the opportunity to initiate policy of their own. They constitute the vital link between theory and practice of military policy. It was this link which broke down in these years when the army was for the first time faced with the need to adapt itself to peacetime conditions.

After 1954 the veteran PLA marshals had virtually handed over day-to-day running control of the army to this group of officers. Su Yü had succeeded Hsu Hsiang-chien as chief of staff in 1954; T'an Cheng replaced Lo Jung-huan as political director in December 1956, and Lo at the same time handed over his concurrent post as cadres director to Hsiao Hua. Liu Po-ch'eng was succeeded by Hsiao K'o as training director in November 1957. Huang K'o-ch'eng, a deputy chief of staff from November 1952, succeeded Su Yü as chief of staff when the latter was dismissed in October 1958. Huang's concurrent post of rear services director, held since 1954, was taken over by his own deputy, Hung Hsueh-chih. With the exception of Hung, who served as rear services director of the CPV in the later stage of the Korean war, these officers had all understudied their leading roles since at least 1953 or earlier.[16] Yet at the first major test of army loyalty, during the first year of the Great Leap Forward, all except Hsiao Hua appear to have been unable to go along with the new party policies. They did not necessarily constitute a homogeneous group—variations in the way that they were subsequently treated suggest that they opposed party policies in differing degrees. But the fact remains that this sensitive level of PLA leadership came unstuck and lost office within the short space of time between the Great Leap and P'eng Teh-huai's dismissal.[17]

The departments of PLA headquarters for which they had been responsible now reverted to stricter party control. First, their number was cut down to the three departments which had existed before 1950, General Staff, Political and Rear Services. The Cadres Department became part of the Political Department, and the Training Department was absorbed into the

[16] Huang and Su were appointed deputy chiefs of staff in November 1952; Hsiao Hua a deputy political director since September 1949. T'an Cheng had been deputy political director of the 8th Route Army, 1937–45, and from 1949 served in Central-South China with the 4th Field Army as political commissar. He returned as first-ranking deputy to the Political Department in Peking in 1955. Hsiao K'o was training director in 1953–4.

[17] Su Yü was dismissed in October 1958; Hung and Huang at the same time as Marshal P'eng in September–October 1959. Hsiao K'o and T'an Cheng were not officially dismissed, but have not been active since P'eng's removal.

Only Hung and Huang appear to have been officially regarded as members of the so-called 'P'eng-Huang anti-party clique'. Hsiao K'o lost his position as a Deputy Minister of National Defence in September 1959, but he remained a member of the NDC, even after the National People's Congress of January 1965, when some changes were made in the Council's composition. Su Yü also remained a member of the Council, and in addition has continued as Deputy Minister of National Defence.

T'an Cheng is probably the mysterious 'XX' referred to in the *KTTH* (Cheng, pp. 53, 228, 230, 651), who is described as having exerted an 'erroneous influence' and as having an indifferent attitude towards ideological work. He seems to have been replaced by Lo Jung-huan as director of the Political Department. (Lo died in December 1963, and his active deputy Hsiao Hua was officially appointed director in September 1964.) T'an, together with Huang K'o-ch'eng, was dismissed from the party secretariat in September 1962. He was removed from the NDC in January 1965, and from his post as deputy Minister of Defence in March 1965.

General Staff. Two other departments of lesser importance, Ordnance and Finance, which had existed independently since 1954 or before, were merged with the Rear Services Department. The position of chief of staff was given to General Lo Jui-ch'ing, the Minister of Public Security since 1949 and commander of the Public Security Forces since at least 1953. P'eng Teh-huai was replaced by Marshal Lin Piao, veteran of the civil war whose party loyalty was unquestioned and prestige within the army equally high. Lo Jung-huan resumed control of the Political Department, actively supported by Hsiao Hua, who succeeded him, after his death, as political director.

The new Rear Services Department director was Ch'iu Hui-tso, a relatively unknown officer who had served with the Fourth Field Army in South China from 1949–54. It may perhaps be deliberate policy not to appoint a senior officer to such a pivotal position, or Ch'iu may possibly be a personal protegé of Marshal Lin Piao.[18]

This reversion to greater political control by the Military Affairs Committee has not solved the problem of finding suitable GHQ directors to bridge the awkward gap between policy-making and implementation. The five officers who lost their positions were in no sense 'young Turks' defending the new professional army against political encroachment. All had distinguished careers in the Red Army, dating back at least to the Long March, and all were members of the Central Committee,[19] two of the secretariat. All were at least 50 years old, and belonged to roughly the same generation as the military marshals of the Military Affairs Committee. If they had represented an organized army movement against party policy, one would expect other leading officers to have been demoted with them. In

---

[18] Ch'iu's name is first recorded in April 1949 as director of the Political Department of Honan Military District. By 1952 he was assistant director of the South China Military Region Political Department, and by the end of 1953 deputy political commissar of Kwangtung Military District. In September 1955 he received the Liberation Medal (1st Class) for meritorious service in the war of liberation (Union Research Service, Hong Kong: Biographical Service No. 400, 27 Oct. 1959).

[19] The early career of Hung Hsueh-chih cannot be traced, but he was awarded in 1955 the August First Honour, 1st Class, for military services rendered in the 1927–37 period. All five were full members of the CC except for Hung, who was an alternate member. Su Yü, Huang K'o-ch'eng and T'an Cheng had been CC members since the 7th Congress of April 1945.

fact, only two other officers can be identified as being implicated in the downfall of Marshal P'eng Teh-huai, and both were associates of his when he was commander-in-chief of the CPV in Korea.[20] Some special ties of friendship can perhaps be inferred between members of this group. Thus Huang and Hung were respectively commander and chief of staff of the New Fourth Army 3rd Division from 1941 to 1945, and Hung served under P'eng Teh-huai in Korea as rear services director during the war. But many other officers with equally close connexions to this group have remained in power. Nor have any of their colleagues, deputy directors or deputy chiefs of staff, been removed.

It is unexpected that a major shift of personnel should take place only at the highest level, without involving at least the most closely connected subordinates. One may therefore speculate that these officers were removed not so much because they differed with the Great Leap policy as because they found it impossible to carry it out satisfactorily. The latent conflict between military and political priorities, which could be either ignored or accepted as a necessary evil by those in lower positions of authority, crystallized at the threshold of top-ranking leadership. In this sense, Su Yü, Hsiao K'o, and the others may be no different from the majority of military leaders who are still one step below on the promotion ladder. Perhaps significantly, these have not since been given the opportunity to assume the key posts of chief of staff or department director. Thus Lo Jui-ch'ing succeeded Huang K'o-ch'eng as chief of staff over the heads of five deputy chiefs whose tenure of office dated back at least to 1955, of whom two were full and two alternate Central Committee members.

2. SECOND ÉCHELON LEADERSHIP—GENERAL STAFF, REGIONAL AND SERVICE ARM COMMANDS

The second échelon of military leadership is here taken to include the deputy chiefs of staff, deputy directors of PLA departments, the commanders and political commissars of the military regions and of the service arm headquarters. Also included are

[20] Li Ta, P'eng's chief of staff in Korea, was dismissed from his post as Deputy Minister of Defence in October 1959, and appointed vice-chairman of the Physical Culture Commission. Teng Hua, P'eng's deputy commander in Korea, was replaced by Ch'en Hsi-lien as commander of Shenyang Military Region sometime in late 1959.

the heads of the most important military academies and General Department bureaux, the president of the Supreme Military Court, and the ministers of a select group of government ministries of military significance. This definition appears to be justified by the rank, seniority, and importance of the officers holding such posts, and it also covers almost all the active senior personnel of whose biographies we have at least some sketchy knowledge. It is also the group which is responsible for interpreting and carrying out the instructions of the present high-level leadership, and from which one may expect the future leadership to emerge.

From this group 70 officers have been selected for analysis. They comprise all those who were identified in the above categories after the dismissal of Marshal P'eng in September 1959 and up to 1962 (with a few exceptions). This is not an exhaustive list, but it can be considered as a representative cross-section of the PLA leadership.

The overall picture which emerges is that of a generation of senior officers whose military training and political environment has been almost entirely confined to the communist army and party for a very long time. Unlike the Soviet Red Army in its early days, there are no known instances of leading officers at this level who transferred their allegiance from the Kuomintang at any time after 1927–30. Over three-quarters of the group are known to have served with the Red Army since the Long March or before (54 out of 70), 9 held command positions during the Yenan period, and 7 can be identified only since 1945.[21]

This long tradition of service in the Red Army suggests obvious advantages in terms of loyalty and esprit de corps. It also means that the majority of the leading officers have reached a relatively advanced age, which may be a disadvantage for the future. Of the 37 officers in the group whose dates of birth are known, 32 were born in the first decade of this century, and their average date of birth lies between 1906 and 1907. A further 9 were awarded the August 1st Order (1st Class) for service in the 1927–37 period, and 2 more are known to have joined the party

[21] In compiling these and other statistics, the military awards made in September 1955 for meritorious service in the revolutionary wars have been taken as evidence of membership of the Red Army at a given time. There were three awards for the three periods of revolution: August 1st Order (1927–37), Independence and Freedom Order (1937–45), and Liberation Order (1945–50).

in 1927–9. Thus over two-thirds (48 out of 70) are probably at least in their 50s. Both in the cases of army service and of age, many who are not identified in the early period of the revolution may still have a longer record than our information reveals, so that these figures are probably underestimated.

As might be expected from the origins of the Red Army in Central-South China, the majority of these officers come from that area. Out of 44 whose provincial homes can be identified, 27 were born in either Hunan (18) or Hupeh (9). Only seven come from north of the Yangtze river. The preponderance of Hunanese reflects the military tradition and geographical location of that province, and should not be construed as implying any sort of military clique.[22]

The group is well represented on the Central Committee of the party with 9 full and 22 alternate members. (This includes three who have since died.) This is not an excessive representation; it amounts to about one-tenth of the full Central Committee and one-fifth of the alternates. Yet only five of these were on the Central Committee in any capacity before the Eighth Congress of 1956, which suggests that as a group its influence has increased rapidly since Liberation. (Although it was not unique in this respect. Altogether 129 new members of the Central Committee were created at the Eighth Congress and subsequently.)

The numerical proportion of the PLA in the Central Committee has however declined since 1949, but this is due in the main to the promotion of former army leaders to party and governmental posts.[23] The army's influence does not extend to the innermost party ranks—the Politburo, the Control Committee, and the secretariat of the Central Committee—on a significant scale. Only the Minister of Defence and two of the Military Affairs Committee marshals (Liu Po-ch'eng and Ho Lung) are Politburo members. The former chief of staff, Huang K'o-ch'eng, and political director, T'an Cheng, were members of the secretariat

---

[22] The other provincial origins are: Anhwei (1), Fukien (2), Kiangsi (4), Kwangtung (1), Honan (3), Hopeh (1), Inner Mongolia (1), Szechwan (2), and Shensi (2).

[23] Donald W. Klein, in 'The "Next Generation" of Chinese Communist Leaders', *CQ*, Oct.–Dec. 1962, shows that the relative proportion of army personnel in the Central Committee élite has declined from 64 persons or about 37 per cent in 1949–50 to 42 persons or about 25 per cent in 1962. These figures include some officers not considered in the analysis under discussion.

until their dismissal in September 1962, and the present political director, Hsiao Hua, is a deputy secretary and member of the Control Committee's Standing Committee. Only one out of the seventy officers in the sample of second échelon military leadership (Wu Lan-fu, commander of Inner Mongolia Military Region and alternate member of the Politburo) has attained this high rank of party office. On the other hand the majority of Politburo and secretariat members held military command posts until at least 1949 or in some cases 1954. Just as specialization has occurred in the army and the government, so it can be observed at the upper party level. Dual tenure of party and military executive positions is now the exception rather than the rule.

Perhaps the most significant feature of this group is its high degree of continuity of office. Since at least 1954 or earlier, most officers have tended to stick in the position or department in which they had arrived, and there is a marked lack of mobility. Out of the 20 commanders or political commissars of service arm headquarters identified in 1962, 13 had held their positions or served as deputies since 1951–4. In the military regions, there have been rather more transfers of personnel, but in only one out of the 13 regions has there been a wholesale change of leadership. A similar picture is revealed among the deputy chiefs of staff, departmental deputy directors, and heads of bureaux. Here 16 out of the 27 incumbents identified in 1962 had been in office at least since 1955. (With fuller biographical information, it is very probable that the tenure of office would in most cases be seen to be even longer.)

Where transfers do take place, they do so impartially between departmental, service arm or military region posts, except for the officers in this group who have become ministers of civil ministries which carry military significance (State Farms and Land Reclamation, Petroleum, 4th, 5th, and 6th Ministries of Machine Building) and four who have since 1959 been promoted to deputy chief of staff. Indeed, one can only talk of 'promotion' with reference to this particular position. Otherwise the departmental, service arm and military region positions all appear to be of roughly equal importance and status.

This continuity of office can best be explained by the fact that the specialized sections of the PLA (general staff and service arms) developed simultaneously and rapidly from their previous embryonic form in the years 1949–54. The officers who were originally assigned to these different fields were few in number and all approximately of the same age and rank, and most of them have since then stayed put within their own specialized sphere of command. As representatives of the pre-Liberation PLA, they ensure, at any rate in theory, that, in a phase of increasing expertise and specialization, party control and adherence to revolutionary philosophy remain undiminished in their departments. In some cases, notably the navy and air force, they had to start completely from scratch, with the additional complication that the ships and aircraft acquired in 1949 were manned and crewed largely by ex-KMT personnel. Wherever possible, however, they possessed at least some technical qualifications for their new posts. Wang Cheng, the Signals HQ commander, had been in charge of the Communications Department in Yenan, where he had supervised the construction of Yenan's first wireless transmitter. Ch'iu Ch'uang-ch'eng, political commissar of the Artillery Corps, had graduated in his youth from the Artillery Class at the Moscow Eastern University. Wang Chen, as a former railway worker, was a natural choice for the Railway Corps.

The continuity is even more impressive in the case of the military region commanders, if one examines their military careers after Liberation and before the establishment of the regions in 1954. Ten out of the thirteen commanders in the period 1954–8 (of whom eight are still in office either as commander or political commissar) had held leading military positions within the region since Liberation. Thus Huang Yung-sheng, commander of Canton until 1958 and again after 1962, had been deputy commander and then commander of Kwangsi Military District since 1950. Ch'en Tsai-tao, commander of Wuhan since 1954, had commanded the Honan Military District from 1950 onwards. Two more, Teng Hua (Shenyang) and Hsieh Fu-chih (Kunming), were appointed to their military regions after service with the CPV in Korea. Only one of the thirteen original commanders, Wang Hsin-t'ing (Tsinan), was moved directly from one part of China to another (from Szechwan to Shantung). The commanders of Tibet, Inner Mongolia, and Sinkiang have held continuous office in one form or another in their regions since communist control was established. New appointments since 1958–9 have in the main been chosen from ex-CPV officers—Han Hsien-ch'u (Foochow), Yang Yung (Peking), and Yang Teh-chih (Tsinan). Only in Shenyang, as previously noted, has there been a wholesale removal of commander and political commissar, bringing in the ex-commander of the Artillery Force (Ch'en Hsi-lien) and an ex-deputy director of the Cadres Department (Lai Ch'uan-chu).

Information on political commissars of military regions is less revealing. It seems that in many cases until 1958 the post of commander and of commissar was held concurrently, and that their functions were separated at the time of the Great Leap Forward. (In Inner Mongolia and Sinkiang the posts are still concurrent.)

In general, most leading military officers in the field have remained almost stationary within their particular region since the early 1950s. Those who have been transferred in this period have usually been promoted from positions in the CPV. Indeed, if it had not been for the Korean war, the degree of mobility might be even less than it has been.

It also appears that the same degree of continuity can be found among the staff members of the service arm headquarters and regional commands. In the navy, for instance, many of the staff officers seem to have been transferred *en bloc* from the Twelfth Army Group in 1950, under their commander Hsiao Ching-kuang, and have remained since then in the same departments.[24] Similar instances can be found in other service arm and regional commands, suggesting a high degree of cohesion among their

[24] The following senior staff on the navy command were identified in 1960 and subsequently:

	1st identification
Commander:	
Hsiao Ching-kuang (former 12th AG commander)	9/50
Dep. commanders:	
Lo Shun-ch'u (former 12th AG army commander)	8/52
Liu Tao-sheng (former 12th AG polit. commissar; from 3/53– 1954 dep. polit. com.)	1954
Li Tso-p'eng (former 12th AG dep. commander)	1965
Fang Ch'iang	10/53
Wang Hung-k'un	1954
Political commissar:	
Su Chen-hua (from 1953–3/57 dep. polit. com.)	3/57
Chief of staff:	
Chou Hsi-han	8/50
Political Dept head:	
Tuan Te-chang (from 3/53–12/58 deputy)	12/58

staffs. The fact that this is so, and that regional and service arm commanders have been allowed to remain static for so long, implies that their political loyalty can never have been in serious doubt. It is legitimate to infer from the evidence of such considerable cohesion and continuity at this level of command that the PLA has not been troubled by the phenomenon of 'regionalism' to which the geographical division of military authority would appear to lend itself.

In a tightly-knit group of officers of this nature, close personal and service connexions tend to reflect themselves in the pattern of appointments. For example, the commander of Kunming region from 1954–8, Hsieh Fu-chih, had previously commanded the Tenth Army of the Second Field Army in the South-west Military Region which from 1950–4 comprised the area later subdivided into Kunming and Chengtu regions. Hsieh was also political commissar of Szechwan Military District before 1954, and the commander of the district, Ho Ping-yen, became commander of Chengtu region at the same time as Hsieh was appointed to the equivalent post in Kunming region. In October 1958 Hsieh was removed from Kunming region, becoming Minister of Public Security in the following year. He was succeeded in Kunming by his former deputy commander of the Tenth Army, Ch'in Ch'i-wei, who had accompanied that army to Korea and returned with it to Kunming to serve in Hsieh's staff.

The commander of the army group garrisoning Kweichow province in the same South-west Military Region in 1950 was Yang Yung. During the anti-Japanese war, Yang had been deputy commander of the Hopeh–Shantung–Honan military zone along the Yellow river, whose commander was Yang Teh-chih. Meanwhile Yang Teh-chih in 1950 commanded an army group in the North-west province of Ninghsia, and moved to Korea in 1951 when he became chief of staff and subsequently deputy commander of the CPV.

In 1954 he was joined by Yang Yung, who also served as a deputy commander, subsequently becoming commander of the CPV. Both were given adjacent military region commands at the time of the Great Leap Forward. Yang Teh-chih took over the command of Tsinan (Shantung) Military Region from Wang Hsin-t'ing, who had also served in the Hopeh–Shantung–Honan area during the anti-Japanese war, and who now became political commissar of the region. Yang Yung took command of the neighbouring region of Peking a few months later. This is only one example of the ramification of service connexions in this group which could be reproduced on a much larger scale. However, these connexions are a very different phenomenon from that of officer 'cliques', which it is impossible to identify at this level of leadership. None of the four dominant Field Armies which existed before 1954 appear to have been especially favoured in promotion. Of the present group of officers, 14 served with the First Field Army, the same number with the Fourth, 11 with the Second, and 8 with the Third. There is no evidence of discrimination in promotion for or against any sector of the army either since Liberation or during the civil war.

The group of ministerial posts held by military officers are concerned with those sectors of the economy which have particular military significance. The work of the Ministry of State Farms and Land Reclamation, under Wang Chen, is closely connected with the PLA Production and Construction Corps in Sinkiang, and other specialized production units of the PLA. Petroleum has an obvious military value, especially since the cut-back in oil supplies from the Soviet Union and the search for native oil resources in China, and the Ministry of Petroleum is closely associated with the PLA Rear Services Department. The exact nature of the 4th–7th Ministries of Machine Building set up since 1963 is unknown, but they are presumably concerned with key technological processes connected with the development of naval, air, and land equipment. The previous positions of their ministers suggests that they may deal respectively with communications, ordnance, naval and aircraft (or possibly missile) development. The 8th Ministry, headed by Ch'en Cheng-jen, who in 1952 directed the PLA's Military Construction and Engineering Department, but was later in charge of agricultural machinery production, may also have military significance, or may be again concerned with agricultural machinery.

3. THIRD ÉCHELON LEADERSHIP—PROVINCIAL AND GARRISON COMMANDS

The third échelon of military leadership, comprising the commanding officers of provincial military district and urban garrisons, is the lowest level at which incumbents can be identified with any regularity, and even then many are no more than once-cited names. Within the limits imposed by this lack of material, a picture emerges in which continuity of office among commanding officers is much the same as that at higher levels of leadership, while party control, especially since the Great Leap Forward, is more emphatic and closely identified with the leading party official in the province concerned.

Of the nineteen commanders of military districts identified in office around 1960,[25] the careers of only four are sufficiently prominent for details of their service before 1949 to be known.[26] A brief obituary notice of one of these, Wang Tao-pang, commander of Hopei district, who died in November 1959, at the age of 48, may be fairly typical.

Wang was a native of Yunghsin *hsien*, Kiangsi. He joined the Chinese Peasant-Workers Red Army in 1930, and joined the Communist Party in the same year. The posts held included squad and company commander, instructor, battalion political commissar, regimental commissar, army corps commander and concurrently army corps political commissar. He was consistently loyal to the cause and worked diligently during the long revolutionary struggle.[27]

In other words, Wang was born in 1911, and joined the communist party and army at the age of 19. He ascended every step of the promotion ladder from platoon to army corps commander before taking charge of Hopei military district. He was experienced both as a military and as a political officer.

Only one of the nineteen received a first-class award for meritorious service in 1955 when honours were accorded to all prominent army veterans.[28] Altogether eleven of these officers are known to have been active in their provinces since at least 1955, of whom five have held their post as commander since that year. As in the case of the military regions, therefore, it seems that the majority of the provincial commanders have remained in the same field of responsibility since the major reorganization of

[25] According to the table in *Communist China: Ruthless Enemy or Paper Tiger?*
[26] Liu Yung-sheng (Fukien), commander of the Fukien–Kwangtung–Kwangsi column in 1948–9, Lu Shao-wu (Kwangsi), a regimental commander on the Long March, and Yang Chia-jui (Shensi), an army commander in the civil war, Wang Tao-pang (Hopei).
[27] NCNA, 13 Nov. 1959.
[28] Chang K'ai-ching (Heilungkiang) Order of Liberation 1st Class.

military control in 1954, if not before. Provincial origins are unknown except for three of the officers identified before 1949, all of
whom now command the provinces in which they were born.

Most of the garrison commanders are also only known by
name. In provincial capitals the post appears to be one rank
lower in importance than that of provincial commander. In the
major cities the garrison tends to be commanded by a more
senior officer. Thus Shanghai is controlled by Wang Pi-ch'eng, a
divisional commander of the New Fourth Army and district
commander of Chekiang province after Liberation. (In 1964
Wang was succeeded by Jao Tzu-chien, also a New Fourth Army
veteran, and probably Wang's second-in-command.) It is note-
worthy that both Wang and Jao have worked continuously in the
Yangtze area around Shanghai since at least 1941.

The post of first political commissar in military districts and
garrisons has since 1958 come increasingly under the control of
the senior party provincial official—the first secretary of the provincial party committee. Out of fifteen commissarships identified
in or around 1960, nine were held by the first secretary of the
province. The commissars of Peking and Shanghai garrisons
were also ranking party secretaries.[29] All these appointments
appear to date from the Great Leap Forward and the increasing
attempts at that time to establish more effective party control
over the army. On a smaller scale, this trend can also be noted in
the military regions, where the most recent appointment to the
post of political commissar (Tsinan region, 1964) was given to
the first party secretary of Shantung, T'an Chi-lung.[30] Earlier,

[29] Tseng Hsi-sheng (Anhwei), Wu Chih-p'u (Honan), Chang P'ing-hua (Hunan),
Yang Shang-k'uei (Kiangsi), Chiang Wei-ch'ing (Kiangsu), Wu Te (Kirin),
Chou Lin (Kweichow), Huang Huo-ch'ing (Liaoning), T'ao Lu-chia (Shansi),
Liu Jen (Peking garrison, 2nd party secretary), Ch'en P'i-hsien (Shanghai, party
secretary).

Chang Teh-sheng (Shensi) was identified as political commissar of Shensi
Military District on his death in March 1965.

Yang Chih-lin (Tsinghai) was identified as political commissar of Tsinghai
Military District in August 1965. The 2nd party secretary, Wang Chao (also
governor of Tsinghai) was similarly 2nd political commissar. Wang Jen-chung
(Hupeh) was identified as political commissar of Wuhan garrison in April 1965.

[30] Following this trend, Li Ching-ch'üan, 1st party secretary of Szechwan and of the
South-west Party Bureau, was identified in August 1965 as political commissar of
Chengtu Military Region. Sung Jen-ch'iung, 1st party secretary of the North-
east Party Bureau, was identified in December 1965 as political commissar of
Shenyang Military Region.

T'ao Chu, the first secretary of Kwangtung province and of the Central-South Bureau, became political commissar of Canton region, relinquishing the post again in 1962. In the key defence areas of Inner Mongolia, Sinkiang, and Foochow, the commander and/or commissar since 1954 has also been the party secretary (Wu Lan-fu, Wang En-mao, and Yeh Fei).

It is only in the military districts, however, that the appointment of the most senior party official as watchdog over the military district is widely practised. This is the only area in the entire range of army leadership where the incumbents are primarily party rather than military men, in the sense that these commissars have specialized in political rather than military duties over the past decade.

CONCLUSION

China's military élite has shown a remarkable lack of disaffection since the Liberation. There has been only one major upset, that of P'eng Teh-huai in 1959. P'eng's dismissal involved only seven other leading officers at the most generous estimate. Apart from these, no one else among the more than seventy strong military élite in power since 1954 has fallen from favour.

The revolutionary *esprit de corps* has apparently persisted at this level of leadership despite the very different atmosphere and conditions of the post-Liberation PLA, although it may now be beginning to disintegrate. The élite shares a common experience of revolutionary struggle and of personal co-operation since the earliest and formative phase of the Red Army. There can be no serious question of the élite's fundamental loyalty to the party and government. At all levels down to but excluding that of the military district, it is allowed to operate without the system of checks and counterbalances by which the military in China was traditionally controlled. Officers sometimes serve in the provinces of their origin, and they are not rotated in order to diminish their influence. Most commanders of the specialized service arms still control the units which they helped to create.

Although many of the members of the military élite are also high in the party structure, very few hold concurrent party or government office. Since 1954 especially, their day-to-day preoccupation with military affairs has made them 'experts' to an

v

extent previously unknown in the PLA. If they do not question the extent of political control over the army, they may nevertheless find it difficult to reconcile political and military priorities, especially when placed in the key positions of chief of staff or of departmental director.

The first test of the strength of the élite is bound to come when the senior PLA marshals are forced by age to retire from close supervision of military affairs through the Military Affairs Committee. If they are replaced by second échelon leaders, there is likely to be a slight shift of emphasis away from the present one-sided party control. The real test is, however, likely to come when the entire élite passes into retirement. Assuming that the majority will continue to work until they are 65, this must still come within ten to fifteen years at the outside. Even if their immediate successors—the staff members of the regions, service arms, and army departments at present largely unknown to us— are also loyal veterans, they too will be getting on in years. The young recruit to the Red Army of 1930 will be some 60 years old by 1970.

The wide-scale appointment of provincial party secretaries as political commissars of the military districts—especially during the Great Leap Forward—suggests that there is already a greater need for party control at the district level and below. This suggestion is reinforced by similar appointments more recently in military regions. This need can hardly fail to increase, as long as present policy-making remains in the hands of the revolutionary hard core. In the long-term view, it seems inevitable that present policies must be modified as younger men rise to the top, but this is unlikely to be accompanied by any dramatic breakdown of party control over the army.

Appendix

TABLE I

Communist Strength during Anti-Japanese War, 1937–45

	8th Route Army strength	New 4th Army strength	Total strength	8th Route net increase	New 4th net increase	8th Route casualties	New 4th casualties	Total turnover
1937	80,000[1]	12,000	92,000	—	—	—	—	—
1938	156,700	25,000	181,700	76,000	13,000	12,539		117,011[2]
1939	270,000	50,000	320,000	113,300	25,000	46,079	59,085	199,150[2]
1940	400,000	100,000	500,000	130,000	50,000	49,187		243,958[2]
1941	305,000	135,000[3]	440,000	−95,000	35,000[3]	59,732		14,503[2]
1942	340,000	110,960	450,960	35,000	−24,040	63,847	17,601	92,408
1943	339,000	125,892	464,892	−1,000	14,932	29,485	16,029	59,446
1944	320,800	153,676	474,476	−18,200	27,784	28,919	17,073	55,576
1945[4]	600,000	260,000	880,000[5]	279,200	106,324	33,838	11,091	430,453
Total 1937–45	—	—	—	520,000	248,000	323,626	120,879	1,212,505[6]

[1] Only 45,000 out of the 80,000 in the 8th Route Army in 1937 were officially recognized as part of the National Revolutionary Army.

[2] These figures are reached by including one-quarter per annum of total New 4th Army casualties for the four years 1937–41.

[3] The figures for the New 4th Army can only be true if they apply to January 1941, before it was broken up in the South Anhwei incident of February.

[4] The figures for 1945 apply to the position in March. The figures for all other years apply to the position in June.

[5] The figure for March 1945 total strength includes 20,000 guerrilla forces in South China.

[6] No figures are available for casualties who later returned to duty. Total turnover figures in this column may therefore be in excess of real recruitment.

Sources: Calculated from official statistics in Yeh Chien-ying, 'Report on the general military situation of the Chinese Communist Party in the war of resistance', 18 June 1944, in Gelder, Chinese Communists, pp. 73–102: K'ang-Jih chan-cheng shih-ch'i ti Chung-kuo jen-min chieh-fang-chün, pp. 219–20; Stein, Challenge of Red China, p. 269; Peabody Report, pp. 2432–4.

TABLE 2

PLA Strength during Civil War

	Regular strength	Guerrilla strength	Total strength	Net annual increase	Annual casualties	Total turnover[1]
June 1946	612,000	665,000	1,278,000	—	—	—
June 1947	1,000,000	950,000	1,950,000	672,000	357,000	1,029,000
June 1948	1,490,000	1,310,000	2,800,000	850,000	542,600	1,392,600
June 1949	2,100,000[2]	1,900,000[2]	4,000,000	1,200,000	533,300	1,733,300
June 1950	—	—	5,000,000	1,000,000	89,600	1,089,600
1946–50	—	—	—	3,722,000	1,522,500	5,244,500

[1] The calculated figures for total turnover—i.e. for total recruitment—do not take into account the proportion of annual casualties which returned to duty. According to PLA claims, 200,000 wounded in 1946–7 and 243,750 wounded in 1947–8 returned to duty. No figures are available for 1948–50. Assuming that over the entire period 1946–50, roughly 50 per cent returned to duty, the real turnover in terms of actual recruitment for the same period would be approximately 750,000 less than as given above, making a total of about 4½ million. On the other hand, my calculated figure for total turnover 1946–8 (2,421,000) does correspond closely to the figures for total recruitment in those years (2,400,000, *MAO IV*, p. 271). This suggests either that PLA claims for the 'returned to duty' category are exaggerated, or that they were returned to the auxiliaries or militia.

[2] At February 1949.

Sources: MAO IV, pp. 141, 223, 269, 337; NCNA, 30 July 1950; NCNA, 16 July 1949, communiqués issued by PLA Headquarters on 15 July 1949 (*FE* 14); Rigg, *Red China's Fighting Hordes*, p. 274; Sheng Li-yu, *Chung-kuo jen-min-chieh-fang-chün san-shih nien shih-hua*, p. 72.

TABLE 3

PLA Statistics, 1950–8

	Strength	Demobilization	Recruitment
1950	5,000,000[1]	—	—
1951	—		
1952	—	2,940,000[2]	1,750,000*
1953	3,500,000*		
1954	—	1,820,000[3]	830,000[2]
1955	3,000,000*		500,000[4]
1956	2,750,000*[5]	740,000[6]	500,000*
1957	2,500,000*	800,000[7]	500,000*
1958	2,500,000*	500,000[8]	500,000*
1950–8	—	6,800,000[9]	4,580,000*

Note: Figures marked * based on the author's calculations, the remainder on official Chinese sources. All figures must be regarded as very approximate. No official figures of any kind are available since 1958.

Sources:
[1] *The Chinese People's Liberation Army* (Peking), 1950.
[2] P'eng Teh-huai, report to NPC on draft military service law, NCNA, 16 July 1955 (*SCMP* 1090).
[3] Calculated from P'eng Teh-huai above, and from unaccounted portion of total demobilization 1950–8.
[4] Hong Kong sources quoted in *Communist China 1955*.
[5] Calculated from P'eng Teh-huai, 'The Chinese PLA', NCNA, 19 Sept. 1956 (*CB* 422).
[6] NCNA, 30 Jan. 1957; Peking radio quoted in *NYHT*, 1–2 June 1957.
[7] NCNA, 5 Nov. 1956 (*SCMP* 1407).
[8] Ibid., 19 May 1958.
[9] Fu Ch'iu-t'ao, 'Everyone is a Soldier', *Hung Ch'i*, 16 Oct. 1958 (*ECMM* 150). By 1959 'over 7,000,000 demobilized servicemen' had been resettled since 1950, according to NCNA, 25 Sept. 1959 (*SCMP* 2108).

TABLE 4

Political Control Structure of the PLA

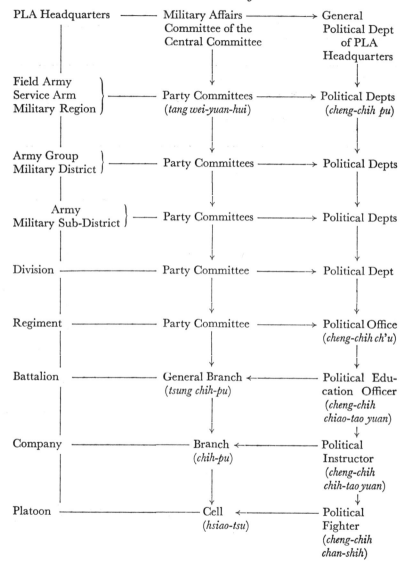

PLA Headquarters ———— Military Affairs ————→ General
                       Committee of the   Political Dept
                       Central Committee   of PLA
                                                Headquarters

Field Army   ⎫
Service Arm   ⎬ ———— Party Committees ————→ Political Depts
Military Region ⎭   (*tang wei-yuan-hui*)   (*cheng-chih pu*)

Army Group   ⎫ ———— Party Committees ————→ Political Depts
Military District⎭

Army   ⎫ ———— Party Committees ————→ Political Depts
Military Sub-District ⎭

Division ———————— Party Committee ————→ Political Dept

Regiment ———————— Party Committee ————→ Political Office
                                          (*cheng-chih ch'u*)

Battalion ———————— General Branch ←———— Political Edu-
                   (*tsung chih-pu*)   cation Officer
                                           (*cheng-chih
                                           chiao-tao yuan*)

Company ———————— Branch ←———— Political
                 (*chih-pu*)   Instructor
                                 (*cheng-chih
                                 chih-tao yuan*)

Platoon ———————— Cell ←———— Political
                 (*hsiao-tsu*)   Fighter
                                 (*cheng-chih
                                 chan-shih*)

TABLE 5

PLA and Regional Government, 1950–4[1]

Central People's
Government Council

PRMC   SAC

PLA GHQ

Field Armies	Military regions	Regional administrations[2]
1st Com.: P'eng Teh-huai Pol. Com.: Hsi Chung- hsun	North-west Com.: P'eng Teh-huai Pol. Com.: Hsi Chung- hsun	North-west MAC Chairman: P'eng Teh- huai Vice: Hsi Chung-hsun & others
2nd Com.: Liu Po-ch'eng Pol. Com.: Teng Hsiao- p'ing	South-west Com.: Ho Lung Pol. Com.: Teng Hsiao- p'ing	South-west MAC Chairman: Liu Po-ch'eng Vice: Teng Hsiao-p'ing, Ho Lung, & others
3rd Com.: Ch'en Yi Pol. Com.: Jao Shu-shih	East China Com.: Ch'en Yi Pol. Com.: Jao Shu-shih	East China MAC Chairman: Jao Shu-shih Vice: Ch'en Yi & others
4th Com.: Lin Piao Pol. Com.: Lo Jung-huan	Central-south Com.: Yeh Chien-ying Pol. Com.: Lo Jung-huan	Central-south MAC Chairman: Lin Piao Vice: Yeh Chien-ying & others
North China—direct army groups under control of PLA GHQ, Peking, sometimes referred to as 5th Field Army Com.: Nieh Jung-chen Pol. Com.: Po I-po	North China Com.: Nieh Jung-chen Pol. Com.: Po I-po	North China administered by central government offices
North-east China garrisoned by units of 4th Field Army	North-east Com.: Kao Kang Pol. Com.: Kao Kang	North-east People's Government Chairman: Kao Kang

[1] Names of incumbents accurate for 1950.
[2] MAC's and the North-east People's Government replaced in Nov. 1952 by 'administrative committees'.

TABLE 6

Military Organization since 1954

Military Affairs Committee of the Central Committee	National Defence Council[1]	State Council

PLA GHQ ←———————————————— Ministry of National Defence

General Staff Dept
General Political Dept
General Rear Services Dept

Military Regions

Military Districts

Military Regions / Districts		Service Arms
Canton	Kwangtung	Air Defence
	Kwangsi	Air Force
	Hunan	Armoured Force
Chengtu	Szechuan	Artillery Force
Foochow	Fukien	Engineer Corps
	Kiangsi	Navy
Kunming	Kweichow	Railway Corps
	Yunnan	Signal Corps
Lanchow	Chinghai	Public Security Forces
	Kansu	ABC Warfare
	Ninghsia	Coastal Defence
	Shensi	Technical Services
Nanking	Chekiang	People's Militia
	Anhwei	
	Kiangsu	
Peking	Hopei	
	Shansi	*Garrison Commands*
Shenyang	Kirin	Canton
	Liaoning	Chengtu
	Heilungkiang	Lanchow
Tsinan	Shantung	Lhasa
Wuhan	Honan	Mukden
	Hupeh	Peking
Inner Mongolia Autonomous Region		Shanghai
		Tientsin
Sinkiang Autonomous Region		Wuhan & other major towns
Tibet Autonomous Region		

Note: In September 1954 the PRMC (see Table 5) was formally replaced by the NDC. This body is elected by the National People's Congress on the recommendation of the Chairman of the Republic. It appears to be an honorific organ with no effective powers.

TABLE 7

Military Expenditure, 1950–60 (according to official statistics)

	Million yuan	Per cent of budgetary expenditure
1950	2,827[1]	41·53[2]
1951	5,061[1]	42·52[2]
		48·00[3]
1952	4,371[1]	26·04[2]
1953	5,680[1]	26·43[2]
	6,176[4]	28·00[4]
1954	5,814[1]	23·60[2]
1955	6,500[1]	24·30[2]
		22·1[5]
1956	6,117[1]	19·91[2]
1957	5,509[6]	19·24[6]
	5,523[4]	18·85[4]
1958	5,000[4]	15·12[4]
1959*	5,800[7]	11·2[7]
1960*	5,826[8]	8·3[8]

* Advance estimates in draft budgets.

Note: No figures for budgetary expenditure have been released since 1960. According to a report by the Rear Services Dept, the national defence budget for 1961 was 'adjusted and reduced', *KTTH,* 26 Aug 1961 (Cheng, p. 749). No information of any kind is available for subsequent years.

Sources:

[1] Budget figures quoted in William W. Hollister, *China's Gross National Product and Social Accounts, 1950-7* (Glencoe, Ill., 1958), p. 121.
[2] Percentages calculated in Li Choh-ming, *Economic Development of Communist China; an Appraisal of the First Five Years of Industrialization* (Univ. of California, 1959), Table xxxvii.
[3] P'eng Teh-huai, 'The Chinese People's Liberation Army', 18 September 1956, *CB* 422.
[4] Kan Szu-ch'i, 'Army building with diligence and thrift and participation of servicemen in national construction', 8 February 1958, *SCMP* 1724.
[5] P'eng Teh-huai's speech at Army Day Rally, NCNA, 31 July 1957 (*SCMP* 1584).
[6] Li Hsien-nien, 'The implementation of the State Budget for 1957 and the Draft State Budget for 1958', 1 February 1958, *CB* 493.
[7] Li Hsien-nien, 'Report on Final State Accounts, 1958, and the Draft State Budget 1959', 21 April 1959, *CB* 562.
[8] Tseng Shan, 'Report on Examination of the 1959 Final State Accounts and the Draft 1960 State Budget', 10 April 1960, *SCMP* 2240.

TABLE 8

Military Leadership, 1954–66

1. FIRST ÉCHELON MILITARY LEADERSHIP SINCE 1954

Military Affairs Committee (at 1960–1)
Standing Committee
Lin Piao (vice-chairman)
Ho Lung (vice-chairman)
Nieh Jung-chen (vice-chairman)
Liu Po-ch'eng
Lo Jung-huan   d. 12/63
Hsu Hsiang-chien
Yeh Chien-ying
Lo Jui-ch'ing
Hsiao Hua

Minister of Defence
P'eng Teh-huai   11/54– 9/59
Lin Piao   9/59–

Chief of Staff
Su Yü   11/54–10/58
Huang K'o-ch'eng   10/58– 9/59
Lo Jui-ch'ing   9/59–

General Political Dept Director
Lo Jung-huan   11/54–12/56, also director since 1950
T'an Cheng   12/56–1960(?)
Lo Jung-huan   at 1960–1961 (d. 12/63)
Hsiao Hua   9/64–

General Cadres Dept Director
Lo Jung-huan   11/54–12/56
Hsiao Hua   12/56–?

Training Dept Director
Liu Po-ch'eng   11/54–11/57
Hsiao K'o   11/57– 9/59(?)

Rear Services Dept Director
Huang K'o-ch'eng   11/54–12/56
Hung Hsueh-chih   12/56–10/59
Ch'iu Hui-tso   10/59–

Armed Forces Inspectorate Director
Yeh Chien-ying   11/54–

2. SECOND ÉCHELON MILITARY LEADERSHIP SINCE 1954

Note: Starred names are not included in the analysis of second échelon military leadership in ch. 14. Comm.=Commander, Pol. Com.=Political Commissar.

	Date of appointment or 1st identification	Comments
(a) *General Staff Dept*		
Deputy chiefs of staff		
Chang Ai-p'ing	6/55–	
Chang Tsung-hsun	11/52–	
Ch'en Keng	5/55–d.3/61	
Li K'o-nung	6/55–	
Han Hsien-ch'u	1965–	ex-Foochow MR Comm.
Li T'ien-yu	1964–	ex-Canton MR Pol. Com.
P'eng Shao-hui	10/55–	
Wang Hsin-t'ing	1964–	ex-Tsinan MR Comm.
Yang Ch'eng-wu	3/59–	ex-Peking MR Comm.
Yang Yung	1964–	ex-Peking MR Comm.
Sub-department heads		
Fu Ch'iu-t'ao (mobilization)	10/58–	
Kuo T'ien-min (training, dep. director)	6/57–	
Li Ta (training, dep. director)	7/58– 9/59	
P'eng Shao-hui (training, dep. director)	11/56–	
Wang Shang-jung (milit. ops.)	5/59–	
(b) *General Political Dept*		
Deputy directors		
Fu Chung	7/49–	
Hsiao Hua*	9/49–9/64	Promoted to Director
Hsu Li-ch'ing	6/54–	
Liang Pi-yeh	1962–	ex-Tsinan MR staff
Kan Szu-ch'i	8/53–d.2/64	
Liu Chih-chien	5/58–	
T'an Cheng*	1/55–12/56	Promoted to Director
Sub-department heads:		
Liu Ch'i-jen (organization)	2/54–	
Liu Chih-chien (propaganda)	2/53–	
Lai Ch'uan-chu (cadres, dep. director)	3/53–11/59	Promoted to Shen-yang MR Pol. Com.
(c) *Rear Services Dept*		
Deputy directors:		
Chang Ling-pin	2/54–	
Chou Ch'un-ch'uan	2/54–	
Jao Cheng-hsi	1/58–	At 12/53 head of RSD health sub-dept
T'ang T'ien-ch'i	6/57–	

Political commissar:

Yu Ch'iu-li	1954–2/58	Transferred to Minister of Petroleum
Li Chü-kuei	2/58–	ex-Minister of Petroleum

(d) PLA Inspectorate
Deputy directors:

Chou Shih-t'i	1958–
Yang Chih-ch'eng	11/57–
P'eng Shao-hui	1962–

(e) Service Arms†
Air defence HQ:

Comm.: Chou Shih-t'i	1951–9/56; 2/59–	
Yang Ch'eng-wu	9/56–2/59	
Pol. Com.: T'ang T'ien-ch'i	10/53–	

Air force HQ:

Comm.: Liu Ya-lou	1950–d.5/65	
Wu Fa-hsien	9/65–	
Pol. Com.: Wu Fa-hsien	7/59–9/65	Dep. Pol. Com. at 2/54

Armoured force HQ:

Comm.: Hsu Kuang-ta	1951–	
Pol. Com.: Hsiang Chung-hua	3/58–	Dep. Pol. Com. at 2/54

Artillery force HQ:

Comm.: Ch'en Hsi-lien	1951–1959	Transferred to Shenyang MR Comm.
Wu K'o-hua	1965–	
Pol. Com.: Ch'iu Ch'uang-ch'eng	1958–	Dep. Pol. Com. at 2/54

Engineer corps HQ

Comm.: Ch'en Shih-chu	3/53–	
Pol. Com.: Huang Chih-yung	1958–	Dep. Pol. Com. at 11/55

Navy HQ:

Comm.: Hsiao Ching-kuang	9/50–	
Pol. Com.: Su Chen-hua	3/57–	Dep. Pol. Com. at 1953

Public Security forces HQ:

Comm.: Lo Jui-ch'ing*	8/53–9/59	Promoted to PLA chief of staff
Pol. Com.: Lo Jui-ch'ing*	8/53–9/59	

Railway corps HQ:

Comm.: Wang Chen	2/54–8/57	Also Pol. Com.
Li Shou-hsuan	8/57–	Dep. Comm. at 5/54

Signal corps HQ:

Comm.: Wang Cheng	1954–
Pol. Com.: Chu Ming	3/59–

† Occupants unidentified for Coastal Defence, ABC Defence, People's Militia, and Technical Services HQ's.

(*f*) *Military Region Command*

Canton
Comm.: Huang Yung-sheng	1954–1958, 1962–	
Li T'ien-yu	1958–1962	
Pol. Com.: T'ao Chu*	1958–1962	
Li T'ien-yu	1962–	

Chengtu
Comm.: Ho Ping-yen	1954–d.7/60	
Pol. Com.: Kuo Lin-hsiang	1960–	
Li Ching-ch'üan*	8/65–	1st Sec. South-west party bureau

Foochow
Comm.: Yeh Fei	1954–1960	
Han Hsien-ch'u	1960–	
Pol. Com.: Yeh Fei	1960–	

Kunming
Comm. Hsieh Fu-chih	1954–10/58	
Ch'in Ch'i-wei	10/58–	
Pol. Com.:		

Lanchow
Comm.: Chang Ta-chih	1954–	
Pol. Com.: Hsien Heng-an	12/58–	

Nanking
Comm.: Hsu Shih-yu	1954–	
Pol. Com.: T'ang Liang	7/57–	

Peking
Comm.: Yang Ch'eng-wu	1954–3/59	
Yang Yung	3/59–	
Pol. Com.: Chu Liang-ts'ai	10/55–	

Shenyang
Comm.: Teng Hua*	1954–1959	
Ch'en Hsi-lien	1959–	
Pol. Com.: Chou Huan*	1956–1959?	
Lai Ch'uan-chu	1959?–d.12/65	
Sung Jen-ch'iung*	12/65–	1st Sec. North-east party bureau

Tsinan
Comm.: Wang Hsin-t'ing	1954–7/58	
Yang Teh-chih	7/58–	
Pol. Com.: Shu T'ung*	1958–?	1st Sec. Shantung party committee
Wang Hsin-t'ing	1962–1964	
T'an Chi-lung*	1964–	1st Sec. Shantung party committee

Wuhan
Comm.: Ch'en Tsai-tao	1954–	
Pol. Com.: Li Ch'eng-fang	1960–	

Inner Mongolia
Comm. & Pol. Com.: Wu Lan-fu	1954–	

Sinkiang
    Comm. & Pol. Com.: Wang En-mao   1954–
Tibet
    Comm.: Chang Kuo-hua   1952–
    Pol. Com.: T'an Kuan-san   1952–

(g) *Military Academies*
Nanking General Staff and War College
    Comm.: Liu Po-ch'eng*   1951–1957
          Liao Han-sheng   1957–1960?
    Pol. Com.: Chung Chi-kuang 1957–1961?
Peking Academy of Military Sciences
    Comm.: Yeh Chien-ying*   3/57–
    Pol. Com.: Yeh Chien-ying*   3/57–?
          Li Chih-min   1963?–
Dairen People's Naval Academy
    Dep. Comm.: Sung Shih-lun   4/58–

(h) *Supreme Military Court*
    President: Ch'en Ch'i-han   at 10/58

(i) *Key Ministerial posts*

Min. of State Farms & Land Re-clamation: Wang Chen	5/56–	
Min. of Petroleum: Li Chü-kuei	7/55–2/58	Transferred to RSD Pol. Com.
Yu Ch'iu-li	2/58–	Formerly RSD Pol. Com.
4th Min. of Machine Building Minister: Wang Cheng	1963–	Signal Corps Comm.
5th Min. of Machine Building Minister: Ch'iu Ch'uang-ch'eng	9/63–	Artillery Corps Pol. Com.
6th Min. of Machine Building Minister: Fang Ch'iang	9/63–	Formerly a Deputy Commander of the Navy
7th Min. of Machine Building Minister: Wang Ping-chang*	1/65–	Formerly a Deputy Commander of the Air Force

Select Bibliography

1. Bibliographies

Chesneaux, Jean and John Lust. *Introduction aux études d'histoire contemporaine de Chine.* Paris, Mouton, 1964.

A wide-ranging general bibliography of contemporary Chinese studies with critical notes.

Communist China: Ruthless Enemy or Paper Tiger? A Bibliographic Survey. Washington, Headquarters, Dept of the Army, 1962.

Especially ch. 5 (pp. 63–76) 'Armed Forces'; and App. C (pp. 125–35): 'Korean War, 1950–1953, a Bibliography'.

Hsueh Chun-tu. *The Chinese Communist Movement, 1921–37: An Annotated Bibliography of Selected Materials in the Chinese Collection of the Hoover Institution on War, Revolution, and Peace.* Stanford 1960.

Chinese-language materials, including many military items, for the period 1921–37.

The Chinese Communist Movement, 1937–49 .... Stanford, 1962.

The continuation of the preceding item.

Rhoads, Edward J. M. *The Chinese Red Army, 1927–63: an Annotated Bibliography.* Cambridge, Mass., Harvard UP, 1964. (Harvard East Asian Monographs.)

A comprehensive and critical bibliography covering all facets of the Chinese communist army, its origins, development, and present status.

2. Primary Sources*

Books

Chang Chün-ying. *Ko-ming yü fan-ko-ming ti chüeh-chan.* Peking, Chung-kuo ch'ing-nien ch'u-pan she, 1961.

China, People's Republic. *The First Year of Victory.* Peking, FLP, 1950.

Chu Teh. *Lun chieh-fang-ch'u chan-ch'ang.* Chieh-fang she, 1949.

Chung-kuo hsien-tai shih-liao ts'ung-k'an. *K'ang-Jih chan-cheng shih-ch'i chieh-fang-ch'u kai-k'uang.* Peking, 1953.

——, *K'ang-Jih chan-cheng shih-ch'i ti Chung-kuo jen-min chieh-fang-chün.* Peking, 1953.

Chung-kuo jen-min chieh-fang-chün tsung-pu. *Chung-kuo jen-min chieh-fang chan-cheng san-nien chan-chi.* 1949.

Ho Kan-chih. *A History of the Modern Chinese Revolution.* Peking, FLP, 1959.

Hu Hua, comp. *Chung-kuo ko-ming shih chiang-yi.* Peking, Chung-juo jen-min ta-hsueh, 1959.

* FLP—Foreign Languages Press.

Hung-ch'i p'iao-p'iao she, ed. *Chieh-fang chan-cheng hui-i-lu.* Peking, 1961.

Lei Feng jih-chi 1959–62. Peking, Chieh-fang-chün wen-i she, 1963.

Li Tu and others. *Tung-pei ti hei-an yü kuang-ming.* n.p. 1949.

Liao Kai-lung. *From Yenan to Peking.* Peking, FLP, 1954.

Mao Tse-tung. *Chung-kuo kung-ch'an-tang hung-chün ti-ssu chün ti-chiu-ts'u tai-piao ta-hui-i chüeh-i-an* (Resolution for the Ninth Conference of the Communist Party Organization of the Fourth Army of the Red Army, December 1929). Hong Kong, Hsin-min ch'u-pan she, 1949.

——, *Selected Works of Mao Tse-tung.* Peking, FLP, 1961–5. 4 vols.

—— *Selected Military Writings of Mao Tse-tung.* Peking, FLP, 1963.

—— and others. *Chung-kuo kung-ch'an-tang yü t'u-ti ko-ming* (The Chinese Communist Party and the Land Revolution). 1947.

—— and others. *Tsen-yang fen-hsi chieh-chi* (How to Analyse Classes). Hong Kong, 1948.

—— On Guerrilla Warfare (*Yu-chi chan*), trans. and with an introd. by Samuel B. Griffith. New York, Praeger, 1961.

Also translated in *Chinese Communist Guerrilla Tactics*, a source book compiled by Gene Z. Hanrahan (Washington D.C., US Army G.L., July 1952), pp. 5–62.

Mu Hsin. *Chin-Sui chieh-fang-ch'u min-ping k'ang-Jih tou-cheng san chi.* Shanghai, Jen-min ch'u-pan she, 1959.

Nan-ching lu-shang hao-pa-lien. Peking, Chieh-fang-chün wen-i she, 1963.

Shang-hai chieh-fang i-nien. Shanghai, Chieh-fang jih-pao she, 1950.

Sheng Li-yu. *Chung-kuo jen-min chieh-fang-chün san-shih-nien shih-hua.* Tientsin, 1959.

Ti-san-tz'u kuo-nei ko-ming chan-cheng ta-shih yüeh-piao. Peking, Jen-min ch'u-pan she, 1961.

Wang Ping and Kao Fan. *Kuang-jung ti san-shih-nien 1927-57.* Peking, Chieh-fang-chün hua-pao she, 1957.

Chinese newspapers and periodicals, and translated material

Ch'ang-chiang Jih-pao (Yangtze Daily), Wuhan.

Che-hsüeh Yen-chiu (Philosophical Studies), Peking.

Chiang-su Ch'un-chung (Kiangsu Masses), Nanking.

Chieh-fang-chün Chan-shih (Liberation Army Soldier), Peking, 1950–

Chieh-fang-chün Hua-pao (Liberation Army Pictorial), Peking, 1950–

Chieh-fang-chün Pao (Liberation Army Newspaper), Peking. Nos. 1–26 (trial series), 28 Sept.–23 Dec. 1955; No. 1, 1 Jan. 1956–

Chieh-fang-chün Wen-i (Liberation Army Literature), Peking, 1950–

Chieh-fang Jih-pao (Liberation Daily), Shanghai, 1949–

Chieh-fang Jih-pao (Liberation Daily), Yenan, 16 May 1941–27 Mar. 1947.

Chinese Press Review, Shanghai, US Consulate General, Nos. 1–1080.

Chung-kuo Ch'ing-nien Pao (China Youth Newspaper), Peking.

Chung-kuo Nung-pao (Chinese Agricultural News), Peking.

Current Background, Hong Kong, US Consulate General, 1950–

Extracts from China Mainland Magazines, Hong Kong, US Consulate General, Nos. 1–212; changed with No. 213, 7 June 1960, to *Selections from China Mainland Magazines*.

Hei-lung-chiang Jih-pao (Heilungkiang Daily), Harbin.

Ho-nan Jih-pao (Honan Daily), Chengchow.

Hsin-chiang Jih-pao (Sinkiang Daily), Urumchi.

Hsin Hu-nan Pao (New Hunan News), Changsha.

Hsin-Hua Jih-pao (New China Daily), Chungking.

Hsin-Hua Yueh-pao (New China Monthly), Peking.

Hua-pei Jen-min Jih-pao (North China People's Daily), No. 1, 15 June 1948–

Hung Ch'i (Red Flag), Peking, June 1958–

Jen-min Jih-pao (People's Daily), Peking.

Kuang-ming Jih-pao (Kuangming Daily), Pcking.

Kung-jen Jih-pao (Workers' Daily), Peking.

Kung-tso T'ung-hsün (Bulletin of Activities), Peking, PLA General Political Dept, No. 1, 1 Jan. 1961–

> An irregular secret publication for PLA officers with party membership at regimental level and above, replacing *Pa-i Tsa-chih*. Nos 1–8, & 10–30, available at the Library of Congress. For full English translation, see entry under J. Chester Cheng, ed. (p. 319).

Nan-fang Jih-pao (Southern Daily), Canton.

Pa-i Tsa-chih (August First Magazine), Peking, PLA General Political Dept, ?–1960.

People's China, Peking, 1950– (title changed to *Peking Review* in 1958).

Shih-shih Shou-ts'e (Current Affairs Handbook), Peking.

Summary of World Broadcasts, Part V: *The Far East*. London, BBC Monitoring Service, No. 1, 26 Apr. 1949—No. 862, 14 Apr. 1959. 2nd series (renamed Part III: *The Far East*), No. 1, 15 Apr. 1959–

Survey of the China Mainland Press, Hong Kong, US Consulate General, 1950–

Ta-kung Pao (Takung Daily), Tientsin.

Tung-pei Jih-pao (North-east Daily), Mukden, 1946-

Wen-hui Pao (Wenhui Daily), Hong Kong.

3. *Secondary Sources*

General

Ch'en, Dr Jerome. *Mao and the Chinese Revolution*. London, OUP, 1965.

w

Garvey, J. E. *Marxist-Leninist China, Military and Social Doctrine.* New York, Exposition Press, 1960.

O'Ballance, Edgar. *The Red Army of China.* London, Faber, 1962.

Rigg, R. B. *Red China's Fighting Hordes.* Harrisburg, Military Service Publishing Co., 1951.

Ting Li. *Militia of Communist China.* Hong Kong, Union Research Inst., 1955.

Before 1949

Band, Claire and William. *Dragon Fangs: Two Years with Chinese Guerillas.* London, Allen & Unwin, 1947.

Belden, Jack. *China Shakes the World.* London, Gollancz, 1950.

Carlson, Evans Fordyce. *The Chinese Army, its Organization and Military Efficiency.* New York, IPR, 1940.

—— *Twin Stars Over China.* New York, Dodd, Mead & Co., 1940.

Chassin, L. M. *La Conquête de la Chine par Mao Tse-tung 1945–9.* Paris, Payot, 1952.

Chiu, S. M. *Chinese Communist Revolutionary Strategy, 1945–9.* Princeton University, Center of International Studies, 1961 (Research Monograph, No. 13).

Compton, B., ed. *Mao's China; Party Reform Documents, 1942–4.* Seattle, Washington UP, 1952.

Crook, Isabel and David. *Revolution in a Chinese Village; Ten Mile Inn.* London, Routledge & Kegan Paul, 1959.

Epstein, Israel. *The Unfinished Revolution in China.* Boston, Little, Brown, 1947.

Forman, Harrison. *Report from Red China.* London, Hale, 1946.

Gelder, Stuart. *The Chinese Communists.* London, Gollancz, 1946.

Johnson, Chalmers A. *Peasant Nationalism and Communist Power; the Emergence of Revolutionary China, 1937–45.* Stanford UP, 1963.

Liu, F. F. *A Military History of Modern China 1924–49.* Princeton UP, 1956.

Payne, Robert. *Journey to Red China.* London, Heinemann, 1947.

Smedley, Agnes. *The Great Road; the Life and Times of Chu Teh.* New York, Monthly Review Press, 1956.

Snow, Edgar. *Red Star Over China.* New York, Random House, 1938.

—— *The Battle for Asia.* New York, Random House, 1941.

—— *Random Notes on Red China (1936–45).* Cambridge, Mass., Harvard East Asian Research Center, 1957.

Stein, Gunther. *The Challenge of Red China.* London, Pilot Press, 1945.

Taylor, George E. *The Struggle for North China.* New York IPR, 1940.

US Dept of War, Military Intelligence Division. *The Chinese Communist Movement, 5 July 1945, in* US Senate, Committee on the Judiciary, Subcommittee to Investigate the Administration of the Internal

Security Act and other internal security laws [Chairman: Brig. Gen. P. E. Peabody], *Institute of Pacific Relations, Hearings* . . . 82nd Congress, 2nd session, pt 7a, app. 2, pp. 2305–474, 1952.

Wales, Nym [Mrs Helen Foster Snow]. *Red Dust; Autobiographies of Chinese Communists*. Stanford UP, 1952.

After 1949

Bobrow, Davis B. Peking's Military Calculus. *World Politics*, Jan. 1964.

—— The Good Officer: Definition and Training. *China Quarterly*, Apr.–June 1964.

Charles, David A. The Dismissal of Marshal P'eng Teh-huai. *China Quarterly*, Oct.–Dec. 1961.

Chen, Wen-hui C. *Wartime "Mass" Campaigns in Communist China: Official Country-wide "Mass Movements" in Professed Support of the Korean War*. Texas, Air Force Personnel and Training Research Center, Lackland Air Force Base, Oct. 1955.

Cheng, J. Chester. Problems of Chinese Communist Leadership as Seen in the Secret Military Papers. *Asian Survey*, June 1964.

——, ed., *The Politics of the Chinese Army: a Translation of the Bulletin of Activities of the People's Liberation Army*. Hoover Inst. on War, Revolution, and Peace, Stanford Univ., Calif., 1966.

Chiang I-shan. Military Affairs of Communist China. *Communist China 1949–59*, vol. 1. Hong Kong, Union Research Institute.

Chin Ta-k'ai and Chang Ta-chun. *Chung-kung chün-shih p'ou-shih*. Hong Kong, Tzu-yu ch'u-pan she (Freedom Press), 1954.

Chiu, S. M. Political Control in the Chinese Communist Army. *Military Review*, Aug. 1961.

—— The Chinese Communist Army in Transition. *Far Eastern Survey*, Nov. 1958.

Chung-kung Wen-t'i (Problems of Red China). Vols. 1–3 in Chinese, Vol. 1 in English. Hong Kong, Freedom Press, 1954–5.

Erickson, John. Sino-Soviet Military Relationships. *Journal of the Royal United Services Institute*, Nov. 1959, Feb. & May 1960.

Evans, Gordon Heyd. China and the Atom Bomb. *Journal of the Royal United Service Institute*, Feb. & May 1962.

Garthoff, Raymond L. Sino-Soviet Military Relations. *Annals of the American Academy of Political and Social Science: 'Communist China and the Soviet Bloc'*, Sept. 1963.

Gittings, John. China's Militia. *China Quarterly*, Apr.–June 1964.

—— The 'Learn from the Army' Campaign. *China Quarterly*, Apr.– June 1964.

—— Political Control of the Chinese Army. *The World Today*, Aug. 1963.

Griffith, Samuel B. The Military Potential of China, *in* Alastair Buchan, ed. *China and the Peace of Asia.* London, 1965.

Halperin, Morton H. *China and the Bomb.* London, Pall Mall, 1965.

Hsieh, Alice Langley. *Communist China's Strategy in the Nuclear Era.* RAND, Prentice Hall, 1962.

—— China's Secret Military Papers: 'Military Doctrine and Strategy', *China Quarterly*, Apr.–June 1964.

Joffe, Ellis. The Communist Party and the Army. *Contemporary China*, vol. IV, 1959–60. Hong Kong UP, 1961.

—— The Conflict between Old and New in the Chinese Army. *China Quarterly*, Apr.–June 1964.

—— Contradictions in the Chinese Army. *Far Eastern Economic Review*, 11 July 1963.

—— *Party and Army: Professionalism and Political Control in the Chinese Officer Corps 1949–1964.* Harvard East Asian Research Center, 1965.

Kashin, A. The Atom and China. *Bulletin: Institute for the Study of the USSR*, Aug. 1961.

Leckie, Robert. *Conflict: the History of the Korean War, 1950–3.* New York, Putnams, 1962.

Lewis, John Wilson. China's Secret Military Papers: 'Continuities' and 'Revelations'. *China Quarterly*, Apr.–June 1964.

Powell, Ralph L. China's Bomb: Exploitation and Reactions. *Foreign Affairs*, July 1965.

—— Commissars in the Economy: 'Learn from the PLA' Movement in China. *Asian Survey*, Mar. 1965.

—— Communist China as a Military Power. *Current History*, Sept. 1965.

——Communist China's Mass Militia, pts 1–2. *Current Scene*, 15 Nov. & 1 Dec. 1964.

—— Everyone a Soldier. *Foreign Affairs*, Oct. 1960.

—— *Politico-Military Relationships in Communist China.* US Dept of State, Bureau of Intelligence and Research, 1963.

Rees, David. *Korea: The Limited War.* London, Macmillan, 1964.

Shih Ch'eng-chih. *Lun Chung-kung ti chün-shih fa-chan.* Hong Kong, Yu-lien chu-pan she, 1952.

—— *People's Resistance in Mainland China 1950–5.* Hong Kong, Union Research Inst., 1956.

Skinner, G. William. Aftermath of Communist Liberation in the Chengtu Plain. *Pacific Affairs*, Mar. 1951.

Whiting, Allen S. *China Crosses the Yalu; the Decision to Enter the Korean War.* New York, Macmillan, 1960.

Wilson, Dick. China's Nuclear Effort. *Far Eastern Economic Review*, 19 Aug. 1965.

Subject Index

Index of Names

Acheson, Dean, 40

Bator, Osman, 35
Bulganin, 128 f.
Burke, Admiral, 143

Chang Ai-p'ing, 311
Chang Chih-chung, 283
Chang Hsiu-shan, 277 f.
Chang K'ai, 279 n.
Chang K'ai-ching, 299 n.
Chang Kuo-hua, 37, 39, 314
Chang Kuo-t'ao, 52 n., 111
Chang Ling-pin, 311
Chang Ming-yuan, 278
Chang P'ing-hua, 300 n.
Chang Ta-chih, 313
Chang Teh-sheng, 300 n.
Chang Tsung-hsun, 311
Chang Wen-t'ien, 129, 232
Chao Te-ts'un, 278
Ch'en Cheng-jen, 298
Ch'en Ch'i-han, 314
Ch'en Hsi-lien, 291 n., 296, 312, 313
Ch'en Keng, 7 n., 284 n., 311
Ch'en Li-fu, 5 n.
Ch'en Ming-jen, 72
Ch'en P'i-hsien, 300 n.
Ch'en Po-ta, 264
Ch'en Po-ts'un, 278
Ch'en Shih-chü, 312
Ch'en Tsai-tao, 195 n., 295, 313
Ch'en Yi, 77 n., 122, 124 n., 280;
    commander of East China Field
    Army, 7 n., 67; — of 3rd Field
    Army, 41, 44, 307; and Shanghai,
    19, 265, 266 n.; Marshal of PLA,
    155 n., 287
Ch'en Yi (head of PLA Cultural
    Dept), 147 n., 285 n.
Ch'en Yun, 26, 125
Cheng Chieh-min, 34
Cheng Chien, 283

Chi Chien-hua, 145
Chiang Kai-shek, 4–5, 10 ff., 45
Chiang Wei-ch'ing, 300 n.
Ch'ien Jsueh-sen, 140 f.
Ch'in Chi'-wei, 297, 313
Ch'iu Ch'uang-ch'eng, 135 n., 295,
    312, 314
Ch'iu Hui-tso, 290, 310
Chou Ch'un-ch'uan, 311
Chou Chun-ming, 279
Chou En-lai, 13, 43, 86, 100, 207 n.,
    228 n.; and civil war, 5 n., 10, 11,
    15; and retrocession of Port
    Arthur, 124 n., 128; and PRMC,
    269, 283
Chou-Hsi-han, 296
Chou Huan, 277, 313
Chou Lin, 300 n.
Chou Pao-chung, 4 n.
Chou Shih-t'i, 312
Chu Liang-ts'ai, 313
Chu Ming, 312
Chu Teh, 26, 41, 55, 283; and Japan-
    ese surrender, 2 n.; in civil war,
    11, 15 n.; and foundation of Red
    Army, 99, 101; 1950–6, Orders of
    the Day, 116–18; 1950–1, on
    Soviet Union, 121 ff.; on modern-
    ization, 132, 146; on PLA and
    politics, 174–5; on militia, 204,
    206, 214; Marshal of PLA, 155,
    287
Chung Chi-kuang, 314

Dalai Lama, 37

Engels, 212

Fan Ming, 39
Fang Ch'iang, 296, 314
Fu Ch'iu-t'ao, 152 n., 209 n., 211 n.,
    213 n., 311; investigation of Honan
    militia, 216–17, 218
Fu Chung, 241 n., 243 n., 311